Kentucky Records

Early Wills and Marriages
Copied from Court House Records by Regents, Historians and the State Historian

Old Bible Records and Tombstone Inscriptions

Records From

BARREN, BATH, BOURBON, CLARK, DAVIESS, FAYETTE, HARRISON, JESSAMINE, LINCOLN, MADISON, MASON, MONTGOMERY, NELSON, NICHOLAS, OHIO, SCOTT AND SHELBY COUNTIES

Compiled By
MRS. WILLIAM BRECKENRIDGE ARDERY

GENEALOGICAL PUBLISHING CO., INC.
BALTIMORE   1977

Originally Published
Lexington, 1926

Reprinted with Permission
Southern Book Company
Baltimore, 1958

Reissued
Genealogical Publishing Co., Inc.
Baltimore, 1965
Baltimore, 1969
Baltimore, 1977

Library of Congress Catalogue Card Number 65-24115
International Standard Book Number 0-8063-0005-1

Made in the United States of America

PREFACE

When this work was begun, nearly two years ago, it was not our intention to publish the information contained in this book, but merely to gather together as many early Kentucky records as possible; to create new interest in research among our chapters, and to preserve the material thus gathered in the archives of the Kentucky State Historical Society, and Memorial Continental Hall.

As the work grew in volume, and in value, we realized the importance of publication, so that these records might be accessible to all.

Many sources of information available at the present time will soon be closed to us. The family burying ground is now a part of the past; the farmer's plow has already erased the graves of countless Revolutionary heroes; grave-stones lie crumbling, with inscriptions almost illegible; valuable old Bibles containing family records are growing fewer with each succeeding year.

So, from the beginning of what we considered a worthy undertaking, this work has grown, and continues to grow. Many chapters unrepresented in this publication have not completed their research, and their records will be too late to be incorporated in this book. It is our earnest desire, however, that this volume may prove so helpful that it may be the fore-runner of others.

If slight errors have crept into this compilation, we ask your forbearance, for it must be remembered the greater part of the manuscript was sent to us in longhand.

We desire to express our appreciation for the work of those loyal women who have labored in the offices of county clerks and elsewhere, giving freely of their time and energy to make it easier for the descendants of early Kentuckians to trace their lineage; and if this little book proves helpful to those descendants, now scattered over every state in the Union, then shall we feel that it has performed its mission, and we have not labored in vain.

JULIA SPENCER ARDERY.

BOURBON COUNTY INDEX TO ESTATES
From 1785 to 1840

(Contributed by Mrs. William Breckenridge Ardery, Jemima Johnson Chapter, Paris, Kentucky)

As the primary object in making the following index was to complete, as far as possible, a list of Revolutionary soldiers who died citizens of Bourbon County, the names of all women who died between these dates, leaving estates, have been omitted.

Abbott, Robert
Aker, Jacob
Alexander, James
Alexander, James
Alkire, Hammons
Allen, Samuel
Allen, T. Gabriel
Allen, Robert
Allen, James M.
Allen, James
Allen, John M. Sr.
Allen, John
Allen, Tandy
Allen, David
Allentharp, William
Allentharp, Jacob
Allison, Charles
Alty, Emanuel
Ament, Philip
Ament, George
Ammerman, Philip
Ammon, Thomas
Amos, Nicholas
Amos, Thomas
Anderson, George
Anderson Thomas
Anderson, William
Andrews, Jacob
Armstrong, James
Armstrong, Plunkett
Arnold, Thomas
Arrasmith, Richard
Ashbrook, Aaron
Ashcraft, Henry
Ashcraft, Josiah
Ashcraft, Josiah
Ayers, Daniel
Ayers, Harmon
Ardery, John
Ardery, Alexander

Baird, John
Barbee, Joseph
Barbee, Thomas
Barclay, Ben H.
Barclay, James
Barlow, Alvin
Barlow, Tompkins

Barlow, Henry
Barnett, Alexander
Barnes, John
Barr, Daniel
Barton, Andrew
Barton, Elijah
Barton, William
Baseman, John
Bayse, Elizmon
Bayse, Newton
Bates, Warren
Battson, Robert M.
Batterton, Ben
Batterton, Moses
Batterton, Henry
Batterton, Wm. G.
Baylor, Walker
Baylor, Geoorge W.
Beatty, John
Beckett, John
Beckett, Robert
Beckett, Joseph
Bedford, Henry
Bedford, Sidney
Bedford, Robert
Bedford, Franklin P.
Bedford, Littleberry
Bedford, Henry P.
Bedford, Benjamin
Bedford, Archibald
Bedinger, Daniel P.
Bell, Archibald
Bell, Thomas
Bell, James
Bell, Robert
Bellis, Wm.
Belt, John G.
Benear, Wm.
Benson, Wm.
Berry, Basil
Berryman, John E.
Besharer, John
Biddle, Richard
Bishop, Isaac
Bivins, Charles
Black, John
Black, James
Black, Alexander
Black, John

Black, Samuel
Black, William
Blue, Jacob
Boardman, Joseph
Boaz, James
Boone, George
Boone, Lincoln
Boulden, George
Boulden, Jesse
Bowles, David
Bowles, David
Bowles, Jesse
Bowles, Joseph
Bowles, Thomas
Bowman, Christian
Boyd, William
Bradley, John
Bramblett, Reubin
Brest, John
Bramblitt, Hugh
Branham, Aug. W.
Brand, Richard
Brand, Andrew
Brand, Jeremiah
Brand, Keziah
Breckenridge, John
Breckenridge, Alex.
Breckenridge, John
Bridges, John
Bristow, John
Brown, Abil
Brown. James
Brown, Samuel
Brown, Abil
Brown, Beverly
Brown, Alexander
Brown, James
Browning, Joshua
Browning, William
Bruce, Henry C.
Brush, James
Buckhannan, Wm.
Bunch, Douglas
Burch, James K.
Burgess, Henry W.
Burke, Robert
Burns, Andrew
Burris, Hezekiah
Bewnoe, George

Burton, John
Butler, Francis
Butler, Moses

Caldwell, Isaac
Caldwell, Wm.
Call, Daniel
Call, John
Call, Samuel
Callis, Wm.
Campbell, Hugh
Campbell, John G.
Campbell, William
Canady, James
Carter, Hebe
Carter, Robert
Carter, Thomas
Carter, John
Carter, John T.
Case, Samuel
Case, Joseph
Chambers, Daniel
Chambers, Robert
Chambers, Francis
Chambers, Silas
Chamblin, George
Chamblin, James
Chamblin, Wm.
Chamblin, John B.
Chamblin, Francis
Champ, Cushenberry
Champ, Robert
Champ, John
Champ, Thomas
Chinn, Joseph
Champ, George W.
Chany, Ambrose
Chinowith, Samuel
Chowning, William
Chowning, Wm.
Christian, Ishmæl
Clark, Robert
Clark, Wm.
Clark, John
Clark, John
Clark, Robert
Clarkson, Julius
Clarkson, John
Clarkson, Julius M.
Clay, John
Clay, Henry
Clay, Henry, Sr.
Clay, Hanibal
Clay, Samuel
Clay, Sidney P.
Clay, Thomas
Clay, Thomas
Cleveland, George
Clendenin, Thomas
Clifford, Robert
Clinkenbeard, Joseph
Clinkenbeard, Lucus

Clinkenbeard, Isaac
Closby, Robert
Cochran, Andrew
Coil, Jacob
Cogswell, Joseph
Coleman, John H.
Colville, John
Collier, Elizend T.
Collier, Franklin
Collins, John
Collier, John J.
Collins, Elijah
Colp, John C.
Coney, Samuel
Coney, Samuel
Congleton, John
Congleton, Wm.
Congleton, William
Conn, Hez.
Conn, John M.
Conn, Notley
Conn, Thomas
Conn, Thomas, Jr.
Constant, John
Constant, Jacob
Cook, John
Coons, James
Corbin, William
Corbin, Lewis
Corbin, Nathan
Corbin, Nathan
Corlis, Geo. W. R.
Cornick, Thos.
Cosby, Alner
Couchman, Andrew
Couchman, Malichi
Couchman, Wm. M.
Couchman, John
Craig, John
Crewser, Michæl
Cropper, Levi
Crose, Michæl
Crose, James M.
Crose, Levi
Crow, John
Crump, Sherwood
Crutchfield, Thomas
Culbert, George
Culton, Robert
Cummins, James
Cummins, Daniel
Cummins, John
Cummins, Jacob
Cummins, Joseph
Cunningham, James
Courl, Jecerson
Courl, John
Current, John
Current, Eli
Current, Thomas
Curry, James
Curtright, Henry

Curtright, Samuel
Cusenberry, Moses
Custer, Conrad
Custer, George
Custer, Jacob

Dalton, Carter
Darnell, Henzie
Darnell, Thomas
Darnell, Thomas, Sr.
Darnell, Isaac
Darnell, Isaac R.
Daugherty, Alexander
Daugherty, Hugh
Daugherty, Levi
David, William
Davidson, Elias
Davidson, James
Davidson, William
Davis, Lodowick
Davis, Umphry
Davis, James
Davis, Wm.
Dawson, John
Dawson, Samiel
Dazey, Jonth.
Dearborn, John T.
Debruler, George
Deley, James
Drimitt, Richard
Dennison, Daniel
Dennison, James
Dennison, John
Desha, John
Dickerson, John
Dickerson, Swat
Dickey, David
Dillon, Samuel
Dinwiddie, John
Dinwiddie, Thomas
Dinwiddie, Wm.
Dodge, John M.
Dodge, James C.
Dodge, Edwin M.
Donald, James
Donaldson, John
Donaldson, Wm.
Donnell, James
Dorsey, William P.
Douglass, John
Douglass, Samuel
Douvall, John
Dowden, Thomas
Downing, Nelson
Dudley, James
Dudley, James, Jr.
Duffield, Robert
Duke, John B.
Duncan, James
Duncan, Joseph
Duncan, Thomas
Duncan, Joseph

(6)

Duncan, John
Duncan, Roger
Duncan, Washington
Dunlap, Robert
Dunlap, John

Eales, John
Eastin, Augustine
Eastin, Mahala
Eastin, Thomas
Edmonson, Robert
Edwards, Haden
Edwards, George
Eldridge, John
Elliott, Arch.
Elliott, Thomas
Elliott, Edward
Ellis, William C.
Elliss, James
Ellis, David
Ellis, John
Endicott, Moses
Epperson, Thomas
Esham, Jonathan
Estes, Clement
Estill, Benj.
Evans, William
Ewalt, Richard
Ewalt, Henry, Sr.
Ewalt, John

Fearn, John
Feenster, Lucian J.
Fencher, John
Field, John
Field, Larkin
Field, Reubin
Fight, Jacob
Fight, John
Finch, Henry
Finch, Samuel
Finch, William
Finley, Jas. H.
Fishback, Jesse
Fisher, William
Fisher, Wm. L.
Fisher, William
Fisher, Nathaniel
Fisher, Thomas
Fisher, Thomas
Fisher, James
Fisher, Hillery
Ford, Charles F.
Ford, Charles
Ford, Edward
Ford, John
Ford, Thos. R.
Forden, John
Forgey, Hugh
Forgey, John
Forman, John
Forman, Aaron

Forman, Joseph
Forman, William
Foos, Nicholas
Forgueran, John
Forgueran, John
Forgueran, Peter
Forsythe, Isaac
Forsythe, Benja.
Foster, Asa
Foster, Jesse
Foster, James
Foster, Thomas
Foster, Nathaml
Foster, John P.
Frakes, Nathan
Frame, George
Francis, Thomas
Francis, William
Franklin, Robert
Friend, Andrew
Fry, Abrm.
Fry, Jacob
Fugate, Edward
Fulton, James
Furnace, Jacob

Gaines, Francis
Gallagher, Miles
Galloway, Joseph
Galloway, William
Garrard, Daniel
Garrard, James
Garrard, James, Jr.
Garrad, George
Garrard, Thomas
Garrard, Stephen L.
Garrard, William
Garth, Thomas
George, Alfred
George, Reubin
Gilbert, Barney
Gill, Erasmus
Gilledon, Samuel
Gillispie, Daniel
Gillispie, Gabriel
Giliock, John
Gillner, Abrm.
Gist, Nath.
Gist, Thomas
Givens, Samuel
Givens, James
Glasgow, John
Godman, Jeremiah
Goodman, Nathan
Gorham, Sanford
Gosney, William
Graffort, Thomas
Graham, Robt.
Grant, Peter
Graves, David
Graves, Richard
Graves, Richard

Graves, Rice
Gray, John B.
Green, John, Sr.
Green, John
Gregg, Nathan
Green, John
Gregg, John
Griffing, Aaron
Griffith, Abel
Griffith, Soloman
Griffith, Manassa
Griffith, Robt.
Griffith, Burrell
Griffith, Amos
Griffith, William
Griles, John
Grimes, Avory
Grimes, John
Grimes, Stephen
Grimes, Nicholas
Grimes, Washington
Grimes, William
Grimes, John S.
Grooms, William
Grosjean, John

Hall, John
Hall, Acquilla P.
Hall, Jas.
Hall, William
Hall, Joseph
Hall, Moses
Hall, Isaac
Hall, Robt. C.
Hall, Samuel
Hall, Caleb
Hall, William
Halleck, Benj.
Halleck, Franklin
Halleck, Jacoby
Ham, Jacob
Hamilton, John
Hamilton, William
Hamilton, John M.
Hamilton, Thomas
Harcourt, John
Hardesty, Benjamin
Hardesty, Benjamin
Hardin, Daniel
Hardwick, John
Harker, James G.
Hammond, Peter
Harney, Selby
Harp, John
Harris, Richard
Hasty, John
Hawker, Jacob
Hawkins, Henry
Hawkins, John
Hawes, James M.
Hayden, Nehemiah
Hazelrigg, John

Hearne, Cannon
Hearne, Urius
Heathman, George
Heddleston, William
Hedges, Joseph
Hedges, John Sr.
Hedges, James
Heedington, Wm.
Henderson, Thomas
Hendricks, Daniel
Hendricks, Peter
Henderson, Alex.
Henderson, Alex.
Henderson, Howard M.
Henderson, Samuel
Henderson, Jesse
Henry, Elizha
Henry, Hugh
Hibler, Daniel
Hibler, William
Hicks, David
Hickman, John L.
Hickman, David
Higgins, Joshua
Higgins, James
Hone, Christopher
Highland, Denman
Hicklin, Hugh
Hicklin, John
Hicklin, Thomas
Hildreth, Jeffrey
Hildreth, John
Hildreth, William
Hill, Abrm.
Hill, Robert
Hill, Warren
Hillis, William
Hinkson, John
Hitchcock, Abel
Hitt, Jesse
Hitt, Samuel
Hitt, William
Hodges, Francis
Holloway, George
Holloway, Robert
Hopper, Elijah
Howe, Christopher
Holmes, Erastus
Holman, Ebenezer
Honey, John, Sr.
Honey, John, Jr.
Honey, Thomas
Hopkins, John
Hopper, James
Hornback, Daniel
Hornback, John
Hornback, Samuel
Hornback, Simon
Horton, Alexander
Houston, Samuel
Howard, James
Huffman, John

Huffman, William
Hupptutter, Ulerick
Hughes, Thomas
Hughes, John
Hughes, Kinzea
Hughes, John
Hughes, Ralph
Hughes, Ralph
Hughes, James
Hughes, Ralph
Hughes, George
Hughes, William
Hulaner, John
Hull, George
Humble, Conrad
Humble, Uriah
Hume, Jesse
Hume, Wm. P.
Humphreys, Charity
Humphreys, John
Hutchcraft, Thomas
Hutchinson, James
Hutchinson, Samuel
Hutchinson, Nathan
Hutchinson, Wm. Jr.
Hutchinson, Lewis
Hutchinson, William
Hutsell, Gabriel
Hutsell, John
Hutsell, Michæl,
Hutsell, George
Hyzer, Peter

Ingels, Boone
Irvin, David
Irvin, Joshua

Jacks, William
Jackson, John
Jackson, Wm. D.
Jackson, Columbus
Jackson, Samuel
Jackson, John, Jr.
Jackson, Israel
Jackson, William.
Jacobs, John
Jacoby, Jacob
Jacoby, Francis L.
Jacoby, Jacob
Jacoby, Ralph
Jacoby, Henry
Jameson, David
Jameson, Jno. M.
Jameson, Samuel
Jameson, Elisha
Jenkins, William
Jenifer, John J.
Johnson, Benj.
Johnson, John
Johnson, Isaac C.
Johnson, William
Johnson, Jas.

Jolly, David
Jones, Garrard
Jones, Thomas
Jones, William
Jones, William
Jones, John
Jones George
Jones, Thomas
Jones, Thomas
Jones, Jacob
Jones, Charles
Jones, Benj.
Jones, James
Jones, Jno. III
Juett, David

Kenny, David
Kenney, Moses
Kenney, James, Sr.
Kenney, Nathan
Kenney, Nathan
Kenney, James, Jr.
Kerr, Jas.
Keathley, Joseph
Keith, George
Keizer, Jacob
Keizer, William
Keller, Abrm.
Keller, Isaac
Kelly, James
Kelly, William
Kelly, William
Kemp, Reuben
Kendall, Jesse
Kendall, Jos.
Kenderick, Benj.
Kendrick, Berwin
Kendrick, Lewis
Kennebrook, John
Kennedy, John
Kennedy, Jas.
Kennedy, Washington
Kennedy, Eli
Kennedy, Thos.
Kennedy, Joseph
Kennedy, Hugh
Kimbro, John
Kincaid, David
Kincaid, Joseph
Kincaid, George
Kincaid, Joseph
Kirby, James
Kirby, Thomas
Kirkpatrick, Alex.
Kirkpatrick, John
Kirkpatrick, Thomas
Kirkpatrick, Joseph
Kirtley, Francis
Kirtley, Richard
Kirtley, Simeon
Klizer, George
Klizer, Henry

Knight, John A.
Knight, Shadrick
Kuykendall, Henry

Lail, George
Lair, Dan'l
Lair, John
Lair, Mattheas
Lairy, Dennis
Lairy, Dennis
Lamme, James
Lamme, Robt.
Lamey, William
Lander, Henry
Layson, Robert
Layson, Isaac
Lander, Charles
Lapsley, Jos. B.
Lawson, Isaac
Layson, John
Laytham, James
Laytham, Thomas
Laytham, John
Layton, Spencer
Leach, John
Letton, John W.
Levesque, Samual
Lewis, Anzie
Lewis, Thomas
Lewis, Reubin
Lilly, Jas. M.
Lindsey, Nimrod L.
Lindsey, Reubin
Lindsey, Preston
Lindsey, William H.
Link, Jacob
Linthicum, Joshua
Liter, Henry
Liter, Henry
Liter, John
Liter, Reubin
Liter, Lewis
Liter, Henry
Lockett, Thomas
Lockwood, Samuel
Logan, Wm.
Longmore, Hugh
Love, Alexander
Love, John S.
Lovely, Jonathan
Loyd, Jefferson
Loyd, James
Luckie, John
Luckie, Robert
Lunsford, Lewis
Lydrick, Andrew
Lyle, John
Lyne, Edmond
Lyon, John
Lyon, Jacob

Malcolm, James

Mallory, Hy H.
Mann, Henry
Madden, Richard
Magill, Alexander
Manlove, Mark
Manlove, William
Maple, William
Marshall, David
Martin, John
Mark, William
Markee, Jonas
Marney, Robt.
Marsh, Beal
Marshall, David
Marshall, Samuel
Martin, David
Martin, Hiz
Martin, John G.
Martin, Gearge
Martin, John
Mason, Enock
Masoner, Campbell
Mason, George
Mason, Enock
Mason, Joel
Masquerier, Lewis
Massie, Thomas
Matheny, Daniel
Matheny, Moses
Matheny, Thomas
Matson, James
Matson, Thomas
Maxwell, John
Maxwell, Samuel

McCann, John
Mclanhan, Thos. Sr.
McClanahan, Thomas, S
McClanahan, Thos., Jr.
McClanhan, William
McClanhan, William
McClanhan, William
McClelland, Wm. M., Sr.
McClelland, Wm. M., Jr.
McClintock, Alex.
McClintock, Joseph
McClintock, Hugh
McClintock, Samuel
McClintock, Daniel
McCloud, John
McCloud, John
McClung, Samuel
McClure, Jas., Sr.
McClure, Jas., Jr.
McClure, Andrew
McClure, William
McConnell, Wm.
McConnell, Samuel
McConnell, Samuel
McConnell, Wm.
McConnell, Arch
McConnell, John
McConnell, Samuel

McConnell, Edward
McCracken, Hugh
McCoy, John
McCoy, Daniel
McCoy, Daniel
McCrary, James
McCullough, George
McCutchen, Jas.
McDaniel, Enos.
McDowell, Joseah
McDowell, Daniel
McDowell, Daniel
McDowell, Thomas
McFall, David
McKee, James
McKee, James
Miller, Henry
Miller, John
Miller, John
Miller, John
Mock, Rudolf
Morris, Thomas
Moss, Thomas
McFarland, John
McGinnis, John
McGreffin, Joseph
McHatton, William
McIlvain, Hugh
McIntyre, Alexander
McIntyre, Nicholas
McIntyre, Ezekiel
McKee, James
McKee, John
McKee, William
McKim, Francis
McKinney, John
McKinzey, John
McKinzey, Adam
McLaughlin, Jas.
McMillan, Jas.
McMillan, John
McMullen, John
McMay, John
McMay, Joseph
McMay, Samuel
McMay, David
McNickle, Auther
McPherrin, John
McShain, Edward
Medlin, Richard
Menary, Chas.
Merick, George
Merick, Roswell
Meredith, Thomas
Merry, Prettyman
Miller, Barnabus
Miller, Jacob, Sr.
Miller, Jacob A.
Miller, Horace
Miller, Henry
Miller, John
Miller, George

(9)

Miller, William
Million, Francis
Mills, Nathan
Mills, Benj.
Mitchell, Alex.
Mitchell, Joseph
Mitchell, John
Mitchell, William
Mitchell, Samuel
Mitchell, George
Mitts, Adam
Mock, Andrew
Mock, Rudolf
Mock, Jacob
Mock, George
Monroy, William
Moore, John, Sr.
Moore, Andrew
Moore, James
Moore, Jacob
Moore, Thomas
Moore, John
Moore, Peter
Moore, McClanahan
Moore, Benjamin
Moore, John G.
Moore, William
Moran, Edward
Morehead, John
Morgan, James
Morin, James
Morris, John
Morris, Thomas
Morris, Morris
Morrison, John
Morrison, Thomas
Morrow, Hiram
Morrow, Robert
Mountjoy, Edmd.
Mountjoy, Nicholas
Mountjoy, John W.
Mountjoy, Wm.
Mountjoy, George Sr.
Mountjoy, George, Jr.
Munson, Samuel, Jr.
Murdock, John T.
Musick, Jedediah
Musick, Jona
Myers, William

Neal, Benj. Y.
Neal, Tavner
Neal, William
Neal, Thomas
Neal, John
Nelson, Charles
Nesbitt, William
Nesbitt, William
Nesbitt, Samuel
Nesbitt, Jeremiah
Newell, Stephen
Nichols, Amos

Night, Shadrack
Nooe, Ziphemiah
Nooe, Zephemiah
Norris, Joseph
Northcutt, George
Northcutt, Jeremiah
Norton, John
Nunn, Edmund
Nunn, Ilai

Ogle, Benj.
O'Neal, Ludwick
Osborne, Thomas
Owings, Edw. C.
Owings, Thomas C.
Owings, John C.

Padgett, Henry
Palmer, John
Palmer, Joseph
Palmer, John
Palmer, George
Parish, Henry
Parish, Nath
Parish, William
Parker, Scarboro
Parker, Lemuel
Parker, Levi
Parker, William
Parker, Thomas
Parks, Jas.
Parks, John
Parsons, Isaac
Paton, John
Paton, William
Paton, William
Paton, William
Paton, William
Paton, Jos.
Patterson, James
Payne, George
Payne, John
Payne, Joseph
Perry, Robert
Penn, Eli
Penn, Joseph
Peyton, Timothy
Phelps, John
Phemister, Jesse D.
Phillips, Elijah
Phillips, Jenkens
Phillips, William
Piant, John
Pickett, Nathan
Pierce, Jno.
Pilcher, Jno.
Pinchard, George
Piper, Israel
Piper, William
Porter, Austin C.
Porter, Jas.
Porter, Henson

Porter, John
Porter, Edw.
Porter, Carter
Porter, Thomas
Poston, Elijah
Powell, William
Prather, Jas.
Prather, Walter
Price, George
Prichart, William
Pritchard, Alfred
Pritchard, Jas.
Protzman, John
Pryer, Joseph
Pryor, Edawrd
Pryor, Joseph
Pugh, Gustavins
Pugh, Joseph
Pugh, William
Pullen, Jedediah
Purdy, Isaac
Purdy, Robert
Purdy, Robt.
Purnell, Thos.
Pursley, William
Purviance, James
Pyke, Samuel

Quiett. James

Rader, Alexander
Rangee, Anthony
Rankin, Reubin
Rankin, Reubin
Rannels, John
Rannels, Thomas
Rannels, Samuel
Ravencraft, John
Rawlings, Joshua
Reading, George
Redhead, David
Redmon, Frank H.
Redmon, George
Reed, John
Reed, William
Reed, John
Respess, Machen C.
Respes, Thomas
Ribling, William
Rice, George
Rice, John
Richards, Burton
Riffle, Peter
Riggs, Benj. M.
Rigs, David M.
Riley, Levin
Riley, George
Ritchie, James
Ritchie, John
Ritchie, Robert
Ritchie, William
Robb, Robert

Ritchie, Philip
Roberts, Frances
Robey, Hiz.
Robey, Leonard
Robinett, Jas. M.
Robinett, Joseph
Robinett, Samuel
Robinet, Johin, Jr.
Robison, James
Robison, Joseph
Rogers, William
Rogers, Ezekiel
Rogers, William
Rogers, Nath.
Rogers, Samuel
Rogers, Jas.
Rogers, Thos.
Ross, Clement
Ross, John
Ross, James
Ross, Henry
Roundtree, Charles
Routt, Wm. (No date)
Rowe, Jno.
Rowland, Abm.
Ruby, Henry
Rucker, Daniel
Ruddell, George
Ruddell, Arch
Ruddell, Isaac
Ruddell, Isaac, Jr.
Ruddell, John
Rule, William S.
Rule, John
Rust, John K.
Rymel, Elias
Ryon, William

Sadler, Jesse
Sandousky, James
Sampson, Richard
Sanford, Reubin
Sanford, Willoughby
Savary, John
Schooler, Benj.
Schooler, Benj.
Schooler, John
Schooler, John
Sconce, John
Sconce, John
Sconce, Robert
Sconce, Robert
Sconce, Thos.
Scott, James
Scott, James D.
Scott, John
Scott, John
Scott, Andrew
Scott, James A.
Scott, John
Scott, William, Sr.

Scott, William B.
Scott, William C.
Scott, Robert C.
Scott, Robert
Scott, Samuel
Scott, Samuel
Scott, Samuel D.
Scott, Vincent
Scott, Wm.
Scott, William
Scott, Wm.
Scrogin, Robert
Seamons, Manion
See, George
See, Jacob
Seldon, George
Self, Vincent
Settles, John
Shanks, Christian
Shanks, John K.
Sharrer, Peter
Sharp, Wm. P.
Shaw, Thomas
Shaw, John
Shaw, John
Shawhan, Daniel
Shawhan, John
Shepherd, George
Shields, William
Shirley, John
Shrader, Conrad
Shropshire, John E.
Shropshire, Benj.
Shropshire, Abner
Shrout, Peter
Sidener, Martin
Sidwell, John
Simpson, Lewis
Simpson, James
Simpson, Levi
Simpson, William
Simpson, Silas B.
Simpson, Hiram
Simms, Craven
Simms, William M.
Skillman, Christopher
Skinner, Elijah
Slater, Samuel
Sledd, Thomas
Small, Samuel
Smalley, Joshua
Smeades, Abrm. K.
Smedley, David
Smelser, Joseph
Smelser, Peter
Smith, John
Smith, John
Smith, Abrm.
Smith, Thomas P.
Smith, Thomas
Smith, Thomas
Smith, Alexander

Smith, Joseph
Smith, Weathers
Smith, Weathers
Smith, Joshua S.
Smith, Ephriam
Smith, William
Smith, Jamen M.
Smith, Wharton
Smith, Jacob
Smith, Nicholas
Smith, Richard B.
Smith, Nicholas
Smith, Isaac
Smith, Jesse
Smoot, Philip B.
Snyder, George
Sadousky, Andrew
Sadousky, Thomas
Soper, Charles
Soper, Thomas
Sonder, Solomon
Sparks, John
Sparks, Thomas
Sparks, Hiz., Jr.
Speakes, Hiz., Jr.
Spears, Christian
Spears, Jacob
Spears, Solomon
Spencer, Benja.
Spencer, John
Spruill, William
Spurgin, Zephania
Spurgin, William
Spurgin, Wm.
Spurgin, George
Squires, William
Stamps, John
Standiford, George
Standiford, Nathan C.
Stark, James
Stark, Thomas
Stark, Thomas
Stark, Thomas, Rev.
Starr, Jacob
Steele, James
Steele, Soloman
Steele, William
Steele, James
Stephens, Daniel
Stephenson, George
Stuart, Jeremiah
Stuart, Peter
Stuart, William
Stuart, James
Stuart, Richard
Stuart, James R.
Stipp, George
Stipp, Sidney
Stokes, John
Stone, Howard
Stone, John

(11)

Stone, Edward
Stone, Elijah
Stone, Asa L.
Stone, James M.
Strother, Thomas
Sturges, Henry
Summers, John
Sutton, Nathaniel
Swiney, John

Talbott, Abrm.
Talbott, John
Talbott, Henry
Talbott, Henry
Talbott, Nicholas
Talbott, Hugh
Talbott, Pressly
Talbott, French
Talbott, William
Talbott, Jona.
Talbott, John
Talbott, Thomas
Talbott, D Movill
Taliaferro, Robert
Tarr, Frederick
Tarr, James
Tarr, Jas.
Tate, John
Tevebaugh, Jacob
Thomas, George
Thomas, Kizeah
Thomas, Poucy P.
Thomas, Moses
Thomas, William
Thomas, David
Thomas, Thomas
Thomas, James
Thomas, Samuel
Thomas, Henry
Thomason, Reubin T.
Thompson, Joseph
Thomorhill, John
Thornton, Anthony, Jr.
Thornton, Lewis
Thornton, Tho. Towles
Thornton, Walker
Thurman, Joshua
Tillett, John
Timberlake, Richard
Todd, Andrew
Todd, John
Todd, John
Todd, Edward
Todd, Benj. B.
Todd, David
Todd, Samuel
Towles, Henry
Towles, Larkin
Trabue, James
Trabue, Robert
Trester, Wm.
Trimble, Isaac

Trimble, Thomas
Trimble, David
Trimble, George
Trimble, Robert
Trotter, Joseph
Trotter, Joseph
Trotter, William
Tucker, Absalam
Tucker, Jeremiah
Tucker, Thomas
Tucker, Acquilla
Tucker, Edward
Tucker, Jon
Tucker, John
Tucker, Alexander
Tull, Isaac
Tully, David, (no date)
Turner, Jesse
Turner, Richard
Turner, Robert
Turner, Joseph
Turney, Peter

Underwood, Francis
Underwood, Reubin
Utterback, Reubin

Vanhook, Benj. S.
Vanlandingham, Jas.
Varnon, John
Vaughan, Erwin
Vivion, Thos. J.

Wade, John
Walton, John
Wallace, os.
Wallace, Stephen
Wallace, William
Wallace, Joseph
Wallace, Stephen
Wallace, Andrew
Waller, Edward
Ward, Benj.
Ward, Isaac
Warren, Henry
Warth, John
Wassen, James
Wasson, James
Wasson, Charles
Watkins, John
Watson, James
Way, John
Way, William
Weakland, Bowles
Weakland, Wm. C.
Webb, Isaac
Webb, Wm. E.
Webb, James
Welch, Michæl
Wells, Benj.
Wentling, Charles
West, Alvin

West, John
Whaley, James
Whaley, William
Whaley, Daniel
Wheat, Hezekiah
Wheat, Zahariah
White, John
White, Robert
White, William
Whitledge, John
Wickerman, John
Wigginton, Allison
Wigginton, Elijah
Wigginton, William
Wigginton, Henry, Sr.
Wilcox, David D.
Willett, Edward
Willett, Acquilla
Williams, Charles
Williams, Sanford
Williams, John
Williams, Hubbard
Williams, Roger
Williams, Jesse
Wilmott, John
Wilmott, Robert
Wilson, George
Wilson, Jeremiah
Wilson, Jeremiah
Wilson, Thomas
Wilson, John
Winchester, John
Winn, Owen
Winston, Andrew T.
Wood, Jacob
Wood, John W.
Wood, Adam
Wood, Malcolm
Woodbridge, William
Woodgate, Jonathan
Wool, Atwell
Workman, Jacob
Wornall, Alfred
Wright, And. H.
Wright, Joseph
Wright, Jas., Sr.
Wright, Thos.
Wright, Lewis C.
Wright, William
Wright, Robert
Wright, John
Wright, Hugh
Wright, Jas.
Wyatt, Thomas T.
Wyckoff, John
Wyckoff, Jacob

Yancey, Thomas
Yelton, Charles
Yocum, Francis
Young, Samuel
Young, Jas. G.

BARREN COUNTY WILL ABSTRACTS

(Contributed by Mrs. W. S. Smith and Miss Ruth Bybee, Edmund Rogers Chapter, Glasgow, Ky.)

WILLIAM BELL—Gives to Wm. Henry Bell, "if he should ever come forward and claim any part of my estate," etc., should have, "two lots in town of Chaplington on Big Barren River." Other legates—my step-mother, Sarah Bell; two sisters, Fanny Roberts and Elizabeth Bell. Proved 1819. WitnessesDavid Logan, James Dodd, Jr.

JAMES BRIDGES—Names—wife, Nancy; children, Sookey, Elizabeth, Polly, Caty, Anne. Written December, 1802. Proved January 20, 1803. Executors—Moses Bridges, Jonathan Cox. Witnesses—Maragaret Bridges, James Walker. Property appraised by—William Allen, Elisha Allen, Simeon Buford.

WILLIAM BROWNING—Names—wife, Louann; children, James E., Henry, William. Written 1851. Proved January, 1852. Executors —James E. Browning, Jas. W. Scrivener. Witnesses—Wm. Lyon, Isaac B. Ellis, Henry Eubank.

JOHN COURTS—Will—Names wife, Fanny; children, Nancy, Clara, CharlesH., William T., Richard W., John, Amanda, Emely, Jane, Zerilda. Written February, 1817. Proved April, 1817. Witnesses —William Grey, Joseph Crockett, J. R. Underwood.

ALEXANDER DAVIDSON—Will—Names—wife, Mary; children, Jesse, Albert, Elizabeth, Sarah Abraham, Ellice, Asa. January 15, 1811. Attest—George Maurell, William Trigg, William Depp, Clement Montague.

WILLIAM DEPP—Will—Names—children, Nancy, Fanny, Elizabeth, Joel, Peter, Susan, Polly, John, Patsey, Sally Thomas, Pemelia, Jane; grand-son, William Davidson; mother, deceased. Written April 10, 1833. Proved October. Executors—Joel Peter and John Depp. Witnesses—Joseph Wooten, Robert Robinson, Thos. W. Wade.

WILLIAM HENDRICK—This indenture, 1798, between William Hendrick and Ann, his wife of Hanover County, Virginia, to Lipscomb Nowell of County of Garrard, State of Kentucky, a certain parcel of land, 600 acres, on Beaver Creek, Warren County, Kentucky, 1798.

JOSEPH HIGDON—Will—Names—wife, Margeret; children, Thomas, Gabriel, John M., Ishmæl, Joseph, Enoch E., Polly Davis, Susanna Foster, Rebecca Smith, heirs of Jane T. Smith, deceased, Margerett Bennet, Sally D. Higdon. Written October, 1835. Proved 1836. Executors— Ishmæl Higdon, James Smith. Witnesses—James Frazier, Isaac Smith.

JAMES JAMES—Will—James James of the County of Bourbon and State of Kentucky, but now in the County of Green and State aforesaid. Dated April 24, 1799. Names—wife, Mary; children, not named. Witnesses—Louis Bryan, Thomas Midleton. At the sale the following purchasers are named: James Chism, Richard Mulinix, Isaac Cook, Thomas Bartley, Stephen Howard, Benagy Burchman, Barney Flin, James Morris, Wm. Harris, Thos. White, Hugh Smith,

David Burchan, Robert Sharp, Edward Wade, James Bundle, James Carter, Isaac Jackson, Jacob Grider, Elizabeth Burcham, Nathaniel Mullinix, Daniel Wray, Moses Beldeer, James Lewis, James Harrison, Francis Harris, John Byers, Wm. Stewert, Lewis Bryam, Daniel Wray, Legetee. Barren County Court, 1804.

SAMUEL LUCKETT—Will—Names—wife, Elizabeth; children, Ann Ware Luckett, David Luckett, William Luckett, Frances H. Luckett, Samuel Luckett, Susanna Parnell, Polly Elms, John L. Luckett, Nancy Creek. Written April 17, 1828. Proved October, 1828. Executors—Elizabeth Luckett, David Luckett. Witnesses—Loammi Whitney, Michel Pinkley.

JOHN McMURRY—Inventory and Appraisement—Appraisers—Samuel Scott, Alexander McKay, Francis Latimore, Wm. Renick. "In Barren County Court, July 23, 1799."

ANDREW NUCKOLS—Will Book 4, page 1—Names—wife, name not given; children, Hezekiah Nuckols, Polly Huffman, Pouncy Nuckols, Nancy Smith, Susannah Pace, Martha Harrison, Andrew B. Nuckols. May 24, 1852. Executor, A. B. Nuckols. Witnesses—R. N. Sanders, W. H. Sanders, Wm. A. Norvell.

POUNCEY NUCKOLS—Will—Names—children A. V. Nuckols, John A. Nuckols, James E. Nuckols, Martha A. Gardner, Susan W. Kirtley, Joseph O. Nuckols, Elizabeth P. Hodges. Written May 21, 1881. Proved May 28, 1881. Attest—B. B. Duke, H. Y. Davis.

WILLIAM B. REYNOLDS—Nuncupative Will—Names—wife, Elizabeth. Proved 1829. Signed—Meridth Reynolds, Sally Ritter. Attest—Willis Bush, William Browning.

ABRAHAM RITTER—Will—Names—wife, Margeret. Written December 30, 1805. Proved April, 1810. Executors—Margeret Ritter, Joseph Ritter. Witnesses—John Kelley, Ralph Petty, John Ritter, Isaac Ritter, Tetre Huffman, Henry Tudor.

JOSEPH RITTER—Will—Dated July 16, 1839—For love he has for her, his daughter Cleina Wilson and for consideration that she will care for him the rest of his life, "I, the said Joseph Ritter, have granted, bargained and sold to the said Clenia Wilson, etc., a certain tract and parcel of land on Glovers Creek which was deeded to me by Edmund Rogers, etc." Witness, John W. Ritter.

JOHN SANDERS—Will—Names—wife, Patsey Sander; children, Hetty Nuckols, Michæl Sanders, Jesse Sanders, other sons not of age. Proved 1834. Attest—Jesse Everett, Samuel Everett.

ISAAC SMITH—Inventory taken May 6, 1811—Names—wife, Sarah Hampton. In obedience to an order of Barren County Court, we, the undersigned Commissioners for appraising the estate of the Isaac Smith, deceased, attended at the dwelling, etc. Given under our hand this 6th day of May, 1811.—Leonard H. Murry, Andrew Nuckols, Joseph Higdon.

WILLIAM SMITH—Will—Names—wife, Rachel; children, Mary Jane, Missinia. Written September 8, 1801. Proved November, 1801. Witnesses—John Howe, John Smith.

ROBERT SNODDY—Will—Names—wife, Sophia; children, Nancy Lewis, (husband John Lewis), Elizabeth Thurman (of Virginia), Caray Snoddy, John Snoddy, Polly Snoddy, Robert Snoddy. Written August 26, 1820. Proved October, 1820. Executors—Carey Snoddy, John Snoddy, Thomas Bransford. Attest—A. P. Beachamp, Horatio Clelland.

DANIEL STOCKTON—Will—Names—wife, Susan; children, Newberry, Hugh and an unborn child. Written April 24, 1800. **Proved** November, 1800. Witnesses—Robert Hill, Thomas Stockton.

NAT V. BOWLES—Power of Attorney, November, 1816—Given by Nat V. Bowles and wife, Jane, daughter of Hezekiale Puryor of Goochland County, Virginia. Hezekiah Puryor, deceased; Thomas P.; Ann Puryor and Robin Puryor, deceased.

SAMUEL MURRELL—Power of Attorney, given by Samuel Murrell and wife, Susanna Puryor, daughter of Hezekiah Puryor of Goochland County, Virginia, to Andrew Nuckols of Barren County—Barren County Court, 1816.

GEORGE BUSH, SR.—Will Book 2, Page 441—Inventory September 5, 1826. Administrators: Walton Bush and George Bush, Jr. Appraisers: Matthew Williams, James Fisher, James Gillock. Notes and accounts on the following to wit: an account on Loammie Whitney; James D. Smith; Wm. Moseby; John Barrett and Wm. Martin; Walton and William Bush; George Bush, Jr.; John Brown; John and William Tredate and Thomas James; Wm. H. Courts; Wm. Anderson; Thomas Williams; W. Filbert, account. Property previously received by Asa Ellis; property previously received by Walton Bush; property previously received by Wm. Bush; property previously received by Loammie Whitney; property previously received by George Bush, Jr.; property previously received by Archibald Bush; property previously received by Josiah Bush.

ALEXANDER E. SPOTTSWOOD and wife, ELIZABETH WASHINGTON SPOTTSWOOD—Deed Book E, Pages 135-6—September 10, 1816. Power of attorney to Robert Lewis to sell land in Virginia on or near the Kenhaway River in which Elizabeth Washington Spottswood has "interest in as heir and representative of her deceased brother, John Lewis, who died in possession of such land," etc. * * * * "whereas, Fielding Lewis, decd. became in his life time under the last will and testament of General George Washington, decd. entitled to a certain portion and interest in his Kenaway lands therein devised and whereas a division took place subsequent to the death of said Fielding Lewis of such lands and thirteen hundred acres thereof the heirs and representatives of the said Fielding Lewis, decd. became entitled to at that time one of whom being Elizabeth W. Spottswood, formerly Elizabeth W. Lewis, who intermarried with Alexander E. Spottswood, formerly of the State of Virginia, by reason of which said division the said Elizabeth W. Spottswood became entitled one seventh part of said thirteen hundred acres of said land, etc. Indenture made 15th of September, 1816, between Alexander Spottswood and wife, Elizabeth of Barren County, Ky., to Bushrod Washington, Jr., of Virginia, all interest in aforesaid thirteen hundred acres of land.

BOURBON COUNTY WILL ABSTRACTS

(Contributed by Mrs. William Breckenridge Ardery, Jemima Johnson Chapter, Paris, Kentucky)

JACOB AKER—Will Book L, page 442—Those mentioned—wife,

Maragaret Aker; nephew, Jacob Aker now in Missouri; two neices, Margaret Wordlin and Polly Goodrich. Will written 11th day of May 1839. Proved May Court, 3rd May, 1841. Witnesses—John Ingels, Anthony McGinty, Wm. Burr.

HAMMONS ALKIRE, SR. (Hammonious Alkires)—Will Book B, page 82—Those mentioned—six sons, William, John, Adam, Michael, Morris, George; six daughters, Catty, Elizabeth, Deborough, Maragaret;Sally; Liddy. Written May 29, 1800. Proved July Court, 1800. Executors, Wm. Alksire, Wm. Clarkeson. Witnesses—John Wallace, Jedediah Pullen, Jesse Fitzgerald, Edward Campbell.

ROBERT ALLEN—Will Book H, page 22—Those mentioned—wife, Elizabeth W. Allen. Made December 14, 1827. Executor, father-in-law, John M. Jameson. Proved February Court, 1828. Witnesses—Elijah Covington, Henry Batterton, Jeremiah D. Sadler, A. W. Bills.

JOHN ALLEN—Will Book E, page 334—Those mentioned—wife, Jane Allen; children, Thomas (Thos. Otway Allen) Allen, William S. Allen, Granville Allen, Sterling Allen, Tandy Allen, (Frank Jones Allen) Allen, Julia Ann Allen, Jane Quarles Allen, John B. Allen, George Allen, Gabriel Allen,. Written August, 1815. Proved September, 1815. Executors—Wm. S. Allen, Sterling Allen, Tandy Allen, Frank Allen. Witnesses—Z. Easton, W. Sanford, John Parrish, Wm. Mosby.

WILLIAM ALLENTHORP—Will Book J, page 160—Those mentioned—Samuel Allenthorp, Betsy McDaniel, Anna Beasley, Polly Miller, Lucy Porter, sister Betsy Allenthorp. Made April 26, 1833. Proved September Court, 1833. Executors—John B. Raine, Henry F. Wilson. Witnesses—Thos. P. Smith, Thos Elliott.

CHARLES ALLISON—Will Book A, page 5—Those mentoned—wife, Jane Allison; my children (property equally divided), son John Allison; son Alexander; Michael Hogg (agreement with); Colby Ship (lawsuit with). Made 2nd October, 1787. Proved Tuesday, 18th of December 1787. Executors—wife, Jane Allison, Son, John Allison. Witnesses—Benjamin Harrison, Mary Allison.

PHILIP AMENT—Will Book K, page 174—Those mentioned—daughter, Sally Lyter (Liter) and her heirs; son, Henry Ament; children of my two daughters, now dead, to wit Polly Liter and Susan Huffman; Henry Liter (husband of Polly Liter); John Huffman (husband of Susan Huffman); son-in-law, John Childers; daughter, Catherine Childers; son, George and his child (a daughter); son-in-law, David Halderman and Elizabeth Halderman. Made June 5th, 1833. Proved April Court, 1836. Executor, son, Henry Ament. Witnesses—Benjamin Howe, Harrison S. Crafton, Peter Clarkson.

THOMAS AMOS—Will Book H, page 409—Those mentioned—wife, Catherine; son, Nicholas Amos; daughter, Betsy Current and John Current; remaining eight children, John Amos, Mordeca Amos, Harriott Allen, Christiana Prudent, Ann Giles, Kitty Demmitt, Abraham Amos, William Amos; son-in-law, John Allen. Made December 21st, 1827. Witnesses—Alexander McClintock, Nicholas Amos, John C. Demmitt. Codicil September 8th, 1830. Witnesses—Jas. Houston, Jr., Nicholas Amos, Alexander McClintock, Proved October Court, 1830. Executor—John Allen.

JACOB ANDREWS—Will Book A, page 110—Those mentioned—friend, Eleanor Brown; Gaspie Hendershott (property now in possession of); friend John Brown. Made 21st September, 1791. Proved March Court, 1792. Executor— John Brown. Witnesses— John Quinn, Luke Merryman, Keziah Reese.

ALEXANDER ARDERY—Will Book K, page 564—Those mentioned— wife, Sarah Ardery; son, James Hervey Ardery; daughter, Eliza- beth; "my heirs." Made September 1838. Proved November, 1838. Executor—son, James Hervey Ardery. Witnesses—H. Parker, Thomas H. Matheny.

JOHN ARDERY—Will Book H, page 363—Those mentioned—son, Alexander Ardery; daughter, Betsy Griffith; daughter, Peggy Watts; daughter, Jane Purdy; daughter Katy McConnell; son, John Ardery; son Thomas Ardery; son James Ardery. Made August, 1827. Proved March 1st, 1830. Witnesses—John Nesbit, Barnard Vandarin, Joseph Robinson.

PLUNKETT ARMSTRONG—Will Book H, page 396—Those men- tioned—wife, Margaret, property for benefit of schooling Eliza Ann, Rebeca and Plunket Armstrong, all my children now liv- ing with their mother; children who have formally been given property, William Armstrong, Robert Arstrong, Margaret Sidner, Monros, Armstrong, Lucinda Armstrong, Caroline Amnent, John H. Armstrong. Written April 18th, 1828. Proved September 6th, 1830. Witness—Aquilla Talbott.

THOMAS ARNOLD—Will Book L, page 202—Those mentioned—wife, Susan P. Arnold, farm bought from John B. Raine, land purchased of Miller heirs. To wife and her heirs. Made 17th of February, 1836. Witnesses—Chas. S. Brent, Hubbard Taylor, Jr. Codicil made to will November 10th, 1839, mentions notes against Hezekiah Martin. Proved 2nd March, 1840. Witnesses—J. M. Arnold, W. B. Arnold.

RICHARD ARROWSMITH—Will Book E, page 50—Those mentoned —wife, Carander Arrowsmith; 12 children, viz: Mary Longnecker, William Arrowsmith, Rebecca Garriott, Alexander Arrowsmith, John Arrowsmith, Margaret Arrowsmith, Elizabeth Arrowsmith, Smithy Arrowsmith, Livina Arrowsmith, Alva Arrowsmith, James Arrowsmith, Sary Arrowsmith. Extrix. wife, Carander Arrowsmith. Made April 15th, 1814. Proved May Court, 1814. Witnesses— Chas. Howard, Anne Howard, William Arrowsmith.

AARON ASHBROOK—Will Book D, Page 63—Those mentioned— Elizabeth, Aaron and Felix, infants of my daughter, Elizabeth Wells; 4 children, Thomas, Felix, Hannah (portion to be in hands of her brother Thomas to manage), Rachel; living children of two daughters, Mary and Betsy. Made 4th day of January 1810. Proved February Court, 1810. Executors—sons, Thomas and Felix. Witnesses—Richard Biddle, William McConnell, William Browning.

DANIEL AYERS—Will Book D, page 467—Those mentioned—wife, Matilda Ayers; children, Mary Ann Ayers, Harmon Hitt Ayers, Matlda Elizabeth Ayers; Mrs. Dorcas Howard's legacy, my former wife's mother to my daughter Dorcus Rebecca Howard Ayers. Made 21st December, 1813. Proved January Court, 1814. Wit- nesses—Thomas Routt, Samuel Rannels, Jacky S. Hitt. Executrix, wife.

JOHN BAIRD—Will Book D, page 172—Those mentoned—Andrew Cochran,, Samuel Gibson, Thomas Baird, Samuel Ross; two grand- daughters, Polly Cochran and Jane Cochran. Made 7th September,

(17)

1810. Proved June Court 1811. Executor—Thomas Baird. Witnesses—Samuel Donnell, Samuel Knox, Charles Wasson.

JOSEPH BARBEE—Will Book E, page 115—Those mentioned—wife, Leeannah; son Jesse; other sons and daughters. Made February 1st, 1814. Proved September 1814. Witnesses—Asa Foster, Tobias Strader.

ALEXANDER BARNETT—Will Book G, page 433—Those mentioned —son, John Barnett, his mother to live with him during her life; grandchildren, children of my daughter Elizabeth M. Brown, deceased; children of son, John Barnett; wife, Dorcus; Agnes Glky, formerly the wife of my deceased son, William Barnett; Martha Ward, formerly the wife of my deceased son, Robert Barnett; grandson, Alexander Montgomery Brown. Made 28th September, 1826. Proved December, 1826. Executors—John Barnett, John G. Brown. Witnesses—William B. Branham, Thomas Roger, Richard Brand.

JOHN BARNES—Will Book C, page 422—Those mentioned—wife, Dean Barnes; daughter, Polly. Written April 20th, 1808. Proved October Court, 1808. Executors—Wife and William Gamble Witnesses—George Smizer, Nathan Seller.

DANIEL BARR—Will Book C, page 290—Those mentioned—wife, Amy; sons, Robert and Abram; daughters, Polly, Rachel, Nancy, Letty. Made August 19th, 1806. Proved September Court 1806. Executor, Robert Barr. Witnesses—Samuel Donnell, John Hopkins, George W. Hopkins.

ANDREW BARTON—Will Book H, page 387—Those mentioned— son, David Barton; son, William Barton; to the children of Sarah Sparks, deceased, when they come of age, by name, James, Hiram, William, Margaret; having given portion to son Elijah, now deceased; children of Sanford Gorham, deceased; son Stephen Barton. Made June 16th, 1829. Proved June 7th, 1830. Executors— sons, David and William Barton. Witnesses—Elizabeth Gray, Augustine Eastin, Mary Kinnaird.

ELIJAH BARTON—Wll Book G, page 434—Those mentioned—friend, William Alexander to manage my Bagging Factory and the estate of my family. Made August 21st, 1823. Proved December Court 1826. Executors—brothers, David and William Barton. Witnesses —Thomas P. Smith, William Sharp Sparks, John Breckenridge.

WARREN BATES—Will Book J, page 630—Those mentioned—wife, Rosanna; son, Ashford G. Bates, when he comes of age; daughter, Mariah Rule, wife of William S. Rule; daughter, America Grimes, wife of Thomas A. Grimes; granddaughter Catherine Cumins. Made August 25th, 1831. Proved March, 1835. Witnesses— Alexander McClintock, M. T. Willett, James Houston, John Current, Joseph Culbertson, James Coons, Benjamin Bowen, James Mahan, Nicholas W. Bowen, William McConnell, William W. Bowen. Executors—Wife and William S. Rule.

HENRY BATTERTON—Will Book J, page 172—Those mentioned— Henry Todd Batterton, son of my brother, James Batterton, tavern property, after decease of my wife, Dulcinea; Acquilla Willett carry on the store in partnership with my wife; brother James; my only living sisters, Elizabeth Batterton and Nancy West; brother, Moses Batterton's two heirs, Sary Jane and Nancy Batterton; land

(18)

I received as an heir of William B. Graves, deceased. Made June 13th, 1833. Proved September, 1833. Executors—wife, Dulcinea and James McClure. Witnesses—Robert M. Batterton, Samuel C. Trotter.

WILLIAM GUTHRIE BATTERTON—Will Book L, page 357—Those mentioned—wife, Matilda Batterton; three children, Julia Ann Batterton, William Henry Batterton, Sarah Ellen Batterton. Made August 10, 1840. Proved 7th of September, 1840. Executrix, wife. Witnesses—J. Huntington, Peter Smith, George Rymel.

WALKER BAYLOR—Will Book G, page 78—Those mentioned—son, Robert B. Baylor; son, Joseph Addison Baylor; son, William M. Baylor; son, Robert Baylor, guardian for son, Patrick Henry Nelson Baylor until he comes of age; daughter, Betsy N. Baylor, she my youngest child, son Robert to be her guardian until she comes of age; balance of my children. Made 23rd February, 1821. Proved February, 1823. Witnesses—Walker Baylor, Frances N. Metcalf, J. W. Baylor, N. B. Coleman.

JOSEPH BECKETT—Will Book E, page 384—Those mentioned—son, Joseph, if he is alive, portion to be held for five years, hoping to hear from him; wife, Elizabeth; daughters, Sarah and Elizabeth, at this time unmarried; seven daughters, excepting Fainey (Fanny). Made December 22nd, 1815. Proved February Court, 1816. Witnesses—John Hamilton, Humphrey Lyon, Wm. Hamilton.

ARCHIBALD BEDFORD—Will Book G, page 440—Those mentioned—wife, land bought of John Strode; two youngest sons, Green and Paul; five daughters, Polly, Nancy, Henrietta, Rachel and Patsy; sons, Thomas, Benjamin and Littleberry, land in Lewis County, on Ohio River, John Barnes now occupying this land and son Benjamin wishes to settle thereon; sons Archibald Coleman, Hillery, Moseby, Asa and Henry C. Bedford. Made 7th October, 1826. Proved January, 1827. Witness, William Reid.

SIDNEY BEDFORD—Will Book H, page 220—Those mentioned—brother, Thomas J. Bedford; father-in-law, Thomas Brice; brother, Benjamin F. Bedford; wife, Susan; son, Sydney Bedford, when twenty-one; all my brothers now living. Written February 15th, 1829. Proved April 6th, 1829. Executor, brother, Benjamin F. Bedford. Witnesses—Archibald C. Bedford, Thomas Bedford.

ARCHIBALD BELL (BEALL)—Will Book L, page 351—Those mentioned—wife, Milly; children, Delilah King, William Beall, Archibald Beall, Jemima Riddle, Nathaniel Bell, Betsy Poston, Nancy Gentry, Milton Beall, grandchildren, children of daughter Anna Colvertson, deceased, William, James, Jane and Rocksey Colvertson; grandchild, James Buckannan, son-in-law, Andrew Buckannan. Written June 5, 1838. Proved September, 1838. Executrix, wife, executors, sons, Archibald Bell, Milton Bell. Witnesses—Peter Hedges, H. F. Wilson, Mason Talbott.

THOMAS BELL, SR.—Will Book G, page 388—Those mentioned—land deeded me by William Rogers, wife, Mary Ann Bell; son, Thomas Bell; other children. Written September 7th, 1819. Proved July, 1826. Witnesses—William Rogers, Kitty M. Rogers.

JAMES BELL—Will Book C, page 26—Those mentioned—wife, Peggy Bell; brother, Thomas Bell. Written July 9th, 1805. Proved September, 1805. Executors—friends, Julius Clarkson, Alexander McPheeters. Witnesses—Charles Jones, James A. McClure.

WILLIAM BELLIS—Will Book G, page 270—Those mentioned—wife, Jenny Bellis; two children by last wife, Charles (B. or H.) Bellis, Margaret Bellis; son, John Bellis, to be under care of William Markham until he comes of age. Written June 24, 1824. Proved February 1825. Executor, William Markham. Witnesses—George Holloway, James Vance, Robert Dudley.

WILLIAM BENEAR—Will Book G, page 49—Those mentioned—son, Henry to be bound to Elijah Webb, to be taught art of a gunsmith until he comes of age; wife, Julia; daughters, Susan, Polly Ann, Margaret; business dealing with Joel Preivitt, William S. Bryan, George Davis. Written June 2, 1821. Proved September, 1822. Executor, friend, John Acor. Witnesses—A. C. McCoy, William Wheat, Z. Wheat.

WILLIAM BENSON—Will Book D, page 162—Those mentioned—son, Thomas; daughter, Betsy Hord; son, Jame; son, Zachariah; daughter, Polly Benson. Written August 24th, 1808. Proved April, 1811. Executors—Edward Hord, Thos. Benson, Thos. McClanahan. Witnesses— Richard Biddle, William Hume, William Jones.

JOHN BESHARER—Will Book C, page 463—Those mentioned— daughter, Rhoda Carr; daughter, Sarah Robbins; grand-daughter, Mary Cummins; grand-daughter, Sarah Cummins; four grand-children, children of daughter, Caty Cummins, John, Mary, Nancy, Cynthia. Written December 18th, 1808. Proved January, 1808. Executor, friend, William Elliott. Witnesses—Richard Biddle, Martha Elliott, Jonathan Judkins.

ALEXANDER BLACK—Will Book C, page 84—Those mentioned— wife, Sarah; son, Samuel; sons, John, William, Craig and Joseph Howe; daughters, Catherine, Sally Polly. Written January 12th, 1806. Proved March, 1806. Executors—wife and son, Samuel. Witnesses—John Alllison, John Scott, Joseph P. House.

JOHN BLACK—Will Book A, page 332—Those mentioned—wife, Martha; our two sons, Samuel and William; grand-son, John Black, son of my son Robert; eldest son, Robert, land in Woodford County, adjoining Robert Gwinn; son, Samuel, land in Bourbon and Mason Counties; son, William, land in Bourbon and Mason Counties. Written May 22nd, 1795. Proved January 1797. Executors—wife, Martha, sons, William and Robert; kinsman, Alexander Black. Witnesses—Walter Cunningham, Samuel Thompson, William Erwin.

JOHN BLACK—Will Book H, page 441—Those mentioned—wife, Milly Black, for support of three youngest children; Christopher, when comes of age; Thomas C., Hiram and Sally; Samuel Black and John Black's son, William Hervey (grand-son); son, William; son, Alexander; son, John; daughter, Elizabeth; Samuel, Christopher and Mary (youngest children); to James Wmy. Written April 3rd, 1829. Proved December 6th, 1830. Witnesses—Bennett Maupin, John P. Wycoff.

JAMES BLACK—Will Book B, page 36—Those mentioned—wife, Anne; son, Alexander; son, John; son, James. Written November 29th, 1797. Proved March, 1799. Witnesses—James Hamilton, Isaac Tull.

JACOB BLUE—Will Book G, page 278—Those mentioned—wife, Isabella Blue; Ephriam Harriett; brothers and sisters, Peter Abraham, David, Benjamin, William, Jesse, Elizabeth Woods, Hannah Harriotte, Peggy Bird. Written March 6th, 1825. Proved May, 1825. Executors—John and Ephriam Harriotte. Witnesses—James Houston, Alexander Dickey.

JOSEPH BOARDMAN—Will Book F, page 120—Those mentioned—wife, Elizabeth and legal heirs. Proved April, 1818. Executors—wife and son, Benjamin Boardman. Witnesses—Henry Bonta, F. Hall, Peter Bonta.

JAMES BOAZ—Will Book H, page 111—Those mentioned—wife, Polly; four married children, Austin Boaz, Elizabeth Henry, Nancy Higgins, James Boaz; other living children, Parmelia Boaz, Jiney Boaz, Julia Ann Boaz, Thomas Boaz, Sareptha Boaz, Dulcinea Boaz, Sally Boaz. Written June 28th, 1828. Proved September, 1828. Executors—wife, son Austin.

GEORGE BOULDIN—Will Book M, page 40—Those mentioned—wife, Julia G. Bouldin, property in Millersburg and Montgomery County; son, George Thomas Bouldin; father and mother-in-law, George and Polly See; wife and father-in-law guardian to son, George Thomas. Written December 19th, 1841. Proved April, 1842. Executors—wife and George See. Witnesses—William Peyton, Matthew Taylor.

DAVID BOWLES—Will Book C, page 195—Those mentioned—wife, Winney, property purchased of Chapman Austin; mother-in-law, Molly Rice, widow; son, Nelson Bowles; son, Thomas; daughter, Elizabeth; grand-daughter, Elizabeth Thomas; great grand-son, David Thomas; son Jesse Bowles; support of my law suit family; three children, Nelson, Thomas and Elizabeth. Written February 20th, 1806. Proved January, 1807. Executor, friend, Richard Thomas, guardian of my children. Witnesses—Michael Hornback, Jr., Abraham Cofman, John Parker.

DAVIS BOWLES—Will Book G, page 129—Those mentioned—wife, Elizabeth; surviving heirs; son, Thomas M. Bowles; daughter, Harriett Payne; son, Benjamin; all my heirs. Written October 2nd, 1823. Proved November, 1823. Executors—brothers, Hughes and Stephen Bowles. Witnesses—Abraham Miller, Robert Green.

JESSE BOWLES—Will Book F, page 353—Those mentioned—wife, Hannah; son Hughes; daughter, Elizabeth Thomas; son, Jesse; son, David; daughter, Sarah A. Turpin; children, Stephen and Robert, Mourning Sandusky and David; children of daugther, Mourning Sandusky, Sally, Betsy, Isaac. Written 29th March, 1820. Proved June 1820. Executors—sons, David, Stephen and Hughes. Witnesses—Thomas Lankford, Augustine Eastin.

ALEXANDER BROWN—Will Book E, page 179—Those mentioned—daughter, Janey; daughter, Hester Alexander; grand-son, Alexander Alexander; grand-sons, John, James Brown; step-son, William Henry; son, John Brown; step-son, James Junkins. Written August 29th, 1807. Proved December, 1814. Executors—grand-son, John G. Brown and step-son, William Henry. Witnesses—William Henry, Samuel Frame, John G. Brown.

THOMAS BOWLES—Will Book G, page 70—"I, Thomas Bowles, son of David Bowles, deceased." Those mentioned: Wife, Nancy, male heirs of brother, Nelson Bowles; friend Henry Parker. Written September 14th, 1822. Proved January, 1823. Executor, Henry Parker. Witnesses—Asa Parker Harlem M. Branham.

JOHN BRADLEY—Will Book L, page 364—Those mentioned—son, Hiram, land to old Daniel Bradley's line; son, Daniel and Joseph Wilson, trustees for daughter, Frankey Henry and her children, Volney Henry, husband of Frankey; Martha Ann Stewart, eldest daughter of John Fulton, deceased. daughter Souckey Judy; son, William Bradley; grand-daughter, Mary, daughter of son, Walter, deceased; Daniel Bradley's two eldest children, John and Hardin; son, Shelton; sons of Hiram Bradley; daughter of William Bradley; Mary, daughter of Walter Bradley, deceased. Written October 15th, 1840. Proved November, 1840. Executors—son, Samuel S. Bradley and Joseph Wilson. Witnesses—William P. Payne, Lewis Wilson, William G. Heges.

REUBEN BRAMBLETT, JR.—Will Book C, page 198—Those mentioned—wife, Peggy; son-in-law, John Grinstead; son, Hugh; three children in South Carolina, Reuben, Jr., Milly Robertson and Polly Robertson; son, William; son, Lewis, land I claim from heirs of Martin Pickett, deceased; son, Henry. Written December 10th, 1806. Proved January, 1807. Executors—John Grinstead, Henry and Hugh Bramblett. Witnesses—Will Mitchell, Edward Riley, Reubin Bramblett, Jr.

ANDREW BRAND—Will Book J, page 567—Those mentioned—mother; father, the late Richard Brand; brothers and sisters. Written February 7th, 1834. Proved September 1st, 1834. Executor, brother, Jeremiah Brand. Witnesses—J. C. Frazier, Thomas Brand.

JEREMIAH BRAND—Will Book K, page 236—Those mentioned—deceased mother; sister, Rachel; her boy, Harry; brother George Brand; brother Richard; brother, Rezin; brother Eliphalet; Rev. Richard Tidings of Sharpsburg, money to Methodist Episcopal Church or American Colonization Society; Washington Bradley. Written September 17th, 1836. Proved October 3rd, 1836. Executor, brother Richard Brand. Witnesses—John Barnett, Victor M. Kenney, John Terrill.

HEZEKIAH (KISEAH) BRAND—Will Book K, page 238—Those mentioned—son, Elephalet; daughter, Rachel; son, Jeremiah; three grand-children, viz: Reason Brand's daughter, Kiseah Wells; Richard Brand's daughter, Kiseah Wells; James Brand's daughter, Mary Ann; son, George. Proved October 3rd, 1836. Witnesses—W. B. Branham, John Barnett, Maria T. Hedges.

ALEXANDER BRECKENRIDGE, SR.—Will Book D, page 416—Those mentioned—wife, Polly; son, Eddy Linn; sons, George Robert, James, Alexander, and John; daughters, Ann, Rachel and Elizabeth; sons, Preston, Washington and Roddy H., land in Murry County, Tennessee; daughter, Jenny. Written June 2nd, 1813. Proved October, 1813. Executors—sons, Alexander and John. Witnesses—John Gass, Henry Clay, Jr., James Alexander.

JOHN BRECKENRIDGE—Will Book G, page 217—Those mentioned—daughter, Elizabeth Orr; daughter, Susan Graves; son, George. Written July, 1824. Proved September, 1824. Executor, son,

George Breckenridge. Witnesses—Benjamin Couchman, Thomas Canaday, John Canaday.

JOHN BRIDGES—Will Book D, page 490—Those named—wife, Nancy; son, William, given him notes on one Martin in South Carolina; son, John; rest of my children, Henry Thomas, Mathew, Betsy, Neddy, Patsy, when they come of age. Written January 6th, 1814. Proved February, 1814. Executors—wife, Nancy and son, Henry. Witnesses—William Boggess, Henry Hennis.

JAMES BROWN—Will Book A, page 284—Those named—wife, Rachel; son, James; daughter, Catherine McCoy; grand-son, James McCoy, when he comes of age; grand-son, Samuel David Brown when of age. Written August 21st, 1791. Proved January, 1796. Executors—wife and Samuel Henderson. Witnesses—Enock Haydon, Peter Smellser, Milchiah Couchman.

ALEXANDER BROWN—Will Book A, page 287—Those named—wife, Elizabeth; sons, James and John; daughters, Nancy, Jane and Elizabeth; children to be educated. Written October 29th, 1795. Proved March, 1796. Executors, William Henry, Jeremiah Frame, David Purviance. Witnesses—William Campbell, John Adams.

JAMES BROWN—Will Book G, page 290—Aged three score and nineteen years—Those mentioned—son, Henry; daughter, Elizabeth Pollard; daughter, Rachel Leach (for particular attention to her stepmother in her last illness, formerly the wife of Edward Dobbins); heirs of deceased wife; daughter, Mary Theobalds; son, James (deceased); widow; son, George; son, William; daughter, Sally Browning; daughter Anna Moore; daughter, Kitty Griffing. Written May 31st, 1821. Proved June, 1825. Executors—sons, George, William, Henry. 1823 codicil, daughter, Isabella Pollard, deceased, her female heirs, Elizabeth Pollard, Mary Porter and Kitty Pollard.

ANDREW BRYAN—Will Book K, page 336—Those mentioned—wife, Cloe; daughter, Elener Piercy; son, William Bryan. Written April 6th, 1836. Proved December 5th, 1836. Executor, son, William Bryan. Witnesses—William Crouch, S. Bowles.

WILLIAM BUCHANNON—Will Book H, page 5—Those mentioned—William Yocum and Jesse Yocum; Betsy McCloud, late Betsy Yocum; wife; all my children; children my wife had by her first husband, Yocum. Written November 7th, 1824. Proved December, 1824. Executors—friends, Andrew Scott of Fayette County and Nicholas Talbot of Bourbon. Witnesses—William Pierce, William A. Menzies.

SPENCER BUCHANNON—Will Book L, page 344—Those mentioned—daughter, Betsy Anderson's children, when they come of age; daughter, Catherine Jones' children; daughter, Rebecca Williams; daughter Polly McCloud; daughter, Jane Buchannon and her children; children of William Buchannon, deceased; son-in-law, Daniel Anderson. Written February 2nd, 1839. Codicil written 31st July, 1840, Jane Buchannon, Noah (lame grand-son); Green Buchannon. Proved September 7th, 1840. Executor, John Cunningham. Witnesses—Dabney Dickerson, Andrew Scott, R. A. Gibney.

ROBERT BURKE—Will Book G, page 104—Those mentioned—wife,

Lucy; son, Robert Burke (son to Juda Stanly, deceased); John and James Humphrey; grand-son, Thomas. Written March 13th, 1820. Proved July, 1823. Executors—friends, William Johnson, Roger Williams. Witnesses—Franklin Williams, George W. Williams.

GEORGE BERNOE (BOURNAUGH)—Will Book D, page 134—Those mentioned—my dear companion; daughter, Polly C. Bournaugh; son, George Bournaugh; son, Thomas; daughters, Peggy, and Susan; my five children that now live with me; son, John; daughter, Betsy. Written November 3rd, 1810. Proved December, 1810. Executrix, wife. Witnesses—William Adair, Jeremiah String, Catron String.

HEZEKIAH BURROUGHES (BURRIS)—Will Book E, page 406—Those mentioned—wife, Polly, she to give as much property to rest of children when they marry as I gave daughters Peggy and Polly. Written March 7th, 1816. Proved May, 1816. Executors—wife, Polly and son, James. Witnesses—Thomas Musick, Joseph Crouch, And. Bryan.

JOHN BURTON—Will Book A, page 144—Those mentioned—children, John, Moses, Charles, Elijah, Elizabeth, Lucy; wife, Martha. Written 1792. Proved October, 1793. Executrix, Martha Burton. Witnesses—Caines Brandon, Thomas Fleming, Samuel Fleming.

MOSES BUTLER—Will Book H, page 292—Those mentioned—wife, Margaret; children, Susan, Catherine, Henry, Alexander, Sarah, Elizabeth and Stephen Waller Butler. Written July 10th, 1828. Proved October 5th, 1829. Executrix, wife, Margaret. Witnesses —Silas Stark, Samuel Stark.

ANN CALDWELL—Will Book L, page 77—William Lyle trustee for three grandchildren viz, Sarah Jane Hall, Margaret Ann and Benjamin Warfield Hall; daughters, Lucretia and Margaret Ann. Executors: sons-in-law, William C. Lyle and Luther Smith. Written September 15, 1837. Proved June 3, 1839. Attest: Thomas P. Smith, John L. Walker.

ISAAC CALDWELL—Will Book E, page 413—"Advanced in life." —Names wife, Rachel, land to descend to her grandson, John Jump; Isaac Seeright, Andrew Seeright and David Seeright, sons of William Seeright (minors). Executors: James Robinson, John Jump. Written August 14, 1811. Proved May, 1816. Witnesses—William and Joseph Nesbitt, Andrew Robinson.

WILLIAM CALDWELL—Will Book H, page 185—Wife, Ann; daughters, Lucretia and Margaret Ann, land purchased from Robert Trimble, married daughters; daughter, Jane Holt; grandsons, William L. Caldwell and John N. Caldwell, sons of Samuel; J. H. Holt; Jane Holt's children, lot in Cynthiana and land in Ohio; son-in-law, Benjamin Warfield; daughter, Betsy Hall. Executors: friends, Geo. W. Williams and Thos. Kelly. Written December 8, 1828. Proved March, 1829. Witnesses—John G. Martin and William Hamilton.

JOHN CALL—Will Book F, page 10—Names friend, William Call; Greenberry Call, son of Wm. Call; Henry F. Wilson; Hety Wilson. Written December 24, 1816. Proved January Court, 1817. Witnesses—Henry Wilson, John and Mary Parker, Harvy Wilson.

SAMUEL CALL—Will Book F, page 165—Names wife, Pricella; "my present family," eldest son, William, farm purchased of Ellis; son, Samuel; son, Daniel; youngest sons, John and Hamilton; daughters, Dorcus, Mary, Ailsey, Hannah and Catherine. Executors: son, Samuel Call, Jr., and Robert Scott. Written June 11, 1818. Proved September Court, 1818. Witnesses—John S. Bristoc, Hugh Folgey.

HUGH CAMPBELL—Will Book C, page 538—Names wife, Jean; two youngest sons, Charles and Greenberry; "all of my family," eldest son, William; daughter, Sally Homes; five eldest sons, William, Hugh, John, James and Lewis; children of age and those not; brother, Charles Campbell. Executors: sons, William and Hugh. Written January 10, 1807. Proved June 1809. Witnesses—Joseph Wallace, David Jameson, Jas. Malcom.

JOHN G. CAMPBELL—Will Book G, page 395—Names wife, Anne Campbell; children. Executors: Anne Campbell and James Campbell. Written July 22, 1826. Proved September, 1826. Witnesses—James Brown, Mason Talbott, Peter Hedges.

WILLIAM CAMPBELL—Will Book E, page 316—Names son, William Campbell, land where John Lyons now lives, adjoining James Lamme and Thos. Dawson; son, Robert; son, James, son John; daughter, Sally Campbell (Bible), daughter, Anna, deceased; daughter, Molly Simpson. Executor—Son, Robert Campbell. Written April 13, 1815. Proved June Court, 1815. Witnesses—Thos. Wornall, Lander Barber, Jas. Lamme, John Lyon.

JAMES CANADAY (KENNEDY)—Will Book G, page 130—"Advanced in age." Sons, John and Thomas; daughters, Lydia and Polly Kennedy; daughter Rebecca Dunaway; daughter, Susannah Garner; sons, Wm., David and James. Written April 9, 1823. Proved November, 1823. Witnesses—Massena Garrard, Wm. Hearn, Jas. Garrard.

HEBE CARTER—Will Book D, page 426—Names six children; land in Greenup County, any land I may have inherited in Maryland or Virginia from my uncle, General Smallwood; land owned in these states and elsewhere; young friend, Susan Peers; cousin, Mrs. Eleanor Peers; Mr. Lyle to educate my children; Benjamin Peers, 4th son of my friends; Mr. James Barns, (religious instructor); brother, Robert. Written October 12, 1813. Proved November, 1813. Executors: Rev. John Lyle, Robert Trimble, Valentine Peers. Witnesses—Thomas Holt, Andrew Todd.

ROBT CARTER—Will Book H, page 196—Names wife, Susannah; son, Thos. Carter, slave in possession of James Carter; my children and their children. Written February 19, 1829. Proved April, 1829. Witnesses—Robt. Toliaferro, R. Bridges.

GEORGE CHAMBLIN—Will Book F, page 469—Names five youngest sons, plantation purchased of Nicholas Bryant; wife, Frances; eight youngest children, viz, Polly, George, Lucy, James, Braxton, Fanny, John, Coleman; son, William; daughter, Nancy Win; daughter, Betsy Foster. Executors: wife and sons, William and George. Witnesses—Wm. Northcutt, John H. Jones, Isaac Webb.

MARY CHAMBLIN—Will Book G, page 229—Names mother, Frances Chamblin; brother, Coleman; sister, Nancy Winn; brother, William; brother, Braxton; sister, Frances Mellean; brother, John. Written March 29, 1824. Proved October, 1824. Witnesses—Willis Prichart, Joseph Forman, Isaac Webb.

JAMES CHAMBLIN—Will Book G, page 83—Names sisters, Polly, Lucy Chamblin and Braxton Chamblin and Nancy Million, land inherited from father; George Chamblin; mother, Frances; Brothers, John and Coleman Chamblin. Written December 6, 1822. Proved March, 1823. Witnesses—Isaac Webb, Thos. Pullen, Joseph Robnett.

ROBERT CHAMP—Will Book H, page 53—Names wife, Sarah; son, Thomas; grandson, Thos. Jefferson Champ, land purchased of Lewellen Porter, land where James Matson lives; grandson, Robert Champ. Executors: son, Thomas and wife, Sarah. Written March 15, 1828. Proved May 1828. Witnesses—Foster Collins, Hezekiah Martin, Wm. G. Burkshire.

JOHN CHAMP—Will Book D, page 196—Estate left by father. wife, when youngest child, Artemetia, comes of age; all my children. Executors: brothers, Thomas and Robert Champ. Proved July, 1810. Witnesses—Jno. Mayfield, Jno. L. Fielder, Robt. Olive.

THOS. CHAMP—Will Book J, page 82—Eldest son, Robert, land willed heretofore by his grandfather; son, Thomas, plantation where my mother, Sarah Champ resides; wife; four sons, viz, Robt. Thos., George, Henry. Executors: Geo. Hughes, Geo. Redmon. Written June 25, 1832. Proved September, 1832. Witnesses— B. H. Hall, Jas. H. Gentry.

JOSEPH CHINN—Will Book J, page 170—Names two youngest children, Elviry and Richard, land bought of Wm. Rossel, Alexander Chinn, "property I gave him which he sold to Henry S. Hawkins;" "all my children," property previously given. Executors: Alexander Chinn and Coleman Chinn. Written August 26, 8131. Proved September 1833. Witnesses—Elijah Chinn, J. M. Chinn.

MARGARET CHINN—Will Book J, page 568—Sister, Matilda Chinn, property from father's estate; sister, Sally Hawkins; neice, Mary Catherine Hawkins; neice, Margarett Ann Shropshire; five brothers, Alexander, Coleman, Christopher, Milton, Benjamin. Written July 7, 1833. Proved September 1834. Executor: brother, Milton Chinn. Witnesses—Jno. H. Hamilton, Betsey Chinn, Elvira Hamilton.

WILLIAM CHOWNING—Will Book H, page 42—Theophilus Chowning, beloved grandson. Executor: grandson, Theophilus Chowning. Written December, 1824. Proved March 1828. Witnesses—R. H. Yancey, Shadrack Shearman.

WILLIAM CHOWNING—Will Book L, page 66—My seven heirs: mother; sister, Elizabeth George; neice, Matildy Chowning; brothers and sister, Lucy's (late Lucy Givens) children; Brady Cummin. Executor: friend, William Hart. Written March 19, 1839. Proved April 1, 1839. Witnesses—Peter Smith, Geo. Moore.

ANN CLARKE—Will Book E, page 104—Sister, Ibby Langston, land left by brother, John Clarke; sister, Margaret Bellis; neice, Ruth Wilson. Executor: brother-in-law, Abraham Langston. May 16, 1814. Witnesses—Eli Hughes, Wm. Ford.

JOHN CLARKE—Will Book D, page 331—Land left by father, brother, Robert Clarke; sisters, Margaret and Ann; neice, Ruth Wilson; brother-in-law, Abraham Langston. Executor: brother Robert. Written August 14, 1812. Proved February 1813. Witnesses— John Hughes, William Ford.

ROBT CLARKE—Will Book B, page 116—Wife, Agnes; son, Robert;

son, John; daughter, Agness; son, James; daughter, Margaret; daughter, Ann; sons-in-law, Daniel Wilson, Benjamin Hardin, Abraham Langston, Noah Lyon. Executors: Jno. Boyd and son, Robert. Written June 17, 1800. Proved January, 1801. Witnesses—Jno. Hamilton, Reubin Duncan, Jno. Row.

JOHN CLARKSON—Will Book B, page 254—"Aged 42 years." Agreement with Rene Mahan, in hands of Robt. McDaniel; land sold Wm. Cummins; land bought of William Mahan; to Agness Mahan; to John Mahan when of age; children, Samuel, Elizabeth and Caty; wife, Agness care of children until 18 years or married. Executors: wife and Roger Williams. Written August 13, 1804. Proved December, 1804. Witnesses—Chas. Clarkson, William Mahan, Jno. Wells.

JULIUS M. (MATTOCK) CLARKSON—Will Book H, page 19—Wife, Lycy Ann Clarkson. Executors: Wife and brother, Charles S. Clarkson. Written at home of brother, Charles C. Clarkson in county of Wilkinson, Miss., January 31, 1827. Proved February 1828. Witness: Charles S. Clarkson.

POLLY CLARKSON—Will Book G, page 471—"Mature age." Husband, Peter Clarkson and "such of my children as may live with him," (youngest child under age); "all my children.". Executor: son, Benjamin B. Written April 3, 1827. Proved 1827. Witnesses—Wm. Moreland, Joseph Russell.

MARY CLARKSON—Will Book G, page 275—Sister, Mourning Clarkson; brother, Julius Clarkson. Executor, nephew, Reubin Clarkson. Written August 1, 1822. Proved April, 1825. Witnesses—John H. Carr, Julius C. Bristoe, Abner Cunningham.

SIDNEY P. CLAY—Will Book J, page 564—Wife, Isabella, property paid me by John Keen's administratrix as guardin for my daughter Sally, amount yet due her from estate at Mrs. Keen's death, Brutus J. Clay and wife Isabella trustees for Sally; sons, Sidney, Elias and Green. Executors: wife, Isabella and Brutus J. Clay. Written April 12, 1834. Proved September, 1834. Witnesses—Jno. Cunningham, Peter Clarkson.

JOHN CLAY—Will Book E, page 1—Three sons, John Samuel, George; son-in-lawHenry C. Bruce. Slaves purchased in Virginia. Written August 23, 1809. Proved March, 1814. Witnesses—Arch O. Bedford, Henry Clay, Jr., Jno. Bedford.

HENRY CLAY, SR.—Will Book F, page 331—"Aged and infirm." Wife, Rachel; son, Henry Clay, Jr.; daughter, Rebecca Finch, land purchased of Col. Jas. Garrard; daughters Sally Martin and Tabitha Bedford, land in Montgomery County; daughters Elizabeth Bruce, Rachel Martin, Mary Anne Dawson, Martha Dedford, Henrietta Bedinger, Letty Bedford; sons, John and Samuel. Executor: Henry Clay, Jr. Written August 7, 1809. Proved February 1820. Witnesses—Jospeh McConnell, Samuel McConnell, Sampson McConnell, Geo. Thomas, Josiah Berryman.

SAMUEL CLAY—Will Book D, page 89—Son, Henry, land on which Anthony Thornton lives; wife; daughter, Lititia; son, Samuel, land on which Zedic Smith lived; son George, land on which Robert Athey formerly lived; son, Littleberry, land on which Wm. Reid lives; son, John, land on which Emanuel Wyatt lives; son, Richard, Hutchison place; daughter Rachel, farm in Madison County; son,

Thomas, land in Henderson County; youngest son, Wm. Green. Executors: Brother Henry Clay and Benj. Bedford. Written April 7, 1810. Proved June, 1810. Witnesses—Emanuel Wyatt, Robt. Nichols, John O. Hancock, Jno. Wyatt, Moses Thomas.

ELIZABET CLEMONS (ELIZABETH COMBS)—Will Book G, page 351—Nuncupative will—Names Jane Norrin. Written July 25, 1825. Proved April, 1826. Witnesses—Margaret Combs, Esther Norrin, Ann Black.

GEORGE CLEVELAND—Will Book D, page 94—Wife, Sally; friends, Captain Maurice Langhorne and William B. Branham, Esq. Written March 19, 1810. Codicil to Maurice Langhorne, "my small sword, presented to me by my father, and my military uniform;" to his son, John M. Langhorne; to Wm. Branham, rest of arms, etc.; to his son, Webb Branham, James King, "bound to me;" mentions wife's relatives. Written March 20, 1810. Proved September, 1810. Executors: Maurice Langhorne, Wm. B. Branham.

ROBERT CLIFFORD—Will Book A, page 64—All my brothers and sisters; brother James Clifford; sister Jane Clifford. Executors: brother, James and William Miller. Written February 13,1790. Proved July, 1791. Witnesses—Joseph Whitesitt, Jas. McCutcheon, John P. Steele.

ISAAC CLINKENBEARD—Will Book M, page 414—Land purchased of Benjamin Forman and Everett Palmer; William and Isaac Clinkenbeard, sons of my nephew, John Clinkenbeard; son of my brother, William, deceased; Nancy Cloud, wife of Prior B. Cloud; late Nancy Pullin; James L. Brown for the three daughters of my nephew, Lucus Clinkenbeard, deceased, son of my brother, John Clinkenbeard, deceased; namely, Mary Ann; and Elizabeth; and Lucinda; Poly Jacob Wilson and Eliza ane Wilson, daughters of my niece, Druzella Smith, daughter of brother, William; Polly Jacob, wife of Isaac Wilson, and Eliza Jane, wife of Tarlton Wilson; Polly Forman tract to niece, Polly Stip, wife of Frederick Stipp; to niece Jane Smith, wife of John Smith; daughter of brother William, deceased; nephew, Jonathan Clinkenbeard, son of brother, William; Isaac Stipp, son of Frederick Stipp. Executors: Nephew, John Clinkenbeard and John Smith. Written May 17, 1845. Proved March, 1846. Witnesses—A. Adams, James Scott, J. L. Brown.

ANDREW COCHRAN—Will Book E, page 121—Daughters, Sally Ferguson; Peggy Raybourn; daughter-in-law, Polly Cochran; three sons; Polly Jubenall. Executors: Clemens Ferguson and Cornelius Raybourn. Written August 24, 1814. Proved September, 1814. Witnesses—Samuel Knox, David Knox, Samuel Ross.

JACOB COIL—Will Book H, page 86—Wife, Elizabeth; seven children, Soloman, Polly ,Noah, John, George, Elijah and Margaret; grand-daughter, Elizabeth Kiplinger (minor); Philip Kiplinger, her father; daughter Polly Allen. Executors: Soloman, John, Elijah Coil and Adniram (Abraham) Allen. Written November 17, 1827. Proved July, 1828. Witnesses—Robt. Scrogin, Joseph and John Cantrill.

MARY M. COLLIER—Will Book K, Page 16—Deceased husband Franklin Collier; daughter Nancy F. Collier; son, John J. Collier; daughter, Elizabeth B. Ellis; daughter, Mary W. Collier, property coming from father's estate now held by mother, land in Illinois; son,

Benj. F. Collier when 21; children: Elizemond T. Collier; Edmond Collier's children and Benjamin F. Collier; Nancy F.; John J.; Mary Wand. Executors: John Breckenridge, Wm. Kenney. Written February 25, 1835. Proved April, 1835. Witnesses—Vale S. Peyton, Elizabeth Peyton, Thos. Basye.

JOHN COLLINS—Will Book E, page 261—Only son, Josiah Collins; eldest daughter,Rodah Hopkins; granddaughter, Ann Swansell, daughter of John Swansill; Nancy (youngest daughter), deceased. Executors: son, osiah Collins, Benj. Miller, Sr. Written June 29, 1807. Proved March, 1815. Witnesses—Andrew G. Mills, Caty Mils.

JOHN COLVILLE—Will Book K, page 59—Estate of sister, Pancy; wife Martha; three sons, Samuel, Sanders, Daniel when of age. "All mychilldren." Written May 22, 1835. Proved July, 1835. Witnesses A. W. Bills, Daniel Summers, Jacob Duncan.

JOHN CONGLETON—Will Book A, page 282—Wife, Margaret; son, William; daughter, Elizabeth Congleton; daughter, Mary Congleton. Executors: James Congleton and William Spenser. Written March 20, 1796. Proved May, 1796. Witnesses—Alexander Bryan, Chas. Payton, Andrew Bryan.

WILLIAM CONGLETON—Will Book D, page 181—Wife, Jean; son, John; son, James; son, William; daughter, Agness, wife of Bennet Roberts; daughter Jean, wife of James Brown; daughter, Mary, wife of John Scott. Executrix: wife and daughter, Elizabeth Congleton. Written June 20, 1804. Proved July, 1811. Witnesses—Patrick Scott, Philip Cox.

WILLIAM W. CONGLETON—Will Boog J, Page 5—Youngest children when of age; wife, Mary; son, John N. Congleton. Executors: wife and son, John N. Congleton. Written September 13, 1831. Proved October 1831. Witnesses—Duncan O. Richart, S. Bowles, Wm. Crouch.

THOMAS CONN—Order Book E, page 416—May, 1815—Heirs were: Thomas, John, Cassandra Flournoy (late Conn), Hezekiah Conn, Sally Ware (late Conn), William Conn, James Conn. Sworn to by Thomas McClanahan.

SARAH CONN—Will Book F, page 389—Daughter Cassandria Flournoy; daughter, Sally Ware; son, John M. Conn; sons, William and James; Fanny Conn, wife of son, William; grand-daughter, Sally Broadus; grand-daughter Kitty Todd Ware, son, Hezekiah. Executor: son, William. November 8, 1820. Witnesses—Jacob Myers, Robert Hill, Jr., James H. Cary.

THOMAS CONN—Will Book E, Page 318—Children: Sally Broadus, eldest; Polly Hallax and Notly Conn (minors), land in Livingston County; wife, Lucy Conn; two youngest children, Oberia Conn and Hezehea (Hezekiah) Conn, money due from John B. Armistead. Executor: Augustine Respess who will sign deed with John, Hezekiah, William, James Conn; David Flournoy and Thomas Ware for land in Culpepper County, Virginia. Written May 31, 1815. Proved July, 1815. Witnesses—David Hickman, Henry S. Hawkins, Wm. Higgins.

JOHN CONSTANT—Will Book A, pages 11-12—Nuncupative will—styled "Captain John Constant."—All his children; Abegail, wife. Signed Van Swearingen and Isaac Constant, October 21, 1788.

FAYETTE COUNTY WILL ABSTRACTS

(Contributed by Mrs. Joseph Beard and Mrs. Ernest Dunlap,
Bryan Station Chapter)

JOHN ALEXANDER—Will Book B, Page 67—Names wife, Mary; nephews, James Campbell, Samuel Gibson, William Campbell, William Alexander, John Campbell. Written October 11, 1809; probated November Court, 1809. Executors—Samuel Hind, Robert Alexander, Wm. Alexander. Witnesses—Wm. Boon, Will Alexander, Charles Campbell, Jane Wilson.

JAMES ANDERSON—Will Book C, Page 529—Names wife, Molly; children, William, Margaret, Samuel Logan, George; friend, David Logan; Esther, Anne, John, James. Written September 28, 1815; probated February, 1816. Executors—James Logan, James Wallace. Witnesses—David Logan, David McMurtry, Thos. McIlroy.

NATHANIEL ASHBY—Will Book B, Page 233—Names wife, Ann Ashby (second wife); daughters, Betsey January, Polly Taylor; sons, Mozie Ashby, William B. Ashby; daughters, Sally, Peggy; son, John G.; daughters Nancy, Jane; sons, Nathaniel, Haman J. Written May 24, 1811; probated July, 1811. Executors—Mozie Ashby, William R. Ashby (sons). Witnesses —Robert Tilton, Brice Steele, Levi Calvert, William Stone.

ELIZABETH ATWOOD—Will Book B, Page 349—Names daughter, Sally Bowlin; grandchildren, Jane B. Bowlin, John G. Bowlin, Elizabeth K. Bowlin, Samuel S. Bowlin, Felicia Bowlin, William Bowlin, Malinda Bowlin. Written April 2, 1811; probated February, 1812. Executor: William Bowlin. Witnesses—Hiram Mitchell, Lewis Hargdon, Robert Chipley, Henry Reed, Charles Betty, Richard Eran.

HENRY BARTLETT—Will Book A, Page 183—Names father, Henry Bartlett; mother, Sarah Bartlett; brother, John Crane Bartlett; sisters, Elizabeth, Phebe, Polly, Sally, Franky. Written July 25, 1792; probated December, 1794. Executors—Thomas Bartlett (brother), James Wood. Witnesses—James McCrosky, Lucky McCrosky.

SARAH BEARD—Will Book A, Page 406—Names sons, William Beard, Joseph Beard; grand-daughters, Nancy McGowan, Sally Beard, (daughter of Joseph), Sally Beard (daughter of Wm. Beard). Written September 30, 1805; probated October, 1806. Executors—Wm. Beard, Joseph. Beard. Witnesses— F. Cosby, John Bryant, John Henderson.

ROB BELL—Will Book C, Page 265—Names daughter, formerly living in Baltimore; brother, John; sister, Mary. Written April 3, 1814; probated August, 1814. Executors—Harvey Weir, Robert Batley, Ed Howe. Witnesses—John Hill, Mary Hill.

JOHN BENDTELL—Will Book B, Page 17—Names Solomon Bental. Written March 3, 1809; probated May, 1809. Executor, Joseph Allen. Witnesses—George Pickett, Charles Bush, John Bush, Josiah Sketer.

JAMES BERRYMAN—Will Book B, Page 377—Names wife, Margaret; Sons, Thomas H., James S., John H., Upshur, Ethelmer, Prancis, and Newton Berryman. Written April 2, 1812; probated July 1812. Executors—Thomas Threshly, Thomas Berryman. Witnesses—Wm. Boon, Geo. G. Boon, Samuel Berryman.

ANTHONY BLESTE—Will Book B, Page 350—Names wife, Judith Bleste. Written short time before death; probated February, 1812. Witness, Jacob Mordecai Harris.

WILLIAM BOBB—Will Book C, Page 74—Nuncupative—Names wife; son, John B. Bobb; daughters, Sarah and Isabella. Written January 8, 1814; proved by oaths of Joseph Connor, Polly Long, David Barton, February, 1814.

WILLIAM BOULWARE—Will Book A, Page 77—Names wife, Nettie Boulware; sons, John, William and Jacob; daughters, Lucy Wortham, Frances Grubbs, Phebe Pemberton and Fannie Boulware; grand-son, Hyram Wortham. Written March 29, 1790. Executors —Son, John Boulware, Samuel Ayres, Nettie Boulware. Witnesses— Alexander Nod, Sally Nod, Sarah Pemberton.

WILLIAM BOYCE—Will Book B, Page 348—Names wife, Elizabeth; sons, John and William; daughters, Betsey Wilson, Patsy Moody and Nancy Wrenn. Written December 9, 1811; probated February, 1812. Executors—John and William (sons) Thomas Wren (son-in-law). Witnesses—William Smith, Stephen Smith.

JOSEPH BRADBOURN—Will Book B, Page 535—Names wife,Gracy. Written December 31, 1811; probated October, 1813. Witnesses— William Cotton, Jacob Yeager, William Cleoff.

JANE BRADSHAW—Will BookA, Page 247—Names daughters, Isabella Burns and Sally Hoblett; sons, Samuel Bradshaw and son. Written June 13, 1804; Probated, April, 1805. Executor, John Gorham. Witnesses—John McDowell, Priscilla Gorham, Frances Simpson.

NICHOLAS BRIGHT—Will Book A, Page 193—Names first wife, Priscilla; second wife, Rebecca; son, George Young Bright, daughter, Catherine Bright (both children of first wife). Written August 4, 1804. Probated August, 1804. Executors—Major James Morrison, Samuel Ayres, George Young, Sr. Witnesses—Allen Magruda, Robert Holmes, C. Kiser.

MORGAN BRYANT—Will Book A, Page 176—Names wife ;daughter, Rebecca; sons, Morgan Bryant, Jr., and Joseph Bryant; grand-daughter, Mary Bryant (daughter of Joseph). Written September 29, 1794; probated July, 1804.

GEORGE BRUCE—Will Book A, Page 501—Names wife, Temperance Bruce; daughters, Helby Bruce, Parmelia Bruce and Polly Grant; sons, Warren (military land), Waddle and Bengamine. Written October 16, 1808; probated November, 1808. Executors, Samuel Blair, Temperance Bruce (wife). Witnesses—Alexander Colbard, James Gibson.

JAMES BULLOCK—Will Book B, Page 501—Names wife, Anne; sons, Thomas, Wringfield and Walter; daughters, Milly Winn, Barbara Wilson, Agnes Bullock, Anne Redd and Martha P. Bullock; son-in-laws, Robert Bullock and Samuel Redd; grand-daughter, Catherine Redd. Written May 18, 1813; probated July, 1813. Executors—

Samuel R. Overton, Walter Bullock. Witnesses—John Todd, Stapleton C. Burch, Benjamin P. Miller.

CHARLES CADE—Will Book A, Page 325—Names wife, Catherine Cade; son, David and his wife Lydia. Was married twice; daughter of first wife could not be found. Written May 17, 1803; probated July, 1806. Executors—Catherine Cade, James Whaley. Witnesses—Thomas Foster, John Hay, C. Morgan, C. Grimes, Job Carter, James Whaley, Benjamin Laughliin..

JOHN CALDWELL—Will Book A, Page 88—Names wife; daughter, Polly, Mary Kelly's daughter, Rebecca; brother, Samuel; brothers. Written 1795; probated February, 1799. Executors—Hugh McIlvain, Samuel Caldwell. Witnesses—John Cooper, John McNair, James Pollock.

CHARLES CAMPBELL—Will Book B, Page 379—Names wife, Mary; sons, James, Robert and William; daughter, Polly Watson (wife of David); daughter, Rachæl; sons, Charles and Hugh; Written March 12, 1812. Probated July, 1812. Executors—Mary Campbell (wife), Hugh Campbell (son), Andrew Wallace (son-in-law). Witnesses—Richard Hunter, James B. Bruster, William Boon.

ROBERT CAMPBELL—Will Book B, Page 358—Names wife, Elizabeth; sons, Arthur and James; step-daughter, Rachæl Kyman; step-son, John Brumfield. Written October 17, 1811. Probated February, 1812. Executors—Elizabeth Campbell, Samuel Ayre. Witnesses—William Beard, L. McCullough, John Carty, Richard Higgins.

HENRY CAMPER—Will Book A, Page 334—Names sons, William, Reuben and Henry; daughters, Nancy, Letty, and Alcey. Written Novvember 24, 1792. Probated January, 1793. Executors—wife (not named), son, William. Witnesses—Wm. Triplett, Tilman Camper, Deniah Camper.

LETITIA CAMPER—Will Book B, Page 390—Names sons, John, William, Reuben and Henry Camper; daughters, Nancy Martin, Lettice Coons and Alice Roach. Written March 4, 1812. Probated May, 1812. Executors—Reuben Camper, Henry Camper (sons). Witnesses—Wm. R. Davenport, Nimrod Camper, Tilman Camper.

JOB CARTER—Will Book B, Page 271—Names wife, Sarah Newton; children, Isaac Newton, and Polly Fairfax; daughter, Creath (who had received her portion); brothers, Solomon and Peter; sister, Elizabeth Dawson; nephew, Elisha Carter (son of Solomon). Written July 27, 1808. Probated October, 1811. Executors—George Webb, Hubbard Taylor, Sr., Henry Payne, William N. Lane. Witnesses—William Watson, James Jenkins, Zacaraish Spiers, Robert Stuart.

MILLY CHINN—Will Book A, Page 489—Names Jane Tandy, mother, from whom she received 200 acres of land to do with as she wished; John Allen, trustee; at the death of Milly Chinn, Asa Wilgns inherited the 200 acres of land willed to him by Milly Chinn; William Tandy, husband of Jane Tandy. Written June 17, 1807. Probated August, 1808. Witnesses—W. W. Tandy, David Castleman, Gab. Tandy, W. D. Young.

WILLIAM CHINN—Will Book B, Page 423—Names wife, Sarah; son,

Alfred; daughter, Nancy. Written February 1, 1812. Probated October, 1812. Executors—Sarah Chinn (wife), Alfred Chinn (son). Witnesses— John Ransdell, Mary Bradford.

JAMES CLARKE—Will Book B, Page 146—Names wife, Susannah; son, John; daughter, Lucy; sons, Edmond and William; daughter, Delphy; sons, James, Wipkin, Thomas, Peter, Samuel, and Sidney; daughters, Betsey and Suckey. Written April 30th, 1810. Probated July, 1810. Executors—Susannah Clark (wife), John Clark, Edmond Clark, Wm. Ellis. Witnesses—John Darnaby, John Edmiston.

JOHN CLARK—Will Book A, Page 323—Names wife, Catherine; sons, John, Charles, William and Alexander; daughters, Polly, Jane and Margaret; Written June 14, 1806. Probated July, 1806. Executors—Catherine Clark (wife), Samuel Blair, Wm. Gibson. Witnesses—Robert Frazer, Elizah McClelachan, John Atchinson.

WILLIAM CLARKE—Will Book A, Page 513—Names sons, George, William and James; son-in-law, John Holmes and wife Fanny. Written October 27, 1808. Probated December, 1808. Executors: William Clarke (son), John Holmes (son-in-law), Thomas Loux (nephew), George Elliott. Witnesses—George Elliott, David Bell, Betsey Allen.

JOHN S. COCKRELL—Will Book B, Page 58—Names wife, Catherine; children, names not given. Written February 25, 1809. Probated October, 1809. Executors—Elmond Bullock and wife Catherine. Witnesses—John Hendley, James Whaley, Robert Nichols, James G. Hardin.

WINDER CROCKETT—Will Book A, Page 47—Names wife, Annie Crockett; son, Newbold; daughters, Betsy Eavins, Nancy Dingle, Eliza Eavins and Lottie Hutchenson. Written January 18, 1800. Probated August, 1803. Executrix—Annie Crockett (wife). Witnesses—Thomas Nutter, John Simieon, Robert Scott.

WILLIAM DANGERFIELD—Will Book B, Page 392—Names mother, Mary Dangerfield; brothers, Henry and John Dangerfield, both of Frederick County, Virginia. Written June 4, 1807, Probated May, 1812. Executor—John Dangerfield of Frederick County, Virginia. Witnesses—Wm. Todd, Abner Legrand.

JOSEPH DAVIESS—Will Book B, Page 307—Names wife; nephews, Samuel and John Daviess (sons of William Daviess). Written July 18, 1811. Probated December, 1811. Witnesses—Joseph H. Hawkins, James Fishback, John F. Bell.

JAMES DOWNING—Will Book B, Page 432—Names wife, Charity; daughters, Keziah Higbee and Sinthea Downing; sons, Jeremiah, John and James Downing. Written July 21, 1812. Probated November, 1812. Executors—wife, Charity, Joseph Higbee (son-in-law), David Bryan. Witnesses—Abraham Bowman, Joseph Faulkoner, Thomas Lincoln, John Higbee.

JOHN EDMISTON—Will Book B, Page 467—Names wife, Margaret; son, Alexander (deceased); daughters (two), names not given. Written August 13, 1812. Probated April, 1813. Executors—wife, Margaret, James Richardson (son-in-law), William Prewett, Walter Preston. Witnesses—Robert Wickliffe, Margaret P. Wickliffe.

ROBERT ELROD—Will Book B, Page 102—Names wife,Sarah; daughters, Elizabeth Jones, Mary Jones, Hester Tanbush. Susannah Rainey, and Rachel Eddleman; step-daughter, Milly Baker. Written December 11, 1809. Probated January, 1810. Executors—Samuel Boon, Peter Eddleman. Witnesses—John House, William Robinson.

RICHARD EPPERSON—Will Book A, Page 341—Names wife; children. Verbal Statement. Probated October, 1806. Witnesses—Sally McNeil, Mary Baxter, Patsey Brink.

SUSANNA EPPERSON—Will Book A, Page 225—Names sons, Francis and John Epperson. Written June 2, 1803. Probated November, 1804. Witnesses—B. Abesnathy, Chesley Epperson, Francis Epperson.

JOHN ESTES—Will Book B, Page 52—Names wife, Ann Estes; John Thomas, Molly, Middleton, Nancy, Abraham, Clement, Betsey and Bartley. Written July 22, 1808. Probated August, 1809. Executors—John and Middleton Estes (sons). Witnesses—Richard Hulet, Robinson Hulet.

JOSIAH FERGUSON—Will Book A, Page 17—Names daughters, Judith Wilson, Mary Duhamel and Jane Tomkins; sons, Thomas, Josiah and William; daughters, Betsy, Nancy; daughter, Catherine Jones. Written July 25, 1802. Probated April, 1803. Witnesses—Thos. Clark, George Muir, Robert Marshall.

JOSEPH FRY—Will Book B, Page 420—Names wife, Susanna, children. Written July 8, 1812. Probated October, 1812. Executors—wife, Susanna, John Devore, Abraham Byrd, Jr. Witnesses—Joseph Cabell, James G. Leach, Chas. Mayersback. Witnesses to codicil—James T. Leach, Abraham Byrd, Samuel Patterson, August 5, 1812.

WILLIAM FRYE—Will Book A, Page 222—Names wife, Rachel Frye; sons, Jacob, Joseph and Henry; daughters, Rebecca, Elizabeth, Catherine and Rachel; son, Benjamin. Written March 28, 1796. Probated May, 1796. Executors—Rachel Frye (wife), Jacob Frye (son). Witnesses—David Boone, Robert McGill, Peter Goodnight.

WILLIAM FULLERTON—of the Commonwealth of Pennsylvania but now in Kentucky—Will Book A, Page 452—Names John Jordan, Sr., 1125 acres of land of the 10,000 that tract patented in my name, lying on Main Rough Creek opposite to Hartford; to sisters. Written August 12, 1801. Probated November, 1805. Executors—John Jordan, John Helm. Witnesses—Henry Clay, Thomas Wallace, Sam Brown.

STARKE GILLIAN—Will Book B, Page 16—(Noncupative)—wife and children. Probated May, 1809 by oaths of witnesses. Witnesses—Thomas Gilliam, David McCoy, Edward Payne, Ellen Payne, Nancy Barns.

THOMAS GOODLOE—Will Book B, Page 463—Names wife, Dolly; son, Henry Goodloe; daughters, Agnes Yates, Nancy Mitchell and Fanny Goodloe; son, John Goodloe. Written October 8, 1812. Probated April, 1813. Executors—wife, Dolly, Walter Bullock, Jesse Bryant. Witnesses—Robinson Hulet, Charles Ellis, Walter E. Ellis, Robert Jones, Lewis C. Ellis.

THOMAS GRAVES—Will Book A, Page 5—Names wife, Isabel Graves;

sons, William, Bartlett and John; daughters, Rosannah Randolph, Isabel Hall, Ann Hancock, Sally Graves, Mary Beeler and Siddy Graves. Written October 24, 1801. Probated December 14, 1801. Executors—Bartlett Graves (son), Bartlett Collins (friend). Witnesses—James Martin, Wm. Dickey, Jeremiah Buckley.

PHILIP GRIMES—Will Book B, Page 53—Valinda Grimes, widow of son John, and children of John, also Warren Bates, son of Valinda by former marriage; sons, James, Avory, Charles and Benjamin; deceased sons, Stephen and Phillip; deceased daughter, Mary Grimes Payne; grand-daughter Polly Grimes. Written February 20, 1805. Probated August, 1809. Executors—Charles Grimes, James Grimes (sons). Witnesses—H. Harrison, Christian Cooper, John Hay, Daniel Lay, Archibald Parker.

MORRIS GWYN—Will Book A, Page 25—Names nephew, Morris Garrett, tract of land in Kenhawa County, containing 1080 acres by patent; Eli Garrett; Lewis Garrett; Wm. Garrett; Morris Garrett; Thomas Garrett; Rebecca and Phebe Garrett. Written January 3, 1798. Probated April 16, 1803. Executor—William Hamilton. Witnesses—Anne Hamilton, Peggy Hamilton, James Hamilton.

WILLIAM HALEY—Will Book A, Page 79—Names wife, Henrietta Haley; son, Benjamin Haley; daughter, Orinda Outon. Written April 6, 1803. Probated November, 1803. Executor—Benjamin Haley. Witnesses—Wm. Haley, James Weathers.

PETER HARPER—Will Book B, Page 66—Names mother, Betty Harper. Written October 10, 1785. Probated March, 1790. Witnesses—Isaac Harper, Sarah Harper.

HEZEKIAH HARRISON—Will Book A, Page 527—Names mother, wife, Jane Harrison; children (five); brothers, Micajah, Hosea; sons D. J. J. P. Harrison; Hezekiah Harrison, son of Hiram Harrison; daughters, Nancy, Dulcinia, Polly and Peggy Richardson Harrison; sons, John, Dudley, Josiah, Jilson Payne Harrison, owned land in Fayette, Jessamine and Jefferson Counties. Written August 2, 1806. Executrix—Jane Harrison. Witnesses— Henry Clay, John Pope, James Hughes, Will Payne, John Glover, Micajah Harrison, Col. Will Dudley, Lawrence Young, Ambros Young.

NATHANIEL G. HART—Will Book B, Page 465—Names wife, Anna Edwards Hart; children. Written October 1, 1812, at St. Mary's, Ohio. Probated April, 1813. Executors—wife, Anne Edwards Hart, Henry Clay, John Hart. Witnesses—Henry Clay, Charles S. Humphreys, David Todd.

THOS. HART, SR.—Will Book A, Page 480—Names sons, Nathaniel, John and Thomas Hart; daughters Susanna Price, Elizabeth Pindell's heirs; sons-inlaws, James Brown and Henry Clay; daughters, Anne Brown and Lucretia Clay; grand-sons, Nathaniel Hart and John Hart, sons of Elizabeth Pindell. Written August 31, 1807. Probated July, 1808. Executors—Thos. Hart, Henry Clay, Witnesses—John W. Hunt, Thos. C. Graves, Samuel Wilikinson.

THOMAS HART—Will Book B, Page 91—Names wife, Eleanor Hart; children, Thomas Pindell Hart; sisters, Eleanor Hart and Louisa Hart; mother, Susanna Hart; brothers, Nathaniel T. Hart and John Hart; sisters, Susanna Hart Price and Sophia Hart Clay (wife of Porter Clay). Written June 26, 1809. Probated December, 1809. Executors—Eleanor Hart (wife), Henry Clay, John W.

Hunt, Abraham Stout Barton, John Hart (brother). Witnesses—
Eleazer Baker, William Hart, Elizah Noble, Henry Clay.

JOHN HENDERSON—Will Book A, Page 482—Names wife, Elizabeth; daughters, Jane and Elizabeth Perkins; son-in-law, Garret Perkins. Written May 12, 1808. Probated July, 1808. Executors —Garrett Perkins, Isaac McIsaac. Witnesses—John Boulware, Isaac McIsaac, Jr.

AZARIAH HIGGINS—Will Book B, Page 328—Names wife, Sarah; son, Azariah Stout Higgins; daughters, Catherine Brown and Grace Stone. Written September 20, 1811. Probated January, 1812. Executors—wife, Sarah, son, Azariah, sons-in-law, Micajah Stone and Benjamin Stout. Witnessses—Jediah Stout, Clare Oxley, David Stout.

JAMES HILL—Will Book A, Page 494—Names wife, Margaret; daughter, Elizabeth, wife of James Henderson; sons, David and John; daughters, Isabella and Polly; sons, James, Henderson and William, my three youngest sons. Written September 22, 1808. Probated October, 1808. Executors—wife, Margaret Hill, son-in-law James Henderson. Witnesses—David Logan, J. McCracken, James Lonney.

HENRY HILLOCK—Will Book A, Page 203—Names James Hambleton Hillock and his mother; Sarah Hambleton. Written June 11, 1800. Probated July, 1800. Witnesses—Walter Karrick, Joshna Judd, Josiah Sketer.

SOPHIA W. HOLDER—Will Book A, Page 340—Names sisters, Lydia Holder, Fanny Holder and Kitty Holder. Written August 3, 1806. Probated October, 1806. Executors—Col. Richard Hickman, Major Robert Caldwell, John W. Holder, John Hart. Witnesses—John W. Holder, John Hart, Polly Hart.

ANN HUFFORD—Will Book A, Page 431—Names children in the old settlement, to wit: Adam, Catherine, Susanna, Mary and Hannah Hufford; other children are: George Elizabeth, Jacob, Barbara and Rebecca. Written March 18, 1807. Probated October, 1807. Executors—John Burger, John Bostian (son-in-law). Witnesses—John Parker, John Collins, Jos. Craig.

GEORGE HUNTER—Will Book A, Page 184—Names wife, Rachel Hunter, son, George Hunter, son, Richard Hunter, daughters, Rachel and Mary Hunter; son, William Hunter; daughter, Elizabeth Hunter; son, Thomas Hunter; grand-sons, George and James Hunter. Written May 11th, 1804. Probated August, 1804. Executors—Rachel Hunter (wife), Thomas Hunter (son). Witnesses —H. Harrison, Wm. Alexander, Chas. Campbell.

JAMES IRWIN—Will Book A, Page 339—Names sister, Martha Irwin; brother, William Irwin; sister, Jane Wood and daughter Jully Wood. Written July 30, 1806. Probated October, 1806. Executor—John Bryant. Witnesses—Henry Pogue, John Napper, Elizabeth Napper.

PETER JANUARY—Will Book A, Page 243—Names wife, Margaret January; sons, Thomas and Derrick P. January; daughters, May Payne and Jennet Thurston; sons, Peter and James B. January; daughter-in-law, Hannah, Ann McGregor (sister). Written May 10, 1802. Probated January, 1805. Executors—Thomas January (son) David Payne (son-in-law).

WILLIAM JENKINS—Will Book A, Page 308—Names wife, Patty Jenkins; daughters, Sally and Amy; son, Downey (oldest son); Avry Webster (alias Jenkins); David Jenkins. Written January 10, 1806. Probated April, 1806. Executors—Patty Jenkins and Downey Jenkins (son). Witnesses—John Foley, Elijah Foley, Wm. Foley.

MATHEW JOHNSON, SR.—Will Book B, Page 101—Names wife, Nancy Johnson; son, Mark Johnson; grand-daughter, Patsy Wood; daughters, Nancy Anderson and Betsey Woodridge; sons, Joseph and Mathew Johnson; daughters, Lucy Robinson, Jany Edrington and Rachel Raney. Written June 7, 1804. Probated January 1810. Executors—Wife, Nancy and son, Mark Johnson. Witnesses—A. Thompson, Adam Hays.

JOHN KAY—Will Book B, Page 361—Names wife, Mary Kay; son, Robert Kay; daughters, Polly Curd and Margaret Gatewood; son, John Kay; daughters, Jane Kay and Lucy Kay; sons, James, William F. and Andrew G.; grand-daughter, Overela Gatewood. Written January 29, 1812. Executors—wife, Mary, sons, Robert and James, son-in-law Merryman B. Curd. Witnesses—Robert A. Gatewood, Will Gist, Larkin Adams.

KATHERINE KELLEY—Will Book A, Page 18—Names sons, John, William, Samuel and Bobb; daughters, Margaret, Eleanor, Rebecca, Sarah and Jane. Written December 5, 1802. Probated April, 1803. Executors—Wm. Kelley, Samuel Kelley. Witnesses—R. Batterson, Jane Riche, Sarah Higgins.

CASPER KERSNER—Will Book A, Page 393—Names wife, Eve Kersner; mother, Margaret; children. Written April 14, 1797. Probated July 10, 1797. Witnesses—Levi Todd, Jonathan Ralston, Henry Kent.

PETER LAUGHLIN—Will Book A, Page 36—Names wife, Sarah Laughlin; sons, John Wilson Laughlin, Benjamin Laughlin; daughters, Margaret, Sarah, Isabel and Elizabeth, wife of John Forsythe; grond-children, Sarah and William Forsythe, Robert Forsythe, son of Peter Laughlin Forsythe; daughter, Mary; John Wilson Laughlin's son, Peter Laughlin. Written June 8, 1802. Probated September, 1802. Executors—John Wilson Laughlin, Benjamin Laughlin, Sarah Laughlin. Witnesses—Wm. Watson, Leu K. Bradley, James Whaley, Jr.

JOHN LEGRAND—Will Book B, Page 167—Names wife, Jane Legrand; daughter, Mary Jane Legrand; son, Peter Legrand. Written April 14, 1810. Probated November, 1810. Executors—wife, Jane P. Legrand, Abner Legrand (brother), James Craig. Witnesses—John McDowell, Jesse Lannine.

THOMAS LEWIS—Will Book B, Page 57—Names wife, Elizabeth; sons, Hector, Asa, Stephen, Thornton, Alphens and Douglas; daughters, Nancy Garrard, Sally Clay, Kitty Payne, and Sophia Lewis; son-in-law, Jepthal Dudley; grand-son, Edward Ambrose Dudley. Written April 25, 1809. Probated October, 1809. Executors—wife, Elizabeth, Henry Payne, Sr., Hector Lewis, Asa Lewis (sons). Witnesses—Levi Calvert, James Beatty, Henry Payne.

JAMES LOWRY—Will Book A, Page 59—Names mother, Melvin Lowry; brothers, John Lowry (oldest), Melvin Lowry; sister, Mary

Lowry. Written February 2, 1795. Probated October, 1796. Witnesses—Alexander Boteler, Thomas Boteler, Elizabeth Lusk.

STEPHEN LOWRY—Will Book A, Page 63—Names wife, Kitty; daughters, Margaret, Mary, Kitty and Sarah; sons, John (oldest), Abram, Stephen and William. Written March 1796. Probated October, 1803. Executors—Samuel Wilson, Joseph Wilson, John Lowry. "A copy, the original will being destroyed by fire."

SUSANNA LUCAS—Will Book A, Page 467—Names son, Charles Lucas; daughters, Jemimah Lucas, Polly Moore and Nancy Cook will. Written June 6, 1806. Probated April 1808. Executor—Charles Lucas (son). Witnesses—James Whaley, Joseph Scragham, Chas. B. Givens.

ROBERT LYLE—Will Book A, Page 270—Names wife, Jane Lyle; son, John Lyle, his mother; daughter, Julia. Written October 29, 1804. Probated August, 1805. Executors—John Lyle, Sr., John Eakin. Witnesses—John Lyle, Sr., John Eakin.

HENRY MARSHALL—Will Book A, Page 322—Names wife, Catherine Marshall; son, John Marshall; daughter, Polly W. Marshall; to children of my brother, Wm. Marshall. Written May 17, 1806. Probated July, 1806. Executors—friend, Henry Clay, George Trotter, Jr., George Heytel, John M. Boggs. Witnesses—Daniel Bradford, C. H. Bradford, John M. Boggs.

JOHN MARSHALL—Will Book A, Page 62—Names wife, Elizabeth Marshall; daughter, Jane McCullah; sons, James and Joseph Marshall; daughters, Elizabeth, Margaret, Sarah and Mary. Written July 6, 1803. Probated October, 1803. Executors—Wm. Barbee, Robert Wilson, Elizabeth Marshall. Witnesses—Wm. Patterson, Moses Randolph, John Lyle.

CHARLES MASON—Will Book B, Page 59—Names wife, Polly Mason. Written September 14, 1804. Probated October, 1809. Executors—wife, Polly Mason, John Higbee, John Mason, Abraham Bowman, Sr., John Parker. Witnesses—David Smith, Elizabeth Cartmell, Evan Price, David Bryan.

EDMOND MASON—Will Book A, Page 318—Names cousin, John Mason of Fayette County, all of my estate. Written January 16, 1805. Probated May, 1806. Witnesses—Daniel Hodges, Sally Mason.

OBEDIENCE McCANN—Will Book B, Page 69—Names daughter, Phebe Baenard; grand-daughter, Polly Bernard; grand-son, Valentine Parren Bernard; grand-daughter, Frances McCann; son, Neal McCann. Written May 8, 1809. Probated November, 1809. Executors—Neal McCann (son), Roger Laughlin. Witnesses—Frances McDonnall, James C. McDonald.

KENNETH McCOY—Will Book B, Page 101—Names brothers, William McCoy, Daniel McCoy; nephew, Kenneth McCoy (son of Daniel). Written August 12, 1809. Probated January, 1810. Executors—Daniel McCoy (brother), Thomas Bodley, Charles Humphreys. Witnesses—B. W. Dudley, Peter Bailey.

PATRICK McCULLOUGH—Will Book A, Page 226—Names niece, Jane Workman; other relatives in Ireland, Margaret Workman, Agnes Drummond, Jane McCullough who married Mr. Couney Weir; James

McCullough. Written September 17, 1803. Probated January, 1805. Executors—John Bradford, Andrew Holmes. Witnesses—MaGrudar, Allen MaGrudar, John Bradford, Wm. Leavy, Lewis Saunders, Archibald Williams.

JOHN McDANIEL—Will Book B, Page 393—Names wife, Mary McDaniel; daughter, Elizabeth McDaniel; sons, Enoch and Boon; grand-children, Mary Johnson, James Johnson, Ennice Johnson; daughter, Sarah Rucker. Written July 9, 1811. Probated May, 1812. Executrix—wife, Mary McDaniel. Witnesses—George Clarke, James Trotter, Mark Whittaker, George McDonald.

JOSEPH McMURTRY—Will Book A, Page 8—Names wife, Isabella McMurtry; sons, James, John, William, Samuel, David and Levi; daughter, Nancy. Written December 4, 1800. Probated January, 1801. Executors—James McDowell, John McDowell, Wm. Hamilton. Witnesses—Wm. Logan, John Gardnes, John Hagerty.

JOHN McNAIR—Will Book A, Page 413—Names wife, Jane McNair; sons, David, Robert and John; daughters, Polly and Eliza. Written August 19, 1801. Probated December, 1801. Executors Robert Patterson, Samuel Ayres, Alexander Parker, Thomas Wallace, Jane McNair. Witnesses—Levi Todd, John Rennick, Robert Hunter.

ROBERT MEGOWAN—Will Book B, Page 187—Names wife, Mary Megowan; sons, two, not named. The home was called Belfast and contained 51 acres, just outside of Lexington, Ky. Written February 24, 1804. Probated August 1804. Executors—Mary Megowan, John Bradford, James Hughes, Wm. Morton, Thos. Bodley, Witnesses—Thomas Bodley, Wm. Todd.

ARCHILAUS MOORE—Will Book B, Page 277—Names wife, Ann Moore; daughter, Betsey Ann Moore; son, Josiah Pleasant Moore; daughters, Patsy Morton Moore, Polly Venable Moore; son, John Anderson Moore; daughters, Fanny Poindexter Moore, Nancy Dabney Moore, Kitty Anderson Moore, Sally Moore, and Susanna Cobb Moore. Written May 8, 1796. Probated July, 1796. Executors—wife, Ann, Thomas Ammon, John White, Joseph Higbee, John Miller. Witnesses—John Washington, Henry Brock, Benjamin Long, Elisha Cavens.

DANIEL MORRIS—Will Book A, Page 363—Names wife, Ann Morris; sons, David, John, William and Robert; daughters, Mary Hopkins, Rhoda Polk and Sarah Beanchamp. Written May 21, 1802. Probated December, 1806. Executors—John Morris, Robert Morris. Witnesses—Wm. Lindsay, Wm. Chambers, Daniel Mc. Payne.

JOHN NICHOLS—Will Book B, Page 267—Names wife, Rebecca; sons, Amos, James and John Fields Nichols; daughters, Winifred Clark. Written December 4, 1807. Probated October, 1811. Executor—James Nichols (son). Witnesses—Leonard Young, Mehaley Mead.

ELIJAH NUTTLE—Will Book A, Page 38—Names wife, Mary Nuttle; sons, Price and Thomas; daughters, Sarah Rollings, Martha Dements, Mary Lamb, Elizabeth Faulkner, Rebecca Nuttle, Susanna and Nancy Nuttle; grand-daughter, Mima Lamb; sons-in-law, Jacob Lamb, Daniel Rollings and Jno Faulkner; Owned land in Shelby and and Fayette Counties. Written September 5, 1796. Probated July, 1803. Witnesses—Henry Brock, Armstead Sharp, Francis Pickett.

THOMPSON PARISH—Will Book B, Page 460—Names brothers and sisters. Written September 24, 1810. Probated February, 1813. Executors—Robert Dudley, James Weaver, Jonathan Parrish. Witnesses—W. C. Dudley, James Dudley.

JAMES PARKER—Will Book A, Page 4—Names wife, Elizabeth; daughter, Margaret; brothers William and Alexander Parker; sisters, Mary and Margaret. Written February 19, 1797. Probated February, 1803. Executors—Alexander Parker, John Coburn, John Bradford. Witnesses—Hugh Brent, Sr., H. McIlvain, John Calhoon, Jr.

DANIEL McC. PAYNE—Will Book B, Page 213—Names wife, Elizabeth Payne; brothers, Henry, Wiliam, Edward, Jilson and Jimmy; friends, Thos. January, Courtney Norton January; sisters, Theodosia Turner, Elizabeth Lewis; nephew, Daniel Payne; children of brother, Sanford Payne, deceased; Peggy, Edward Luicy, Polly, Sally, Nancy, Sanford, Silas and Ellen. Written April 9, 1811. Probated May, 1811. Executors—Henry Payne, Edward Payne (brothers). Witnesses—Randolph Harris, Jacob McConathy, Major Donoho.

SALEM PEYATT—Will Book B, Page 457—Names Kitty Peel; James Kelly; eldest daughter of John Bodley; youngest son of John Bodley. Written February, 1813. Probated January, 1814. Witnesses —Samuel Q. Richardson, W. Montgomery, David Steele.

JOSHUA PILCHER—Will Book B, Page 152—Names wife, Nancy Pilcher; son, Joshua Pilcher; grand-sons, Merritt Pilcher and Prestley Pilcher. Written May 3, 1810. Probated August, 1810. Executrix, wife, Nancy. Witnesses—Elijah Cartmell, Lucy Casey.

CHRISTIANNA PRICE—Will Book B, Page 57—Names son, James Price; niece, Sarah Bryan. Written May 4, 1809. Probated October, 1809. Witnesses—Abr. Bowman, Eliza Ryman, Evan Price, John Gatewood, Elijah Foley.

WILLIAM ROSS—Will Book B, Page 115—Names daughters, Margaret Ross, Mary; son, Daniel; daughter, Elizabeth; sons, William and Thomas; daughter, Emily and John Balmerino Ross and daughter Ann Haley. Written February 2, 1810. Probated February, 1810. Executors—Samuel Patterson, Robert Wilson. Witnesses—Samuel Meredith, Samuel Patterson, Robert Wilson, Mary Peebles.

J. H. RUNYAN—Will BookB, Page 236—Names brother,Francis Runyan. Written April 27, 1914. Probated July, 1811. Witnesses— Thos. H. Burbridge, Richard Baird, Benjamin Atkinson.

GUY SMITH—Will Book A, Page 275—Names son, Guy Smith, daughters Sarah Coffie, Ann Vaughn and Elizabeth Mitchell. Written January 19, 1780. Recorded September 2, 1803. Executors—John Smith (son), John Young. Witnesses—James Smith, Lewis Amis, John Young. Proved Granville County, N. C., 1787, afterwards a copy recorded Fayette County, Ky., 1805.

DANIEL SPENCER—Will Book B, Page 421—Names wife, Mary; son, Giles Spencer; daughters, Margaret Lawrence, Katherine Spencer and Elizabeth Anthony; sons, Daniel and James; daughters, Ann, Lydia, Susannah and Welther Spencer. Written April 20, 1796. Probated October, 1812. Executor—William Huston. Witnesses—John Bradford, David Sutton.

RICHARD SPURR—Will Book A, Page 336—Names wife, Frankey Spurr; sons, James, William Cotton Spurr; daughter, Mary Spurr; son, Richard Spurr; daughter, Judith Spurr, sons, John and Daniel Spurr. Written May 7, 1790. Probated June, 1791. Executors—Owen Winn, James Whaley. Witnesses—Wm. Jinkins, Dennis Bradley, Elijah Holtsclaw.

ANDREW STEELE—Will Book A, Page 20—Names son, John Steele; sons, John and William; daughters, Margaret, Elizabeth, Anne, Jane, and Priscilla; Brice Steele. Written September 12, 1793. Probated December, 1794. Executors—Rev. Samuel Shannon, Robert Patterson. Witnesses—George Wilson, Robert Patterson, Levi Todd.

RICHARD STEELE—Will Book B, Page 24—Names wife, Martha; sons, Adam, Richard, Joseph, John and Robert M.; daughters, Esther Steele and Nancy Pollock Steele; son, William; daughters, Polly Sutherland and Patsy Beal. Written November 15, 1808. Probated May, 1809. Executors—wife, Martha, Adam, Richard and Joseph (sons). Witnesses—Joseph Patterson, Jr., Will Gibson, Joseph Patterson.

JOHN STONE—Will Book B, Page 537—Survey of land made and recorded for heirs of J. Stone, deceased and ordered to be recorded, October, 1813. John D. Young, Clerk.

WILLIAM TANDY—Will Book B, Page 417—Names wife, Jane Tandy; sons, John, Achilles and Gabriel; daughter, Lucy; son, Moses; daughters, Francis Lipscomb, Sally B. Bledsoe and Jane Allen; Written May 2, 1792. Probated October, 1812. Executors—wife, Jane, Achilles Tandy, Moses Tandy (sons), Moses Bledsoe. Witnesses—John Mason, William Bush, Jas. Arnold, G. N. Tompkins,

CHARLES TATHAM—Will Book B, Page 4—Names wife, Nancy Holmes Tatham (daughter of John Holmes); in case of death without heirs to go to Mary Holmes, also a daughter of John Holmes; afterwards to Cuthbert Banks of Lexington, Ky., and Captain Samuel Coleman of Richmond, Va., and brother, Col. Wm. Tatham of Richmond, Va. Written February, 1800. Probated April 28, 1809. Executor—Cornelius Beaty, Capt. Samuel Coleman, Cuthbert Banks, Col. Wm. Tatham. Witnesses—Jos. Boswell, Allen M. Magruder, Lewis Marshall.

ASA TAYLOR—Will Book B, Page 313—Names wife, Hannah Taylor; son, John L. Taylor; daughters, Elizabeth Barry Taylor, Rebecca Taylor and Sarah Taylor. Written September 23, 1811. Probated December, 1811. Executors—wife, Hannah, son, John L. Witnesses—Robert Alexander, Robert Campbell.

GEORGE TEGARDEN—Will Book B, Page 48—Names son, William Huston Tegarden; nephew, William, son of Aaron Tegarden; nephew, William, son of Moses Tegarden. Written March 31, 1813. Probated May, 1813. Executors—William Morton, Charles Wilkins. Witnesses—Thomas January, Samuel Patterson, Elexander Walker.

JAMES THOMPSON—Will Book B, Pape 439—Names son, James Thompson; daughter, Polly; sons, Josiah and John; daughters, Jane Utley, Cathy Veal, Hannah May and Sally Medole; sons, William and Daniel Thompson. Written April 17, 1812. Probated December, 1812. Executors—James Thompson (son), William Ellis. Witnesses—William Ellis, Rebecca Taylor, Hannah Taylor.

WILLIAM TOMLINSON—Will Book B, Page 17—Names sons, Elijah and Ambrose;daughter Nancy's heirs; sons, George, John, William and Richard; daughters, Mary and Sarah. Written April 1, 1809. Probated May, 1809. Witnesses—John Dogel, John Forsyth, Wm. Gordon, Edmond Wainman.

JOHN VIVION—Will Book A, Page 248—Names wife, Martha Vivion; nine children; sons, John, Flavel (youngest son); daughter Frankey. Written May 24, 1789. Probated April, 1805. Executors—Philip Bush, Sr., John Vivion, Jr., Thacker Vivion, and wife, Martha. Witnesses—John McGuire, Benjamin Combs, Presly Anderson.

RICHARD YOUNG—Will Book B, Page 391—Names son, John Young; daughters, Molly Young, Jenny Young and Lucy Young; son William. Written December 2, 1811. Probated May, 1812. Executors —Richard Young (enphew), Molly, Jenny and Lucy Young. Witnesses—Ambrose Young, William Clubb, Sr.

WILLIAM YOUNG—Will Book A, Page 30—Names wife, Milley Young; son, Minor Young; daughter, Judah Martin, James, husband of Judah Martin; sons, Richard and John; daughters, Lettice and Patsy;; son, Douglas. Written May 15, 1793. Executors —John Young, Leonard Young (brothers). Witnesses—Hezekiah Harrison, Polly S. Smith, W. Smith, Lawrence Young.

MARY BELLOWS—Will Book L, Page 459—Names daughter, Elizabeth Pence; son, John; daughter, Mary Kelley; daughter, Sally Black; daughter, Susanna Smith; Mary Elizabeth Owens (if she lives till of age); son, Henry. Written June 13, 1833. Probated September, 1834. Executors—son, Henry Bellows and friend, John Graves. Witnesses—G. W. C. Graves and L. J. Graves.

HARRISON COUNTY WILL ABSTRACTS

(Contributed by the Cynthiana Chapter)

JOHN ADAMS—Will Book C, Page 63—Names wife, Barbara; son, James; son, John; daughter of John, Mary Ann; daughter, Jane Lemon. Written September, 1833. Probated October, 1823. Executor—John Curry. Witnesses—James J. Ralston, Henry Y. Elbert, John Zumwalt, Pontius Clarke.

MOSES ALLEN—Will Book C, Page 329—Names wife, Priscilla. Written Sept. 20, 1834. Probated November, 1834. Witnesses—Josephus Perrin, C. C. Martin.

JOHN ANDERSON—Will Book B, Page 501—Names daughter, Matilda Forest, wife of Wm. Forest; mentions William K. Wall and James R. Curry. Written March, 1831. Probated, June, 1831. Witnesses —James B. Nichols, John Monrow.

ROBERT ANDERSON—Will Book C, Page 39—Names wife, Margaert; sons, William, John, Alexander, George, James; daughters, Jane, Polly, Sally, Rebecca. Written May 14, 1833. Probated June, 1833. Witnesses—John Anderson, A. A. Harmon.

WILSON ALEXANDER—Will Book B, Page 521—Names, daughters, Prudence, Ann Johnson; son, Robert. Written May 5, 1832. Probated June, 1832. Executors—Prudence Alexander, William English. Witnesses—William Grey, Samuel C. McMillin.

HENRY ASBURY—Will Book B, Page 407—Names wife, (no name); sons, Squire, John; daughter, Elizabeth Lenter. Written March 24, 1829. Probated April, 1829. Executors—Elijah Asbury, William Asbury. Witnesses—A. M. Camron, Thomas Harding.

WILLIAM ASBURY, Sr.,—Will Book B, Page 203—Names sons, William, Henry, Jeremiah and Thomas; daughters, Charlotte and Susannah; wife, Mary. Written November 1, 1822. Probated October, 1824. Executors—Wife, Mary and brother, Henry Asbury. Witnesses—Archibald Duncan, Patrick Watson, Henry Shell, John Reitzel.

JACOB ASHCRAFT—Will Book B, Page 420—Names wife, Elizabeth; Written June 18, 1827. Probated October, 1829. Witnesses—William Wood, John Retzel, Benjamin Ellis.

LINDSAY AZBY—Will Book A, Page 312—Names wife, Jane; daughters, Nancy, Betsy, Polly, Sally; son-in-law, Robert Clifford. Written March 12, 1816. Probated April, 1816. Executrix—Jane Azby, wife. Witnesses—James McMurtry, David McKee, Henry Seller.

JOSEPH BACON—Will Book B, Page 436—Names sister, Betsy Bacon. Written, 1821. Probated December, 1829. Executor—Barton Ingraham. Witnesses—James R. Curry, Thomas Smith.

AUGUSTEN BAILEY—Will Book B, Page 247—Names wife, Ann; and children, not named. Written October 17, 1825. Probated December, 1825. Executors—Ann Bailey, Lewis Conner, William Furnish. Witnesses—John Conner, Joseph Ralston.

JOHN BARNES, (Pensioner)—Will Book A, Page 394—Names wife, Hannah; sons, Abraham and John; daughters, Elizabeth, Rebecca and Anna. Written August 28, 1813. Probated December 1817. Executors—Charles Miller, Abraham Barnes. Witnesses—Robert Scott, William Gormany.

JOHN BARNES—Will Book A, Page 394—Names wife, Hannah,; sons Abraham, John; daughters, Elizabeth, Rebecca, Anna; mentions Drusilla. Written August 28, 1813. Executors—Abraham Barnes, Charles Miler. Probated, December, 1817. Witnesses—William Garmany, Robert Scott.

MICHAEL BEAVER—Will Book A, Page 149—Names wife, Christian; sons, Michael and Abraham; daughters, Martha, Betsy Brummer Kelly, Barbary Coon and Nancy Armstrong; son, Matheas. Written March 5, 1811. Probated March, 1811. Executors—Wife, Christian, John Chinn. Witnesses—Piler Smieser, Joshua Lilly, William Curry, Jeremiah Morgan.

WILLIAM BENNETT—Will Book B, Page 517—Names wife, Polly; sons, Joesph, William and James; daughters, Catty Houston, Jane Shuffett, Elizabeth Shuffett, Frankie Renaker; grandchildren, Mary Ann Bennett, John Bennett, (children of Joseph). Probated April, 1832. Witnesses—John Berry, Thomas Williams, Nathaniel Berry. Executors—James Bennett, William Bennett.

JAMES BLACKBURN—Will Book A, Page 146—Names wife, Jane;

daughter, Jean; sons, William, Thomas, James and Ramkin. Written August 8, 1810. Probated December, 1810. Executrix—Wife, Jane. Witnesses—Gavin Morrison, Thomas Rankin, Charles Kelso.

JOSEPH BLAIR, Will Book A, Page 223—Names wife, Hannah; children. Written January 17, 1814. Executors—Hannah (wife), James Wiglesworth, Richard King. Witnesses—Samuel Blair, Thomas Moore.

SAMUEL BLAIR—Will Book B, Page 491—Names, wife, Susan; sons, John R., Joseph and Greenville; daughters, Nancy Baird, Sally Liforce, Margaret Todd, Luvinia Brown and Jane Brown. Written February 27, 1831. Probated April, 1831. Executors—John R. Blair, Joseph Blair, James Baird. Witnesses—Frances Edwards, Sally Edwards.

WILLIAM B. BOONE—Will Book C, Page 321—Names, Mary Boone Godman. Written September 2, 1834. Probated October, 1834. Executor—Capt. John Ingles. Witnesses—F. C. Huey, William Denny, Edward Walter.

JACOB BOYERS, SR.—Will Book C, Page 63—Names wife, Dorothy; daughter, Milly; son, John. Written Sept. 25, 1833. Probated October 3, 1833. Executor—John (son).

WILLIAM BROWN—Will Book C, Page 126—Names sons, William and James; daughters, Ruth Anne Smith and husband, James D., Mary Wilson and husband, Barton Wilson; Rebecca, Sarah, Eliza and Harriett; son, Elisha; mentioned wife, no name. Written October 16, 1833. Probated October, 1833. Executors—Wife, H. B. Brown, William Brown, (son). Witnesses—Mat Stacy, Thomas W. Buckner.

DAVID CALDWELL—Will Book C, Page 160—Names son, David Caldwell; daughters, Rachael, Kitty. Written July 15, 1833. Probated December, 1833. Witnesses—James Poindexter, John Wiglesworth, Meeke Love.

JOSEPH CALDWELL—Will Book A, Page 142—Names wife, Mary. Written February 10, 1810. Probated December, 1810. Witnesses—Josephus Penn, John Williams, Jonas Hoffman, William Perrin.

DANIEL CARPENTER—Will Book B, Page 479—Names wife, Hannah, Written July 16, 1830. Probated December, 1830. Witnesses—Benjamin Brandon, Samuel Ewalt.

JOSEPH CARR—Will Book B, Page 417—Names wife, Catherine. Written May 14, 1825. Probated August, 1829. Executors—Catherine Carr (wife) and Joseph Coonrad. Witnesses—A. Biggs, James Pollard.

JOHN CARTWILL—Will Book A, Page 86—Names wife, Susanah; sons, William, John and Thomas; daughters, Peggs, Elizabeth, Nancy, Mary, Martha, Jenny and Nelly. Written December 27, 1807. Probated February, 1808. Executors—Wife, Susanah, and Samuel —— Witnesses—William Ward, David Hawkins, Joseph Ward.

ARCHIBALD CASEY, (Pensioner)—Will Book B, Page 226—Names wife, Hannah; daughter, Delila; sons, George H. and Archibald. Written April 15, 1825. Probated July, 1825. Witnesses—Sam V. Timberlake, James Marsh.

JANE CATHERWOOD—Will Book B, Page 82—Names son, Jesse; daughters, Ruthy and Jane. Written November 26, 1821. Probated January, 1822. Executor—Jesse Catherwood. Witnesses—Stephan Barton, A. M. Camron.

JOSIAS CHAMBERS—Will Book B, Page 15—Names sons, Samuel, John Alloway and William; daughters, Molly Watkins, Sally West, Elizabeth Hardwick, Nancy, Mildred and Rebecca Chambers; wife, Patsy. Written June 11, 1817. Probated February 1819. Executors Patsy Chambers and Samuel Chambers. Witnesses—John Smith, Elijah Chinn, George Coons.

CLAIBORNE CHANDLER, (Pensioner)—Will Book E, Page 157—Dated May 16, 1844. Inventory and Appraisal Record Book E.

SUSANNAH CHANDLER—Will Book A, Page 364—Names son, Henry; daughter, Sarah. Written October 23, 1807. Probated April, 1817. Executor—Henry Chandler. Witnesses—John Crenshaw, Lewis Day, Nancy Day.

WILLIAM CHINN—Will Book B, Page 452—Names wife, Sally, son, Joseph G.; daughters, Matilda Wilmott, Fannie Harcourt, Polly Barton and Susan McHattan; son, David, (wife, Barbara P. Chinn); grandsons, William Wilmott and Joseph David Wilmott; William Chinn and David Davis Chinn, (sons of Joseph Chinn); William Barton and William McHatton. Written February 6, 1830. Probated March 1830. Executors—Joseph G. Chinn, William Barton. Witnesses—Roger Williams, John Chinn, James Duvall.

JOHN CLARK—Will Book A, Page 245—Names son, William T.; son-in-law, James Kelly; son, Augustine. Written July 5, 1814. Probated August, 1814. Witnesses—Joseph Taylor, T. M. Timberlake, Samuel Broadwell.

THOMAS CLARKE—Will Book B, Page 101—Names sons, John and Irvin; daughters, Peggy McIntire, Delila Pierce and Polly Boyd. Written October, 1821. Probated May, 1822. Executors—John, Irvin, Peggy and Delila. Witnesses—Ben Warfield, John Frazier, Robinson Magee.

JOHN CLEVELAND, (Pensioner)—Will Book B, Page 523—Names wife, Jane. Written June 26, 1832. Probated July, 1832. Executor—Lewis Day. Witnesses—I. H. Blair, S. C. McMillain, George Smiser, George Cleveland.

JOHN CLEVELAND—Will Book B, Page 531—Names daughters, Abigail, Frances, Hannah McDonald, Elizabeth Bennet and Sarah Way; sons, William, George and John. Written July 31, 1832. Probated September, 1832. Executors—Wife, Wm. Cleveland (son), Joel Frazier. Witnesses—William Bodkin, Wesley Sparks.

LEROY COLE—Will Book B, Page 450—Names wife, Susanna Brooks Cole. Written June 13, 1826. Probated, 1829. Executrix—Wife, Susanna Cole. Witnesses—Robert Jones, Richard B. Jones, Andrew Boyd, Joel C. Frazier.

HENRY COLEMAN—Will Book A, Page 95—Names wife, Mary, son-in-law, William Moore; daughters, Polly Green and Caty Miller, Lucy, Sallie, Peggy, Suckey Colman; sons, William and Edward; son-in-law, John Miller and Napoleon Coleman, son of William Coleman. Written November 14, 1807. Probated April, 1808. Executors

—William Moore, Thomas Miller, William Colman, Edward Colman. Witnesses—Joseph Boyd, Christopher McCannico.

JAMES COLEMAN—Will Book B, Page 405—Names wife, Eliza; sons, Nicholas D. and James C.; daughter, Mary Ann. Written November 12, 1827. Probated March, 1829. Executors—Wife, Eliza, Nicholas and James (sons). Witnesses—Lucy A. Coleman, Polly Ann Coleman.

JOHN CRAIG—Will Book B, Page 324—Names wife, Mary; daughters, Margaret, Jane, Violet, Elizabeth, Esther and Mary; sons, James and John. Written August 12, 1824. Probated November, 1827. Executors—Wife, Mary, and son, John. Witnesses—James Craig, Cabel Jennings.

JOHN CRAIG—Will Book B, Page 227—Names wife, Margaret; sons, Moses Henry, Andrew Jackson and James Perry Craig; daughters, Mary Dils and Betsy. Written January 3, 1825. Probated July, 1825. Witnesses—John McIlvain, John Jones.

ABRAHAM CROSSDALE—Will Book A, Page 177—Names wife, Margaret; son, Abram; duaghter Ann. Written May 27, 1811. Probated November, 1812. Witnesses—David Holstead, John Cross, Richard Marsh, James Kelly, James Finley, G. W. Timberlake.

JAMES DARROUGH—Will Book C, Page 225—Names wife, Margaret, sons, John Darrough and James Darrough; daughters, Sarah Heger, Jane Thornly and Elizabeth Faulconer; grandchildren, John Rose, James Rose, Thomas Rose, Stanford Rose, Margaret Brown, Lemory Brown, Elizabeth Brown, John Brown and Josephus Brown. Written July 29,1833. Probated January, 1834. Executor—James Darrough. Witnesses—Thomas Thompson, Andrew H. Garnett, Newton Garnett.

JACOB DAVID—Will Book B, Page 303—Names wife Mary; daughters, Catherine, Mary and Sarah; sons, William, Thomas, David and Simeon. Written June 19, 1827. Probated August, 1827. Executor William (son) and Henry Spears (son-in-law). Witnesses—Joseph Patterson, Benjamin Snodgrass, Robert Snodgrass.

LEWIS DAY, SR.—Will Book B, Page 467—Names John M. Day, Lewis Day, Benjamin Day, Lucy Coleman, Patsy Anne Eliza Keene, Written June 4, 1829. Probated October, 1830. Executors—Lewis Day, Benjamin C. Day. Witnesses—Sidney S. Fisher, Burrel Carter, John Crenshaw.

CHRISTIAN DECK—Will Book B, Page 366—Names, wife, Elizabeth; sons, John, Michael and Jacob; daughters, Fanny Patterson, Barbary Rutledge, Rebecca Bigham, Elizabeth, Susanna, Lena, Anna and Polly. Written February 26, 1828. Probated April, 1828. Witnesses— Daniel Huffman, George Huffman, Hamon Million. Executor—John Deck.

MORGAN DESHA—Will Book A, Page 372—Names wife, (no name); daughters, Nancy and Nelly Gannon; son, William. Written December 7, 1816. Proven October, 1817. Executor—Mr. Kilgore. Attest —W. M. Edmondson, James Agnew.

EDWARD DIAL—Will Book A, Page 1—Names wife, Betsy; sons, Alexander and William; daughter, Polly. Written June 27, 1796. Will proved Oct. Ct., 1796. Executors—John Stephenson, John Massey.

Witnesses—Edward Dyal, Jr., Alexander Dyal, James Curry, Simon Dyal.

DAVID DILLS—Will Book A, Page 68—Names daughter, Jane; wife, Rachael (my third wife); sons, John and Elijah. Written October 15, 1806. Proven January, 1807. Executors—Rachael (wife) and John Walton. Witnesses—John Miller, David Dills.

DAVID DRYDEN—Will Book A, Page 45—Names wife, Jean Dryden; son, James; daughters, Peggy, Nancy, Patsy, Jenny, Rughanna and Elizabeth. Written November 14, 1803. Proven December Ct., 1803. Executors—James Stephenson and wife, Jean Dryden. Witnesses— W. E. Boswell, Nat McClure.

JOSEPH DUNCAN—Will Book B, Page 119—Names daughters, Lydia, Nancy Harp, Charlotte Parker, Susanna Whitley; sons, Washington, James and Archibald; son-in-law, Claiborne Collier. Written March 30, 1818. Probated October, 1822. Executors—Sons, Archibald and Washington, and Claiborne Collier, son-in-law. Witnesses—Taylor King, James Watson, William Watson.

WILLIAM DUNCAN—Will Book B, Page 453—Names wife, Lydia; daughter, Lavinia Taylor; sons, Toliver, Mason and Watson; daughters, Elizabeth, Helen, Matilda, Judia Armfred; grandchildren, Reuben Miles, Lydia and Gabriel Miles, and Wesley Duncan. Written December 18, 1828. Probated March, 1830. Executors—Mason Duncan, John Breitzell. Witnesses—A. M. Cameron, Ellis Ashcraft, Blair Breitzell.

HUGH SMITH DUNN—Will Book A, Page 216—Names daughter, Elizabeth Merchant; son-in-law, Benj. H. Hickman; grandson, Hugh Smith Duncan Hickman; grandson, Eals Hickman; son, Arichibald Dunn; son, Thomas Dunn. Mentions Sarah Margaret Linginfelter, Mary Peck and Elsha Dunn. Written August 5th, 1813. Probated October, 1813. Executors—Benjamin Hickman, John Whittaker. Witnesses—Robert M. Duffee, John Whitaker.

I. J. W. DUNN, Will Book B, Page 489—Names wife, Eliza Dunn, daughter, Hannah Jane; daughter, Susan P. Written January 8, 1831. Probated March, 1831. Executor—Thomas Dunn. Witnesses —James Dunlap, Hugh Hickman.

SAMUEL DUNN—Will Book A, Page 64—Names Dorothy, wife; sons, Ezeriah, Samuel, Jr.; daughters, Ann Massey, Mary Gossett, son Abram. Written November 22, 1805. Proven April, 1806. Witnesses—Aquilla Perkins, William Douglas, James Woodson.

DANIEL DURBIN— Will Book B, Page 301—Names, wife, Elizabeth; sons, Hosah, John Bonaparte, Napoleon Mirabo; daughters, Cassandra Sappington, Sarah Phillips, Ann Easton, Corella Boracia. Written March 5, 1822. Probated July, 1827. Executor—Wife, Elizabeth. Witnesses—George Rees, Wm. Minter, James Coleman.

BOSWELL EADS—Will Book B, Page 238—Names brothers, Austen, John, Martin and Burket; brother-inlaw, Caswell Thomas Graves, husband of sister Delphy, and their daughter, Sarah (Mrs. Samuel Dehart). Written August 20, 1825. Probated October, 1825. Executor—Samuel Dehart. Witnesses—John Wilson, Mary Wilson, James Endicott.

SOPHIA ECHTLE—Will Book A, Page 203—Names, sons, Valetine and Daniel; daughter, Sophia McCann; granddaughters, Sally McCann,

Betsy, Sallie. Written April 20, 1813. Probated July, 1813. Executors—Nathaniel Glasgow, William Bayman and Samuel Lewis. Witnesses—Nathaniel Glasgow, William Bayman, Samuel Lewis.

HENRY EDGAR—Will Book B, Page 260—Names wife, Polly; sons, Samuel and John T.; daughters, Jane, Peggy, Polly and Betsy Lyle. Written June 23, 1825. Probated May, 1826. Executor—Samuel D. Edgar. Witnesses—William Lowry, Robert Crogin.

JACOB ECKLER—Will Book A, Page 19—Names son, Ulery; daughter, Mary; five sons and two daughters not named. Written August 24, 1798. Proven October, 1798. Executors—Jacob Eckler and France Hostater. Witnesses—Samuel Moore, George Ruppert.

FRANCIS EDWARDS—Will Book C, Page 286—Names children, Frances, Susanna, Thomas, Polly, Eleanor, Emmalen and Amanda Edwards; wife, no name. Written September 10, 1831. Probated May, 1834. Executor—Wife.

WILLIAM ELLIS—Will Book A, Page 196—Names wife, Lucy. Written August 14, 1812. Probated May, 1813. Witnesses—Jo David Ellis, Robert Ellis, John McKinney, Lewis Hendrick.

DISEY ELLIS—Will Book B, Page 233—Names sons, John, Reuben, Nathonel, Edward, William nad Cleveland; daughters, Caty and Susan. Written April 7, 1825. Probated August, 1825. Executors—G. M. Clerkson, Wm. Anderson. Witnesses—Griffin Robinson, William Cogswell.

SAMUEL ELLIOTT—Will Book C, Page 42—Names John, brother; children of John, Elizabeth, Martha, James and William. Written August 8, 1833. Probated September, 1833. Executors—Andrew Moore, John Elliott. Witnesses—Henry Haines, George H. Mountjoy, John Moore.

WILLIAM ENGLISH—Will Book B, Page 299—Names wife, Nancy; sons, Joshua, James, John, William and Robert; daughters, Sally McHatton and Betsy Hufford. Written December 25, 1826. Probated May, 1827. Executors—William English, John Hufford. Witnesses Abraham Miller, Abraham Fry, Jacob Fry.

RICHARD FALCONER—Will Book B, Page 535—Names wife, Ann; sons, James, Nathaniel, Benjamin and Absalom; daughter, Milly Jones, Elizabeth Snyder, Polly and Jane. Written Septemer 2, 1826. Probated October, 1832. Executors—Nathaniel Falconer, Absalom Falconer. Witnesses—Reuben Falconer, Edmund Falconer, John Burgess.

JAMES FOWLER—Will Book B, Page 79—Names son-in-law, Valentine Leonard; grandsons, James Leonard and Michael Leonard; daughter, Polly; wife, Nancy Fowler; granddaughter, Polly Leonard. Written November 1, 1821. Probated December, 1821. Executors—William Asbury, Arch Alexander. Witnesses—Stephen Barton, John Oliver.

JOHN H. FOWLER—Will Book A, Page 187—Estate in Virginia. Names, sister, Elizabeth; brother, William R. Written August 7, 1812. Probated April, 1813. Witness—Miranda Lewis.

GEORGE FINLEY—Will Book A, Page 415—Names wife, Polly; daughters, Jane and Polly. Written May 19, 1819. Probated July, 1818.

Executors—George Parmer and wife, Polly Finley. Witnesses—
Benj. Oversake, George Parmer, Polly Barry.

ARMSTED FRAIZE—Will Book C, Page 266—Names cousin, Polly
Alerson and husband Otko Alerson, Elizabeth Young and husband,
Charles S., Mildred Taylor and husband, George; uncle, Valentine
and wife, (all of the above of State of Illinois). Written February
11, 1834. Probated March, 1834. Executor—John Chowning.

ROLAND B. GEORGE—Will Book B, Page 349—Names mother, Mary;
sisters, Nancy Williams, Penelope Coppage and Louisa George.
Written December 23, 1827. Probated February, 1828. Executor
—Joseph G. Chinn. Witnesses—James Carey, Minor Hearne.

JOHN GIVENS—Will Book A, Page 417—Names wife, Ruth; sons,
George Givens, Alexander, James; daughters, Isabella, Letitia and
Maria; brother, Alexandra; brother-in-law, Francis Grey. Written
August 3, 1818. Probated October, 1818. Executors—Ruth Givens
(wife) Alexander Givens, Francis Grey. Witnesses—William Bot-
kins, John Chinn.

GERARD GREEN—(Pensioner)—Will Book E, Page 284—Names
wife, Virlinda; sons, James, William, Fielding, George and Lilburn;
daughters, Mildred Holliday, Elizabeth McLoney and Parthena Kenney. Written March 23, 1845; Probated August, 1845. Executor—
James Green. Witnesses—Burwell N. Carter, Jacob Renneckar.

JAMES GUNSAULUS—(Pensioner)—Will Book D, Page 190—
Names daughter, Hanner Maran and husband, Augustus Maran,
daughter, Polly. Written May 11, 1837. Probated March, 1839.
Witnesses—Benjamin Daley, Orvil Camrom.

JOHN HALL—Will Book B, Page 382—Names wife, Ellanor. Written
February 14, 1828. Probated October, 1828. Witnesses—Lewis
Day, Jr., Joseph Marin.

JOSHUA HALL—Will Book A, Page 196—Names wife, Sarah; daughters, Rebeccah, Kuturah, Elizabeth Jones and Mary Kemper; sons,
John, Joshua, Thomas, Charles and William. Written September,
24, 1812. Probated May, 1813. Witnesses—William Vinard, John
Thomas, James Furnish.

DAVID HAMBLETON—Will Book A, Page 220—Names wife, Mary,
sons, William, Thomas, Alexander, Elijah and David; daughters,
Elizabeth, Janey, Martha, Sally, Margaret, Mary and Nancy. Written December 14, 1813. Probated April, 1814. Executors—Mary
(wife), John Miller, John McDaniel and Wm. E. Boswell. Witnesses—Will E. Boswell, Joseph Currey.

THOMAS HAMILTON—Will Book A, Page 43—Names wife, (name
not given); sons, David, John William, James and Andrew. Written
November 16, 1802. Proven October Ct., 1803. Executor—Wm. E.
Boswell. Witnesses—William E. Boswell, Joshua McDowell.

MARGARET—HANNON, Will Book B, Page 193—Names sons, John,
Archamedions and Thomas; daughter, Maryann. Written January,
1824. Probated April, 1824. Executor—John Redmon, (son).
Witnesses—David McFall, Isaac Thompson, Silas J. McCandless.

SARAH HANSON—Will Book B, Page 298—Names sister, Jane Hawkins; niece, Polly Ship; brother, John Hanson; Polly H., and Fanny
Taylor; Albert Hanson. Written February 5th, 1827. Probated

May, 1827. Executor—Thomas Hawkins. Witnesses—Benjamin Hodges, A. S. H. Hawkins, Devall Hodges.

RICHARD HARCOURT, SR.—Will Book B, Page 296—Names sons, Richard and William; daughter, Sarah Reese. Written October 19, 1822. Probated April, 1827. Executors—Peter Barrett and Richard Harcourt, Jr. Witnesses—John Shurts, Rachel Shurts, Albert Barrett.

JOHN HARDING—Will Book A, Page 351—Names wife, Harriet. Written October 14, 1816. Probated November, 1816. Executors— William Harding and Harriet Harding (wife). Witnesses—Thomas Harding, Robert McDuffee, Braxton King.

ALEXANDER SMITH HENDLEY HAWKINS—Will Book A, Page 83 —Names wife, Nancy Hawkins; sons, John, Milton, Alfred, Francis, Basil W., Alexander and Thomas; daughters, Elender, Jane, Betsy Grubbs, Elizabeth Miller, and Nancy Jackson. Written November 1, 1807. Probated December, 1807. Executors—Wife, Nancy, Isaac Miller. Witnesses—Benjamin Hodges, Henry Edger.

ALEXANDER HAWKINS—Will Book B, Page 275—Names wife, Patsy; son, Alexander; daughter, Susan. Written March 12, 1827. Probated April, 1827. Executors—Benjamin Hodges, Isaac Miller. Witnesses—H. Warfield, Joseph Van Deren, Thomas Hawkins.

JONATHAN HEDGER—Will Book B, Page 228—Names wife, Mary; sons, George, Jonathan, Sanford and Jacob; daughter, Phoeby. Written June 15, 1825. Probated July, 1825. Executors—Wife, Mary Hedger; son, Jacob Hedger. Witnesses—Francis Edwards, Reuben Hedger.

FANNIE HENDERSON—Will Book B, Page 510—Names sister, Elizabeth Grant, Written October 12, 1831. Probated February, 1832. Executors—Andrew Moore and Wesley Roberts. Witness—A. Moore.

RICHARD HENDERSON—Will Book B, Page 237—Names wife, Fanny; daughter, Lauretta; son, William H. B. Written May 30, 1820. Probated October, 1825. Executors—Wife, Fanny, John Trimble, Robert Trimble and Joseph Taylor. Witnesses—R. Henderson, G. W. Tilmberlake, Henry Carr, George Pickett, William Stewart, Noah Campbell.

WILLIAM B. HENDERSON—Will Book B, Page 454—Names wife, Nancy; daughter, Catherine. Written January 24, 1830. Probated April, 1830. Executor—William Stewart (father-in-law). Witnesses—James R. Curry, James B. Stuart.

JOHN HENRY—Will Book A, Page 309—Names sons, Thomas, Williams, James and John; daughters, Nancy Northcutt, Betsy Dunn, Polly Dunn and Peggy Henry. Written, 180? Probated January, 1816. Executors—William Henry, James Henry. Witnesses—Will E. Boswell, Wilson Picket.

WILLIAM HERREN—Will Book A, Page 224.—Names wife, Anna; sons, George, Ezeriah and Samuel. Written December 23, 1813. Probated January, 1814. Witnesses—Aquilla Perkins, Jonathan Marsh.

SHADRACK HIEATT, Will Book C, Page 312—Names son, Alfred L. Hieatt, son, Ashford W. Hieatt. Written August 22, 1834. Probated

September 1, 1834. Executors—Alfred and Ashford Hieatt (sons). Witnesses—Patrick Watson, Jacob Duncan, Robert A. Garner.

NANCY HILLEMS—Will Book C, Page 304—Names Thomas Moffett, son-in-law; Angelo and Polly Adams; daughters, Elizabeth Moffett and Nancy Moffett; grandson, William Moffett; granddaughter, Nancy Long. Written December 24, 1831. Probated August, 1834. Executor—Thomas Moffett.

JOHN HIND—Will Book B, Page 294—Names wife, Margaret; sons, Edmond and Franklin; daughter Eleanor. Written February 12, 1827 .Probated April, 1827. Executors—Wife, Margaret and John McMillin. Witnesses—Archilaus VanHook, Moses McOlvain.

JAMES HINTON—Will Book B, Page 381—Names wife, Rebecca; sons, Solomon, Jeremiah, James, Ashert and William; daughters, Rebecca, Deborah, Polly, Eleanor, Caty and Dorcas. Written April 11, 1828. Probated August, 1828. Executor—James Adams. Witnesses—Joseph D. Brockman, William Pavey, Martin Sellers.

ELIZABETH HOGG—Will Book B, Page 394—Names son, Thomas. Written October 13, 1826. Probated November 1828. Executor—Thomas Hogg. Witnesses—Thopilus Chowning, Rebecca W. Harrison, Isaac Miller.

MICHAEL HOGG—Will Book A, Page 263—Names wife, Elizabeth; daughters Polly, Isabella, Nancy Cummins, and Elizabeth; sons, Thomas, David, Robert and Harvey. Written November 2, 1814. Probated February, 1815. Executors—Wife, Elizabeth, and son, Thomas. Witnesses—Herbert Wells, George Payne, Alexander Douglas.

WILLIAM HOLIDAY—Will Book A, Page 161—Names wife, Martha; daughters, Jane Holiday, Rebeccah Holiday, Nancy Holiday and Sarah H. Martin; sons, William P., Joseph, James and Samuel. ("Samuel now lives in Ohio"). Written Dec. 20, 1811. Probated April, 1812. Executors—Martha Holiday and John Patton. Witnesses—George Reading, Henry Edgar, Wm. P. Holiday.

WILLIAM HOLLAND—Will Book A, Page 221—Names wife, Amelia; sons, Anthony, Aaron, and Uuriah; daughters, Mary Greenup, Rachel Wilson, Polly Elliott, Rebecca and Lydia. Written August 4, 1813. Probated May, 1814. Executors—Sons, Anthony and Uriah. Witnesses—Josiah Griffith, James Smith.

JANE MIRANDA HOLT—Will Book B, Page 486—Names sister, Amelia Holt; mentions brother-in-law, Foster Demasters; mentions Paulina Jane DeMasters; mention Jane Mabelia Duncan, daughter of John H. Duncan; brother, Thomas. Written July 2, 1831. Probated Feb. 1832. Executor—Thomas Holt. Witnesses—Alice M. Boyd, John Leach.

THOMAS HOLT—Will Book B, Page 99—Names wife, Pauline; daughters, Jane, Amelia, Pauline, Louisa; sons, Thomas, oseph and David. Written April 13, 1820. Probated May, 1822. Executors—Wife, Pauline and William Lowry. Witnesses—Ben Warfield, Joseph Boyd.

WILLIAM HUDELSON, Will Book B, Page 101—Names daughters, Rebecca Ann and Harriett Eliza. Written April 15, 1822. Probated July, 1822. Executor—William Lowry. Witnesses—Samuel Hudelson, Robert Lowry, William Gray.

MARY HUCHERSON—Will Book A, Page 76—Names daughters, Mary Lewis Crosthwaite and Jane Stears Kinsler. Written February 11, 1807. Probated May, 1807. Executors—Jacob Powers and Robert McKitrick. Witnesses—William Stears, David McKitrick, Margaret McKitrick, Ann Powers.

GEORGE HUTCHERSON—Will Book A, Page 248—Names wife, Mary; son, William; daughters, Sally Edwards and Polly Bennett; grandchildren, James Henry Hutcherson and Sally Hutcherson. Written December 24, 1813. Probated January, 1815. Executors—William Hutcherson and Francis Edwards. Witnesses—Thomas Walden; David Williams, Jonathan Marsh.

JOHN HUTCHERSON—Will Book A, Page 54—Names, wife, Mary; sons, Charles and Edward; daughters, Phoebe, Frances and James White, Sally and John Marsh and Jenny Kensler. Written May 31, 1805. Proven August Ct., 1805. Executors—Edward Coleman, William Moore. Witnesses—H. Coleman, Benjamin Coleman, Samuel Broadwell.

JOHN HUTCHISON—Will Book C, Page 42—Names, wife, Sally; sons, Lindsey, Edward, James and Samuel. Written June 7, 1833. Probated August 1833. Witnesses—David Lemmon, Robert Clifford, James Clifford.

JOSEPH INGLES—Will Book B, Page 378—Names wife, Mary; daughters, Mary, Elizabeth, Nancy, Lucinda, Catherine and Louisa; sons, James, John, Bryan and Joseph; grandson, Joseph (son of James). Written April 14, 1828. Probated July, 1828. Executors—Wife, Mary and son, James. Witnesses—Joseph H. Clair, Harriett Coleman, Barnett Odon, Abraham Sucker, William Victor.

JOSHUA JACKSON—Will Book A, Page 290—Names wife, (name not given); sons, Modica, Jack, Colby, Wingate and Joshua; daughters, July Hall and Phoebe Chopsherr. Written September 4, 1813. Probated April, 1815. Witnesses— Daniel Hall, Henry Hall, John Whitley.

GEORGE JAMESON—Will Book A, Page 27—Names wife, Ellinor, 100 acres on Eagle Creek; sons, James and Andrew; daughter, Nancy, Written October 11, 1799. Proven January, 1800. Executors—Ellinor Jameson, Sqr. Moore. Witnesses—John McClanahan, Francis Hiesler, Peter Price.

JOHN JENKINS—(Pensioner)—Will Book C, Page 397—Inventory and sale bill recorded. Dated October 15, 1835.

JOHN JOHNSON—Will Book B, Page 352—Names wife, Lydia, sons John, Hugh and William; daughters, Margaret Jenkins, Mary Miller, Betsy Parman, Jane Johnson, Lucinda Casey, Nancy and Sefrona. Written October 20, 1827. Probated February, 1828. Executors—David Snodgrass and Benjamin Snodgrass. Witnesses—Lawson Myers, James Dunlap.

WILLIAM JOHNSON—(Pensioner)—Letters of administration in Record Book D.

BENJAMIN JONES—Will Book A, Page 4—Names wife, Sarah Jones; sons, Benjamin, John and Jonathan; daughters, Sarah Pursley, Rebecca and Mary C. Written October 19, 1795. Will proven September, 1796. Executors—Jesse Hume, John Darnaby. Witnesses —George Pursley, Betsy Cole.

DUMAS JONES—Will Book B, Page 490—Names wife, Sarah, daughters, Nancy (and husband, Jesse) Vanderen, Sarah (and husband, John) Turney; America; sons, John, Benjamin Franklin and Dumas. Written March 30, 1831. Probated April, 1831. Executors—Benjamin Franklin Jones and John Jones. Witnesses—J. Veach, J. C. Frazier, J. R. Stewart.

EVAN JONES—Will Book B, Page 80—Names Peggy, wife; sons, Lewis, Evan and John; daughters, Polly, Hannah, Nancy, Peggy, Tempy and Fetney, daughters of Peggy; mentions "6" daughters. Written October 14, 1821. Probated December, 1821. Executors—Lewis Jones, Evan Jones. Witnesses—James McMurtry, Robert Clifford.

JOSHUA JONES—Will Book C, Page 40—Names wife, Mary Ann (land inherited by me from my father in Frederick Co., Md.); son, Joshua. Written July 6, 1833. Probated August 14, 1833. Witnesses— Thomas B. Woodyard, Nath'l Campbell.

URIAH JONES—Will Book A, Page 70—Names, wife, Mary. Written May 19, 1806. Proven January Ct., 1807. Executors—Mary Jones and Robert Stevenson. John Morrow, James McIlvain.

WILLIAM JUETT—Will Book B, Page 72—Names daughter, Nellie Gooch; wife (mentioned, no name). Written January 24, 1809. Probated November, 1821. Witnessed—William Nelson, Robinson Nelson, Elizabeth Nelson.

JOHN KING—Will Book B, Page 511—Names wife, Hannah; sons, Jesse, Silas, George and John; daughters, Rachel, Polly, Susan, Elizabeth, Sally, Jane and Nancy. Written September 21, 1825. Probated February, 1832. Executor—Hannah King. Witnesses— Stephen Barton, Jno. O. Baseman, P. Barrett.

JOSEPH KING—Will Book A, Page 291—Names Selia King, wife. Written February 30, 1815. Probated May 1815. Witnesses—Robert McDuffee, Braxton King, John Snodgrass.

JOSHUA KING—Will Book A, Page 40—Names wife, Rachael. Written June 7, 1802. Proven August Ct., 1802. Executrix—Rachel King. Witnesses—Thomas Mullen, William Hall, Richard King.

RICHARD KING—Will Book B, Page, 292—Names wife, Sally; sons, Daniel, Richard, Bartlett, Paul, Silas; daughter, Elizabeth and husband Ezekiel Turner and Rachael; granddaughters, Rachael Lemon, Lucinda Lemon, Elizabeth Lemon and Polly Lemon. Written Oct. 5, 1826. Probated February, 1827. Executors—Wife, Sally King; son, Paul King. Witnesses—Larkin Garnett, William Marshall.

JOHN KINKADE—Will Book A, Page 415—Names, sister, Allia; nephew, John Kinkade; brothers, Hugh and William; mentions other brothers and sister. Written June 14, 1818. Probated July, 1818. Executors—Hugh Kinkade and William Kinkade. Witnesses—Will E. Boswell, Joseph Carr.

WILLIAM KINMAN—Will Book B, Page 248—Names wife, Elizabeth; sons, David, John, Jeremiah and Samuel; daughters, Elizabeth Henry, Jane McKeller (wife of Hugh McKeller) and Alie Miller. Written October 12, 1811. Probated December, 1825. Executors—

Wife, Elizabeth and son, David. Witnesses—Joseph W. Withers, Joseph Moren, Lewis Day, Samuel Hall, Samuel Williams, Abram Gossee, William Conayers.

SIMEON T. KIRTLEY—Will Book B, Page 265—Names daughters, America, Cordelia and Mariatta; sons, Paseal, Elijah, Wisham, Richard and Simeon. Written April 14, 1826. Probated July, 1826. Executors—William Gray, Joseph Patterson and William Griffith. Witnesses—James Gray, Isaac N. Snell.

ANNE LAIRD—Will Book B, Page 54—Names daughter, Jean; sons, James, David and Samuel. Written September 14, 1811. Probated April, 1821. Witnesses—Samuel C. Lamme, William Garmany, Nancy Lamme.

JOHN LAIR—Will Book B, Page 316—Names wife, Sallie; daughters, Katherine, Sallie, Margaret Anderson and Mary Payton; sons, William, Jacob, Mathias, Paul and John W. Written June 1, 1827. Probated September, 1827. Executors—John W. and Mathias Lair. Witnesses—T. W. B. Carnagy, Daniel McClintock.

SAMUEL LAMME—Will Book B, Page 210—Names wife, Nancy; daughter, Ann Allen and son-in-law, James Allen; daughters, Mary, Nancy and Isabella; sons, David, William and Samuel C.; father, William Lamme. Written April 17, 1823. Probated January, 1825. Executors—Sons, David and Samuel Lamme. Witnesses—John C. Ruddell, James Brannock, James Chowning, N. Campbell.

ANDREW LAUDERBACK—Will Book B, Page 396—Names daughters, Lydia Bradley, Susan Can, Nancy Armstrong, Hannah, Mahala; sons, James, David, Eli, Isaac. Written June 6, 1828. Probated November, 1828. Executor—Son, David. Witnesses—A. M. Camron, John McGuire.

JOHN LAUGHLIN—Will Book B, Page 205—Names wife, Sarah, and children's names not given. Written September 16, 1824. Probated November, 1824. Executor—Wife, Sarah. Witnesses—Absalom Conner, Elijah Allison, Adam Pock.

WILLIAM LEMON—Will Book A, Page 412—Names wife, Elizabeth; sons, John, George. Witnesses—Josiah Whiteker, Andrew Barnett.

THOMAS LILLEL—Will Book H, Page 198—(Bourbon County)— names sons, Joshua, son, Thomas; daughter, Susanna; son-in-law, William May; daughters, Lucy, Anne Gohayn, Elizabeth M., Mary Anne. Written Dec. 1, 1810. Executors—Charles Smith, Rhuben Anderson, Jerimia Morgan. Witnesses—Charles Smith, Rhuben Anderson Jerimia Morgan.

JACOB LANTER—(Pensioner)—Settlement Filed Record Book F, Page 445—Dated September 11, 1846.

ALEXANDER LEWIS—Will Book B, Page 58—Names wife, Elizabeth; daughters, Melvina, Amanda. Written September 20, 1820. Probated May, 1821. Executors—Elizabeth (wife), Wm. R. Fowler. Witnesses—N. Moore, Alex. Lewis, Sr.

JEAN LOWRY—Will Book A, Page 45—Names son, William; William's daughter, Jenny; son, Robert; Robert's daughter, Jean; daughters, Margaret, Jean. Written February 1, 1803. Proved January, 1804. Executor—Son, William. Witnesses—John Craig, Joseph Craig.

HUMPHREY LYON—Will Book B, Page 412—Names wife, Peggy; mentioned Samuel and Susan Hinkson, (wife adopted Humphrey Hinkson). Written April 4, 1829. Probated May, 1829. Executors—Wife, Peggy, Charles Lair, Humphrey Hinkson. Witnesses—Wm. Thornton, James H. Fisher.

ARTHUR McLAIN—Will Book B, Page 394—Names wife, Sarah; sons, Joseph, Samuel, Jonathan; daughters, Jane Dunn, Mary McClain, Susan McClain. Written March 29, 1824. Probated November 1828 Witnesses—Thomas Thompson, Aaron Miller.

CHRISTOPHER McCONNICO—Will Book C, Page 134—Names daugter, Mary Ann Stith; son, Andrew McConnico; grandson, Andrew McConnico; granddaughter, Mary Ann Stith; grandsons, Edwin, Christopher; mentions other grandchild, but gives no name; mentions James Paton; mentions Joseph Boyd; mother, Keziah McConnico, of Williamson County, Tennessee. Written Nov. 30, 1814. Probated November, 1833. Executors—Andrew McConnie McComico, Drury Stith. Witnesses—Bela Metcalfe, James Johnson, Isaac Reed.

FRANCIS McDANIEL—Will Book B, Page 436—Names daughters, Sidney Howard, Polly Hoggins, Rachel Coonrad, Chesiah, Suffrona West, Nancy Parker; sons, Enos, John, James, Andrew. Written July 7, 1826. Probated Oct. 15, 1829. Executor—William Tucker. Witnesses—Samuel Tucker, Benjamin Ward, Dolly Ward.

JOHN McDOWELL—Will Book A, Page 19—Names wife, Catereen. Written June 29, 1798. Will proved August, 1798. Executrix—Catereen McDowell. Witnesses—Wm. McFarland, Esq., John Dance, Robert Boyd.

WILLIAM McFARLAND—Will Book B, Page 233—Names son Thomas; other children previously provided for. Written November 25, 1822. Probated August, 1825. Witnesses—Joel Monson, John Florence.

ROBERT McKETTRICK—Will Book A, Page 2—Names sons, Robert, John, William, James (land Augusta County, Va.); son-in-law, Wm. Metiare, John Wright, John Meglemmery, James Guye; granddaughter, Jenny Guye; daughters, Sarah, Esbell and Margaret. Written March 13, 1795. Will proved July, 1795. Executors—Robert and John McKettrick. Witnesses—John Hutcheson, Sr., Moses McClure, William Schooler.

DANIEL McLONEY—Will Book B, Page 206—Names wife, Elizabeth; sons, John, James, William, Alexander; daughters, America, Eleanor. Written September 28, 1824. Probated November, 1824. Executrix—Wife, Elizabeth McLoney. Witnesses—John B. Talbott, Presley Robinson, Dudley Robinson.

ESTHER McMILLIN—Will Book B, Page 514—Names husband, Samuel; sons, A. F. McMillin, Kennedy McMillin, Marshall T., Samuel; daughter, Mary E. Broadwell; grandchildren, Mary Hester McMillin, Hester Elliott McMillin, (daughter of Kennedy); mentions Hester Eleanor Grey, daughter of Francis Grey. Written July 16, 1832. Probated March 1832. Executors—A. F. McMillin, Thomas R. McGee, Peter Barrett. Witnesses—James R. Curry, A. Adams.

HANNAH McMILLIAN—Will Book A, Page 124—Names James, Thomas, John; grandchildren, sons of John, viz: John, Kenney, Thomas, Samuel, James; daughter of John, Hannah; daughters of Thomas, viz: Hannah, Mary, Betsy, Liday; sons of James, viz: Kinney, Thomas, Samuel, James, John, and daughter, Hannah. Written March 8, 1809. Executors—Joseph Ward, John Adams. Probated April, 1809. Witnesses—George Smith, Benjamin Fry, Isaac Vaughan.

SAMUEL McMILLIN—Will Book A, Page 335—Names wife, Easther; sons, William, Marshall, John, Andrew, Kenady, Samuel; daghters, Polly, Mary. Written August 15, 1816. Probated November, 1816. Executors—Wife, Easther, Andrew McMillin. Witnesses—Joseph Taylor, John Ward, William Lowry, A. F. McMillin.

WILLIAM McMILLIN—Will Book A, Page 369—Names brothers, Kenneda, Marshall, Andrew F., Samuel; sister, Mary. Written June 4, 1817. Probated July, 1817. Executor—Samuel McMillin. Witnesses—G. W. Timberlake, Charles Smith, Jr.

JANE McNEES, Will Book B, Page 21—Names granddaughters and children of her son Abraha, viz: Elizabeth McNees, Sarah, Jane, Patsy, Anna, Nancy, Catherine, John; names of daughters-in-law, Nancy and Peggy; children of her son, Alexander McNees, viz: James Harvey, Nancy, Isaac Newton, Wm. Clapoole, Lucinda, George Washington; children of her daughter, Elizabeth Lemmon, viz: Mary Lemmon, John Lemmon, David Lemmon, Abraham Lemmon. Written July 13, 1816. Probated April, 1819. Witnesses—Josephus Perrin, Cynthia Perrin, Edna Perrin.

JOHN McNEESE—Will Book A, Page 53—Names daughters, Ann McConnac, (wife of John); Elizabeth Lemmon, (wife of John); sons, Abraham, Alexander; wife, Jean. Written September 16, 1804. Proven Nov. 19, 1804. Executors—Abraham McNeese, Alexander McNeese. Witnesses—Josephus Perrin, Hugh Newell, John Berry.

ELIZABETH McNUTT—Will Book A, Page 311—Names daughters, Susanna Dickson, Sarah Cragg; sons, Thomas, Samuel; granddaughter, Betsy McNutt Williams; son-in-law, David Williams. Written March 24, 1815. Probated April, 1816. Witnesses—Jonathan Marsh, John Berry, Sam Williams.

THOMAS R. MAGEE—Will Book C, Page 159—Names wife Nancy Magee; daughter, Maria Louise; sons, Thomas Temple Smith, John Bowan Gustavus Smith, Henry Clay. Written Nov. 17, 1833. Probated December, 1833. Executors—Nancy Magee (wife), Benjamin Robinson, John Hodges.. Witnesses—Eldred Robinson, William H. Rainey.

THOMAS MAHON—Will Book A, Page 246—Names wife, Margaret; children mentioned. Written March 16, 1814. Probated July, 1840. Executor—Benjamin Mills. Witnesses—Charles Smith, Edward Anderson, John Jomdon.

JOHN MAIS—Will Book A, Page 56—Names wife, oldest daughter, Jenny, daughter Betsy; first son, Thomas; second son, John; third son, Samuel; fourth son, David; second daughter, Annie Kirkpatrick. Will written May 15, 1805. Proved Aug. 1805. Witnesses, George Kirkpatrick, Wm. Stewart.

MARSHALL MAKEMSON—Will Book C, Page 41.—Names sister Betsy Brown, her husband Samuel. Written July 11, 1833. Probated Auust, 1833. Executor—Samuel Brown. Witnesses—William Lockhart, Casander Collison.

FRANCIS MANN, (Pensioner)—Will Book C, Page 401—Names daughter, Phebe; son, John Mann; daughter, Nancy Morrow; son,

Ambrose D. Written Sept. 20, 1831. Probated Nov. 12, 1835. Executors—John Mann, Phoebe Mann. Witnesses—Europe Hendricks, James B. Nichols.

GEORGE MARSHALL (SR.)—Will Book C, Page 357—Names daughter Lucy and husband, Thomas Foster; daughter, Clarissy and husband, Stephen Davis; sons, William, George, John; daughters, Alsy Parker, Elizabeth M. King, Polly Tullis, Judith Marshall; granddaughter, Eliza Mitchell; great-grandchildren, Joseph Thomas Jones, Lucy Marshall Jones, Ann Cruse Jones; son-in-law, John Jones; children of Nancy King (daughter) namely: Elizabeth, Alsey Ann, Lucy Ren, George Albert. Written January 18, 1830. Probated March, 1835. Executors—William Marshall, George Marshall, John Marshall. Witnesses—Larkin Garnett, Benjamin Robinson.

JANE MARTIN—Will Book C, Page 154—Names husband, Edmund Martin; sister, Rachael Boyd; niece, Eliza Boyd; niece Mary Boyd; sister, Elizabeth Pollock. Written Sept. 18, 1833. Probated November, 1833. Witnesses—Isaac Delse, Henry Maffet.

JOHN MASSEY—Will Book A, Page 247—Names son, Hugh, daughters, Betsy, Nancy, Delilah, Mary, Rebecca. sons, John, William. Written Sept. 23, 1814. Probated October, 1814. Witnesses—Samuel Rogers, Charles McDaniel.

ABRAHAM MILLER—Will Book B—Page 174—Names wife, Elizabeth; daughters, Charity, Ann Carbough, Rachel Buckner, Rebecca; sons, Abraham, John Aaron, Jacob; daughters, Jane Endicott, Martha Cummins, Lucretia Murphy. Written September, 1823. Probated October, 1823. Witnesses—John Waits, Moses Endicott, Sr.

ELIZABETH MILLER—Will Book B—Page 354—Names son, John; daughters, Rachel Buckner, Rebecca, Ann Carbough, Martha Cummins, Charity; sons, Jacob, Aaron, Abraham; daughter, Jane Endicott; grnadchildren, Mary Cummins, Jane Cummins, Betsy Cummins, Ann Cummins, John William Cummins. Written March 12, 1828. Probated April, 1828. Witnesses—John Waites, Anna Brownfield.

HUGH MILLER—Will Book A, Page 102—Names wife, Margaret Miller; daughters, Rebeccah, Polly McCoy; sons, Isaac; daughters, Elizabeth Anderson, Margaret Frazier, Jane, Ann Harrison; sons, John, James, Alexander; brother, James. Written March 17, 1808. Probated July, 1808. Witnesses—James Caldwell, George Frazier.

JAMES MOORE, "Near Colemansville," (Pensioner)—Will Book C, Page 411—Names son, Thomas; daughter, Peggy Barrett Murley; son, Edwin K. Moore; daughter Betsy G. Brand; son, James Moore; heirs of James Moore (son): Anna Brand Moore, Edwin J. Moore, Benj. Moore. Written January 11, 1834. Probated January, 1836. Executor—James Moore. Witnesses—William A. Dance, Benj. Moore, Edward Waller.

JOSEPH MILLER, SR.—Will Book B, Page 273—Names wife, Molly. Written September 20, 1826. Probated October, 1826. Witnesses—John G. Williams, Joseph Miller.

KITTY MILLER—Will Book, Page 413.—Names sons, John, William, Hugh, Henry, A. A. Frazer; daughter, Elizabeth. Written February 11, 1829. Probated May, 1829. Executor—Hugh M. Frazer. Witnesses—Joel Frazer, W. Moore.

NICHOLAS MILNER, (Pensioner)—Will Book D, Page 421— Names wife, Hannah; daughters, Elizabeth McLain, Polly, Nancy Lanter; son, Amos Milner; granddaughters, grandsons, children of Polly, viz: Mariah Milner, John A. Milner, Nicholas Milner. Probated August, 1841. Executors—James D. Milner, Amos Milner. Witnesses—Thomas Thompson, James Lanter, Samuel McLain, Jeremiah Ramey, Henry Milner.

DORCAS MINTER—Will Book A, Page 160—Names sons, James Minter, William Minter, Robert Minter, Joseph Minter; daughter, Dorcas Ardery; son-in-law, William Ardery and Dorcas, his wife. Written September 27, 1807. Probated December, 1811. Executor—William Ardery. Witnesses—Joseph Dodge, Daniel Duval.

HENRY C. MOORE—Will Book B, Page 525—Names wife, Sarah; son, Thomas; brothers, William, Andrew. Written July 24, 1832. Probated August, 1832. Executors—William Moore, Esq., Sarah Moore, (wife). Witnesses—Andrew Moore, Nopolian B. Colman.

KISIAH MOORE—Will Book A, Page 352—Names sister, Elizabeth, and other heirs; Boston Moore, James Moore, Benjamin Moore. Written October 20, 1815. Probated November, 1816. Executors—Elizabeth Moore, Benjamin Moore. Witnesses—Thomas Wolf, Benjamin Moore, Samuel McMillin.

THOMAS MOORE—Will Book B, Page 188—Names wife, Mary. Written May 20, 1819. Probated January, 1824. Executor—Wife, Mary. Witnesses—P. Barrett, Jenny Barrett.

WILLIAM MOORE—Will Book B, Page 422—Names son, Andrew; son, Samuel; daughter, Polly Boswell, husband, William Boswell; son, Henry C.; daughter, Jane Baseman, husband, John O. Baseman; son, James; daughter, Louisa; daughter, Peggy; son, William. Written March 12, 1827. Probated November, 1829. Executors—Andrew Moore, Samuel Moore, Henry Moore, James Moore. Witnesses —Isaac Miller, Isaac N. Miller, Joseph Wiglesworth, William English.

DAVID MORRISON—Will Book B, Page 265—Names wife, Sally; daughter, Zurelda; son, John; son, Gavin. Written July 1, 1826. Probated July, 1826. Executors—wife, Sally, Thomas Foley. Witnesses—A. Downing, James Chambers.

BENJAMIN NEALE—Will Book A, Page 361—Names wife, Dorcas; sons, George, William, James, Thomas, Benjamin Young Neale, Jonathan; mentions daughter, America; Gabriel George, Reuben Anderson, Joseph Shropshire, Lattice McDaniel. Written December 13, 1816. Probated February, 1817. Executors—Gabriel George, John McDaniel. Witnesses—John B. Tucker, Samuel Tucker, Alfred George.

BENJAMIN NEELY—Will Book A, Page 5—Names son, William. Written March 12, 1797. Proven May Court, 1797. Executors—John McNees, William Arnold. Witnesses—Joshua Swinford, George Huffman, Hezekiah Doane.

JANE NESBITT—Will Book B, Page 354—Names sister, Margaret Nesbitt. Written September 6, 1827. Probated April, 1828. Witnesses —H. Lewis, Henry Perkins, Alex. Lewis.

JOHN NESBIT—Will Book C, Page 265—Names daughter, Nancy, Polly Douglass, Elizabeth Lorey, Samuel Nesbit, Wm. Nesbit, Robert Nesbit, Nancy Nesbit, Sally Shawhan, Hester Cummins, Virginia Nicols. Written February 6, 1834. Probated March, 1834. Witnesses—William Nesbitt, Jacob Righter.

SAMUEL NESBET—Will Book A, Page 244—Names sons, John, Robert, Samuel, James, William; wife, Mary; daughters. Written March 7, 1814. Probated July, 1814. Executors—Wife, Mary, son William. Witnesses—W. Moore, A. Moore, Henry C. Moore.

DANIEL NEAVES—Will Book B, Page 398—Names wife, Mary; daughter, Judith Barrett; grandson, Elijah Barrett; granddaughter, Eliza Neaves; son, James Neaves. Written September 8, 1828. Probated December, 1828. Signed, David Neaves. Witnesses—M. Browning, Harmon Stevens, Eli Forsythe.

JAMES NEVES—Will Book B, Page 325—Names daughter, Eliza Jane; wife, mentioned. Written December 2, 1826. Probated November, 1827. Witnesses—John Washborn, John Beckett, John Ruboy.

SHADRACH NIGHT, SR.—Will Book B, Page 257—Names sons, Jesse, Isaac, Shadrach, Jacob, William; daughters, Sallie Berry, Mary Alder. Written January 12, 1826. Probated April, 1826. Executors—Shadrach Night, Jr., Isaac Night, Jesse Night. Witnesses—Eleasaph Monson, Andrew Moore.

ROBERT NISBIT—Will Book B, Page 139—Names daughter, Eliza Jane; wife, Sarah; son, James. Written Nov. 30, 1822. Probated December, 1822. Executrix—Wife, Sarah. Witnesses—George Reading, James Nolan, John Trimble.

JAMES ODER—(Pensioner)—Will Book C, Page 336—Names Elizabeth (wife of James Oder); son, James; daughters, Polly Porter, Milley Austin, Sarah Milner. Written September 14, 1834. Probated December, 1834. Witnesses—Joseph Kennedy, Harmon Million.

JOHN OLIVER—Will Book B, Page 202—Names wife, Milley; daughter Polley; other children not named, but left equal share of estate. Written, 1822. Probated, 1824. Witnesses—Archibald Duncan, John P. Duncan.

CATHERINE PATTERSON—Will Book B, Page 520—Names sons, William, James; daughter, Jane; son, David W.; daughter, Mary Haynes. Written June 10, 1825. Probated June, 1832. Executors—David W. Patterson, Henry Haynes. Witnesses—James Chambers. Thomas Callant.

JAMES PATTERSON—Will Book A, Page 152—Names brother, William; sister, Polly; brother, David; brother, Robert. Written March 2, 1811. Probated, May, 1811. Executor—Robert Patterson. Witnesses—U. Stevenson, William Lowry, James Craig.

JOSEPH PATTON—Will Book B, Page 158—Names wife, Peggy; son, John; brother, William Patton. Written March 20, 1823. Probated April 1823. Executors—Wife, Peggy, brother, William Patton. Witnesses—William Lowry, John Hughes.

PHILIP PENDLETON—Will Book A, Page 153—Names wife, Agnes; daughters, Elizabeth Hunter, Nancy C. Kennedy; sons, Philip, James, Edmond (land on Potomac); Henry, (lot Hancacktown, Md.); sons--in-law, David Hunter, John Kennedy. Written November 19, 1801. Probated January 26, 1802. Executors—Wife, Agnes, son, Philip,

David Hunter, John Kennedy. Witnesses—Nicholas Orrick Pendleton, R. Pindall.

TEMPLE S. PENN—Will Book B, Page 518—Names wife, Lauretta W. Penn; sisters, Sophia Penn, Jane Penn. Written February 9, 1829. Probated April, 1832. Executrix—Lauretta Penn (wife), Witnesses —J. R. Curry, Nathaniel Campbell, J. Smith.

THOMAS PHILLIPS—Will Book A, Page 370—Names wife, Martha; son, Moses; mentions other children. Written October 25, 1817. Probated August, 1817. Witnesses—Stephen Davis, William Blair.

WILLIAM PHILLIPS—Will Book A, Page 243—Names wife, Ellen; sons, Howard, Hyram, William, Warner, John, James, Austen; daughters, Polly, Ellen, Cordelia. Written March 20, 1814. Probated July, 1814. Witnesses—James Coleman, James Robb.

JOHN PICKETT—Will Book A, Page 108—Names wife, Mary Pickett; sons, Richard, Thomas, George, John; sons-in-law, Nicholas Long; James Wilson, Littleton Robinson, Zachariah Wilson, Philip Samuel; son, Wilson. Written August 22, 1808. Probated October, 1808. Executors—George Pickett, Thomas Pickett, William Brown. Witnesses—Edwin Reynolds, Robert Rankin, Gavin Morrison.

MOURING PIGG—Will Book B, Page 42—Names wife, Nancy Pigg; sons, Lewis Pigg, Moses Pigg, David Pigg, Spencer Pigg, John Pigg, William Pigg; daughters, Sally Patterson, Margaret Adkins, Elizabeth Chinn. Written Oct. 11, 1820. Probated December, 1820. Executors—Richard Faulconer, Francis Edwards, Nancy Pigg. Witnesses—Jonathan Hedges, Edmund Falconer, James Simpson.

PHILIP POCK—Will Book B, Page 350—Names wife, Sarah; daughters Sarah, Milcah Gossett; sons, Philip, John. Written March 10, 1827. Probated February, 1827. Executors—Wife, Sarah, Andrew Guardner. Witnesses—William Furnish, Philip Fightmaster, George Fightmaster.

EDMUND POLLARD—(Pensioner)—Will Book C, Page 382—Name wife, Sarah; daughters, Elizabeth Kinny, Nancy Smith, Patsy Perkins, Mariah Faulconer, Frances Swinford, Emily Faulconer. Written September 25, 1834. Probated August, 1835. Executors—Sarah Pollard (wife), Nathan Faulconer, William Furnish. Witnesses—Samuel Courtney, James Courtney, Whitfield Collins.

CHARLES PORTER—Will Book A, Page 411—Names wife, Sarah; daughters, Catharine, Polly, Frances, Nancy, Malinda; sons, Moody, Stanfield, Owings, Thomas, Lewis, Joseph, Shelton. Written April 4, 1818. Probated July, 1818. Executor—John Smith. Witnesses—Charles Smith, Elijah Chinn.

GEORGE POWELL—Will Book A, Page 371—Names wife, Margaret. Written March 11, 1817. Probated August, 1817. Executors—Jacob Keith, wife, Margaret Powell. Witnesses—Arch Alexandra, Thomas Brinson, Jacob Keith.

JOHN RALSTON—(Pensioner)—Will Book D, Page 135—Names sons, John, Joseph, Andrew, David, William, Robert; daughters, Elizabeth Furnish, Jane Ralston, Rebecca Woods. Written April 10, 1835. Probated September, 1840. Executors—John Ralston, William Furnish. Witnesses—Lewis Conner, Lewis T. Conner.

THOMAS RAVENSCRAFT—Will Book B, Page 304—Names wife,

Margaret; sons, James, Thomas, William, Samuel, Robert, John; daughters, Sallie Milton, Betsy Ranvenscraft, Polly, Peggy, Nancy. Written May 15, 1827. Probated August, 1827. Executor—John Ravenscroft. Witnesses—T. W. B. Carnagy, Conrad Custor.

JAMES RIED—Will Book A, Page 39—Names wife, Elizabeth. Written March 16, 1802. Proved May, 1802. Executors—Elizabeth Ried, David Dryden. Witnesses—Benj. Hamilton, James McClure.

WILLIAM W. RILEY—Will Book A, Page 412—Names wife, brother, brother, Ninian Riley; child mentioned. Written March 26, 1818. Probated July, 1818. Executors—Ninean Riley, John R. Blair. Witnesses—Samuel Hine, James W. Riley.

THOMAS REDMON—Will Book B, Page 192—Names daughters, Elvina Abigail, Hursey Jane (children of John Hurley); daughters, Elizabeth Johnson, Matilda, Sally, Rhoda, Nancy, Polly Ann; sons, John, George W., Wesley W.; brothers, George, William, Charles; wife, Nancy. Written April 29, 1824. Probated May, 1824. Executors—Charles and George Redmon. Witnesses—Joel Frazier, John Frazier.

ZELY RENO—(Pensioner)—Will Book D, Page 16—Names wife, Mary; sons, Christopher, Charles, Lewis; daughters, Sytha Jones, Polly Jones, Pernelepy Calbert, Margaret Lewis. Written June 10, 1834. Probated February, 1837. Witnesses—Benjamin Bradon, William Simpson.

MICHAEL RITTER—Will Book A, Page 162—Names wife, Mary; sons, Lewis, John; daughter, Susanna. Written March 16, 1812. Probated May, 1812. Executors—Lewis Ritter, Thomas Dugan. Witnesses—Joshua Hall, Thomas Kemper, Jacob Martin.

HUGH ROBERTS—Will Book B, Page 288—Names wife, Elizabeth; sons, James, William. Written November 18, 1826. Probated January, 1827. Executors—Sons, James Roberts, William Roberts. Witnesses—David Humphreys, Thomas Roberts.

FRANCIS ROBINSON—(Pensioner)—Will Book D, Page 365— Names sons, Samuel, Benjamin, William; daughters, Nancy Dunn, Sally McCann, Ellen Readnour, Polly Calyar, Frances, Jone Robinson, Agnes Dunn, Catherine Huffman, Betsy; grandsons, Thomas Colson, Samuel Colson. Written December 28, 1840. Probated January, 1841. Executor—Benjamin Robinson. Witnesses—Harmon Million, W. L. Robinson.

JOHN RODGERS—Will Book B, Page 68—Names wife, Ann; sons, George, John, Abner; daughters, Mary Tippett, Sarah Mountague-Fanny Rodgers, Lucy Rodgers, Susanna Rodgers. Written April 17, 1821. Probated April, 1821. Executors—John Tippet, son-in-law, Abner Rodgers. Witnesses—James Veach, Robert Ashurst, Moses Webb.

JESSE ROSE—(Pensioner)—Will Book B, Page 509—Names son, William; daughters, Elizabeth, Sallie, Peggy; son, Thomas; daughter, Pollie; granddaughter, Pollie Seeper. Written October 3, 1831. Probated January, 1832. Executors—Joe Barrett, Jacob Zeller. Witnesses—Victor Barrett, Wesley Barrett.

MICHAEL ROZER—Will Book A, Page 51—Names wife, Caty; son, John; other children (not named); son, Jacob. Proved October

Court, 1804. Executors—Wife, Catey, son Jacob. Witnesses—William Turney, William Raymond, Peter Pope.

ISAAC RUDDLE—Will Book B, Page 14—Names daughters, Sally, Deborah; son, Roberson; daughter, Caty Ingram. Written September 9, 1818. Probated February, 1819. Executrix—Caty Ingram. Witnesses—Wm. F. Asbury, P. Barrett.

ARCHIBALD SCOTT—Will Book A, Page 20—Names sons-in-law, John Morgan, David Lowry, James Martin, Robert Thompson, Robert Russell, John Russell and wife. Written May 1, 1798. Proven March Court, 1799. Executors—John Ellison, Robert Russell. Witnesses—William January, John McGrath, Polly Ellison.

JOHN SCOTT—(Pensioner)—Record Book F, Page 78—Names in division of land, Nancy Scott, Lidia Scott, William Scott, Margaret Scott, Richard Schooler, Jacob Lockhart, Aaron Ashbrook, Hiram Scott, M. M. Baley.

JOHN SELLERS—Will Book A, Page 6—Names wife, Elizabeth; children, Mary, Elizabeth, Jane, Margaret, Sarah, John, Ruth, James Written March 21, 1798. Will proved July, 1798. Executors—Elizabeth Sellers (wife), John Adams, James Brown. Witnesses—William Adams, James Thompson.

JOHN SHERMAN—Will Book A, Page 134—Names son, William, daughters Mary, Anna; brother, Shadrack. Written Nov. 11, 1809. Probated December, 1809. Executors—Shadrack Sherman, Abraham Powell. Witnesses—Thomas Duncan, William Hutcherson, John Tucker.

ARCHIBALD SHIELDS—Will Book B, Page 18r—Names wife, Nancy Edgar Shields; daughters, Margaret, Martha, Polly; sons, John, Robert, Thomas, James. Written Feb. 15, 1824. Codicil written Feb. 16, 1824. Mentions children of Nancy Thompson Shields, daughter, Polly, one unnamed. Probated April 1824. Executors—Wife, Nancy Shields, James M. Clarkson. Witnesses—L. H. B. Clarkson, J. G. Chinn, William Sewell.

JAMES SHROPSHIRE—Will Book B, Page 272—Names wife, Milly; daughters, Polly Reno, Nancy, Betsy; son, James, daughters, Julia Simms, Milly, Lucinda, Huldah; son, John Elliott; daughter, Kitty; grandchildren, James Edward and William Simms. Written July 27, 1826. Probated October, 1826. Executors—Brothers, George Shropshire, John Shropshire. Witnesses—Edward Shropshire, Joseph Shropshire, John Conner, Hubbell Shropshire, William Essex, Abner Shropshire.

JOHN SHURTS—Will Book B, Page 254—Names wife, Rachael. Written Nov. 20, 1824. Probated February, 1826. Executors—Peter Barrett, Abraham Dilse. Witnesses—Alexander McDaniel, William H. Casey, George King.

CHARLES A. SMITH—Will Book B, Page 206—Names wife, Mary; Children unnamed, but mentioned. Written August, 1824. Probated November, 1824. Executors—Mary Smith, Noah Spears. Witnesses—John Walton, John Frazier, Sarah C. Frazier.

GEORGE SMITH—Will Book A, Page 197—Names wife, Polly; brother, Charles—Written June 8, 1813. Probate July, 1813. Executor—Charles Smith. Witnesses—William Brown Bennett, John Smith.

JOHN SMITH—Will Book B, Page 451—Names daughter, Patsy Davis; sons, James, William; daughter, Elizabeth. Written January 5, 1830. Probated March, 1830. Witnesses—Achilles Chinn, Alexander Chinn, John Chinn.

JOHN SMITH—Will Book B, Page 532—Names daughters, Zelinda Ann Payne, Peggy Dickerson, Eliza; son, Thomas P.; daughter, Mary Theobald; son, John N.; son, Nathan; mentioned Nancy Porter, daughter of Patsy Porter. Written July 5, 1832. Probated September, 1832. Executors—Thomas P. Smith, Nathan Smith. Witnesses —G. K. Perrin, James Ingles, Frank L. Combs.

JOHN SMITH—Will Book B, Page 536—Names wife, Ruth; sons, Ephraim, John, William, Thomas; daughters, Sarah, Mary, Hannah. Written January 31, 1832. Probated October, 1832. Executors— John Smith, Ephraim Smith. Witnesses—J. C. Frazier, J. R. Curry.

MICHAEL SMITH—(Pensioner)—Will Book E, Page 52—Names sons, Peter, Martin, Nicholas, Michael, John, Manuel, George; daughters, Catharine, Betsy, Anna, Amanda; wife, Nancy. Written August 11, 1834. Probated December, 1842. Executor—Peter Smith. Witnesses—Elias Batterton, Nicholas Smith.

LEWIS SNELL—Will Book B, Page 32—Names wife, Mary Kirtley Snell; daughters, Elizabeth and son-in-law, James Jameson; Sarah Logan, Lucretia, Nancy Fry and son-in-law, Abraham Fry; Mary Thomas; sons, Joseph, James, Taverner, John, Newton. Written April 8, 1819. Probated April, 1820. Executors—Mary Snell, Joseph Snell, James Snell. Witnesses—Joel Frazier, Joseph Patterson.

RICHARD SNEED—Will Book A, Page 74—Names wife, Patsy; brother Thomas. Written August, 19, 1806. Proven April, 1807. Executors—Wife, Patsy, brother, Thomas. Witnesses—William Adams, Larkin Price, James Adams.

ROBERT SNODGRASS—Will Book B, Page 121—Names sons, David, James, John; daughters, Patsey, Salley, Peggy, Polley, Nancy; son, Bott; wife, no name given. Written October 3, 1822. Probated November, 1822. Witnesses—Elijah Ferrell, John Waggoner.

LIMEN STEADYCORN—Will Book A, Page 110—Names wife, Rachel; son, Samuel. Written November 27, 1808. Probated December, 1808. Executors—Wife, Rachel, John Shanly. Witnesses—James Galley, Samuel Endicott, Samuel Jamison.

JOHN STEPHENSCN—Will Book A, Page 35—Names wife, Mary. Written October 26, 1800. Proved November Court, 1801. Executors—Mary (wife), John Minter. Witnesses—Samuel McIlvain, John McIlvain, John Ermon.

ROBERT STEWART—Will Book B, Page 375—Names sons, Thomas L. Stewart, Robert C. Stewart; daughters, Annie McClintock, Nancy Merchal, Maria Stewart, Jane Stewart, Louisa N. Stewart; sons, James R. Stewart, William C. Stewart, Arthur F. Stewart, John L. Stewart, David B. Stewart; wife, Margery. Probated July, 1828. Executors—Wife, Margery, son, David B., son, Robert C. Witnesses —John Eads, Dumas Jones.

WILLIAM STUART—Will Book A, Page 364—Names, wife, Eilzabeth; son, Benjamin; daughters, Sally, Nancy; sons, Henry, William; daughters, Jenny Shields, Isabella Nisbits, Polly Anderson; grandsons, William Shields, William Nisbit, Jeremiah Nisbit. Written

March 12, 1817. Probated April, 1817. Executors—John Huddelson, Alexandra McDaniel. Witnesses—Isham Tyree, George Kirkpatrick.

WILLIAM SUTTON—(Pensioner)—Invoice and Appraisement— Record Book E, Page 74. Dated February 16, 1842.

JOSHUA SWINFORD—Will Book, Page 44—Names wife, Elizabeth; sons, James, John; daughters, Peggy, Jane, Eliza. Written, Oct. 11, 1820. Probated December, 1820. Executors—Elizabeth (wife), James Swinford. Witnesses—James Marshall, William Adams.

JOHN TAYLOR—(Pensioner)—Will Book B, Page 301—Names wife, Ruth. Written May 9, 1827. Probated July, 1827. Witnesses— Wm. Asbury, David Clark, A. M. Camron.

JOSEPH TAYLOR—Will Book B, Pages 188 and 189—Names brother, James. Written December 9, 1815. Probated January, 1824. Executor—Brother, James. Witnesses—Benjamin Henry, William J. Clarke, Dennis Forest.

OBEDIAH TERRY—Will Book B, Page 256—Names wife, Sarah, daughter, Nancy Carter; grandson, Burret N. Carter; son, William. Written January 12, 1823. Probated April, 1826. Executor— Lewis Day, Jr. Witnesses—Benjamin Hutcherson, Stephen White, John Cason.

ANTHONY THORNTON—Will Book B, Page 398—Names daughter, Lucy Dickson Thornton; son, John Rootes Thornton; grandsons, Henry Melkar Thornton, Lewis Read Thornton; granddaughters, Mildred R. Whitney, Mary Rootes Thornton. Written February 18, 1828. Probated January, 1829. Witnesses—John McKee, Alexander McClain.

SAMUEL TIMBERLAKE—Will Book B, Page 300—Names brother, John; sister, Elizabeth Broadwell. Written Jan. 4, 1827. Probated May, 1827. Executor—Wesley Broadwell. Witnesses—Joel Frazier, William B. Hunt.

HARRIET TISDALE—Will Book C, Page 306—Names sister, Mary Cason; mother, Sarah; nieces, Sally Ann Cason, Harriett Ellen Cason. Probated August, 1834. Executor—Sarah Tisdale, (mother). Witnesses—Lewis Day, Leonard Stump.

JOHN TONEY—Will Book B, Page 54—Names son, Jaret; wife, Mornin Coley. Written January 8, 1821. Probated April, 1821. Executor—Alijah North. Witnesses—Thomas E. Ferguson, John Douglas.

JOHN TRIMBLE, SR.—(Pensioner)—Will Book E, Page 26—Names daughters, Susanna, Mary, Jane; sons, Isaac, William, John. Also names brother, William; grandchildren, John and James Trimble, John M. Trimble Gregory; son-in-law, John Fry. Written May 10, 1836. Proved, 1842. Executors—William Trimble, Susannah Trimble. Witnesses—John Ballinger, James Dawson, A. Dawson.

SAMUEL TUCKER—Will Book B, Page 519—Names wife, Matilda A. Tucker; brothers, John Tucker, William Tucker; father-in-law, Harmon Dills. Written April 13, 1832. Probated May, 1832. Executors—William Tucker, Harmon Dills. Witnesses—Joseph Tucker, James Arnett.

GEORGE TURNER, "County of Culpepper, Va."—Will Book B, Page 1

—Names son, Thornton, William, Ezekiel, Daniel, John; daughters, Polly Rodgers, Rachael Bryant, (Jesse, husband), Levina Kinnard; wife, Elizabeth. Written May 20, 1815. Proved June 19, 1815. Executors—Daniel Turner, Jesse Bryant. Witnesses—John Rodgers, John Boyd.

MARY TURVEY—Will Book A, Page 308—Names son, Braxton King. Written December 11, 1815. Probated January, 1816. Witnesses—William Raymon, Robert McDuffee, John Heading.

WILLIAM TURVEY—Will Book A, Page 88—Names wife, Mary; son, William. Written September, 26, 1807. Probated February, 1808. Executors—Wife, Mary, Braxten King. Witnesses—Benjamin Hickman, William Raymond, Isaac Taylor, Zackus Key.

JESSE M. VANDEREN—Will Book B, Page 419—Names wife, Nancy (Jones); brothers, Bannard, Joseph; brother-in-law, Benjamin Jones. Written September 9, 1829. Probated October, 1829. Executrix—Nancy Vanderen (wife). Witnesses—Joel Frazer, M. C. Thomas, J. I. Sparks.

WILLIAM VENARD—(Pensioner)—Will Book D, Page 72—Names wife, Dorothy; sons, John, George; daughters, Hannah Mitchel, Druzilla Steward, Polly McNeese, Rebecca Eads; son, William; children of William: America Hayden, Dudley. Written, 1839. Probated March 12, 1841. Executors—Dorothy (wife), Lewis Conner, John McNeese. Witnesses—George Marshall, Lewis Conner.

JOHN WADKINS (WATKINS)—(Pensioner)—Record Book C, Page 66—Inventory dated August 28, 1833.

JOHN WARD—Will Book B, Page 225—Names wife, Margaret; daughter, Mary; sons, Carey Allen, James, Joseph, Archibald. Written October 30, 1824. Probated February, 1825. Executors—Carey Allen Ward, son, and wife, Margaret. Witnesses—William Gray, William Lowry.

JOSEPH WARD—Will Book B, Page 163—Names wife, Margarette; sons, John, James, Newton, Carey; brother, John. Written October 1, 1821. Probated May, 1823. Executors— Wife, Margarette; brother, John Ward. Witnesses—Francis Gray, Nathaniel Campbell.

JAMES WATSON, SR.—Will Book A, Page 370—Names sons, Patrick, James, David, Joseph, William; daughters, Elizabeth Blackburn, Peggy Jameson, Mary Ardry, Marth Linn; daughter-in-law, Nancy Watson. Written Sept. 9, 1816. Probated July, 1817. Executors—James Watson, Patrick Watson. Witnesses—William Asbury, Shadrick Hieatt.

WILLIAM H. WEBBER—Will Book C, Page 285—Names mother, Sarah Johns; mentions David Kinman's heirs; mentions Sanford, son of Sarah Huffman; mentions William Anderson, son of Anne Burgess. Written January 29, 1833. Probated May, 1834. Witnesses—Reuben Faulconer, George Hedger, John Burgess.

JOHN WHITEKER—Will Book C, Page 120—Names wife, Nancy, sons, Isaac, Peter; daughter, Nancy Groghegan; sons, John Wesley and Josiah, son-in-law, Hugh Hickman. Written April 30, 1829. Probated November, 1833. Executors—Hugh Hickman, Peter Whiteker. Witnesses—Hugh Hickman, James Dunlap.

JAMES WHITSON—Will Book B, Page 459—Names sons, John Curle

Whitson, Basil; daughter, Sally Rankin (hubsand, David Rankin); son, Willis. Written June 18, 1830. Probated July, 1830. Executors—Nancy Whitson, (wife), John Curle Whitson. Witnesses—J. C. Frazer, Samuel Rankin.

PHILIP WIGGINS—Will Book B, Page 41—Names daughters, Mary Chambers, Hannah Williams, Sarah Martin, Rachel Osbourne, Christen Martin, Drusella Harnes, Rutha Kernes, Elenor Reeves; son, James H. Wiggins. Written July 17, 1820. Probated August, 1820. Executors—John Martin, John Horas, James H. Wiggins. Witnesses—Larkin Garnet, Thomas Gibson, Edward W. Martin.

JAMES WIGLESWORTH—Will Book B, Page 225—Names wife, Priscilla; sons, Thompson, John; daughter, Anna Holeman; son, William; grandson, Thompson Wiglesworth. Written October 18, 1824. Probated April, 1825. Executors—Sons, Thompson and John. Witnesses: James Poindexter, Larkin Garnett.

ELIZABETH WILLIAMS—Will Book B, Page 122—Names sons, Samuel, John, Thomas, David; daughters, Polly, Ann, Isabella; brother, Thomas W. Nutt. Written September 2, 1822. Probated November, 1822. Executor—David Lamme. Witnesses—Frances Edwards, Susanna Dixon, Joseph Morin.

DAVID WILSON—Will Book B, Page 58—Names, sons, James, David, John, Jacob, William, Samuel; wife, Patsy; daughters, Elizabeth, Margaret, Nancy, Patsy; granddaughter, Nancy Hinkson. Written May 8, 1821. Probated July, 1821. Executor—John Wilson. Witnesses—John Shawan, James Cummins.

HUGH WILSON—Will Book B, Page 30—Names, daughters, Jane, Elizabeth, Rachael, Nancy; wife, Margaret; sons, James, William, John. Written July 28, 1819. Probated October, 1819. Witnesses—John Waits, Daniel McShane.

BENJAMIN WITHERS—Will Book B, Page 473—Names, wife, Nancy; daughter, Alice M. Boyd (husband, Joseph Boyd); sons, William A.; George M; grandson, William T.; granddaughter, Anna F.; grandson, Montgomery Boyd. Written February 28, 1828. Probated November, 1830. Executors—William A. Withers, George M. Withers. Witnesses—Joseph Barnett, John Kindrick, Joseph Leavell, William Lightner.

LEWIS WOLF, SR.—(Pensioner)—Will Book F, Page 82—Names wife, Barbara; daughter, Mary Craford; son, Lewis. Written June 10, 1848. Probated August, 1848. Executors—Lewis Wolf, Isaac Brown. Witnesses—William H. Eskridge, Delaney Wolf, John Beagle.

JAMES WOOD—Will Book B, Page 85—Names brother, James; sons, James, Eli; daughters, Elizabeht, Sarah. Written November 21, 1821. Probated February, 1822. Witnesses—Caleb Jennings, Eleanah Jennings.

THOMAS WOOD—Will Book C, Page 225—Names daughter, Milly Rush; son-in-law, David Rush; daughter, Rebecca; sons, Hiram, Joseph, Benjamin, Samuel, William; daughters, Patsy Ellis, Mary Scott; grandchildren, Susannah, Mary Scott; their father, William Scott. Written April 10, 1827. Probated January 1834. Executor—Hiram Wood. Witnesses—Thomas Smith, W. T. Sutton.

IESI (ISAAC?) YARNELL—Will Book A, Page 125—Names wife, Ann;

sons, John, Samuel, Isaac; daughter, Sallie; son, David. Written April 8, 1809. Probated July 9, 1809. Executors—Benjamin Hodge, S. P. Griffith. Witnesses—Thomas Hawkins, Leonard Stump, sons, Philip, Christian, John, Jacob; daughters, Polly Simmon, Eliza-William Ralston, Jacob Coonrad.

GEORGE ZUMMUTT—Will Book A, Page 310—Names wife, Mary; sons, Philip, Christian, John, Jacob; daughters, Polly Simmon, Elizabeth Fry, Margaret Bever, Christiana Snider; granddaughter, Mary Loiure; son, Henry. Written September 4, 1815. Probated February 1816. Executor—John Zummutt. Witnesses—Charles Smith, Jr., Austin Bradford, Jr., William Mosley.

JESSAMINE COUNTY WILL ABSTRACTS

(Contributed by Mrs. Raymond Burch, Mrs. Edward Lane, Miss Susan McDowell and Miss Kathryn P. Fitch, Trabue Chapter)

WILL BOOK A

CHARLES WEBBER—Page 1—date of will, June 17,1779; date of probate, 1799—names brothers.

GEORGE WALKER—Page 3—date of will, December 22, 1798; date of probate, March, 1800—names wife, Priscilla and children.

MICHAEL COGER—Page 5—date of will, February 19, 1801; date of probate, September, 1801—names wife, Mary and children.

CHIRLEY GATES—Page 7—date of will, April 4, 1800; date of probate, October, 1800—names wife, Susanna and daughters.

JOHN HAYDON—Page 13—date of will, June, 1801; date of probate, September, 1801—names wife, Lucy and children.

JAMES CARNES—Page 22—date of will, December 22, 1800; date of probate, April, 1801—names Jno. Ficklin, Executor.

THOMAS WILLIAMSON—Page 24—date of will, October 31, 1800; date of probate, November, 1800—names wife, Elizabeth and children.

DAVID TAYLOR—Page 26—date of will, December 31, 1801; date of probate, February, 1802—names brothers and sisters.

JAMES McELHANY—Page 41—date of will, August 11, 1801; date of probate, May, 1802—names wife, Ann.

AUGUSTINE GATEWOOD—Page 42—date of will, March 18, 1802. date of probate, May, 1802—names wife, Betty and children.

JOHN STONESTREET—Page 49—date of will, March 1, 1802; date of probate, May, 1802—names wife, Anne and children.

JONAS DAVENPORT—Page 57—date of will,April 5, 1802; date of probate, August, 1802—names wife, Alice and children.

PETER ALLISON—Page 64—date of will, June 4, 1802; date of probate, October, 1802—names children.

DAVID WALTERS—Page 74—date of will, November 5, 1802; date of probate, January, 1803—names wife, Betty and children.

DANIEL HULSE—Page 80—date of will, March 7, 1805; date of probate, May, 1805—names wife, Dinah and children.

FRANCIS BOURNE—Page 85—date of will, June 2, 1803; date of probate, September, 1807—names wife, Frances and children.

ELIZABETH GILMORE—Page 92—date of will, September 19, 1804; date of probate, December, 1805—names children.

COURTNAY WALKERS—Page 100—date of will, February 17, 1804; date of probate, March, 1804—names brothers and sisters.

SAMUEL WALTERS—Page 100—date of will, June 11, 1804; date of probate, February, 1805—names wife, Sarah and children.

JAMES WILLIAMS—Page 103—date of will, January 20, 1803; date of probate, May, 1802—names wife and children.

WILLIAM SCOTT—Page 105—date of will, October 3, 1804; date of probate, December, 1804—names wife, Grezel and children.

GABRIEL MADERSON—Page 111—date of will, April 21, 1801; date of probate, May, 1802—names wife, Mariah and children.

JOHN GILMORE—Page 114—date of wil, June 16, 1807; date of probate, August, 1807—names sisters.

ISAAC SMITH—Page 116—date of will, January 14, 1806; date of probate, February, 1807—names wife, Polly and children.

AGULLA GILBERT—Page 118—date of will, December 29, 1806; date of probate, February, 1807—names children.

REUBEN BOURNE—Page 125— date of will, March 31, 1807; date of probate, June, 1807—names wife and children.

WILLIAM EDMON—Page 129—date of will, September 21, 1806; date of probate, November, 1808—names brothers and sisters.

WILLIAM T. TURNER—Page 132—date of will, May 15, 1807; date of probate, June, 1807—names wife, Action and sons.

JAMES LOCKHART—Page 154—date of will, August 1, 1804; date of probate, November, 1804—names children.

SHEROD WILLIS—Page 160—date of will, March 3, 1806; date of probate, June, 1806—names wife, Maryann and children.

JAMES DUNN—Page 195—date of will, November 6, 1806; date of probate, February, 1808—names wife, Martha and children.

JOSEPH PREWITT—Page 197—date of will, January 31, 1808; date of probate, February, 1808—names wife, Polly and children.

JOHN FOSTER—Page 205—date of will, April 25, 1808; date of probate, June, 1808—names wife, Leanah and children.

JAMES BRUSTER—Page 206— date of will, August 15, 1807; date of probate, August, 1808—names wife, Elenor and children.

CORNELIUS EMPSON—Page 219—date of will, May 27, 1808; date of probate, August, 1808—names wife, Hannah and children.

SAMUEL SODUSKY—Page 223—date of will, April 1, 1803; date of probate, December, 1803—names wife, Margaret and children.

MARY COGER—Page 229—date of will, January 19, 1804; date of probate, May, 1806—names children.

THOMAS DILLIN—Page 231—date of will, July 27, 1796; date of probate, September, 1803—names wife, Ezabella and children.

ELIZABETH SMITH—Page 241—date of will, June 1, 1807; date of probate, November, 1808—names children.

EDWARD HOCKERSMITH—Page 241—date of will, October 13, 1808; date of probate, November, 1808—names children.

WALTER CUNNINGHAM—Page 250—date of will, June 27, 1807; date of probate, June, 1808—names wife, Jean and children.

JOSEPH THOMPSON—Page 268—date of will, March 3, 1808; date of probate, December, 1809—names wife, Mary and children.

TURNER MORRIS—Page 279—date of will, January 25, 1810; date of probate, February, 1810—names sons.

GEORGE STOVAL SMITH—Page 286—date of will, January 24, 1809; date of probate, March, 1810—names wife and children.

THOMAS STEELE—Page 294—date of will, April 12, 1809; date of probate, March, 1810—names wife, Frances and children.

NATHANIEL LOWERY—Page 297—date of will, June 2, 1810; date of probate, August, 1810—names wife, Mary and sons.

JOHN SCOTT—Page 298—date of will, February 22, 1811; date of probate, March, 1811—names brothers and sisters.

ELENOR BRUSTER—Page 300—date of will, April 5, 1809; date of probate, August, 1811—names children.

MARTEN DICKENSON—Page 302—date of will, July 21, 1810—date of probate, August, 1811—names wife and children.

HENRY HUNTER—Page 304—date of will, October 15, 1810; date of probate, January, 1811—wife, Sara and children.

JAMES JOHNSON—Page 337—date of will, December 7, 1808; date of probate, November, 1811—names wife, Sarah and brothers.

ROGER PATTON—Page 387—date of will, December 4, 1811; date of probate, February, 1812—names children.

AQUILA KERTLEY—Page 396—date of will, March 24, 1812; date of probate, May, 1812—names sisters.

ZACHARIAH BARR—Page 410—date of will, April 1, 1812; date of probate, August, 1812—names wife, Sara and children.

GEORGE HARBISON—Page 415—date of will, November 6, 1812; date of probate, November, 1812.

SHADRACK MOORE—Page 417—date of probate, November, 1812—names wife, Rebecca and children.

THOMAS BICHOLS—Page 419—date of will, August 8, 1812; date of probate, September, 1812—names wife, Nancy and children.

DUDLEY GATEWOOD—Page 421—date of will, May 25, 1812; date of probate, November, 1812.

CHARLES WEST—Page 422—date of will, January 1, 1803; date of probate, November, 1812—names wife, Susanna and children.

DAVID HOOVER, SR.—Page 425—date of will, April 14, 1813; date of probate, May, 1813—names wife, Elizabeth.

DAVID STEELE—Page 426—date of will, November 23, 1812; date f probate, February, 1813—names wife, Mary and children.

ABRAM FULKERSON—Page 428—date of will, April 6, 1812; date of probate, February, 1813—names wife, Ann and sons.

JOSEPH WOODS—Page 430—date of will, April 6, 1812; date of probate, January, 1813—names wife, Martha and children.

JOHN CHILES—Page 432—date of will, January 4, 1813; date of probate, June, 1813—names wife, Elizabeth, and children.

JOHN STONESTREET—Page 434—date of will, February 15, 1812; date of probate, February, 1813—names wife, Betsy and daughter.

PATRICK GRAY—Page 436—date of will, August 14, 1812; date of probate, March, 1813—names wife, Margaret and children.

POWHATAN NETHERLAND—Page 442 date of will, February 27, 1813; date of probate, November, 1813—names brother.

BENJAMINE STEWART—Page 444— date of will, April 4, 1813; date of probate, June, 1813—names wife, Milly and children.

WILL BOOK B

CHAS. BARNES—Page 143—date of will, 1813; date of probate, 1814 —names wife, Mary.

J. EDMOND SINGLETON—Page 152—date of will, 1814; date of probate, 1814—names wife, Margant.

ISAAC JOHNSON—Page 157—date of will, 1814; date of probate, 1814—names wife, Elizabeth.

JOHN HUCKSTIP—Page 159—date of will, 1810; date of probate, 1813.

JOHN SALE—Page 161—date of probate, 1812.

G. W. BARKLEY—Page 164—date of will, 1814; date of probate, 1815 names wife, Martha.

CHRISTOPHER WEBSTER—Page 172—date of will, 1813; date of probate, 1814—names wife, Hannah.

MARY CARSNER—Page 185—date of will, 1813; date of probate, 1814.

WM. BOWMER—Page 195—date of will, 1814; date of probate, 1816 —names wife, Catherine.

JAS F. WALLACE—page 241—date of will, 1816; date of probate, 1816.

JOSHUA HAWKS—Page 241—date of will,1815; date of probate,1816 —names wife, Mariah.

DAVID THOMAS—Page 243—date of will, 1806; date of probate, 1816 —names wife, Catherine.

JOSEPH BARKLEY—Page 244—date of will, 1815; date of probate, 1816.

HENRY STARR—Page 266—date of will, 1813; date of probate, 1816 —names wife, Nannie.

DAN EASLEY—Page 286—date of wil, 1816; date of probate, 1816.

BRYAN McGRATH—Page 291—date of will, 1815; date of probate, 1816.

SUSANNA PRYOR—Page301—date of will,1809; date of probate, 1817.

THOS. REED—Page 307—date of will, 1817; date of probate, 1817— names wife, Rosanna.

SIMEON—Page 331—date of will, 1810; date of probate, 1817—names wife, Martha.

WM. ANDERSON—Page 335—date of will, 1814; date of probate, 1817 —names wife, Catherine.

SAMUEL PANKEY—Page 360—date of will, 1817; date of probate, 1817—names wife, Mary.

NATHAN BAKER—Page 374—date of will, 1817; date of probate, 1818—names wife, Nancy.

SAMUEL MARRS—Page 376—date of will,1810; date of probate, 1818.

CATY SMITH—Page 394—date of will,1818; date of probate, 1818.

JOHN WITHERS—Page 424—date of will, 1814; date of probate,1818.

PETER BOLLOCK—Page 431—date of will, 1815; date of probate, 1815—names wife, Mary.

WILL BOOK C

WM. COLEY——Page 1—date of will, 1818; date of probate 1818— names wife, Debarah.

ELIZABETH PENISTON—Page 11—date of will, 1818; date of probate, 1818.

JUDETH SALLEE—Page 12—date of will, 1818; date of probate, 1818.

JOHN FICKLIN—Page 18—date of will, 1819; date of probate, 1819 —names wife, Mary.

GU. RAMSEY—Page 19—date of will, 1817; date of probate, 1818.

JOHN EAKIN—Page 26—date of will, 1818; date of probate 1818.

GEO. WALKER—Page 48—date of will, 1819; date of probate, 1819 names wife, Catherine.

SUSANNAH PRICE—Page 49—date of will,1819; date of probate, 1819.

JOHN HOWELL—Page 68—date of will,1819; date of probate, 1820 —names wife, Ann.

GU. HOGHTOWER—Page 69—date of will, 1820; date of probate, 1820.

GU. M. PROCTOR—Page 72—date of will, 1820; date of probate, 1820 —names wife, Elizabeth.

JOHN GORDON—Page 76—date of will, 1820; date of probate, 1820.

HENRY KING—Page 76—date of will,1817; date of probate, 1820.

ELIZABETH GREEN—Page 87—date of will, 1813; date of probate, 1813.

FRANCIS LWOEN—Page 101—date of will, 1820; date of probate, 1820—names wife, Lucy.

JNO. KELLAR—Page 105—date of will, 1820; date of probate, 1820— names wife, Elizabeth.

JAS. SUTTON—Page 128—date of will, 1819; date of probate, 1821.

JOSEPHA LEWIS—Page 135—date of will, 1819; date of probate, 1821—names wife, Jane.

PETER SIMPSON—Page 145—date of will, 1820; date of probate, 1821.

BENJAMINE MERTIN—Page 146—date of will, 1818; date of probate, 1821.

WM. MARSHALL—Page 147—date of will, 1821; date of probate, 1821 names wife, Elizabeth.

SAMUEL BEAL—Page 204—date of will, 1797; date of probate, 1821.

NATHAN EVANS—Page 242—date of will, 1823; date of probate, 1823.

JOS. DUMMIDEE—Page 245—date of will, 1822; date of probate, 1823.

JOHN WALTERS—Page 258—date of will, 1823; date of probate, 1823 —names wife, Mary.

EPHRIAMID JANUARY—Page 265——date of will, 1823; date of probate, 1823—names wife, Sarah.

ELIZABETH McKINNEY—Page 265—date of will, 1822; date of probate, 1823.

JAS. HEMPHILL—Page 276—date of will, 1823; date of probate, 1823.

ALSEY HOWARD—Page 61—date of will, 1807; date of probate, 1827.

RICHARD YOUNG—Page 75—date of will, 1827; date of probate, 1827—names wife, Nancy.

MARTIN WHISS—Page 77—date of will, 1827; date of probate, 1827.

JOSEPH CHRISMAN—Page 79—date of will, 1826; date of probate, 1828—names wife, Jane.

ELISABETH HOGAN—Page 101—date of will, 1825; date of probate, 1828.

CATHERINE BOURNE—Page 106—date of will, 1827; date of probate 1828.

SAMUEL WELLS—Page 110—date of will, 1828; date of probate, 1828—names wife, Elizabeth.

DAVID WATTS—Page 117—date of will, 1828; date of probate, 1828 names wife, Martha.

JOHN BARKLEY—Page 118—date of will, 1827; date of probate, 1828.

THOS. RICKETS—Page 118—date of will, 1827; date of probate, 1828 —names wife, Martha.

JACOB NEED—Page 126—date of will, 1827; date of probate, 1828.

JOHN SCOTT—Page 147—date of will, 1824; date of probate, 1829— names wife, Milly.

W. G. BRUCE—Page 152—date of will, 1829; date of probate, 1829— names wife.

DAVID MEAD—Page 153—date of will, 1829.

THOS. FLETCHER—Page 153—date of will, 1827; date of probate, 1829.

JACOB ZIKE—Page 158—date of will, 1828; date of probate, 1829— names wife, Katherine.

HENRY GREEN—Page 171—date of will, 1829; date of probate, 1829 —names wife, Margaret.

POLLY BARKLEY—Page 176—date of will 1829; date of probate, 1829.

WM. PAYNE—Page 176—date of will, 1829; date of probate, 1829— names wife, Minerva.

GEORGE JAMESON—Page 176—date of will, 1829; date of probate, 1829.

JAS. HOLLOWAY—Page 177—date of will, 1830; date of probate, 1829.

ANN MOREHEAD—Page 180—date of will, 1830; date of probate, 1830—names Henry.

GEO. CHADWELL—Page 279—date of will, 1823; date of probate, 1823—names wife, Ellis.

JOHN MOOR—Page 307—date of will, 1823; date of probate, 1823—names wife, Nancy.

RANDOLPH WALKER—Page 308—date of will, 1822; date of probate 1822—names wife, Lucy.

WM. ROBARDS—Page 313—date of will, 1823; date of probate, 1823—names wife, Polly.

DAVID SHELY—Page 313—date of will, 1823; date of probate, 1823.

ALLEX IRVIN—Page 333—date of will, 1813; date of probate, 1824—names wife, Milly.

THOS. WILSON—Page 342—date of will, 1824; date of probate, 1824.

JOHN CAMPBELL—Page 386—date of will, 1824; date of probate, 1824.

CLAYBORN KERSEY—Page 382—date of will, 1824; date of probate, 1824.

JANE WILKERSON—Page 395—date of will, 1823; date of probate, 1824.

FRANCIS B. KEIRBY—Page 441—date of will, 1825; date of probate, 1825.

AMNEY PITCHER—Page 450—date of will, 1825; date of probate, 1825.

DAVID McKEE—Page 451—date of will, 1825; date of probate, 1825.

GERSHAM LOURY—Page 483—date of will, 1826; date of probate, 1826—names wife, Prudence.

MICALL ROBB—Page 508—date of will, 1826; date of probate, 1826—names wife, Elizabeth.

WM. BOURN—Page 508—date of will, 1826; date of probate, 1826.

WILL BOOK D

THOS. WADE—Page 10—date of will, 1824; date of probate, 1826.

WM. EVANS—Page 14—date of will, 1826; date of probate, 1826—names wife, Ann.

EDMOND GARRETT—Page 15—date of will, 1823; date of probate, 1827.

SAMUEL OFFUTT—Page 30—date of will, 1825; date of probate, 1827—names wife, Elizabeth.

MERRITT HUGHES—Page 38—date of will, 1827; date of probate, 1827—names wife, Mary.

RICHARD MARTIN—Page 43—date of will, 1827; date of probate, 1827—names wife, Eleanor.

MARY O'KELLY—Page 204—date of will, 1850; date of probate, 1850.

THOS. ROBERTS—Page 212—date of will, 1850; date of probate, 1850 —names wife, Sarah.

FOUNTAINE DAVENPORT—Page 231—date of will, 1829; date of probate, 1830—names wife, Nancy.

JOHN NEED—Page 234—date of will, 1830; date of probate, 1830— —names wife, Susan.

JOSEPH CROCKETT—Page 248—date of will, 1826; date of probate, 1831.

WM. SALLEE—Page 258—date of will, 1829; date of probate, 1831— names wife, Elizabeth.

KATHERINE PRICE—Page 262—date of will, 1831; date of probate, 1831—names Dr. John.

ABRAHAM ROHER—Page 266—date of will, 1831; date of probate, 1831.

DAVID WILSON—Page 268—date of will,1828; date of probate, 1831 —names wife, Ellen.

ADAM McCONNELL—Page 269—date of will,, 1831; date of probate, 1831—names Francis.

JAMES KNIGHT—Page 284—date of will, 1828; date of probate, 1831 —names wife, Elizabeth.

SAM BARKLEY—Page 297—date of will, 1831; date of probate, 1831 —names wife, Jane.

GEO. BRONAUGH—Page 314—date of will, 1832; date of probate, 1832—names wife, Sarah.

DAVID JACKSON—Page 316—date of will, 1831; date of probate, 1832.

MAJ. GEN. ADAMS STEPHEN—Page 319—date of will, 1791; date of probate, 1831.

JACOB SONDUSKY—Page 330—date of will, 1832; date of probate, 1832—names wife, Elizabeth.

JOHN WELCH—Page 332—date of will, 1832; date of probate, 1832.

JAS. McCAMPBELL—Page 333—date of will, 1832; date of probate, 1832—names wife, Eleanor.

ANDERSON SALLEE—Page 334—date of will, 1832; date of probate, 1832—names wife, Judith.

HANNAH PHILLIPS—Page 338—date of will, 1832; date of probate, 1832.

THOS. OVERSTREET—Page 339—date of will, 1832; date of probate, 1832—names wife, Zillah.

CHAS CHOWNING—Page 355—date of will, 1830; date of probate, 1832—names wife Tilletha.

STEVE E. JONUS—page 356—date of will, 1832; date of probate, 1832—names wife, Mary Ann.

MARY CHAMBERS—Page 360—date of will, 1832; date of probate, 1832.

HENRY MASCEY—Page 380—date of will, 1830; date of probate, 1833.

JOHN GREEN—Page 408—date of will, 1833; date of probate, 1833.

MASIN SINGLETON—Page 410—date of will, 1833; date of probate, 1833—names wife, Fanny.

ELIAS HITT—Page 419—date of will, 1822; date of probate, 1833.

JOHN WASHINGTON—Page 422—date of will, 1833; date of probate, 1833—names wife, Nancy.

JOHN ROBERTS—Page 424—date of will, 1833; date of probate, 1833.

WM. ROBERTS—Page 441—date of will, 1833; date of probate, 1833.

VINCENT FRANCIS—Page 442—date of will, 1833; date of probate, 1833.

ARCHABEL CRAVENS—Page 470—date of will, 1833; date of probate, 1834—names wife, Phebe.

MONTGOMERY COUNTY WILL ABSTRACTS

(Contributed by Mrs. W. P. Oldham, Col. George Nicholas Chapter)

MATHEW ADAMS—Will Book B, pages 382-390—Names—son, Joseph; daughters, Nancy and Betsy; grand-daughter, Polly Adams, children of Robert Adams. Written March 17, 1821. Probated August 8, 1821. Witnesses—Daniel Wools, Mathew Kirk, John James.

WILLIAM ALLEN—Will Book B, Page 59—Names—wife, Sally. Written December 24, 1813. Probated March 7, 1814. Executor, George Allen. Witnesses—Daniel Wools, John White, Spencer Reid.

WILLIAM ALLISON—Will Book B, pages 413-414—Names—Charlotte (colored). Written May 25, 1822. Probated July 2, 1822. Witnesses—Wm. Wilkerson, Allen Hagan, Sandford Garrett.

JOHN ANDERSON—Will Book B, pages 60-61—Names—wife, Susanna Anderson; sons, Hedgman, John and Josiah; daughters, Nelly, Mildred and Mary. Written February 25, 1814. Executors—Thomas Monly, John R. Poter. Witnesses—Dawson Wade, David Vestal.

DAVID BARROW—Will Book B, pages 314-315—Names—wife; sons, David Gilliam Barrow, Abraham, William and Hinchea Giliam Barrow; daughters, Sarah Heeles and Ann Lee McClum; children of Nathan Barrow. Written August 1, 1817. Probated January 3,

1820. Executors—David Giliam Barrow, Abraham Barrow, William Barrow, Hinchea Barrow.

WILLIAM BRIDGES—Will Book B, page 320—Names—wife, Elizabeth; sons, Charles, Wilis and William. Written January 8, 1820. Probated March 6, 1820. Executors—George Rader, Joseph Bridges. Witnesses—Joseph Bridges, George Rader.

JOSHUA CANTRILL—Will Book A, page 42—Names—wife, Ann; sons, Wyatt, Zebulon, Joshua and William. Written August 20, 1800. Probated October 14, 1800. Executors—James Graham, Zebulon Cantrill. Witnesses—Thomas Isles, I. H. Jinkins, Andrew Biggs.

HENRY COOPER—Will Book B, page 321—Names—wife; granddaughter, Peggy Myers. Written February 7, 1820. Probated March 6, 1820. Witnesses—Daniel Woods, Adam M. Cormack, James Montgomery.

JOHN DARNELL—Will Book A, page 8—Names—wife, Mary Ann; sons, Henry and Cornelius; Thomas Arter Taul and Daughters. Written December 17, 1797. Probated March 6, 1798. Witnesses—Anthony Furtad, Samuel Motin Arwin, Thomas Darnall.

IGNATIOUS DAVIS—Will Book A, page 120—Names—wife, Mary; sons, Luke, John, David, Asa and Joseph; daughters, Nancy, Mary, and Dorcas. Written May 13, 1801. Probated February 28, 1803. Executrix, Mary Davis. Witnesses—John Whitecroft, Elizabeth Brown.

THOMAS DAVIS—Will Book A, page 57—Namessons, Thomas, Lamach and Rezin; daughter, Eleanor; to Effy Lyon. Written February 12, 1801. Probated March 1801. Executor, Jerimiah Davis. Witnesses—I. Crawford, Richard Hays, Robert C. Nicholas.

BENNETT DEWITT—Will Book A, page 24—Names—sons, James, Bennett and Martin; daughters, Sally, Peggy and Rachel. Written December 24,1798. Probated January 8, 1799. Witnesses—John Summans, Sr., Margaret Kent, James Lee.

MARTIN DEWITT—Will Book A, page 33—Names—wife; sons, Peter, Henry and Paul; daughters, Mary Williamson, Hannah Elder and and Sarah Rice. Written October 10, 1799. Probated November 12, 1799. Executors—Robert Dewitt, Henry Dewitt. Witnesses—Edwards Roberts, John Summers, Stephen Strange.

ISAAC DUNCAN—Will Book A, page 124—Names—wife, Margrete; daughter, Sarah and all children. Written March 14, 1803. Probated June 27, 1803. Executors—Margret Duncan, William Duncan. Witnesses—Andrew House, Joseph Love, George Routt.

DAVID ENGLAND—Will Book A, page 84—Names—wife, Lucy; sons, Stephens, Jesse and David; daughters, Deborah, Lucy, Elizabeth, Nancy, Polly and Eleanor. Written August 19, 1801. Probated December 8, 1801. Executors—Lucy England, Stephen England. Witnesses—Thomas Lewis, Zephaniah Ratliff, Valentine Stone, Josiah Collins.

THOMAS FLETCHER—Will Book A, page 30—Names—wife, Ann; son, Thomas; daughters Ann, Mary Moor, Rache Lankister, Rebecca, Catherine, Ruth, David Lorency. Written May 14, 1799.

Probated July 9, 1799. Witnesses—Jacob Lorency, Elijah Adams, Garry Lorency.

ANTHONY FUTARD—Will Book A, page 26—Names—wife, Charlotte; daughters, Nancy, Susannah, Polly and Elizabeth; son, William. Written September 4, 1798. Probated March 12, 1799. Executors—William Bell, wife, Charlotte Futard. Witnesses—John Fuqua, Wm. Bell, Henry Darnall.

PETER GUERRANT—Will Book B, page 325—Names—sons, John, Peter, Stephen, Charles and Daniels; daughters, Magdalen, Mary, Jane and Martha; grand-children, Henry E. Guerrant, Martha Guerrant. Written July 20, 1817. Probated January 3, 1820. Executors—Daniel Guerrant, Thomas Mosley, Charley Glover, James Anderson. Witnesses—Daneal P. Moseley, Edward Hughart, Thomas Moseley.

SAMUEL HARROW—Will Book A, page4—Names—wife, Elizabeth; son, Thomas; daughter, Elizabeth. Written May 29, 1797. Probated October 3, 1797. Executors—wife, Elizabeth, brothers, James and John. Witnesses—N. Hackett, John Allen.

EDMOND JOHNSON—Will Book A, page 128—Names—wife, Sarah; son, Able; daughters, Nancy and Katherine. Written April 12, 1803. Probated June 27, 1803. Executors—Sarah Johnson, Nathan Barrow. Witnesses—Will Orear, Mathew M. Jones.

LEWIS MAYBERRY—Will Book A, page 15—Names—wife, Elizabeth; son, Benny and other children. Written April 2, 1798. Probated May 8, 1798. Executors—Elizabeth Mayberry and son, I. Mayberry. Witnesses—D. Wilcox, Edward Taylor, Thomas Boyd, Wm. Bonge.

WILLIAM METEER—Will Book A, page 122—Names—sons, Robert, Samuel and William; daughters, Mary, Sally, and Jenny, all my sons and daughters. Written June 14, 1803. Probated June 27, 1803. Executors—Thomas Meteer, Robert Meteer. Witnesses—William Smith, Sammie Surgis, Henry Smith.

BENJAMINE OKLEY—Will Book A, page 71—Names—wife; daughters, Mary and Jenny. Written July 3, 1801. Probated August, 1801. Witnesses—Jacob Williams, John Butler, Christopher Okley.

NATHANIEL PEYTON—Will Book B, page 335—Names—wife, Nancy Patten; daughters, Nancy, Mary and Sarah; son, Nathaniel. Written October 28, 1813. Probated June 5, 1820. Executors—Nancy Patten, Samuel Williams. Witnesses—John Campbell, Ason McIlvain, George Howard.

FRANCIS PEYTON—Will Book B, pages 213-214—Names—son, Townshend D. Peyton; daughters, Elizabeth Hale, Lettie Lucket, Ann Peyton; grand-daughter, Mary Peyton; son-in-law, William Hale. Written August 1, 1810. Probated January 8, 1816. Executors—Townshend Peyton, Leven Luckett. Witness, C. Bimms.

ELIJAH SAMON—Will Book A, page 1—Names—wife, Elizabeth; Daughter, Mary; grand-son, Samuel Almond. Written October 16, 1796. Probated May 2, 1797. Executors—David Wilcox, wife, Elizabeth Samon. Witnesses—Thomas Almond, Robert Wood.

JOHN STORBRIDGE (STROBRIDGE)—Will Book B, page 334— Names—wife, Nancy Storbridge; sons, Charles, William, George,

Samuel, Lewis and John; daughters, Suky Harris, Mary Hedges, Masie Fuqua, Polly Butler and Sally. Written April 5, 1819. Probated June 5, 1819. Executors—John Fuqua, James Fuqua. Witnesses—John Fuqua, James Fuqua, Liskon Davis.

JOHN WILLIAMS—Will Book A, **pages 5-6**—Names—wife; Rezen, Thomas, Jesse, Priscilla, Daniel and Nancy. Written August 2, 1797. Probated January 2, 1798. Executors—wife, Sarah Williams, son, Daniel. Witnesses—Benjamine Taul, Porterfield Tolin, Thomas Harrow.

EUCLID WILLS—Will Book A, **page 35**—Names—wife, Betsy Wills; sons, John, James and William; daughters, Caty, Sally, Mollie, Polly and Mina. Written August 31, 1790. Probated March 12, 1799. Witnesses—Alexander Kelly, Thomas Smith, Wm. Wapper, John Whaye.

WILLIAM HOPPER—Will Book A, **Page 206**—Those named, wife, Eleanor; children; $1.00 to Elizabeth Lamberts. Written April 6th, 1805. Proved January 6, 1806. Witnesses—James Fetzjmull, Wm. Hopper, Jr.

HUGH FORBS—Will Book A, **Page 210**—Those mentioned, wife; son, David; daughter, Elizabeth. Written January 22, 1806. Proved March 6, 1806. Executors—John McIntire, Peter Ringo, Jeremiah Davis. Witnesses—Moses Bladsoe, David Cheatham, Peter Ringo.

ROBERT HALL—Will Book A, **Page 213**—Those named, daughter, Rachel (land); daughters, Jane, Ruth, Nancy, Susanna, five shillings apiece. To sons, James, Stephen, Robert and Abraham, $5 each. Written, February 19th, 1806. Proved March, 1806. Executor— B. Burbridge. Witnesses—Elzaphan Offill, Wm. Richards, John Richards, James Burbridge.

MOSES WILKERSON—Will Book A, **Page 221**—Those named, wife, Elethe; sons and daughter. Written May 27, 1806. Proved August, 1806. Executor—Son, William Wilkerson. Witnesses—Julia Hardwick Payne, William Haynes.

JOHN CALDWELL—Will Book A, **Page 224**—Those named, wife, Jane; sons, James, John, Oliver; daughters, Mary, Eleanor and Ann. Written March 20, 1806. Proved September Court, 1806. Executors— David Alexander, Robert Long, James Harrow. Witnesses—Alexander Ferris, James Trimble, John Ferris.

WILLIAM NORRIS—Will Book A, **Page 230**—Those named, sons, Jacob Norris, William Norris. Written Dec. 24, 1805. Proved November, 1806. Executor—Jacob Norris. Witnesses—Betty Ralls, Susannah Ralls.

WILLIAM BELL—Will Book A, **Page 260**—Those named, wife, Louisa; sons, Thomas, John, Patterson, William, Zacharia; daughter, Mary, Elizabeth. Written April 16, 1808. Proved June, 1807. Executrix— Louisa Bell (wife). Witnesses—Henry Jeffries, David Howell, Abraham Wilson.

JOSEPH COLLIVER, Will Book A, **Page 310**—Those named, wife, Sarah; sons, Elijah, Richard, Thomas; daughters, Elizabeth, Mary, Peggie. Written Sept. 18, 1807. Proved March, 1808. Executrix--- Wife, Sarah; son, Richard. Witnesses—Gustavius Elgin, John Hull, Loyd Rowlings.

ROBERT STEEL—Will Book A, Page 334—Those named, sons, Samuel, Gonsey, Nenian, Robert; daughter, Elizabeth. Proved September Court, 1808. Exexcutors—Nenian Steel, John Creasen. Witnesses —John Mills, William Legater, James Armstrong.

PETER HONAKER—Will Book A, Page 344—Those mentioned, wife, Mary; children, Molly, Ellen; John Martin, William and Chesley Wesley. Written August 12, 1808. Proved November, 1808 Executors—Mary Monaker, Charles Holliday, John Evins.

WILLIAM LANE—Will Book A, Page 351—Those named, wife, Letty L. Lane and children. Written May 23, 1808. Proved December 5, 180?. Executors—Wife, Letty Lane; son, Henry Smith Lane; friend, Benjamin Thompson. Witnesses—F. Drake, George Pettel, Cuthe Bank.

ALAXANDER KELLY—Will Book A, Page 362—Those named, wife, Mary; children. Written Nov. 19, 1808. Proved, February, 1809. Witnesses—John Fuqua, John Crossen, Elizabeth Morgan.

JOSEPH WILLIAMS—Will Book A, Page 428—Those named, sons, James and Samuel Williams; son-in-law, Samuel Blackburn; daughters, Jane Baily, Margaret Malden; daughter, Elizabeth Patterson. Written August 1, 1809. Proved November, 1810. Executor—James Williams. Witnesses—Zebulon T. Cantral, Joseph Cantrall, James Bracken.

WILLIAM RAGAN—Will Book A, Page 400—Those named, wife, Milly; son, Charles; legally begotten children. Written January 30, 1809. Proved August 1809. Executors—wife, Milly and son, Charles. Witnesses—James Rice, John Martin, David Rice.

IGNATION BUTLER—Will Book A, Page 430—Those named, wife, Delila; eight daughters, Nancy, Sarah, Fanny, Delila, Rachel, Dadies, Elizabeth, Milinda, Melelda. Written May 29, 1810. Proved Nov. 5, 1810. Executrix—Delila Butler. Witnesses—Jacob Lornecy, Daniel Goodwin, Jerimy Lorency.

HENRY SHULTZ—Will Book A, Page 431-432—Those named, Phoebe Shults and their children. Written July 9, 1810. Proved November 1811. Executors—Phoebe Shultz, John Ledford. Witnesses— Peter Davis, Richard Menifee, John Shultz.

JOHN HODGES—Will Book A, Page 434—Those named, wife Deborah; children, Jesse, Nancy, Lucy England, Mary Logan. Written March 15, 1809. Proved May, 1810. Executor—W. Ralls, Lawsen Robertson. Witnesses—Thomas Sinclair, William Wilcockcon, Thomas Bromagene.

MOSES BLEDSOE—Will Book A, Page 436—Those named, wife, Lucy, and to all his children. Written Feb. 23, 1809. Proved January 17, 1811. Executors—Wife, Lucy, Thomas Jameson, Jr. Witnesses— Richard Hackley, William Hackley, John Young.

WILLIAM YOUNG—Will Book A, Page 439—Those named, wife, Ann; to his sons and daughters. Written February 1, 1811. Proved June, 1811. Executors—Ann Young, wife; James Harrow, David Alexander, Christofer Glover. Witnesses—Thomas Mosley, James Caldwell, James Trimble.

JANE PEABLES—Will Book A, Page 443—Those named, son, John; grandchildren, Jane and Mary Wilson, Jane Davis, James Ervin,

Robert Peables Jane and John Peables Jane. Written November 19, 1807. Proved September, 1814. Executors—Andrew Simpson, Joseph Simpson.

PHILIP PRITCHART—Will Book A, Page 506—Those named, wife, Hannah; son, Alfred, son, Lewis, and all his children. Written Dec. 10, 1811. Proved Jan. 1812. Executors—Wife, Hannah and William Kemper.

JAMES CLARK—Will Book A, Page 176—Those named, brother, John; brother-in-law, James Butcher; sister, Martha; brother-in-law, John Daugherty; William Butcher, son of James; mother, Frances Clark; brother, Samuel Clark; sisters, Prepare Magahey, Martha Butcher, Elizabeth Butcher, Margaret Daugherty and Frances Corell. Written January 9, 1805. Proved June 3, 1805. Witnesses—Absalom Hunt, William Morgan.

JOHN FUQUA—Division of Land, Will Book B, Page 425-426—Those named, daughter, Lavinia; daughter, Polly; son, John; daughter, Susannah; daughter, Matilda; son, James; son, Thomas; son, William. Proved November Court, 1822. Administrators—Thomas and William Fuqua.

PHARIS ROGERS—Settlement of Estate, Will Book B, Pages 428-430— Infant heirs. Proved Nov. 4, 1822.

DAVID HATHAWAY—Will Book B, Page 445—Those named, daughter, Caby Riggs; daughter, Dorcas Riggs; son, John; son, James; daughter, Nancy Anderson; daughter, Delia; daughter Matilda; son, Wesley; daughter, Anna; wife, Rebecca. Written Feb. 22, 1823. Proved July 7, 1823.

JOHN WHITE—Will Book B, Page 448—Those named, wife, Polly, and at her death, to all my childrne. Written Dec. 8, 1822. Proved October Court, 1823.

WILLIAM CALK—Will Book B, Page 450-451-452—Those named, son, Thomas; wife, Sarah; son, William; daughter, Tamer Orear; daughter, Lidia Wilkerson; daughter, Nancy Holley; daughter, Eliza Stevens; daughter, Sally Head. Written June 9, 1822. Proved November 3, 1823. Witnesses—Kenneas Farrow, Wm. Barrow.

NICHOLAS ANDERSON—Will Book C, Page 4—Those named, wife, Rachel, for the purpose of raising his children. Proved December Court, 1823. Witness—David Bradshaw.

JOHN LANE—Will Book C, Page 5—Those named, wife, Margaret; son, Hiram; daughter, Ann Higgins; daughter, Mary Trimble; daughter, Jemima Cook; daughter, Elizabeth Meeks; daughter, Mary Anne Grinstead; daughter, Sarah Priest. Written November 15, 1822. Proved February 2, 1824.

FRANCIS WYATT—Will Book C, Pages 6-7—Those named, daughter, Polly Clyce; grandson, Franklin Clyce; daughter, Elizabeth Means; son, Haden Wyatt; daughter, Sally Fort; daughter, Malinda Helms; daughter Nancy Hanks; son, William; son, Francis; son, Duglas; son John; son, Antony. Written February 11, 1824. Proved April 5, 1824.

JAMES SEWELL— Will Book C, Page 8—Those named, wife, Penelope; son, Joseph and other children. Written Feb. 27, 1824.

HENRY UTTERBACK—Settlement, Will Book C, Page 8-9-10—Those named, son, Henry. Written January 6, 1824.

DANIEL GILLON, Will Book C, Page 13—Those named, wife, Rachel; son, Willis; son, Thomas; son, John; daughter, Nancy; daughter, Lucy. Written August 13, 1823. Proved April 5, 1824.

JONATHAN MALONE—Will Book C, Page 21—Those named, wife, Mary; daughter, Leah; duaghter, Ruth; daughter, Sarah; son, Andrew and other children. Written October 12, 1823. Proved May Court, 1824.

ATWELL ROGERS—Will Book C, Page 57—Those named, wife, Lucy; sister, Lucy Duncan; sister's children, namely, Wm. D. Duncan, James A. Duncan, Edward Duncan. Written July 16, 1824. Proved December Court, 1824.

DAVID PUGH—Will Book C, Page 58—Those named, wife, Sally; daughter, Adaline; son, Charles; son, Spencer; son, Harrison; son, John. Written, January 8, 1824. Proved July Court, 1824.

WILLIAM CASE—Will Book C, Page 71—Those named, wife, Patsy; two children. Proved December Court, 1824.

ENOCH SMITH—Will Book C, Page 82—Those named, wife, Frances; daughter, Nancy Reed; daughter, May Lane; daughter, Sarah Jameson; daughter, Susannah Ferguson; daughter, Frances Ferguson; son, Enoch; son, Sandford; son Betsy Willson; son, Franklin; son, Anna Garrett. Written, July 8, 1824. Proved May, 1825.

JOSEPH HON—Will Book C, Page 95—Those named, daughter, Katherine Farris; daughter, Polly Sip; daughter, Margot Miller; son, Joseph; wife, Mary. Written January 10, 1825. Proved July Court, 1825.

REBECCA WHITSITT—Will Book C, Page 97—Those named, son, Isaac; son, Stewart; daughter, Polly Summers. Written March 16, 1825. Proved July Court, 1825.

DAVID JOHNSON—Will Book C, Page 104—Those named, wife, Nancy; son, Levi; son, Jacob, daughter, Susannah Johnson; son, David Johnson; son, Andrew Johnson; son, John; son, Thomas; daughter, Elizabeth Willson; daughter, Henrietta Pence; daughter, Polly Dale. Written September 6, 1825. Proved October Court, 1825.

ANDREW DUNCAN—Will Book C, Page 106—Those named, wife, Frances; Polly Northcutt, wife of William. Written July 25, 1825. Proved October Court, 1825.

JAMES HIGGINS—Will Book C, Page 107—Those named, daughter, Polly Watson; granddaughter, Sally; son, John. Written August 17, 1825. Proved October Court, 1825.

JILSON PAYNE—Will Book C, Page 110—Those named, wife, Anna; daughter, Ann Holland Payne; brother, Jimmy; nephew, Orlando Payne; nephew, George R. Payne. Written August 12, 1825. Proved October 3, 1825.

JOHN HASTY—Will Book C, Page 170—Those named, son, William; children, Rheady, Clement, Nancy, James, Elizabeth, Merdoc; wife, Rebecca. Written January 6, 1826. Proved February Court, 1826.

HENRY WHITE—Will Book C, Page 171—Those named, wife, Anne; daughter, Erveame. Written July 9, 1825. Proved February Court, 1826.

SQUIRE FORTNER—Will Book C, Page 172—Those named, wife. Written September 17, 1825. Proved February, 1825. Attests: Wm. H. Forkner, Jonas Fortner, Eliza Allen.

ELIZABET CLEMENTS—Will Book C, Page 204—Those named, daughter, Elizabeth; daughter, Gustavius A.; granddaughter, Elizabeth Wilson; daughter, Susannah Dovney; grandson, Thomas Clements Written August 4, 1812. Proved April Court, 1826.

JOHN WELLS—Will Book C, Page 205—Those named, wife, Anne; deceased son, Bennett Wells' children; daughter, Nancy Jenkins; son, John; daughter, Jane Kelsoe; son, Hasten. Written March 24, 1820. Proved April, 1826.

JACOB VIRT—Will Book C, Page 212—Those named, wife, Kesiah; son, Adam; daughter, Sibby Buck; daughter, Polly; daughter, Betsy Willson; son, Jacob; daughter, Sally; daughter, Rebecca Sutton; son, Nathaniel; son, John; son, William; son, Daniel. Written April 1, 1826. Proved May Court, 1826.

WILL DEWITTE—Will Book A. Page 33—Those named, wife, for life; Mary Williamson, Peter Dewitte, Sarah Rice, Hannah Elder, Paul Dewitte, Henry Dewitte. Written October 10, 1799. Proved November 12, 1799. Executors—sons, Peter Dewitte, Henry Dewitte. Witnesses—Edward Roberts, John Summers, Stephen Stranges.

EUCLID WILLS—Will Book A, Page 35—Those named, wife, Betsy, (whole estate); one shilling each to eight children. Written August 31, 1796. Proved March 12, 1799. Witnesses—Alaxander Kelly, Thomas Smith, William Webber, John Whayn.

JOSHUA CANTRIL—Will Book A, Page 42—Those named, wife, Ann; sons, Zebulon, Joshua, Williams, Levy. Written August 26, 1800. Proved October 14,1800. Executors—Son, Zebulon Cantrell, James Graham. Witnesses—Thomas Iles, J. H. Jenkins, Andrew Biggs.

THOMAS DAVIS—Will Book A, Page 57—Those named, sons, Thoams, Lamach, Rezen, Effie Lyon; daughter, Sarah; daughter, Eleoner. Written February 19, 1801. Proved March Court, 1801. Executors— Jeremiah Davis (nephew). Witnesses—I. Crawford, Richard Hayes, Robert C. Nicholas.

BENJAMIN OAKLEY, Will Book A, Page 71—Those named, wife; daughter, Nancy; daughter, Janny. Written July 3, 1801. Proved August Court, 1801. Witnesses—Jacob Williams, John Butler, Christopher Okley.

DAVID ENGLAND—Will Book A, Page 84—Those named, wife, Lucy; daughters, Deborah, Lucy and Sarah, Elizabeth, Nancy, Polly, Elenora; sons, Stephen, Ipse, David, Written August 19, 1801. Proved December 8, 1801. Executors— wife, Lucy, son, Stephen. Witnesses—Thomas Lewis, Zephamiah Ratliff, Valentine Stone, Josiah Collins.

IGNATIOUS DAVIS—Will Book A, Page 120—Those named, wife, Mary; sons, David, Joseph, Asa, John; daughters, Nancy, Mary, Dorcas. Written May 13, 1801. Proved February 28, 1803. Executrix—wife, Mary Davis. Witnesses—John Whitecraft, Elizabeth Brown.

WILLIAM METEER—Will Book A, Page 112—Those named, all surviving children; sons, Robert, Samuel, William, Thomas; daughters, Mary, Sally, Jenney. Written June 14, 1803. Proved June 27, 1803. Executors—Sons Thomas Meteer, Robert Meteer. Witnesses—William Smith, Samme Surgin, Henry Smith.

ISAAC DUNCAN—Will Book A, Page 124—Those named, wife, Margaret; daughter, Sarah; and the rest of his children. Written March 14, 1803. Proved June 27, 1803. Executors—Wife, Margaret, and son, William. Witnesses—Andrew House, Joseph Love, George Routt.

EDMOND JOHNSON—Will Book A, Page 128—Those named, wife, Sarah; sons, Able, Nathan, Kinchin; daughter, Nancy; daughter, Kathrin. Written April 12, 1803. Proved June 27, 1803. Executors—wife, Sarah, Nathan Barrow. Witnesses—Will Orear, Mathew M. Jones.

HENRY RINGO—Will Book A, Page 131—Those named, sons, Peter, Cornelius, John, Major, Samuel, Joseph. Written May 12, 1802. Proved August 22, 1803. Executors—Peter Ringo, John McIntire. Witnesses—Willis Prickett, Cornelius Ringo.

WILLIAM TODD—Will Book A, Page 172—Those named, brothers, Peter Todd, James Todd; Elizabeth Williams. Written October 28, 1804. Proved February 4, 1805. Executors—Rauleigh Williams, Samuel S. Williams. Witnesses—Wm. W. Cook, Arch McIlvan, Jr., Robert Brown.

NELSON COUNTY WILL ABSTRACTS

(Contributed by Mrs. J. B. Brown, John Fitch Chapter)

PETER BROWN—Will Book A, Page 75—Names wife, Brances Brown, Jereboam Brown, Peter Brown, Charles Brown, Francis Brown, Ann Brown, Rose Brown, Elinor Brown, Mary Brown. Written January 15, 1792; probated July 10, 1793. Witnesses—Wm. Miller Read, Ernest Miller, Jerema Greenwall.

SAM L. EWING—Will Book A, Page 38—Names friend, Jacob Yoder. Written April 17, 1790. Executor, Jacob Yoder.

JOHN FITCH—Will Book A, Page 351—Names friends, William Rowen, Eliza Vail, John Rowen, James Nourse, Dr. Wiliam Thortin. Written June 20, 1798; probated July 10, 1798. Executors—James Nourae, John Rowen. Witnesses—James Nourae, Nich. Reutch, Susanna McCown.

MARK HARDIN—Will Book A, Page 86—Names wife, Ann Hardin, Henry Hardin, John Hardin, Mark Hardin, Benjamin Hardin, Mary Hardin, Lyda Hardin, Sarah Hardin, Sarah Catherine Hallet, Hannah Stech. Written March 31, 1790. Executors—Wife, Henry and John Hardin. Witnesses—Benjamin Hardin, John Hardin, Selman Robertson.

SAMULE WILLETT—Will Book A, Page 92—Names wife, Ann Willett, John Willett, Mary Willett, Wm. Willett, Elizabeth Willett. Written November 22, 1792. Executors—Ann Willett, George Willet. Witnesses—Atkinson Hill, M. Carler, Ignatious Hagan.

ABSTRACTS OF WILLS AND INVENTORIES OF REVOLUTIONARY SOLDIERS OF OHIO COUNTY

(Contributed by Miss Lettie Marks and Mrs. Roy Barnhill, Fort Hartford Chapter)

WM. L. BARNARD—January 20, 1843—His children were: Ignatius, Joshua, Silas, Loyd 1799, Garrett, Faluria, Ann, Jamima, Matilda, Emily.

JOHN BENNETT—August, 1828—Estate Settled.

JOSHUA BARNARD—November, 1808—Estate settled.

ROBERT BARNETT—April, 1801—Appraisement and Settlement.

SAMUEL BIGGER—1807—Estate settled.

CHESLEY CALLOWAY—1846.

WILLIAM CARTER—Probated 1842—Names wife, Sarah Carter; Polly, Moses, Peggy, William, Abram, Delilah, George.

MARTIN COLEMAN—February, 1804—Appraisement.

WILLIAM COOPER—May 30th, 1835—Names Wife, (Polly) Mary; children, Alexander, Polly Campbell, son, Cornelius Henry, Elizabeth.

JOSEPH COX—1840—Estate settled.

GORDON DOUGLAS—June, 1802—Appraisement.

JOHN FIELDS—August, 1801—Wife, Sally; children, Elizabeth, Hannah, Nancy, Zacharies, James, Aquila.

PHILIP HOCKER—August, 1821—Sons, Nicholas, Richard, Philip, Weaver; daughters, Delilah, Dorcas, Polly, Betsy.

DANIEL HOLT—January, 1804—Witnesses, Peter Evans, John Vannada, Abram Harmon.

JOHN HOWELL—November,1830—Children, Seely, Francis, Jane W., Susan D.

RICHARD LANHANM—May, 1807—Wife, Rachel; sons, Elias, Elijah.

WM. LEECH—November, 1808—Wife, Alcy; children, William, Leonard, Susan, Patsy Miller, Lisbah Cox.

JOHN MONROE—May 21, 1837—Andrew B. Monroe, Mary Bell, Eleanor Baltzell.

ROBERT MOSELEY—November 3, 1827—Estate settled.

PETER PARKS—April 22, 1844—Ann Parks, Daniel, Quenton.

THOMAS PENDER—1833—Estate settled. Wife, Ann Pender.

THOMAS PARKER—January, 1805—Estate settled.

MATTHAIAS SHULTZ—May, 1834—Wife, Didamah; children, John, Nicholas, Joseph, Charles, Matthais, Dinah, Neel, Nancy Bayes, Mary Mellon.

MRS. RACHEL SPRIGGS—December, 1803—Appraisement.   Son, Joseph Barnett.

CHARLES TRAVIS—November, 1804—Appraisement.

SCOTT COUNTY WILL ABSTRACTS

(Contributed by Miss Hattie Scott, Susannah Hart Shelby Chapter)

Note—Spaces indicate burned places on records.

RICHARD APPLEGATE—Will Book A, Page 103—Wife, Rebecca; daughter, May Applegate, Rebecca Sparks; son, Benjamin; son, Daniel; son, William; daughter, Allela Lantaman; daughter, Catherine Lemon; daughter, Elizabeth McCan; daughter, Also Walls; daughter, Mary. Executor—Joseph Wilson. Witnesses—William Ward, William Fisher. Written July 1, 1798. Recorded December, 1800.

THOMAS BEUBRIDGE—Will Book A, Page 1—All my brothers and sisters, viz: Lunsford Beubridge, George Beubridge Mildred Robinson, Sarah Elley, Frances Smith, Elizabeth Branham, Mary Bullett. Executors—Brothers, Lunsfield, George, and brothers-in-law, Henry Elley, Robert Smith, Benjamin Robinson, Tavener Branham. Written Sept. 27, 1794. Proved January 179?. Witnesses—Edward Elley, Matthew Gale, Sr., William Wood, Thomas and Henry Elley.

JOHN BERRYMAN—Will Book A, Page '74—"Of Spottsylvania Co., Va." Lands in Nelson County bought of James Muse, brothers, Francis and Josias Berryman, nephews, William Monroe and Josias Berryman, Jr., son of Garrard Berryman; nephews, Newton and Waters Berryman, _____ Berryman, sons of my brother Newton Berryman, niece, Elizabeth Berryman, daughter of brother, Garrard Berryman, nephew, Francis Berryman, niece Winefred Berryman, orphans of John Berryman, deceased; nephew, William Berryman of Fauquier County, land in Kentucky (Lincoln County); daughters of my sister, Winifred Monroe and Eliza Berryman, deceased. Executors—Brothers, Newton, Francis and Josias Berryman. Written February 1799. Recorded September 25, 1799, Spottssylvania Count, Va.

WILLIAM BEATTY, SR.—Will Book A, Page 173—Wife, Sarah, 50 acres joining James Beatty; three sons, George, Joseph and Howard; George Beatty, land adjoining Richard Sebree; sons, Joseph, _____ Steward, Howard; daughter, Sally; daughter Nancy; to my children by former wife, John, William, Molly, wife of James Beatty, Betsy Craymiles, James Beatty. Executors—wife, Sarah and son, George. Written August 23, 1800. Proved December, 1803. Witnesses—Mareen Duvall, Cornelius Duvall.

HENRY H. DUVALL—Will Book A, Page ?—"Afflicted in body." To mother Kizeah Duvall; brother John Duvall's children (if he has any); brother Zachareh Duvall; nephew, Henry Clark; brother, Mareen Duvall (if he returns to this state); nephew, John Duvall; brother, John Duvall. Executors—father, Cornelius Duvall and brother, John Duvall. Written October 22, 1806. Recorded October, 1806. Witnesses, Rodes Smith, Samuel Lowey.

ELIZABETH FLOURNOY—Will Book A, Page 46—"Advanced in life." To John P. Smith, Samuel Smith, Peggy Dabney, Samuel Flournoy, Robert Flournoy, Thomas Flournoy, son John J. Flournoy, Martha Wells, Francis Flournoy, "deceased husband's estate", sons, Mathews Flournoy, Lucy Flournoy; daughter, Eliza D. Henry; to Elizabeth P. Henry, my daughter-in-laf _____. Executors—Major William Henry and Francis Flournoy. Written June 4, 1797. Recorded January, 1798.

WILLIAM NEALE—Will Book A, Pages 264-269—Inventory and Appraisement. Bill of sale, page 370. Administrators—Mary and Daniel Neal.

THOMAS OSBORNE—Will Book A, Page 159—Appraisement of property June 20, 1803, by Fielding Bradford, Samuel Daharin and Rhodes Coppage.

PHILIP PATTON—Will Book A—My negro woman Grace, and her three children, James, Jeremiah and Samuel, be free at my death. A note on William Ham of Madison County for 40 pounds, be equally divided between them, also all other property. Written May 22, 1803. Witnesses—John Carckwell, Roda Thomason, Susannah Carckwell (Campkwell).

WILLIAM PAULINGS—Will Book A, Page 112.—Names wife, Susannah; no children at time will was made. Test., James Speed and Mary Speed. Written June 28, 1794. Recorded October 1, 1798. Page 56. Appraisement of William Paulings, deceased, April 14, 1801.

JOHN PEAK—Will Book A. Page 298—Names wife, Jemmia; Isaac, son, 60 acres of land in Montgomery County. Presley Peak, 75 acres of homestead land; Spencer Peak; six daughters, by name, Constance Anderson, Milly Scott, Alsey Sanders, Ellen Cullin, Mally Mulberry and Rachel Drake, seventy acres of land in Ohio which I purchased of Cane Johnson and 200 acres of land on south side of the Kentucky on the waters of Paint Lick in the county of_____ Executors—Spencer and Presley. Written February 15, 1801. Probated March 24, 1806. Witnesses—John Hawkins and Samuel Logan. Logan.

JOSEPH PEW—Administrator bond, January 1809. John R. Ireland, administrator.

JOHN RISK—Will Book A, Pages 392-393—Names wife, Jane; sons, Robert and John. Jane is to have full possession as long as she remains single; otherwise divided between the boys. John having choice. Other children are William and Moses, 100 acres of land on Trade Water equally divided between them. James Risk and sisters Margaret, Elizabeth, Mary Ann, Jane, Martha, Susan, Rebecca and Nancy, Sally, Hetty and Ruth. Appoints as guardians Robert Morris, David Morris, James Daugherty and John Thorn. Written September 4, 1805. Proved March, 1808. Witnesses—John Nesbit, Isaac Beauchamp, Daniel Brown, Sally Brown.

WILLIAM ROSS—Will Book A, Page 128—"Late of Sussch County, Delaware, now Scott County, Kentucky."—Names wife, Anne Ross; Daniel, grandson, son, of Howell Ross; Peggy Layton, daughter; Clement Ross, son; Hewitt Ross, son; Rebecca Ross, daughter; William Ross, son. Written March 9, 1802. Executors—wife, Anne, and son, William. Witnesses—Robert Griffith, John Nutter, and David Layton. Executors' bond given May 24, 1802.

ROBERT SANDERS—Will Book A—Son, Tolliver, 1000 choice of 4000 acres on North Elkhorn or one-half of Dry Ridge tract. Benjamin land on North Bank of Cane Run, (description recorded). Thomas Walter (or Walker). Property of all sons to be as nearly equal as possible. Nancy Sanders, daughter; children to have possession when they become of age or marry. Peter Gatewood to live with children. Cato Haskins paid with first money executors can collect. (Another son is Valentine Saunders). Executors—David Flourney, John Thomason and Peter Gatewood. Written May 11, 1805. Witnesses—Henry Herndon, James Barton, and Benjamin Wharton. Recorded May 27, 1805.

WILLIAM SHIRLEY—Will Book A—Names wife, Margaret; children, Robert, Rebecca, William, Richard, John and Sarah Johnson. Written September 30, 1799. Produced in court, March 25, 1805. Witnesses—John Rodes and Walter Rodes.

THOMAS SMITH—Will Book A, Page 96—Names Lilly Davis; children, James, Peggy, Bryant, Fanny Davis, Thomas and Mary Davis, equal parts of land bought of George Thornton. William Smith, John Smith (sons). James Smith, sole executor of estate. Written Sept. 11, 1799. Recorded, Sept. 22, 1800. Witnesses—William Ward and William McGarrick.

RICHARD THOMASON—Will Book A, Page 137—Names wife, Sarah; children; Frances, only one named; others alluded to. Written June 12, 1802. Recorded Sept. 27, 1802. Executors—Henry Jenkins, Nelson Thomason and David Shelton. Witnesses—Henry Dehoney and Nancy Thomason.

NELSON THOMASON—Will Book A, Page 170_____—Names niece, Winny Gough, Frances Thompson, daughter of Richard Thompson, to receive one-half interest of his father's estate, now in the hands of his mother. Elizabeth Herndon of Scott County. A negro girl named Milly. Executors—Nathaniel Craig, Cornelius Gough and Thomas Herndon. Recorded November, 1803. No witnesses named and no date other than 1803 given.

ANN THOMPSON—Will Book A, Page 134-5—(_____); children, Rodes, William, Clifton, Asa, John, David, Ann Walker, Mary Wigglesworth, Unity Smith, Elizabeth Rodes, Lydia Ferguson. Son-in-law, Rodes Smith and David Thompson, (son) executors. Written

June 12, 1798. Recorded August 23, 1802. Witnesses—Nelson Smith and Sally Webber.

BENJAMIN ALLEN THARP—Will Book A, Page 293—(   ); To William Tharp, brother; Martha and Ann Tharp, sisters; George Tharp, brother. Rest of goods, etc., to his father, John Allen Tharp, who is executor. Written January 5, 1806. Recorded March 24, 1806. Witnesses—John B. Talbott, Samuel Young, Daniel Mitchell.

WILLIAM TROTTER—Will Book A, Page 38—Names wife, Margaret; children, Polly, Joseph, William and David Stephenson, James, John Trotter, land in Woodford County. 100 acres conveyed to John Alexander and 100 acres to Samuel Hinds. Written June 26, 1797. Recorded, Oct. 23, 1797. Executors—Margaret Trotter, and my brother, James Trotter, also William McClure. Witnesses—George Trotter, Samuel Trotter, Robert Kay, James Lindsay.

WILLIAM UTLER—Will Book A, Page 32—Names wife, Margaret; children, Margaret; other children, but not named. Written August 1, 1797. Recorded, Sept. 25, 1797. Witnesses—Wm. Hicklin and Ash Emison.

JOSEPH WALKER—Will Book A, Page 322—Names wife, Grissel; children, Nancy, Womack, wife of Michael Womack, Jane Walker; grandson, Joseph Walker, son of James Walker; grandson, Joseph Henderson, son of Alexander Henderson. Twenty dollars to be paid to Cherry Spring congregation for support of the gospel. Mary Hays, daughter; Jenny Walker, daughter to Samuel Walker and Nancy McCrosky; Samuel Walker, son. Written January 22, 1806. Witnesses—John Hutchinson, Michael Womack, Joseph Womack. Recorded, August 25, 1806.

SAMUEL WARD—Will Book A, Page 167—Names wife, Sarah; children, William and Elizabeth; father of Samuel, William Ward. Written Sept. 19, 1803. Recorded Nov. 28, 1803. Executors—William Ward and Sarah Ward. Witnesses—John Adams and Iva Cook.

VALENTINE WHARTON—Will Book A, Page 66—(_____); children, Benjamin Wharton, Nancy Landers (Saunders), Fanny Wharton. Written July 20, 1799. Recorded July 22, 1799. Administrator—Benjamin Wharton. Witness—Thomas Cavender.

EDWARD WOOLEN—Will Book A, Page __—Names Tabitha Cummo children, Thomas, Trustin, Nancy Harris, Westly. Thomas Harris, husband of Nancy. Written Dec. 26, 1804. Recorded March 25, 1805. Executrix—Tabitha Cumi. Witnesses—John Wallace, John Branham.

HENRY BELLIS—Will Book B, Page 35—Mentions wife, Mary, and children, Betsy Pence, John Bellis, Hannah Bellis, Mary Bellis, Henry Bellis, Lucky Bellis, Sally Bellis, Rebecca Bellis, David Bellis. Written July 1807. Probated December Court, 1809. Executors—wife, Mary Bellis, son, John Bellis and Friend, James Kelly. Witnesses—Hall Richardson, Charles W. Hall, Peggy Hall, Mary Bellis, John Bellis, Jacob Shrawyer.

GEORGE ROBINSON—Will Book A, Page 93—"Advanced Age" Names Margaret Hutchison (young woman who had nursed him); wife, Ann Robinson; daughter, Mary Black; Jonathon Robinson; John Robinson name in burned space; to church at Bethel; Jaul Hutchinson; all children, viz: Mary Black, John Robinson, Margaret

Logan, Agnes (Fisher in burned space), Sarah Fergus' heirs, Esther Logan, George Robinson, Martha Crawford, Thomas Robinson. Written August 10, 1811. Proved May, 1814. Executors—friends, Thomas Dinwiddie and Andrew Armstrong Dinwiddie of Scott and Fayette counties. Witnesses—Jonathan Robinson, Jr., Abegail Robinson, Margaret M. Robinson.

JONATHON ROBINSON—Will Book F, Page 54—To daughters, Abegail B., and Esther Robinson; Francis and R. Palmer and wife, Ann W.; son-in-law, John Robinson and Polly of Ohio; son, George Robinson; son, John M. Robinson; son, Thomas Robinson; George W. C. Graves and Sidney Jane, his wife; son, James F. Robinson; son, Jonathon Robinson, deceased. Written Dec. 30th, 1833. Proved July Court, 1834. Witnesses—Micajah Stone, Jacob Judy.

ROBERT MORRIS—Will Book A, Page 378—Estate appraised 1807. Appraisers, David Logan, _____ White. Administrators—Martha Morris and David Morris.

SHELBY COUNTY WILL ABSTRACTS

SOME MARRIAGES FROM FIRST MARRIAGE BOOK

(Contributed by Mrs. Graham Lawrence, Isaac Shelby Chapter)

JOHN ANDERSON—May 1796—Executrix Margaret Anderson, widow. Sec. Wm. Smiley, Ebenezer Patton. Ap. Hardy Hill, George Cravenson, Samuel Figley.

WILLIAM BOLING (BOWLING)—30 May, 1794; proven March Court, 1795.—Ex. Sim Boling, Daniel Ketcham. Wit., Wm. Morrow, Alex. Montgomery, Moses Warfrod. Names wife, Margaret; son, John Boling.

Mrs. Margaret Boling married 8-28-1795, Elias Neal—1st M. Book

JESSE BUZAN—Inventory, 18th November, 1794—Ap., Samuel McKinley, Nicholas Smith, James Prichard.

WILLIAM BUCHANNON—1-26-1797—proven July Court, 1798—Ex., Agness Buchannon, widow, Victor Buchannon. Sec., James Pringle. Wit., Thos. Robertson, Thos. Allison. Ap., Robr. Lowden, Nicholas Smith, Wm. Huston, John Lawson. Wife, Agnes, 100 acres on Drennon's Lick.

RICHARD BREEDING—Proven 20 March, 1798—Ex., Frances Breeding, widow. Sec., Wm. McCory, Isaac Whitaker. Ap., Peter Bailea, Elijah Whitaker, Thos. Johnston, Wm. Brodie. Wife, Frances; son, William Breeding; son, Paul Breeding; daughter, Elizabeth Breeding.

Wm. Breeding marreid 6-4-1798; Polly Breeding——————; Paul Breeding married 8-19-1799; Elizabeth Stanley, daughter of Joseph.

DAVID BOYLES—Inventory May 15, 1798—Ex., Rebecca, widow.

Sec., George Cravenson, Henry Boyd. Ap. Hardy Hill, Wm. Collings, Thos. Ferguson, Francis Cunningham. Son, William Boyles.

WILLIAM BOYD, SR.—Inventory July, 1798—Ex., Mary Boyd, widow. Sec., Jacob Newland, Benjamin Roberts, Wm. Roberts. Mehitable Boyd, William Boyd, Jr., Jane Boyd John Boyd, Hannah Boyd.

JAMES BROWN—Proved Nov., 1799—Ex., Daniel Colgan. Sec., Morias Hansbrough. Wit., Wingfield Bullock, Thos. Allen, Jas. Moore. Wife, Lydia.

GEORGE BOSWELL—Inventory 9 May, 1803—Ex., Nancy Boswell, widow. Sec., Jacob Tichenor, John Wright. Ap. Chas. Polke, Wm. Polke, Frederick Price, Jas McDavitt. Children: Susanna Boswell, Elizabeth Boswell, Rebecca Boswell Polly Boswell, George Boswell, John Boswell, Edward Boswell.

ELIZABETH BUTLER—Inventory January, 1803—Ex., Wilson Maddox. Dan Butler.

JAMES BRISCOE or BRISCOW—2-23-1804, proven October, 1804—Ex., brothers, John and Edward Briscow. Wife, Catherine; daughter, Mary Briscow; daughter, Massy Briscow; Daughter, Caty Briscow; daughter, Sarah Briscow.

JOHN CONNELLY—proved October, 1798—Ex., Sarah Connelly, Neddy Curd, Andrew Allen. Sec., Jas. Mulligan, Benjamin H. Kerrick. Wit., Benj. H. Kerrick, Jacob Tucker. Wife, Sarah; son, Wm. Connelly; daughter, Mary; daughter Sarah; son, Thompson; daughter, Elizabeth; son, Jesse; son, James; daughter, Nancy; son, Stephen.

JOHN CLARKE—proved 9-3-1798—Ex., Obadiah Clarke, Benjamin Clarke, sons. Sec., Thos. Martin, Hugh Dugan, Stephen Ashby, Josiah Clarke. Ap. Adam Hostedler, Joseph Simpson, Ebenezer Patton. Wife, Elizabeth; sons, Obadiah and Benjamin; brother-in-law, John Ellis.

ROBERT DANIEL—Ex., brother, Martin Daniel. Sec., Benjamin Roberts. Wit., Daniel Farley, Samuel Pryor. Ap. Joseph Smith, David Standiford, John Miller, Bryant O'Neal. Sister, Bessy Meriwether and two sons, John Martin and Reuben Meriwether; brother, Thos. Daniel; sister, Sucky Manes; brother, Coleman Daniel; father, John Daniel.

OLIVER DORNAN—Inventory December,1801—Ex. Daniel Taylor. Ap. John Buskirk, Ebenezer Patton, Jno. Martin, Simon Phiegly.

JOHN DUNN—Inventory November, 1802—Ex., John Stone. Sec., Wm. Stone, Richard Baisey. Ap., John Buskirk, Jas. Stone. John Scott, Ebenezer Patton.

RICHARD ELAM—Inventory November, 1800—Ex. Elizabeth Elam. Sec., Francis Hall. Ap., John Shannon, Moses Hall, Singleton Wilson, Thos. King.

Richard Elam married 10-24-1796, Elizabeth Sorrels, daughter of Nelly Sorrels. Mrs. Elizabeth Elam married 1-5-1817, James H. Toncray.

JOHN FELTY—Inventory March, 1795—Ex., Elizabeth Felty. Ap., Basil Noel, Wm. Butler, Daniel Farley.

HENRY FULLINWIDER—March 16, 1793; proved May, 1793—Ex., Jacob Fullinwider, John Carr. Wit., Caty Fullinwider, Martin Daniel, Jas. Crockett. Ap., Jonathan Boone, William Boone, John Wilcox. Son-in-law, John Carr; son-in-law, Samuel Ryker; daughter, Ann Fullinwider; son, Peter Fullinwider's two children, Henry and Elizabeth; son, Jacob Fullinwider, 264 acres on Lute's Run.

JOHN FORD—4-13-1803; proved October, 1803—Ex., Wm. Ford, Elisha Ford, Samuel Ford. Sec., John Ford, Spence Ford. Wit., Oswald Thomas, David Denny, David Thomas. Ap., Richard Booker, David Thompson, James Robinson. Wife, Catherine; children, Samuel, Edward, Elisha, Spencer, Ann, Jinney, William.

JONATHAN GREEN—proved May, 1798—Ex., Caty (Smith) Green, widow. Sec., Simon V. Smith, Nicholas Smith, Jr., brothers-in-law. Wit., Nicholas Smith, Sr., Nicholas Smith., Jr., Simon V. Smith. Ap., Edmund Wayman, Adam Sill, William Hall. Wife, Caty; oldest son, George Green; daughter, Polly Green; William Green.

CATHERINE GREEN—Inventory January, 1803—Ex., Nicholas Smith, Jr., (brother). Sec., Abraham Smith, (brother). Ap., Jacob Castleman, John Shannon, Edmund Wayman.

JONAH GLOVER—Inventory October, 1798—Ex., Frances Glover, widow, David Reed, Wm. McCoy. Sec., Benjm. Roberts, Jacob Case, Joshua Reed. Ap., Elijah Whitaker, Wm. Polke, Peter Bailea, Daniel Bennett. Children, Sarah, Elizabeth, Jane.

Mrs. Frances Glover married 10-1-1800, John Carlin or Kerlin.

JOHN GARRETT—Proved May, 1799—Ex., Margaret Garrett, Isaac Garrett. Sec., Elisha Whitaker, John Williamson. Wit., Richd. Gasaway, Jas. McQuaid, Isaac Edwards. Ap., Isaac Edwards, James McQuaid, John Howe, Alex. McClain, Jr. Children, Isaac, Nancy, Esther, Margaret.

RICHARD GASAWAY, or GAZAWAY, or GASSAWAY, (spelled all three ways). Proved November 9, 1801. Executrix—Nancy Gasaway. Sec.—Alexander McClain. Witnesses—John Todd, John Hansborough. Appraisers—John Todd, Hugh Dugan, Hugh Redman, John Sharp. Children, John, Nancy, Elizabeth, Nicholas, James, Samuel, Henry and William Garrett.

PHILIP HANEIL—Inventory August, 1796—Ex., Jacob Kephart. Sec., Nicholas Smith. Ap., Joseph Irwin, Robert Irwin, Samuel McKinley.

RICHARD HOAGLAND—Inventory March, 1797—Ex., John McClain, Nancy McClain, his wife late Nancy Hoagland. Sec., Abraham Owen, Joseph Dupuy. Ap. Nicholas Smith, Robert Lowden, James Pritchard.

HARDY HILL—Inventory March, 1799—Ex., Margaret Hill, George Cravenson. Sec., Robt. Jeffries, Wm. El. Collings. Wit., Archibald Cameron, Isaac Miller, Wm. El. Collings. Ap., Richard Basey, Jonathan Bedle, Isaac Miller, Thos, Forman. Wife, Margaret; children, Sarah, Martha, Isaac, Margaret. Sarah Hill married 5-31-1808, Thomas Carrithers. Martha Hill married 4-11-1807, Robert Cunningham. Isaac Hill married 4-11-1807, Margaret Cunningham, daughter of Francis. Mrs. Margaret Hill married 2-26-

1812, John Osborne. Margaret Hill, step-father, John Osborne, married 12-21-1812, Wm. Kester.

MORIAS HANSBROUGH—Proved August, 1800—Ex., Geo. Hansbrough, John Underwood. Sec., P. Hansbrough, Robt. Allison. Wife, Mary; children, George, John, Joel, Susanna.

George Hansbrough married 4-27-1799, Nancy, daughter of Drury and Mary Howard. Joel Hansbrough married 2-13-1810, Lucy Gooch.

ANTHONY HARTMAN—Proved April 11, 1803—Ex., David Harman, Soloman Hartman. Sec., Wm. Bridgewater, Wm. Johnston. Wife, Margaret; children, Abraham, Daniel, Soloman, David, Anthony, Jr., Easther Hatter, Joseph, Jonatha, Catherine Miller, Agenes Hostedler.

THOMAS JACOBS—Inventory May, 1797—Ex., John Cline. Sec., William Hall. Ap., Robt. Tyler, Nimrod Duncan, Anthony Jenkins.

PHILIP JOHNSTON—July 17, 1798—Proved January 15, 1799—Ex., Elizabeth Johnston, widow. Sec., Jesse Payne, Jas. Latham, Rowland Thomas. Wit., Jesse B. Payne, Rowland Thomas. Children, Thomas, Elizabeth Payne, Catherine Thomas, Fanny Payne, Philip, Jr., mother-in-law, Ann Taylor; wife, Elizabeth (Taylor) Johnston.

JOHN LEATHERMAN—January 15, 1798—Proved March, 1796—Ex., David Miller in Hartman's Settlement and George Humphries in Leatherman's Settlement. Sec., John Addams, John Humphries. Wit., Henry Newman, John Harrison, Thos. Craig. Ap. Stephen Ashby, Joseph Thatcher, John Harrison. "I, John Leatherman, of the Leatherman Settlement, Shelby County, Ky." Wife, Hannah, Christian Leatherman, oldest son of brother, Peter, now living in Leatherman Settlement; Basil Tegarden; residue to brother's children.

Christian Leatherman married 7-4-1798, Barbara Houghstalter, consent of Christian Houghstalter. Catherine Leatherman married 11-23-1810, Samuel Gazway, consent of brother Christian Leatherman.

RICHARD LEMASTER—Inventory May, 1795—Ap., Robert Lowden, Jas. Hoagland, Jas. W. Hemphill.

ROBERT LASTLEY or LASSLEY or LASLEY—Inventory November, 1797—Ex., Alexander Lastley, brother. Sec., Robert Jeffries, Francis Cunningham. Ap., George Cravenson, John Johns, Ab. Carr, Caleb Reed. Children, John Lastley, Alexander Lastley, Jr., (both under age at this time).

JOHN LEWIS—Inventory January 9, 1804—Ex., Margaret Lewis, widow. Sec., John Todd, Jas. Morton, Chas. Motherhead. 300 acres on Buck and Gist Creeks. Children, Bluford Lewis, Patsey Lewis, Henry Lewis, Polly Lewis, Keziah Lewis, Catherine Lewis, John Lewis, William Lewis, Fanny Lewis.

Mrs. Margaret Lewis married 11-4-1805, Austin Hall. Guardian's account, 1807; Keziah is 13 years, born about 1794; Catherine is 11 years, born about 1796; John is 9 years old, born about 1798; William is 6 years, born about 1801; Fanny is 4 years, born about 1803.

LAMBERT LANE—Inventory July 9, 1804—Ex., Anne Lane, widow. Sec., Jas. Anderson, Thos. Lane, Isaac Whitesides. Ap., Caleb Reed, Isaac Norman, Henry Johns, David Johnson.

Mrs. Ann Lane marreid 7-21-1806, Henry Johns. Nancy Lane, daughter of Lambert Lane, married 3-25-1800, Jas. McCoy.

DAVID LAWRENCE—November 10, 1804—Proved December, 1804—Ex., John Lawrence, William Crow. Sec., Wm. Henton, George Hansbrough. Wit., Thomas Prather, John Lawrence, Soloman Lawrence. Ap., Thos. Hanna, John Smith, Daniel Ketchum, Benj. Roberts. Wife, Elizabeth; children, Hannah, Lawrence, Charlotte Lawrence, Mary Ann Lawrence, Betsey Lawrence, Thomas Lawrence, James Lawrence, David Lawrence, Jr.

JAMES METCALFE—Inventory October, 1798—Ex., Margaret Metcalfe, John Metcalfe. Sec., Thomas Metcalfe, Wm. Jones. Wife, Margaret Metcalfe.

Peggy Metcalfe, widow of James, married 7-3-1807, Robert Miller in marriage bond and Reuben Miller in First Marriage Book.

SAMUEL McCLAIN—Inventory 9-14-1801—Ex., James McClain. Sec., Joseph Robinson, William Henton.

JESSE MEEKS—Proved March, 1802—Wit., Andrew Holmes, Augustine Shelburne. Wife, Sarah; mentions four children, named only one—Silas Meeks.

SAMUEL McCAMPBELL—Proved August, 1804—Ex., James McCampbell, John McCampbell. Sec., Thos. Gooch, Daniel Colgan. Wit., Daniel Colgan, Andrew McCampbell. Ap., George Wilcox, Alex. Reed, Jacob Fullinwider, Alex. McDowell. Wife, Martha; children, James, John, William, Andrew, Margaret, Jane Logan, Nancy Elliott, Molly Lawson, Washington.

Washington McCampbell married 1-9-1808, Elizabeth Tilford.

JAMES McCLURE or McLURE—Inventory 1796—Ex., Sarah McClure, Hugh McClure. Sec., James Campbell, John McClure. Ap., Bland W. Ballard, Jas. Logan. Wife, Sarah. A receipt from James Legget, James Campbell, John McClure, Elijah Baker, John Skidmore to Sarah and Hugh McClure, Admrs. James McClure, Jr., minor.

JOHN McCLAIN—Inventory July 9, 1804—Ex. Catherine McClain. Sec., James McClain, William Henton. Ap., Joseph Robinson, Albertus Bright, A. McGaughey, Moses Boone.

JACOB NEWLAND—November 10, 1800—Ex., Lusy Newland, widow, John Newland. Sec., Robert P. Allen, Luke Haff, Daniel Colgan. Ap., Jas. Ballard, Samuel Shannon, Luke Haff, Wm. Polke. 300 acres on Brashears Creek. Wife, Lucy; children, Isabella, John, Elizabeth, Isaac, Benoni, Robert, Polly, Abraham, Amy, Jacob, William.

GEORGE OWEN—Inventory May, 1794—Ap., Jacob Fullinwider, Samuel Ryker, William Cooper.

BRACKETT OWEN—Proved May, 1802—Ex., Thos. I. Gwin, Abraham Owen. Sec., Charles Lynch, Samuel Shannon, William Roberts. Wit., Gillon Lively, Daniel Lively, John Lively. Children, Jacob, Nancy Gwin, John, Abraham, David, Joseph, Robert, William, Jesse, Sally Glass, Samuel.

WILLIAM PERKINS—Inventory October, 1795—Sec., William Glem.

Ap., Thos. I. Gwin, Arthur McGaughey, Aquilla Whitaker. Wife, Jane.

MICHÆL PREWITT or PRUITT—Proved August, 1798—Ex. Elisha Prewitt, Daniel Mitchell. Sec., Thos. I. Gwin, Ezek. Talbott. Wit., Jeremiah Crabe, Wm. Gregory, Richd. M. Booker. Ap., John Ford, Richard Booker, Wm. Ford, James Robinson. Wife; children, Betsy Adams, James, Judy, Elisha, Michæl, Jr., Byrd, Joseph, Robert, Joshua.

JOHN POTTS—Inventory October, 1799—Ex., Margaret Potts, widow. Sec., William Taylor, Joseph Winlock. Ap., William Oglesby, Wm. Powell, Fielding Ashby. Settlement of heirs and legal representatives. Beverly Taylor, Abraham Bennett, Thomas Potts, Nicholas Miller, John Potts.

Margaret Potts married 8-17-1815, Nicholas Miller.

ISAAC PENNINGTON—Inventory November, 1801—Ex., Jonathan Bedle or Beadle. Sec., John Crawford, Wm. El. Collings. Ap., Richard Basey, Thomas Forman, George Cravenson, James Starke.

Isaac Pennington married 2-18-1799, Polly Lockhart.

WILLIAM POWELL—Inventory June,1801—Ex., Joseph Oglesby. Sec., Daniel Ellis, Michæl Smiser. Wife, Polly.

Mary Powell, widow of William, married 8-21-1818, Reuben Cowherd. Frances Powell married 4-19-1816, Daniel Caplinger. William M. Powell married 9-20-1817, Nancy Smiser, daughter of Henry.

WILLIAM ROBINS—Inventory October, 1795—Ap., Gerardus Ryker, Mason Watts.

JAMES REED—Inventory May, 1804—Ex., Susannah Reed, Alex Reed. Sec., Samuel Shannon, Jas. McDavitt. Ap., Daniel Colgan, Bland W. Ballard, Christopher Brant. Wife, Susannah.

WILLIAM REDDING—Proved August,1804—Ex., Timothy Redding. Sec., Reuben Redding, Elisha Lindsay, George Clifton. Ap., Daniel Ketcham, Elisha Ford, Masterson Ogden, Thos. Mitchell.

WILLIAM SHANNON—2 September, 1793; proved May, 1794—Ex., brother, Samuel Shannon, David Standiford. Wit., Dorsey Penticost, Joseph Winlock, William Addams. Ap., John Young, Jacob Newland, Peter Balea. Mother, Sarah Shannon; sister, Margaret Byers; sister, AnnBrakin or Brackin or Bracken; nephew, William Shannon, son of Thomas; neice, Sarah Shannon, daughter of Thomas; nephew, John Shannon, son of Samuel.

JACOB SMITH—Inventory—Ap., Robert Lowden, Jas. Hoagland, James W. Hemphill. Wife, Susanna; children, Betsy Smith, Polly Smith, James Smith.

Jacob Smith married Jefferson County, Ky., 9-28-1789, Susanna Dement, daughter of Benoni Dement. Susanna Smith, widow, evidently married before 1797, Peter Kerlin, as Peter Kerlin and Susanna Kerlin are guardians for Jacob Smith's children.

PATRICK SHIELDS—Inventory July, 1797—Ex., Mary Ann Shields, widow. Sec., Richard Worthington. Ap., Richard Rees, Robert Lowden, James Dods. Appraisement value £2000, 200 acres.

JAMES STOUT—August, 1790—Noncupative Will—Brother, Samuel Stout only legatee. Deed from Joseph Simpson to Saml. and Jas. Stout, August, 1797.

WILLIAM SLED—Inventory May, 1799—Ex., Lucy Sled, widow. Sec., John Barbee, Wm. Gaines. Ap., Aaron Martin, John Martin, John Jones, James Brenton. Legal heirs: Seaton Sled, Richard McCaslin, Benjamin Martin.

Lucy Sled, widow, married 11-14-1802, Charles Rice. Elizabeth Sled married 10-14-1811, Benjamin Martin. Nancy Sled married 4-21-1814, Richard McCaslin. Seaton Sled married 12-14-1820, Ann Underwood.

THOMAS SHANNON—September 12, 1800; proved November 10, 1800—Ex., Mary Shannon, widow. Sec., James Shannon, Samuel Shannon, Alex. Shannon. Wit., Matthias Ham, Jacob Canoy, both of Mulenburg (Muhlenburg) County. Wife, Mary; brother, Samuel Shannon; children, James, Samuel, Jane Reid, Agnes Wallace, Mary.

Agnes Shannon married 5-21-1795, Michæl Wallace.

ANDREW SHUCK—March 20, 1803; proved May, 1803—Ex., Peter Banta, Albert Vories. Sec., Peter Banta, Daniel Demaree, John Vories. Wit., John Vories, David Demaree. Wife, Margaret; children, Cornelius, John, Andrew, William, Hannah Batiss, Helena Banta, Margaret Sharp, Matthias, Sarah Banta, Mary Poland.

Mary Shuck married 10-23-1798, Willia mPoland. "Wm. Poland cared for Margaret Shuck, widow, while weak, feeble and infirm, from January 1, 1812 to January 1, 1820." Settlement.

JOHN SQUIRES—Inventory July 1803—Ex., John Gott. Sec., Abraham Rutledge, George Boyd. Ap., Arthur McGaughey, Wilson Maddox, Dyonyssius Shelburn. Wife, Mary; John Squires, Jr., son.

Mary Squires, widow, married 6-9-1803, Henry Caplinger. Margaret Squires, daughter of John, deceased, consent of mother, Mary Caplinger, married 3-31821, Alfred G. Mount.

THOMAS THOMPSON—Inventory November, 1797—Ex., Elizabeth Thompson, widow. Sec., Evan Thompson, Morgan Linville. Ap., Bland Ballard, John Wilcox, William Boone.

RALPH VANCLEAVE—Inventory October, 1798—Ex., Lydia Vancleave, widow. Sec., Benjamin Vancleave. Ap., John Teague, John Ryker, Samuel Ryker.

Mrs. Lydia Vancleave married 7-15-1808, George Staten.

SAMUEL WILSON—August 30, 1794; proved October, 1794—Ex., Hugh Wilson. Ap., Remembrance Wilson, Wm. Caneday, Samuel Kinkade. Wit., William Smiley, Remembrance Wilson. "To wife, Margaret, then to brother, Hugh Wilson."

DAVID WARFORD—Inventory March, 1795—Ex., Joseph Warford. Ap., Daniel Ketcham, John Metcalfe, John Kephart. 600 acres on Simpson Creek, Nelson County, Kentucky.

JOSEPH WALKER—Proved September, 1800—Ex., Polly Walker, widow, James Parke. Sec., Samuel McCampbell, Robert Allison. "Wife, Polly, all property she had before our marriage and all my personality." Daughter, Nancy; son, James; daughter, Polly Hays Walker.

Mary Walker, father deceased, married 2-4-1822, Peter Carnine, son of Richard.

JOHN WHITAKER or WHITACRE—Proved March, 1798—Ex., Jesse Whitaker, Isaac Whitaker. Sec., Benjamin Roberts, Samuel Shannon. Wit., John Stillwell, Jonah Glover. Ap., Jonah Glover, Wm. McCoy, Nath Tracey, Peter Pauly. Wife, Mary; children, John, deceased, Charles, Abraham, Hannah, Aquilla, Elijah, Isaac.
(John Whitaker was one of the early Baptist ministers in Kentucky.— M A C A L).

JESSE WHITAKER—Noncupative Will—December, 1800—Ex., Isaac Ellis. Sec., Aquilla Whitaker, George Walker, Wit., Elijah Whitaker, Isaac Whitaker. Wife, Lydia, 100 acres of Buck Creek. Infants under 21 in 1800: Rachel Whitaker, Squire Whitaker, Lee Whitaker, Mary Whitaker.

Mrs. Lydia Whitaker married 2-18-1804, John McCrocklin. Rachel Whitaker married 11-14-1810, Joshua Chapman. Squire Whitaker married 2-28-1815, Lucy Miles, daughter of Reuben Miles.

WILLIAM WILLIAMS—Proved February, 1801—Ex., Samuel Bryant. Sec., Richard Radford, John Underwood. Wit., John Piercy, Richard Radford, Nicholas Merriwether. Ap., Daniel Ketcham, John Warford, Joseph Warford, Giles Smith. Wife, Elizabeth; children, John Williams, Jenny Davis, Nancy Bryant, Sally Nash, Malinda Williams.

Sally Williams married 2-19-1801, Noble Nash. Malinda Williams married 1-23-1804, James Reynolds.

JOHN WILLIAMS—Proved January, 1804—Ex., Milly Williams, widow. Ap., Isham Talbott, Charles Baird, Jos. Field, George Cardwell.

ELIZABETH WILLIAMS—Proved August, 1804—Ex., Aquilla Whitaker. Sec., Bland W. Ballard. Wit., Isaac Collett. Children, daughter Sidney, Basil, Eli, Sarah, Rebecca. July Court, 1804: Basil Williams, 18 yrs., 6 mos., bound unto Wm. I. Tunstall, housejoiner. Eli Williams, 14 yr., 2 mos., 14 da., bound unto Thos. I. Sturman, shoemaker. Sally Williams, 13 yr., 8 mos., bound unto David Shipman. Rebecca Williams, 7 yrs., 8 mos., bound unto Mrs. Mary Shannon.

ADAM YOUNG—Proved January, 1799—Wit., Wm. Smiley, John McCortney.

MISCELLANEOUS

VALENTINE STONE—**Bath County**—Names wife, Keziah; sons, Richard and Robert; youngest son, James F. Stone; son, Samuel (land in Owen County); daughter, Philadelphia Robinson (land in Owen

County); son, William; daughter, Elizabeth Lewis; daughter, Keziah Ratcliff; daughter, Molly Elie; daughter, Matilda Stone; grandson, Alfred Stone (land in Owen County). Leaves land in Stafford County, Virginia, to son, Samuel. Written July 14th, 1822. Proved September 9th, 1822. Executors—Sons, Samuel and James Stone. Witnesses—Samuel Wilson, William Hagriss, Samuel Hagers.

ZEPHANIAH RATCLIFF—Bath County—Dated May 3d, 1825—Eldest daughter, Mary Ringo; daughter, Susannah Baird; daughter, Elizabeth Bell; heirs of daughter, Eleanor Stone, deceased, viz.: Stephen Joseph, Valentine, Caroline, Richard Stone; son, Joseph Ratcliff; son, Charles Ratcliff; son, Caleb Ratcliff; son, Coleman Ratcliff, and daughter, Nancy Moffitt. Executors—Sons, Joseph and Caleb. Proved, 1831.

THOMAS JAMESON, Sr. — Montgomery County — Will Book C, Page 317 — Eldest daughter, Lucy Jeter, married with John R. Porter; Mildred, married with Danile P. Moseley; Judith Ball, married with Elijah Beldsoe; Elizabeth Ball, married with Lloyd Thompson; Margaret Ball, married with David Stewart; son, James Jameson; heirs of eldest son, Thomas Jameson; heir of son, Hackley Jameson; youngest son, Sanford Jameson; son, John Jameson. Dated June 27th, 1827. Executors—Son, Sanford Jameson, and son-in-law, David Stewart.

JAMES HARDGE LANE, 2nd.—Montgomery County—Will Book E, Page 128—Names wife, Sarah; son, William Lane; son, Henry S. Lane; son, Higgens Lane; son, John Lane; to Mary Carrington, James H. Lane, Elizabeth Goodlow, Nancy Riggs, Evelina Reid, daughter, Sarah Stone; John and Mary Strode, grandparents of my first children; Dated July 22, 1841. Proved, 1850. Executors—Henry S. Lane and Higgins Lane. Witnesses—Hiram Lane, W. N. Lane.

(Contributed by Miss May Stone, Fincastle Chapter)

NANCY MARTIN—Lincoln County—Will Book 1, Page 64—Names Ann, wife of Peter Carter; Peggy Kelly, Hannah Russell, John L. Martin. Recorded March, 1823.
NOTE—Nancy Martin was the widow of John Martin, founder of Martin's Fort.

(Contributed by Mrs. Wade Whitley, Jemima Johnson Chapter)

JOSEPH MILLER—Will Book No. 7, Page 765, Clark County—
—Dated January 17, 1832, probated at July Court, 1832. Mentions his wife, Susanna, and children as follows: Sarah Scholl, Elizabeth Scholl, Samuel H. Miller, Mary W. Miller and Isaac S. Miller. He also mentions Oliver P. Scholl, Sirus R. Scholl, and James R. Scholl, the three sons of his daughter, Rebecca V. Scholl, deceased, who was the wife of Joseph Scholl. He appoints his son, Samuel H. Miller, his son-in-law, Septimus Scholl and his wife, Susanna Miller, as his executors. The witnesses to the will were James Miller, Samuel Ritchie, Edward Elliott and John S. Evans.

GEORGE MILLER—Clark County, Ky.—In a deed dated February 18, 1822, (recorded in Deed Book 18, page 282), George Miller and

Mary Ann, his wife, and William Miller and Polly, his wife, of the county of Clark and State fo Kentucky, conveyed to Joseph Miller, of same county and state, their rights in a tract of land in "Shannando County, State of Virginia," on the waters of Cabin Run, part of a larger tract granted to George Bruce by patent bearing date May 25, 1750, the said Bruce having conveyed it to George Miller, William Miller and Joseph Miller by deed bearing date November 19, 1773.

SIMON KENTON—Mason County—Deed Dated 1794, Book B, Page 58 —Simon Kenton and wife, Martha, to John Curtis.

JAMES EDWARDS, Sr.—Mason County—Deed Dated 1795, Book B, Page 501—James Edwards, Sr., and wife, Sarah, of Mason County, to William Clarke, Sr., lot in town of Washington which was conveyed by James Kay to James Edwards, Sr.

JOHN CURTIS—Mason County—Deed Dated 1804, Deed Book A, Page 251—John Curtis, Sr., of "Loudoun County, Virginia," from John Curtis, Jr., of Mason County, Kentucky.

JOSEPH ROSEBERRY—Mason County—Will Book B—Names wife, Parmelia; children, Michael, Mary, Ebenezer, Hannah, Joseph. Written April 20, 1804. Proved June 10th, 1805.

JAMES EDWARDS—Mason County—Will Book A, Page 79—Names wife, Nancy; daughter, Elenor, when she comes of age. Executors —Father, James Edwards, and brother, George Edwards. Proved December, 1795. Witnesses—John West, John Jacobs, Caleb T. Taylor.

JACOB EDWARDS—Mason County—Will Book A, Page 10—Names wife, Elizabeth; children, Sarah Emily, Milly, Mary, Alexander. To daughter, Sarah Emily, 100 acres on Licking River due on bond from John Curtis assigned by John Harding. To Mary and Milly that which is received from William Wood and Arthur Fox. To son, Alexander, four lots in town of Washington. To Sarah Suddith 100 acres being a military survey, located and surveyed by John O. Banion. Executrix—Wife, Elizabeth. Executors—Father, James Edwards, Richard Marshall and George Edwards. Written April 9, 1791. Proved July 28th, 1791. Witnesses—James Stephenson, John West, John Raine. Securities—Henry Lee and Robert Rankin.

JOHN CURTIS—Mason County—Will Book C, Page 255—Names children, George, Nancy Hill, David, Polly, Julia, Hiram, Nicholas, Eliza, Eleanor, John, James. Wife, Nancy. Father, John Curtis. Executrix—Wife, Nancy Curtis. Written September 9, 1813. Proved October 11, 1813. Witnesses—Joseph Donephan, James Nichols, George Curtis, Joseph Clarke, Walker Reid. Securities— James Key, George Moore, James Nichols, William Shields, Joseph Thomson, Joseph Clarke.

(Contributed by Mrs. W. B. Ardery, Jemima Johnson Chapter)

EDMUND MARTIN, Sr.—Mason County—Will—Names wife, Susannah; son, Edmund Martin, and his brother, Micajah Martin; son, Jerry Martin; son-in-law, Eli Huron; daughters, Nancy Altig, Rachel

Rees, Milly Bland, Isabella Fitch and Hannah Porter; Swells Boaz Brooks and Levi Boone (obligated for land); son, Elijah Martin (formally received portion). Executors—Son, Elijah Martin, and friend, Moses Daulton. Written November 28th, 1811. Proved December 9th, 1811. Witnesses—Charles Gallagher, Adam McFerrin, Sanford Carrell. Security—Sanford Carrell, William Porter, William Grinstead, Jeremiah Martin.

SUSANNAH MARTIN—Mason County—Will—Names son, Edmund Martin; grand-daughter, Susannah Boone, daughter of Levi and Sarah Boone; grandson, Hiram Martin, son of Edward and Rebecca Martin; grandson, William Porter, son of William and Hannah Porter; Jeremiah Martin; sister, Mary Daulton; sisters. Executor— Son, Edmund Martin. Written July 5th, 1821. Proved September Court, 1821. Witnesses—William Tureman, Henry C. Tureman.

(Contributed by Miss Letitia Hedges, Jemima Johnson Chapter)

CLARK COUNTY MARRIAGES

(Contributed by Mrs. William Breckenridge Ardery, Jemima Johnson Chapter)

John Allen-Ann Griffin, 1794.
Richardson Allen-Camelia McCracken, May 6, 1795.
Abijah Arnett-Susannah Femmons, 1795.
Jacob Arlington-Elizabeth Baby, 1794-5.
Randal Alexander-Mary Nelson, January 28, 1796.
John Alexander-Lydia Harris, December 13, 1796.
William Anderson-Rebecky Lisle, October 29, 1795.
William Allen-Martha Allenton, May 25, 1796.
Benjamin Allen-Keziah Clawson, April 11, 1797.
Charles Atchason-Rosanah Scott, September 23, 1796.
John Ard-Deborah St. Duskey, July 7, 1795.
Jeremiah Blan-Gussa Tuicher, January 16, 1794.
John W. Buckner-Mary Ann Martain, February 20, 1794.
Thomas Bell-Agness Whitesides, March 6, 1794.
James Brower-Mary Proler, July 9, 1793.
Oliver Badjer-Sally Roberson, 1794.
Joshua Bartlett-Winny Herring, January 31, 1794.
Zachariah Bell-Nancy Evans, May 15, 1794.
Clark Bunch-Ann Davis, August 26, 1794.
Garland Bullock-Elizabeth Bullock, December 23, 1794.
William Barns-Caty Angel, January 29, 1795.
David Braninburg-Agnes Morton, July 23, 1795.
Bartlett Brundig-Margaret More, August 6, 1795.
Lewis Berry-Agnes Rash, December 24, 1795.
Joshua Bartlett-Betsy Fletcher, January 14, 1796.
William Barker-Peggy Cotton, 1796.
James Burns-Lusy Ray, July 4, 1797.
Joseph Bush-Sary Dunkin, August 3, 1797.
Moses Bledso-Lucy Jamison, 1797.
Joseph Braninburg-Delily Vesser, September 1, 1796.
Jonathan Barker-Sary Quisenberry, June 22, 1797.
John Baker-Polly Combs, August 17, 1797.
John Boyd-Dorcus Hendrix, December 3, 1795.
William Brindle-Nancy Lonsdale, December 27, 1796.
John Barr-Margaret Lemon, 1796.

Richard Boyd-Polly Downie, March 3, 1796.
Mathew Bracken-Nancy Rogers, February 23, 1797.
Edward Bundamon-Nancy Morton, January 20, 1798.
William Boyd-Isabel Hillis, 1799.
James Craig-Rebekah Hill, December 12, 1793.
Thomas Ashley Cassity-Elizabeth Cassity, December 11, 1794.
John Caldwell- Elizabeth Combs, January 27, 1795.
Gustavus Clament-Mary Gross, July 9, 1795.
Andrew Cartwell-Nancy Brown, 1795-5.
Henry Celoy-Jeen Neets, 1794-5.
Abram Cooroy-Rachel Jonson, 1794-5.
John Crow-Patey Bybee, February 29, 1796.
Bowling Clarke-Agnes W. Bullock, 1796.
Francis Cullom-Ellenor Owen, 1796.
Thomas Constant-Margaret Edmonson, June 6, 1796.
Richard Crump-Sarah Smith, April 12, 1796.
John Crawford-Dolly Fort, June 22, 1796.
Thomas Chisholm-Lucy Crim, April 30, 1797.
Edward Cane-Elizabeth Jones, September 7, 1797.
Benjamin Combs-Betsy Payne, 1797.
Peter Cassaday-Mary Armstrong, 1797.
J. Francis Cronch-Jenny Sparks, May 3, 1798.
John Collins-Margaret Daniel, May 11, 1797.
Halley Crump-Prescila Blackburn, August 10, 1797.
Joseph Combs-Susanna Clark, September 27, 1797.
Wm. Clayton-Jenny Nelson, May 27, 1795.
Rupard Crow-Elizabeth Burgess, June 22, 1798.
Daniel Daring-Agness McFadion, August 20, 1793.
Andrew Duncan-Frances Colliver, July 14, 1795.
James Dunlap-MillyJohnson, August 29, 1794.
Jacob Dawson-Abigale Constant, December 20, 1795.
Mathias Davis-Sarah Rulem (Rulon), March 1, 1796.
James Davis-Hannah Smith, 1794-5.
Jeans Downy-Susany Yocum, November 17, 1796.
James Davis-Rachel Atchoson, March 28, 1797.
John Dunken-Sary Bush, February 9, 1797.
Robert Donilson-Sary Donalson, May 12, 1796.
Henry Darnell-Sarah Furpin (Turpin), January 7, 1797.
Daniell Darnell-Nancy Turpin (Furpin), January 7, 1797.
William Dunnaway-Margaret Bratso, August 4, 1796.
Andrew Downing-Emma Cochron, February 2, 1797.
Samuel Eten-Frances Dowell, July 30, 1794.
James Ewalt (Emalt)-Bathshaba Trombridge, 1796.
Thomas Embree-Elizabeth Duncan, 1796.
Joseph Everman-Catherine Wall, January 5, 1797.
William Frazer-Vina Patrick, 1796.
Sherrd Falker-Lydia Wynn, April 25, 1796.
Elijah Friored?-Margaret Board, January 23, 1797.
James Forbes-Elizabeth Magee, July 14, 1796.
James Fitsworth-Jenne Wick, April 30, 1795.
James Forgey-Peggy Rogers, February 23, 1797.
John Fox-Anna Stripling, September 13, 1797.
Thomas Gardner-Susannah Weddel, October 10, 1793.
John George-Lucy Martain, February 7, 1794.
Andrew Goff-Anne Cooker, May 8, 1794.
Peter Goosey-Anna Cotton, 1796.
Clem Griggs-Elisander Hall, 1796.
Joseph Gray-Mary Finnel, February 16, 1796.
Edmund Green-Elizabeth Watson. May 23, 1796.
Lige Genkins-Betsey Myers, November 3, 1796.
James Grimes-Peggy Smith, June 6, 1797.

John Gaines-Patsy Jackson, January 18, 1798.
David Haggard-Amelia Elkin, June 29, 1793.
James Hazelrigg-Leucy Flemmin, October 30, 1793.
John Hooten-Franky Bush, February 27, 1794.
Abraham Heeton (Hooten)-Jane McGuire, 1794.
Samuel Hadden-Anne Anderson, January 17, 1794.
Joseph Hedges-Sally Thursby, August 28, 1794.
Archibald Harris-Franky Wynn, June 6, 1796.
Charles Harper- Jroply ? Shamblin, 1794-5.
John Hatten-Sarah Oldfield, 1794-5.
John Higgins-Jane Parkhurst, 1794-5.
William Hosick-Polly Turner, March 31, 1796.
William Hooten-Caty George, November 15, 1796.
Jonatohn Hampton-Jane Davis, March 30, 1797.
Nathaniel Haggard-Petty Hays, December 30, 1796.
Henary Hunter-Sary Vagwill, August 23, 1797.
Daniel Hearrin-Susannah Hunter, 1797.
Aaron Hand-Keziah Dawson, 1797.
James Harper-Sukey Houghman, February 25, 1797.
Moses Hampton-Rachel Morgan, June 2, 1797.
Robert Hall-Peggy Rinkin, May 10, 1797.
Turner Harper-Mary French, November 5, 1797.
Shadrack Hodsdale-Ann Goff, August 1, 1793.
James Jackson-Pollay Embree, 1796.
John Jackson-Mary Conkright, 1796.
John Jones-Mary Vise, April 14, 1796.
Thomas Johnson-Martha Elkin, November 2, 1797.
Neolon Justion-Polly Morton, December 4, 1797.
Thomas Jones-Sary Hall, 1797.
Phillip Johnson-Margaret Parker, March 22, 1798.
Isaac Keeton-Margaret Wade, August 5, 1793.
Henry Kain-Anne Ramey, April 9, 1795.
David Kees-Kitty Striplin, January 26, 1797.
William Kavanaugh-Hanna Hubbard Hind, March 22, 1798.
William Kindle-Annie Ray, May 10, 1797.
Amergety Lilly-Catherine McCutchen, September 23, 1795.
William Lefore-Jane Watson, November 6, 1796.
Benjamin Lemaster-Polly Langstone, September 21, 1796.
Thomas Laferty-Mander Strode, December 27, 1797.
John Morgan-Sarah Hanley, March 1, 1796.
John Midcalfe-Elizabeth Ramey, July 30, 1793.
James Metcalfe-Peggy Flemmin, October 30, 1793.
Joseph More-Mary Shearley, July 26, 1794.
Jese Melton-Sarah Stone, July 24, 1794.
Zachariah Morris-Sarah Donham, February 29, 1796.
William Morgan-Rachel Feamster, March 1, 1796.
James More-Mary Lewis, August 11, 1795.
Caswel Micks-Elnor Roberts, August 21, 1796.
John Mulroy-Labra Levenstone, April 5, 1796.
Robert Morrow-Margaret Trimbel, February 8, 1797.
John Metcalf-Polly Cummin, October 10, 1797.
Daniel Morris-Polly Crostwait, January 8, 1798.
James Mason-Anna Fishback, 1799.
William Moore-Sarah Colbert, December 6, 1797.
John Mussett-Mary Stoker, February 19, 1797.
John Murphy-Sarah Weddle, March 29, 1798.
David McGee-Elizabeth McMahan, December 20, 1794.
Samuel McMahan-Jane Daniel, February 27, 1796.
William McKinsy-Nancy Lampkin, 1796.
Robert McKinnie-Sally Young, June 29, 1796.
Thomas McDaniel-Jane Rise, December 25, 1796.

Elijah McRay-Nancy Cheaton, November 19, 1797.
John McKinney-Jane Coleman, December 24, 1797.
John McFerran-Sary Huffman, May 23, 1797.
William McMahan-Mary McMahan, May 19, 1797.
William Nelson-Mary Taylor, September 19, 1793.
William Norton-Catherine Srock, January 6, 1794.
John Nelson-Margaret Fisher, October, 1796.
Mehabo Ohorow-Elizabeth Tribit, April 4, 1793.
Elias Oldfield-Rue ? Bigs, March 31, 1796.
Thomas Owen-Nancy Morgan, April 7, 1796.
James Oldham-Mary Burgin, November 22, 1797.
Michæl Pauls-Peggy Hughs, September 30, 1793.
Mathias Pleak-Milley Goff, August 6, 1794.
John Phillips-Elizabeth ————————, January 20, 1796.
Morris Phillips-Prudence Doughty, April 2, 1796.
James Payn-Judith Jamison, 1797.
Michæl Peebler-Esther Sears, November 23, 1796.
George Peck-Nancy Barker, March 15, 1796.
John Price-Anna Fishback, 1799.
George Routt-Margaret Holder, June 11, 1793.
Cornelius Rogers-Caty Lambert, October 20, 1793.
Thomas Rogers-Elizabeth Ament, November 1, 1793.
David Richardson-Nancy Ratlef, October 17, 1793.
Patrick Rogers-Sally Barrier, July 6, 1794.
Jessy Robinson-Sally White, January 3, 1795.
Moses Ray-Nancy Elliotte, March 12, 1795.
Hennery Rockwill-Fanny Lisle, November 17, 1795.
Thomas Roberson-Nancy Croswhite, 1796.
James Rash-Mary Terrel, August 4, 1796.
Alexander Ritchie-Susannah Ritchie, December 21, 1797.
Harny Rice-Betsy Martin, 1797.
Maron Ray-Prissler Breading, May 8, 1797.
Pierson Richardson-Elizabeth Jackson, June 8, 1797.
James Riggs-Caty Hathaway, December 22, 1796.
Samuel Summers-Nancy Middleton, August 12, 1793.
Peter Smith-Susannah Munroy, May 20, 1793.
John Slater-Jane Alderson, July 5, 1794.
John Cusbary Sutton-Anne Dixon, May 1, 1794.
William Stagsdell-Jane Jackson, August 29, 1794.
Welder Smith-Unis Rigs, 1794-5.
Denis Sunbrey-Rachel McCourley, 1794-5.
Jesse Saingon-Elizabeth Payne, January 4, 1796.
Patrick Smith-Charlotty Barnett, June 22, 1796.
Elijah Smith-Sarah Doughaty, August 21, 1796.
Derret Sanford—Luster Bly, October 31, 1797.
Henry Smith-Nancy Davis, February 22, 1797.
Moses Suaim-Caty Berry, September 27, 1796.
William Smythe-Chloe Atchison, November 8, 1797.
Thomas Said-Ann Harris, December 20, 1797.
Eli St. Duskey-Margaret McCallom, April 7, 1796.
John Stepheson-Nancy Pease, January 19, 1798.
William Turner-Sarah Pointer, 1794.
Moses Treadaway-Caty Dewit, 1794.
John Tatmon-Phebe Martin, 1794-5.
John Terrel-Abby Allen, 1797.
John Tipton-Betsey Hall, January 12, 1797.
Thomas Turner-Nancy Myers, January 25, 1797.
Nathl. Vice-Elizeb White, April 4, 1793.
Smith Vivion-Sibby Jones, August 10, 1794.
Milton Vivion-Elizabeth Jones, February 9, 1797.
Elic Vawhan-Rhoda Drake, June 15, 1797.

John Webb-Mary Webb, August 7, 1793.
Jason Wright-Rebeckah McKeny, September 5, 1793.
Joseph Wade-Peggy Mounce, May 28, 1793.
Edward Whaley-Nancy Haney, April 15, 1794.
Joseph Whitesides-Rebecca Stewart, December 20, 1794.
John Williams-Jane Frasier, August 4, 1795.
George Walton-Franky Bush, December 29,1795.
Jesse Wilkoxen-Sarah Hogans, February 6, 1796.
Jesse West-Nancy French, January 28, 1796.
Richard Wills-Elender Patton, October 19, 1796.
Andrew Wilson-Mary Nicols, October 13, 1796.
Benjamin Whittenton-Amey Bunch, December 12, 1796.
James Winn-Nancy Johnson, August 17, 1796.
~ William West-Lidia George, October 15, 1796.
Thomas Winn-Sary Johnson, August 14, 1796.
William Wilkerson-Betsy Striplin, December 21, 1797.
William Wells-Ann Cassaday, 1797.
David Welty-Mary Brown, November 23, 1796.
Jeremiah Webb-Judy Beby, July 23, 1796.
Frederick Wilson-Nancy Lane, October 13, 1796.
Jacob Warrik-Jane Montgomery, March 10, 1796.
George Weaver-Bridget Dohertie, February 6, 1797.
Isaac Wilcoxkson-Rebecah White, May 25, 1797.
Garland White-Sarah Nelson, April 3, 1798.
Jonathon West-Rachel Alexander, 1798.
George Webb-Patsy Lane, 1798.
William Whitesides-Anna McGee, February 28, 1797.
William Yeates-Susannah Higgins, July 11, 1793.
James Yarbrough-Elizabeth Kilpatrick, August 30, 1794.
Benjamin Yates-Verlinga Ford, January 16, 1794.
Henry Yaakey-Polly McClure, June 9, 1795.
Edward Young-Mary Rash, January 19, 1797.
Charles York-Polly Everman, 1797.

DAVIESS COUNTY MARRIAGES

(Contributed by Mrs. W. T. Mastin, Gen. Evan Shelby Chapter)

NOTE: In the following records the bond dates only are given, as in every instance the marriage was recorded during the year, with the exception of those marked *. As there is no record of these having been returned, they were, no doubt, recorded in some adjoining county.

Samuel McCoy-Jane Helm, June 23, 1815.
Robert Galloway-Catherine Sonerheber, July 27, 1815.
Caleb Hedges-Polly Davis, August 7, 1815.
William Lock-Elizabeth Mothrell, August 7, 1815.
John Arbono-Harriett C. Lumpkins, August 9, 1815.
John Tribble-Nancy Barnett, September 11, 1815.
John Field-Rachael McFarland, November 27, 1815.
John Neighbors-Catty Liggetts (widow), December 30, 1815.
*John Johnson-Lucy Huston, March 13, 1816.
Banister Wall-Sally Thompson, May 23, 1816.
Hugh Barnet-Polly Cummins, May 18, 1816.
John Gates-Lydia Edwards, June 10, 1816.
Thomas Metcalf-Elizabeth Jones, August 19, 1816.
Joseph Spray-Mary Travis, October 19, 1816.
John McFarland-Elizabeth Griffith, October 18, 1816.

Azel Arterberry-Vina Lay, November 6, 1816.
William Beall-Elizabeth Beall, November 25, 1816.
George Gilmore-Patsey Isbell, November 28, 1816.
Hillary Beall-Margaret Adams, December 6, 1816.
Phillip Thompson-Sally Mosley, December 9, 1816.
John Roberts, Jr.-Mary Mosley, December 9, 1816.
John McDaniel-Jane Adams, December 21, 1816.
Abraham Shutt-Elizabeth Humphrey, January 9, 1817.
Wilston Martin-Polly Pinkston, January 13, 1817.
William Terrell-Ann Coldwell, January 24, 1817.
Ephriam Thompson-Susan Grisby, February 4, 1817.
Cyrus Pinkston-Delila Pinkston, February 4, 1817.
James Jordon, Jr.-Jane Glenn, February 26, 1817.
Samuel Piles-Elizabeth Calhoun, March 15, 1817.
John Briant-Milly Pinkston, March 21, 1817.
Benjamin Stidham-Leanna Holmark, March 21, 1817.
Ralph C. Calhoun-Lucy Glenn, May 5, 1817.
John B. Blackwell-Nancy Hellms, May 15, 1817.
James Hellms-Rachael Taylor, July 8, 1817.
William McFarland-Francis Field, July 8, 1817.
David Hamilton-Elizabeth Crabtree, July 10, 1817.
James Bartlett-Una (Unis) Lay, July 21, 1817.
William Sisk-Ann Brown, August 1, 1817.
John Barnett-Leah Howard, September 11, 1817.
James C. Barnett-Delila McFarland, September 31, 1817.
John W. Crow-Cynthia McCreery, October 30, 1817.
John Roman-Elizabeth Brooks (widow), November 20, 1817.
Gabriel Hart-Mary May, December 30, 1817.
Robert Wood-Millay Briant, January 5, 1818.
Abner Bassett-Nancy Galloway, January 5, 1818.
Joseph Davis-Sally Myer, February 3, 1818.
William McAfee Jones-Ollie May, February 3, 1818.
John Totten-Esther Vandike, May 24, 1818.
Robert Lamb-Polly Briant, May 17, 1818.
Joseph Riggs-Lucy Dicken, March 4, 1818.
Reuben Field-Agnes Barnett (widow), April 8, 1818.
Harrison Adkins-Polly Smith, April 11, 1818.
George Tribble-Elizabeth Bingham, April 15, 1818.
Jesse Lockett-Sallie Bates, May 8, 1818.
Nathan Arterberry-Levica Arterberry, May 30, 1818.
Willis Duncan-Frances Frazier, June 3, 1818.
James Newton-Fanny Field, June 25, 1818.
William R. Duncan-Kitty Roberts, August 2, 1818.
Grover Howard-Elizabeth Moore, August 4, 1818.
David Brown-Jane Hale, August 22, 1818.
Joseph S. Webb-Ann Vandike, August 26, 1818.
Thomas W. Palmer-Sarah Wells, September 5, 1818.
Nace Overall-Amelia H. Daviess, September 8, 1818.
Benjamin P. Lockett-Jane Carey, September 8, 1818.
George Calhoun-Mary Gilmore, October 28, 1818.
John Gabbert-Polly McKinney, December 14, 1818.
John Howard-Margaret Moore, December 15, 1818.
Joseph McDaniel, Jr.-Rhody Kirk, December 15, 1818.
Baptist Mattox-Leah McDaniel, December 15, 1818.
Michael Coyle-May Polly Black, December 26, 1818.
Jeremiah Lucas-Sussanna May, December 29, 1818.
John Downs-Polly Bassett, December 30, 1818.
Aaron Taylor-Lydia Maxon, January 8, 1819.
Pleasant Cox-Charlotte Wiley, January 13, 1819.
William Metcalf-Elizabeth Brown, January 18, 1819.
William Tanner-Anny Brown, March 21, 1819.

John T. C. Priest-Isabelle Grigsby, March 27, 1819.
Morgan Hawkins-Sallie Holmes, March 28, 1819.
Elisha Barker-Polly Huff, April 16, 1819.
William McFarland-Patsy Chambers, April 25, 1819.
John W. Patton-Nancy Anderson (widow), May 8, 1819.
Moses Long-Isabel McAntyre, May 13, 1819.
William Glover-Sarah McFarland, May 10, 1819.
Julius C. Jackson-Harriett McCreery, January 13, 1819.
Lewis Riley-Cassandria Pedicord, August 11, 1819.
Jacob Phigley-Elizabeth Gibson, September 11, 1819.
Zachariah Galloway-Margaret Pearson, September 18, 1819.
Martin Richardson-Pammelia Lockett, September 25, 1819.
Hiram Jones-Sally Taylor, October 19, 1819.
Thomas Martin-Sally Winkler, October 18, 1819.
Ezekiel Hedges-Polly Tanner, October 18, 1819.
Joseph Taylor-Elizabeth Galloway, October 23, 1819.
Henry Courtney-Nancy C. Lumpkins, November 8, 1819.
Edward Shown-Phinta T. Phinkston, November 11, 1819.
John Sanders-Hannah Stevenson, November 17, 1819.
*Samuel T. Hynes-Elizabeth Thompson, December 8, 1819.
Leonard Jones-Olly May, December 21, 1819.
*Levi S. Scott-Sally Lawrence, January 3, 1820.
Joseph Taylor-Sally Martin, October 24, 1819 (return).
John J. Jofford-Polly Rice, January 5, 1820.
John Igleheart-Ellen Humphreys, January 5, 1820.
Henry Owen-Eliza Howard, January 10, 1820.
Terry Thorpe-Polly Edmundson Howard, January 10, 1820.
George Metcalfe-Elizabeth Winkler, January 24, 1820.
Richard L. May-Lucy Davis, January 24, 1820.
Owen Howard-Polly Howard, February 2, 1820.
James Nelson-Susanna Crews, February 15, 1820.
Corneleus Head-Mary McDaniel, February 2, 1820.
Zachariah Field-Amelia Tanner, February 21, 1820.
William Brown-Ann E. Atherton, March 22, 1820.
*John McCracken-Peggy Hall, March 25, 1820.
Benjamin Duncan-Nancy Beauchamp, March 20, 1820.
Samuel Cabit-Sally Timmons, March 10, 1820.
William R. Griffith-Arria Moseley, April 13, 1820.
Henry W. Clark-Sally Clark, May 31, 1820.
*Lewis Barnett-Agnes Hedges, June 9, 1820.
John Gaither-Rebecca Bell, June 15, 1820.
Thomas Tanner-Nancy Davis, June 23, 1820.
Nicholas Worthington-Eliza White, July 5, 1820.
William Clark-Catherine Timmons, August 1, 1820.
Andrew O'Neal-Ann Higgins, August 15, 1820.
Russell Isam-Mary Ann Perry, August 24, 1820.
James M. Rogers-Jane Adams, August 24, 1820.
John Owens-Elizabeth Allen, September 13, 1820.
Smith Akers-Martha Chamberlain, September 18, 1820.
Jacob Crabtree-Elizabeth Travis, October 14, 1820.
William M. Helms-Catherine Husk, October 14, 1820.
James Archibald-Patience Taylor, November 11, 1820.
Reuben Harris-Elitha Akes, October 31, 1820.
Hezekiah L. Priest-Patsy Lumpkins, November 3, 1820.
*William Kirkham-Ann Rogers, December 21, 1920.
William Howard-Polly Moore, December 27, 1820.
John May-Polly Davidson, December 27, 1820.
Thomas Daniel-Mary Williams, January 1, 1821.
Absolam Chinoworth-Mrs. Elizabeth Edwards, January 9, 1821.
James McFarland-Betsy Wall, January 22, 1821.
*Levy Voyles-Bathabra Phillips, February 2, 1821.

John Maddox-Nancy Eaton, February 10, 1821.
Silas Hart-Hannah Hourdan, February 12, 1821.
Benjamin Roberts-Rebecca Frazier, February 24, 1821.
Jesse Rogers-Martha Jennison, March 6, 1821.
Lewis Love-Elenor Arteberry, April 7, 1821.
Jarrett Willingham-Marion Friels, April 15, 1821.
John A. Taylor-Polly Buckner, April 20, 1821.
Alexander Adams-Linny Metcalf, May 7, 1821.
James Hall-Charlotte Roland, June 16, 1821.
Solomon Barnett-Sarah McDaniel, July 12, 1821.
Jeremiah Collard-Betsy Baker, August 1, 1821.
Reuben Bennett-Margaret Black, August 4, 1821.
Isaac Kennedy-Lydia Dryson, August 15, 1821
*William Downs-Milly Ann King, October 4, 1921.
William McFarland-Patsy White, October 10, 1821.
Robert Wilson-Margaret L. May, October 13, 1821.
Solomon Brand-Elenor Lynn, October 15, 1821.
William Hansford-Mary Griffith, November 28, 1821.
James Howard-Mary A. Johnston, December 15, 1821.
Able Etkins-Mrs. Margaret Evans, December 28, 1821.
Christopher Jones-Mary Ann Lumpkins, January 10, 1822.
Elisha Adams-Eliza Ball, January 22, 1822.
William Bethol-Patsy Downs, January 25, 1822.
Jesse Bates-Elizabeth Arteberry, January 20, 1822.
Nathanlial Bassett-Rebecca Mothrat, March 16, 1822.
Stephen T. Ogden-Sally Ann Daviess, April 20, 1822.
William R. Duncan-Ann E. Miller, May 4, 1822.
Jeremiah Wayland-Nancy Ann Bartlett, May 4, 1822.
William Winkler-Eliza Adams, May 15, 1822.
William May, Jr.-Polly Gauf, May 22, 1822.
Henry Campbell-Partyaniel Brown, June 3, 1822.
John J. Nelson-Milly Cruise, July 26, 1822.
James Stinnett-Cecelia Briant, August 22, 1822.
John Helms-Elizabeth Stephenson, September 30, 1822.
Isom Fares-Mrs. Nancy Blackwell, October 7, 1822.
Col. Joseph Pollard-Mrs. Ann Daviess, November 4, 1822.
Anthony New-Charlotte Head, November 28, 1822.
Evan McBrown-Nancy Barrett, December 16, 1822.
Nester Clay-Nancy Johnson, December 12, 1822.
William Young-Jane Wickerson, December 23, 1822.
William Bassett-Patsy Galloway, December 25, 1822.
Starling Cardwell-Elizabeth Barker, December 25, 1822.
Jonas Richardson-Phebe Boucher, December 30, 1822.
William Ward-Polly Thompson, January 7, 1823.
John Murphey-Alley Millay, January 18, 1823.
John Brown-Malinda Spradling, January 25, 1823.
Enoch Grigsby-Mrs. Sally Carlisle, February 12, 1823.
Alexander Moreland-Ann Potts, February 13, 1823.
John Taylor-Ruth Bell, February 20, 1823.
John McGraw-Mrs. Nancy Bassett, March 11, 1823.
Bryam Barnett-Harriett Head, June 12, 1823.
George Critser-Polly West, June 28, 1823.
Francis McCormick-Precilla Newton, July 7, 1823.
Elijah Dotson-Sarah King, July 18, 1823.
Owen Davis-Nancy Taylor, August 4, 1823.
Shardrack Rogers-Ruth Raferty, September 16, 1823.
Daniel Stinnett-Harriett McDaniel, October 10, 1823.
James Foster-Polly Kelly, November 3, 1823.
John McFarland-Matilda Moseley, December 11, 1823.
Richard C. Jett-Susan T. Miller, October 24, 1823.
David Arteberry-Elizabeth Clark, December 29, 1823.

Stephen Ashby-Betsy Chaney, January 2, 1824.
James Hatcher-Catherine Jackson, January 5, 1824.
Samuel Harriason-Elenor Allen, February 12, 1824.
Lewis Bryant-Mary T. Morris, February 17, 1824.
John Kincade-Hannah Jones, March 8, 1824.
*Ben Humphrey-Martha Little, March 9, 1824.
Alfred E. Harris-Polly Martin, April 20, 1824.
*Charles Coomes-Fannie Dollin, April 29, 1824.
James Barnett-Mary Bashaba McIntire, May 15, 1824.
John Stevens-Rachael Thompson, February 3, 1824.
*Benjamin Dickens-Lucinda Chamberlain, May 31, 1824.
James B. Wright-Jane Allen, September 1, 1824.
Benjamin Allen-Mary Grigsby, September 1, 1824.
Andrew Goff-Sally G. Pinkston, September 7, 1824.
Thomas T. Thompson-Lucinda Marks, October 9, 1824.
Henry Kelly-Sallie Bingham, October 14, 1824.
*Alexander Landman-Sally Dumend, October 18, 1824.
John Duncan-Elizabeth Beauchamp, October 29, 1824.
James Cannady-Margaret Dennison, November 11, 1824.
John Metcalf-Harriett Winkler, November 29, 1824.
Sterling Hall-Elizabeth Bassett, December 3, 1824.
*Samuel Johnson-Hannah Howard, December 13, 1824.
Isom Barker-Patsy Roberts, December 21, 1824.
William Kennady-Frances Clarkson, December 30, 1824.
*Robert M. Synder-Sarah D. Bye, January 3, 1825.
*John Hathaway-Martha Roley, January 10, 1825.
*Josiah Haynes-Frances Howard, February 3, 1825.
*William Margrave-Margaret Travis, February 7, 1825.
*Joseph Stinnet-Sarah Stearman, March 6, 1827.
Andrew Jones-Hannah Huston, January 1, 1829.
James H. Bourland-Elizabeth Gabbert, January 3, 1829.
Raphael Johnston-Elizabeth Ross, January 5, 1829.
Richard Millay-Mary Murphey, January 5, 1829.
*Barnett Johnson-Sary Howard, January 12, 1829.
Samuel Haynes-Mary Ann Barnhill, January 13, 1829.
Henry T. Priest-Mary Ann Pointer, January 20, 1829.
Harrison Dawson- Sally Bassitt, January 27, 1829.
George Brown-Milly Morgan, January 31, 1829.
*David Williams-Rebecca Doway, February 10, 1829.
Thompson Tucker-Polly Tanner, February 10, 1829.
Jonas McDaniel-Sussanah McIntire, February 14, 1829.
Jesse Gray-Mary Everly, March 2, 1829.
Sanford Tanner-Elizabeth Waltrip, March 7, 1829.
James Hunt-Hannah Minton, March 17, 1829.
Joshua Murphey-Elizabeth Rowland, March 23, 1829.
James Husk-Matilda Lancaster, April 13, 1829.
Stephen Henning-Mariah Drury, April 25, 1829.
John Simmons-Hannah Lynn, May 30, 1829.
Joseph S. Stone-Ann Adkins, June 9, 1829.
Daniel Murphy-Harriett Kelly, July 11, 1829.
Samuel R. Rogers-Sarah Morgan, July 18, 1829.
George Husk-Charlotte G. Kelly, July 27, 1829.
Ignatius A. Spaulding-Ann Allen, August 29, 1829.
William Johnson-Elizabeth Huston, September 7, 1829.
Abraham Hoglan-Catherine Tanner, September 8, 1829.
William Jones-Elizabeth Johnson, September 9, 1829.
Osburn King-Martha Melburn Dawson, September 28, 1829.
Uzal Lusk-Ann Cutley, October 3, 1829.
*Jarrett Floyd-Jane Strain, October 5, 1829.
*John Kennady-Sally Crabtree, 1829.
George Duncan-George Frazier, October 12, 1829.
John T. Mosely-Polly Little, October 20, 1829.

*Thomas P. William-Elizabeth Pointer, October 27, 1829.
Alexander Peacece-Missourie Lawrence, October 28, 1829.
Willett Holmes-Amelia R. Cummins, October 29, 1829.
William Gilison-Jemima Baird, November 7, 1829.
John W. Lanham-Letitia Jackson, November 20, 1829.
Simon Rowland-Lucinda Lottisman, December 8, 1829.
*John Griffin-Sally M. Anderson, December, 1829.
Nathaniel Bingham-Jane Hendrick, December 15, 1829.
Thomas T. Howard-Persis Barnhill, December 22, 1829.
James S. White-Dicy L. McFarland, January 8, 1830.
James W. Dennis-Pricilla Herring, January 12, 1830.
James Baird-Phebe Gilison, January 18, 1830.
Michael Wallace-Treacy Coomes, January, 1830.
Aaron C. Jewett-Lucy C. McFarland, January 24, 1830.
*Catton Peddicord-Elizabeth Kelly, February 2, 1830.
Joel Stinnett-Luticia Nelson, March 3, 1830.
*Benj. Layton-Polly Pots, March, 1830.
*Charles W. Taylor-Lucy Chambers, March 15, 1830.
Wm. Anderson-Susan Horseman, March, 1830.
Jesse L. McCracken-Isabella Harris, March 19, 1830.
Henry Stinnett-Elizabeth Stirman, March 25, 1830.
Eldred L. Glover-Lucinda Griffith, March 31, 1830.
Cornelius Westerfield-Rebecca Cooper, March 31, 1830.
Wm. Bell-Anne Thompson, April 12, 1830.
*John S. Robinson-Barbarry Galloway, May 3, 1830.
James D. Hanna-Martha Moseley, May 17, 1830.
John Bannon-Jane Miller, May 24, 1830.
Henry Lane-Elizabeth G. Nelson, May 26, 1830.
Wm. Royal-Mary Lanham, June 11, 1830.
Geo. W. Carey-Eliza Gabbard, June 14, 1830.
John Roberts-Louisa Bates, June 22, 1830.
*John Henderson-Malinda C. Roberts, August 14, 1830.
Wm. Burrow-Sally Mallay, August 26, 1830.
David Crews-Sally Bryant, September 25, 1830.
David Ewen-Elizabeth Miller, October 2, 1830.
Elisha Adams-Mildred S. Clarkson, October 18, 1830.
Presley Moseley-Polly Crow, October 18, 1830.
Dudley Bevins-Margaret Shadwic, November 1, 1830.
Robert Moseley-Martha French, November 8, 1830.
*John Tanner-Sally Downs, November 22, 1830.
*Luke Waltrip-Elizabeth Wall, November 27, 1830.
*Jackson Dollerit-Kezzy Bartlett, December 2, 1830.
*Wm. T. Patterson-Mary T. Wright, December 15, 1830.
Mathew C. Young-Hannah Likens, December 15, 1830.
Henry Roberts-Delilah Pinkston, December 18, 1830.
John Lucas-Margaret May, December 18, 1830.
Allen Baughn-Elizabeth Baughn, December 29, 1830.
*Wm. Housley-Elizabeth Davis, January 3, 1831.
John Barnett-Susan Short, January 10, 1831.
Thomas Vittetoe-Deborah P. Shop, January 15, 1831.
Richard Norris-Cynthia Epperson, February 15, 1831.
Richard Butcher-Fannie Richardson, February 16, 1831.
Johnathan Tanner-Catherine Hendricks, March 12, 1831.
Jacob Miller-Martha Whitter, March 14, 1831.
Dillas Dyer-Elizabeth Chambers, March 18, 1831.
Solomon Howard-Hannah Johnson, March 22, 1831.
Joseph Dyson-Matilda Smith, March 23, 1831.
George L. Williams-Eliza L. Beckley, March 23, 1831.
John McDowell-Nancy Morris, March 31, 1831.
Daniel Ward-Eliza Ward, April 5, 1831.
Byrd Chambers-Jane Wright, April 21, 1831.

Samuel Barker-Rhoda Kellams, April 23, 1831.
Jesse Fry-Polly Short, June 18, 1831.
James C. Kinneer-May Adams, June 14, 1831.
Louis Early-Milly Stinnett, July 28, 1831.
Lewis Adkins-May Ann McDowell, August 12, 1831.
*Thos. N. Hart-Caroline M. N. Harris, August 15, 1831.
Benj. B. Blincoe-Louisa Juliet Daviess, September 10, 1831.
James Howard-Magdaline Jackson, October 10, 1831.
Benj. Bell-Rachael E. Pierce, October 12, 1831.
Richard Beall-Lucinda Head, October 18, 1831.
Joseph Lanham-Nancy Rice, October, 1831.
William Head-Catherine C. Jarboe, November 10, 1831.
William Lancaster-Fanny Horn, November 21, 1831.
Burrel Jackson-Nancy Croley, November 14, 1831.
William Kirk-Susan Bassett, December 12, 1831.
Samuel Hendrick-Polly Ward, December 26, 1831.
Willis Smith-Phebe Taylor, January 2, 1832.
James Clark-Hannah Adams, January 11, 1832.
*John W. Sallee-Elizabeth Hyatt, January 17, 1832.
Elisha Burton-Elizabeth Barnhill, January 19, 1832.
Cornelius Barker-Rachael Barnett, January 30, 1832.
James M. Kirkham-Malinda May, February 13, 1832.
Amos Bennett-Judith Lloyd, March 12, 1832.
Craven C. Boswell-Margaret Glenn, March 19, 1832.
Robert P. Sharp-Frances Tapscott, April 2, 1832.
Elijah Comstock-Tabina Holmes, May 3, 1832.
Willis Hemmingway-Elizabeth Tompkins, June 4, 1832.
Johnathan G. Taylor-Susan E. Hawes, June 20, 1832.
Nathaniel Wornell-Doris Campbell, June 30, 1832.
Elisha J. Kellams-Lucinda Kelly, July 7, 1832.
Volentine M. Husk-Malinda Kelly, July 7, 1832.
Thos. W. Watkins-Malinda Kirkpatrick, July 9, 1832.
Jacob Shaw-Sophia Black, July 13, 1832.
Henry Martin-Malinda Sheckler, July 14, 1832.
Spottswood T. Heintle-Elizabeth Thompson, July 16, 1832.
Richard Walker-Mary Eperson, July 18, 1832.
Charley K. Newton-Sally Cummins, July 27, 1832.
Alfred E. Harris-Barbary Mortin, August 3, 1832.
George Gabbert-Mary Cooney, August 4, 1832.
Thomas W. Jarvis-Judith Johnson, August, 1832.
Isaac C. Whayne-Harriett E. Pointer, August 28, 1832.
Adam Winkler-Lettie Harrison, September 1, 1832.
Henry Campbell-Abbagail Noble, September 1, 1832.
*Joshua Taylor-Mary Fry, September 15, 1832.
Thomas J. Kirkham-Mary May, September 25, 1832.
Henry Ludwick-Martha Carland, September 18, 1832.
John Tanner-Eliza Downs, September 29, 1832.
John Dobins-Sarah Taylor, October 12, 1832.
Joseph Arnold-Ann Bunn, October 22, 1832.
James Campbell-Margaret Campbell, October 27, 1832.
Stephen Dawson-Catherine Griffin, October 30, 1832.
Charley Sosh-Martha Wornell, November 13, 1832.
Loyd Pelicord-Malina May, November 13, 1832.
Elijah Rafferty-Margaret Howel, November 26, 1832.
Stephen V. Rogers-Lucinda Lenerre, December 3, 1832.
Jefferson Cox-Cynthia Cotrell, December 7, 1832.
Thos. W. Sneed-Aleindia Tapscott, December 13, 1832.
Joshua Baker-C. Griffith, December 22, 1832.
Wm. H. Johnson-Mary A. Ralston, December 25, 1832.
Elisha Barker-Mahala Horn, December 29, 1832.
Samuel Hendricks-Charlotte Shaw, December 31, 1832.
John H. McFarland-Harriett Leaman, January 11, 1833.

James Stewart-Nancy Lashbrook, January 14, 1833.
George Vanada-Lucretia Harris, January 21, 1833.
Jos. M. Potts-Eliza Jane Higdon, February 9, 1833.
James Estes-Elizabeth Jett, February 11, 1833.
James Jordon, Jr.-Sophia Kelly, February 18, 1833.
James Griffin-Anne E. Duncan, February 25, 1833.
Elijah Griffin-Sarah Ann Miller, February 25, 1833.
*Alfred Acres-Mary Person, March 15, 1833.
Balum May-Sarah Evans, March 18, 1833.
Elisha Marks-Elizabeth Lashbrook, March 23, 1833.
Joseph M. Kelly-Elizabeth Newton, April 1, 1833.
William G. Slaughter-Ann G. Tappscott, May 16, 1833.
*Benedict McDaniel-Malinda Leathers, July 5, 1833.
John G. Galloway-Elica Williams, July 8, 1833.
Wm. N. Mason-Emeline Crow-July 9, 1833.
Timothy Oflynn-Miss F. Clary, July 10, 1833.
Henry McManner-Emelina Lockett, March 26, 1833.
*Benedict J. Aud-Lucinda E. Head, August 12, 1833.
George Jones-Mary Jane Johnson, March 17, 1834.
Wesley Lashbrook-Sally Wright, September 2, 1833.
Wm. Taylor-Elizabeth Miller, September, 1833.
Thos. P. Vance-Nancy P. Pinkston, September, 1833.
John May, Jr.-Elizabeth Davis, September 9, 1833.
Nance P. Ramsey-Polly A. Davis, September 13, 1833.
Amos Medcalf-Pamelia Harrison, September 14, 1833.
Wm. Purcell-Ann Haynes, October 5, 1833.
*Chas. H. Wall-Mary Waltrip, October 5, 1833.
R. F. Bibb (Richard)-Sarah Tapscott, October 10, 1833.
*Ralf Crabtree-Frances Wall, October 15, 1833.
*Henry McDaniel-Ann Monarch, October 25, 1833.
Thomas Kelly-Elizabeth Mason, October 20, 1833.
Robert A. Baird-Betsy Crow, October 31, 1833.
*John Keith-Conna Kinney, November 4, 1833.
John Humphrey-Virginia Christian, November 12, 1833.
*Phillip Cripps-Ann Howard, October 8, 1833.
Howard G. Taylor-Elton Riley, November 18, 1833.
Adkins Wall-Elizabeth Chambers, November 22, 1833.
Enos McCormick-Jemmiah Newton, December 9, 1833.
Wm. B. Williams-Mary Miller, December 12, 1833.
*Philip Gray-Lucinda Taylor, December 17, 1833.
Wm. Inglehart-Lydia Shickley, December 23, 1833.
*Elijah Atherton-Mary J. Atherton, December 23, 1833.
Edward Worthington-Alcinda Crabtree, December 24, 1833.
James Polk-Sarah Ann Boswell, January 25, 1834.
George Westerfield-Sally Dawson, January 27, 1834.
*Samuel Hall-Hannah Welch, January 28, 1834.
Richard Vanmeter-Elizabeth E. Fulkerson, February 7, 1834.
Thos. T. Chapman-Prudence T. Huston, February 13, 1834.
William E. Young-Mary Griffith, February 19, 1834.
Thomas B. Haynes-Susan Duncan, February 24, 1834.
Minor E. Pate-Rebecca H. May, March 8, 1834.
Benj. Mors-Sally Short, March 12, 1834.
Joseph Ludwick-Elizabeth McDaniel, March 15, 1834.
John Watkins-Elizabeth Kerns, March 15, 1834.
John Maddox or Maddon-Zilphy Remmington, March 18, 1834.
Jesse Crabtree-Mary Smith, April 7, 1834.
*Samuel Kenney-Prudy Keith, April 12, 1834.
*Henry Higdon-Martha E. Hazel, April 22, 1834.
Issac Hudson-Mary Isbell, April 24, 1834.
George T. Moore-Mary Jane Robertson, April 25, 1834.
James Martin-Nancy Carland, April 30, 1834.
Wm. Protsman-Mary Kelly, May 5, 1834.

Silas Mason-Frances Ashby, May 27, 1834.
James Little-Agnes Morgan, May 31, 1834.
Benjamin Nelson-Ann Turner, June 2, 1834.
Nicholas Richards-Elizabeth Cotter, June 15, 1834.
Robert Roby-Mary T. Wells, June 20, 1834.
John Parker-Rebecca Lancaster, July 9, 1834.
John B. Brand-Sarah Moseley, July 29, 1834.
*Amos Smith-Anna Gray, August 5, 1834.
Benedict J. Clark-Mary Leathers, August 25, 1834.
Henry Hadley-Polly Lynn, September 2, 1834.
Benjamin Rafferty-Margaret Winstead, September 9, 1834.
*John W. Galloway-Lydia Lamb, September 23, 1834.
William G. Kenney-Hannah Gray, October 4, 1834.
Thomas Pierce-Mileha P. Bristow, October 6, 1834.
Napoleon B. Robertson-Elizabeth A. Harris, October 7, 1834.
Zachariah Galloway-Levina Artherbery, October 11, 1834.
*George Little-Betsy A. Leachman, November 5, 1834.
*John C. Robertson-Elizabeth McNalley, October 8, 1834.
William Field-Louisa McFarland, November 17, 1834.
John Lumpkins-Emery Rafferty, December 2, 1834.
James H. Long-Catherine C. Edwards, December 8, 1834.
Shadrack Tennison-Harriett Coateney, December 8, 1834.
James Hiatt-Martha Ann Rolin, December 13, 1834.
B. Duncan-Sarah B. May, December 22, 1834.
Isaac Ambrose-Lucy Huston, December 22, 1834.
Creed Burton-Mary Ward, December 24, 1834.
Richard Millay-Ruth Williams, December 31, 1834.
Isaac Cosby-Susan Jordon, September 8, 1834.
Obadiah Gordon-Mary Ann Miller, January 13, 1835.
*Joseph Hudson-Matilda Vaughn, February 2, 1835.
William Tanner-Susan Layton, February 9, 1835.
Wilson Waltrip-Susan Holeman, February 10, 1835.
Faniel A. T. Fields-Mary Ann McKinney, February 11, 1835.
Wyatt Lucas-Nancy Isbell, February 28, 1835.
J. A. Brook-Ann Fenwick, March 28, 1835.
*C. J. Mason-Ellen Morgan, April 15, 1835.
Owen Thomas-Elizabeth Ashby, April 13, 1835.
David Stone-Sarah Morgan, April 25, 1835.
*Westbery Overton-Fanny Fletcher, April 26, 1835.
James M. Overton-Polly Jane Beauchamp, April 29, 1835.
John D. Marks-Judith A. Leaman, May 11, 1835.
Robert Rodes-Rachael Church, May 21, 1835.
Richard Phillips-Lydia C. Riley, June 23, 1835.
Talbert Atherton-Catherine Taylor, July 15, 1835.
*James Welch-Elizabeth J. Chamberlain, July 20, 1835.
Stephen R. Williams-Malinda Downs, July 29, 1835.
*Nazra Jones-Sally Kelly, August 8, 1835.
*Wesley Chamberlain-Betsy Pearson, August 13, 1835.
Henry Campbell-Elizabeth Lanters, August 19, 1835.
Joseph Fuqua-Nancy Norseman, August 24, 1835.
George Horseman-Tabitha Boone, August 29, 1835, (return).
Richard Tanner-Minerva Jane Jennings, August 18, 1835.
Andrew J. Walden-Elizabeth Winstead, August 31, 1835.
Wm. P. Horseman-Elizabeth J. Morris, September 5, 1835.
*Wm. Barnett-Judith Ann Crabtree, September 5, 1835.
Joseph M. Dawson-Elizabeth Miller, September 7, 1835.
Mathew Murphey-Polly Moore, September 25, 1835.
Jesse W. Chapman-Susan W. Ellis, October 26, 1835.
Wm. Reddish-Polly Ann McDonnall, October 26, 1835.
David Galloway-Lucinda Field, November 2, 1835.
Thomas Blair-Mary Ann Jones, November 4, 1835.
Asa T. Parker-Elizabeth T. Pinkston, October 12, 1835.

William P. Mobberly-Lucy Haynes, November 20, 1835.
Morton Harris-Lavina Keith, November 28, 1835.
Samuel Kennedy-Lavina Scott, December 4, 1835.
Joseph Norris-Sarah T. Beckley, December 21, 1835.
George M. Dawson-Mary Ann Beckley, December 21, 1835.
John L. Kirk-Susan Cottrell, December 28, 1835.
Jordon Pinkston-Elizabeth Field, December 31, 1835.
Edward T. Long-Margaret Jarbo, January 9, 1836.
William W. Jones-Elenor Bristow, January 14, 1836.
George Field-Susan Tenner, January 20, 1836.
Wm. Beall-Katherine Higdon, January 5, 1836.
Jacob Talbott-Elizabeth Field, January 23, 1836.
Edward D. Bennett-Elizabeth McFarland, January 27, 1836.
*Alfred Crabtree-Norsissa Kennedy, January 29, 1836.
Isaac Mills-Sarah Nunn, February 1, 1836.
*Wes P. Bristow-Elizabeth Bristow, February 25, 1836.
Irah H. Moss-Lucy Barnett, February 25, 1836.
Wm. B. Williams-Lucy B. Hendricks, March 4, 1836.
Erasemus D. Beauchamp-Caroline Evans, March 8, 1836.
Soloman H. Bishop-Fanny H. Robertson, May 6, 1836.
Joseph Harrison-Margaret L. Gore, May 7, 1836.
Washington Young-Rachael Simpson, May 8, 1836.
Pleasant P. Frels-Susan J. McKinney, May 17, 1836.
Elliott Ward-Jane M. Ward, May 26, 1836.
John G. Ewing-Mary Jane Crawford, June 9, 1836.
Abraham-Hosley-Levina Bunch, June 25, 1836.
James C. Letcher-Sarah A. Horne, June 27, 1836.
Price Longest-Hannah Isbell, July 5, 1836.
Strawther Humphrey-Hannah Horrell, July 27, 1836.
Daniel A. McCormack-Mary B. Newton, July 27, 1836.
William Ritchy-Jennie Barker, August 29, 1836.
John B. Hall-Margaret Taylor, August 29, 1836.
*John McMillen-Susan Galloway, September 6, 1836.
Hardin Ellis-Elizabeth Dolin, September 9, 1836.
Thomas Tanner-Julia Ann Whitaker, July 16, 1836.
*Miles Pender-Sally Ann Lee, September 23, 1836.
Wm. Henrick-Eliza Williams, September 24, 1836.
*Wesley M. Little-Henrietta Waltrip, October 1, 1836.
Alfred G. Yewel-Mary M. Coomes, October 3, 1836.
Isaac Ambers-Nancy Bishop, October 14, 1836.
*Wm. Galloway-Martha Crabtree, October 24, 1836.
Wm. O. Smith-Mary Jane Wallace, October 26, 1836.
Wm. J. Johnson-Eliza Bristow, October 29, 1836
*Stephen Newton-Polly Crabtree, October 31, 1836.
*Washington Anderson-Patsy Baker, November 7, 1836.
Zachariah Pinkston-Nancy Pinkston, November 14, 1836.
Jeremiah Barnhill-Elizabeth Ann Ware, November 14, 1836.
John Dawson-Bethany Buckhannan, November 21, 1836.
James P. Hays-Susan Norris, November 22, 1836.
Wm. I. Jackson-Audelina B. Adams, November 24, 1836.
E. T. Long,-M. Jarbo, January 9, 1836.
Thomas Howard-Nancy T. Howard, November 20, 1836.
Young E. Davidson-Nancy E. Vance, November 28, 1836.
Robert Barnhill-Mary Ware, November 30, 1836.
Richard Head-Elizabeth Pool, December 12, 1836.
Augustine H. Talbot-Lucinda M. Crawford, December 21, 1836.
Janius B. Alexander-Kucy F. Dades, December 22, 1836.
Edmund Johnson-Elizabeth Johnson, January 2, 1837.
C. R. Clarke (Charles)-Elizabeth McDaniel, January 5, 1837.
George W. Rodes-Lucy Jane Dawson, January 14, 1837.
Edwin Hissley-Martha Hudson, January 23, 1837.
James Roberts-Elizabeth Little, January 27, 1837.

Silas Barker-Mary Horn, January 30, 1837.
Byrd Bunch-Jane Chism, February 4, 1837.
John Ernest-Matilda May, February 7, 1837.
*John Ford-Nancy Haynes, February 20, 1837.
*Henry E. Tanner-Jane Burden, February 22, 1837.
*Robert Hall, Jr.-Sally Jane Foster, February 28, 1837.
John Miller-Cintha Hunt, March 4, 1837.
Henry E. Hamner-Elizabeth Ward, March 23, 1837.
Wm. W. Bonner-Jane H. Griffith, May 11, 1837.
Thomas Norris-Sarah Vittitow, May 23, 1837.
Franville C. Brown-Mrs. Priscilla A. Davis, May 27, 1837.
Elijah Hatfield-Emaline Morgan, May 29, 1837.
*James Campbell-Mrs. Patsy Ash, June 1, 1837.
Wm. R. Riggs-Miss A. C. Scott, June __, 1837.
A. Fitts-Miss Lightfoot, June 3, 1837.
Richard Holdings-Miss Sarah R. Griffith, June 5, 1837.
Alicy Ford-Lindsey Burton, June 15, 1837.
Wm. M. Calloway-Rebecca Myers, June 15, 1837.
James Johnson-Sarah A. Kallams, June 17, 1837.
*J. Crabtree-J. Shadwick, June 19, 1837.
Wm. C. Stowers or Stowart-Miss Judith C. Ennison, July 8, 1837.
Gardner Runnage-Julia A. Owens, July 10, 1837.
Felix G. Davis-Kezia McNett, July 24, 1837.
Edmond W. Frazier-_____ Lashbrooks, August 2, 1837.
Chas. A. Jarbo-Mary Wathen, September 5, 1837.
Washington A. Morgan-Martha A. Haydon, September 4, 1837.
Jackson Talbott-Julian Shomaker, September 20, 1837.
Joseph Hearring-Margaret Morgan, October 6, 1837.
Alexander McDaniel-Elizabeth Weaks, October 9, 1837.
Joseph G. Cassaday-Jane H. Pointer, October 19, 1837.
James T. Overall-Rachael W. Davis, October 22, 1837.
*Sampson Stone-Amanda McKay, November 2, 1837.
Henry Speak-Margaret Blandford, November 9, 1837.
Samuel Lott-Leah Taylor, November 13, 1837.
*Edward Metcalf-Margaret Brown, November 20, 1837.
*James Hillyer-Juliet L. Tapscott, December 5, 1837.
Simpson Lee-Sarah A. Mosley, December 8, 1837.
John Galoway-Susan J. Galloway, December 11, 1837.
Jesse B. Moseley-Joanna Downs, December 14, 1837.
Edward D. Friel-Nancy Davidson, December 15, 1837.
Joseph A. McVar-Sally Davis, December 21, 1837.
Alexander G. Hollis-Catherine M. Roberts, December 22, 1837.
William T. Beauchamp-Sally A. Thompson, December 23, 1837.
*Robert P. All-Sarah E.Steele, January 4, 1838.
Ignatius Mattingly (Benedict)-Eliza Monarch, January 12, 1838.
Bazel B. Malin-Julian Nally, January 27, 1838.
*William Harris-Elizabeth Torrance, February 2, 1838.
*William Torrance-Elizabeth Womal, February 2, 1838.
McGee Agnew-Sarah Ashby, February 3, 1838.
John L. Laywood-Sarah Roberts, February 5, 1838.
Morrison L. Henderson-Caroline Polly, February 7, 1838.
Isaac Miller-Julian Sutton, February 7, 1838.
Henry Howard-Jane M. Felix, February 17, 1838.
David Westerfield-Elizabeth Moseley, February 19, 1838.
William F. Hawes-Aurelia Combe, February 21, 1838.
William B. Head-Margaret A. Bell, February 27, 1838.
William Ward-Mariah Morgan, February 27, 1838.
John Howard-Mary Johnson, March 6, 1838.
Wm. B. Williams-Nancy Jackson, March 8, 1838.
William Morgan-_____ Fuqua, March 12, 1838.
*Randal Turpin-Elizabeth Barnett, March 17, 1838.

(114)

Isaac Strain-Rebecca Brown, March 31, 1838.
James Wallace-Nancy Layton, April 2, 1838.
David J. Miller-Lucy Jane Hull, April 9, 1838.
Jonathan Bozarth-Sally Jones, April 23, 1838.
James Bennett-Jane Tanner, April 28, 1838.
Hardin C. Riley-Elizabeth Smith, May 7, 1838.
John P. Wells-Leona Morgan, May 21, 1838.
John May-Lutitia McFarland, May 23, 1838.
Joseph Fugua-Eliza Jane Ford, May 30, 1838.
Grover Howard-Susan W. Owen, June 1, 1838.
Thomas Ransom-Hannah Faith, June 7, 1838.
*John Bristow-Caroline M. Wilman, June 19, 1938.
William A. Taylor-Nancy B. Porter, June 25, 1838.
Joseph Thomas-Nancy Odin, July 18, 1838.
John G. Duncan-Marah Ann Head, August 10, 1838.
Grayson T. Lashbrook-Emily Forman, August 13, 1838.
John G. McFarland-Delia B. Griffith, August 17, 1838.
James M. Jennings-Rachael M. Cary, August 25, 1838.
Tho. W. Kincheloe-Manerva McFarland, September 18, 1838.
*Enoch Early-Habbach-I. Dunn, September 28, 1838.
Andrew Jackson-Mary Lacklin, October 27, 1838.
James H. Hughes-Sarah M. Worthington, November 1, 1838.
Edw. Oden-Susan Calhoun, November 3, 1838.
*James Holloway-Miss L. M. Smith, September 4, 1838.
Young J. Cravin-Mildred Davis, October 29, 1838.
Addison Burton-Martha Lockhart, November 19, 1838.
John T. Howard-Levina Smith, November 27, 1838.
*Peter Ashby-Nancy Downs, December 3, 1838.
Geo. Scarbough-Miss C. A. Thompson, December 4, 1838.
James J. Bowlds-Elizabeth Jones, December 7, 1838.
Sam'l Denton-Lucy Taylor, September 22, 1838.
William Kimberlain-Susanna Jones, September 25, 1838.
Andrew J. Mahon-Frances Johnson, December 20, 1838.
Robert Williams-Sarah Ann Johnson, December 21, 1838.
John McFarland-Indiana B. Elam, December 23, 1838.
Samuel Henderson-Susan Ann Parker, January 5, 1839.
Preston H. Brown-Matilda J. Liman, January 7, 1839.
Joshua G. Crow-Jemima McCormack, January 7, 1839.
John Allen-Nancy A. Anderson, January 16, 1839.
Luke Waltrip-Margaret J. Faith, January 18, 1839.
William Faith-Jane Wall, January 18, 1839.
Thomas Henry-Elizabeth Polly, January 19, 1839.
*Cecelin Bell-Elizabeth Head, January 19, 1838.
Isaac McDaniel-Nancy McDaniel, January 20, 1839.
Joseph Keith-Eliza Aere, February 11, 1839.
John Gisson-Nancy B. Riggs, February 11, 1839.
Robert M. Duncan-Eliza Jane Bell, February 16, 1839.
John H. Napper-Ann Stone, February 16, 1839.
Stephen Roland-Margaret Tolliman, March 9, 1839.
Jasheth Skinner-Mary Ann Obinskain, March 11, 1839.
Harman Hendrix-Mary Jane Thompson, March 11, 1839.
Austin L. Montgomery-Rosa Ann Carrico, March 21, 1839.
Henry Roberts-Elizabeth Moffett, March 27, 1839.
Willis Roberts, Jr.-Nancy J. Hudson, April 3, 1839.
Alexander Howard-Rebecca Pender, April 10, 1839.
William Ward-Rachael A. C. Helm, April 16, 1839.
William Curry-Mary Jane Roberts, September 12, 1839.
*William W. Chambers-Elizabeth P. Morrison, April 16, 1839.
James Hill-Charlotte McDaniel, May 4, 1839.
John H. Davidson-Nancy Webb, May 6, 1839.
Benj. All-Maria Henning, May 9, 1839.
John B. Higgins-Eliza Higdon, May 10, 1839.

James A. W. Haggard-Emily V. Courtney, May 20, 1839.
Stephen Hansford-Elizabeth Crews, May 21, 1839.
Thomas W. Shoemaker-Elizabeth Lackland, June 1, 1839.
James Ballard-Lydia Casey, June 1, 1839.
Tinson Stout-Harriett Bristow, June 3, 1839.
James Pipes-Rachael Young, June 6, 1839.
James Lackland-Louisa Shomaker, June 8, 1839.
James Bunch-Sarah Bartlett, June 14, 1839.
*Wm. T. Walker-Polly Ann Courtney, June 25, 1839.
Joseph P. Waltrip-Nancy Jane Eidron, July 9, 1839.
Joseph Carlin-Frances A. Porter, July 11, 1839.
James Lasnbrook-Nancy Birkhead, July 13, 1839.
Benj. B. Whitaker-Margaret A. Howard, July 15, 1839.
Lovill B. Nevill-Mary Jane Gabbert, July 13, 1839.
Peter Tichenor-Mariah Shoemaker, July 14, 1839.
*Hugh B. Winstead-Jane Rafferty, July 20, 1839.
Wm. N. Pool-Susan All, July 26, 1839.
Wm. Bartlett-Charlotte Ford, August 5, 1839.
Wm. H. Crabtree-Amanda F. Baird, August 5, 1839.
Geo. W. Chapman-Hannah Ellis, August 12, 1839.
Henry Smith-Elizabeth Marlow, August 14, 1839.
James G. Harrison-Pricilla Dadimager, August 27, 1839.
*Isaac Lambert-Louisa Daniel, August 23, 1839.
Felix Blandford-Mary E. Montgomery, September 7, 1839.
John C. Cary-Mary H. Griffith, September 9, 1839.
Moses Benton-DelphineA. Henry, September 20, 1839.
John Jackson-Mary J.Adams, Septembre 28, 1839.
Lewis C. Anderson-Chanteller J. Gray, September 30, 1839.
Wm. Houston-Stella Crow, October 5, 1839.
Wm. Gibson-Mary M. Huston, October 5, 1839.
Thomas H. Hinton-Cynthia M. Miller, October 7, 1839.
James H. Hinton-Elizabeth Miller, October 7, 1839.
Benj. T. Gore-Nancy Hale, October 11, 1839.
Wm. Johnson-Lucreta Jarbo, October 11, 1839.
Joshua Bright-Martha Waltrip, October 22, 1839.
Joseph Wayne-Mary Rhodes, October 22, 1839.
Aaron Short-Nancy Steele, October 23, 1839.
Nathaniel Scales-Anney Shouts, September 25, 1839.
Wm. H. Torrington-Catherine C. Hollis, October 25, 1839.
John Taylor-Eliza Wilson, November 18, 1839.
*Aquilla Spray-Alcy Ann Williams, November 29, 1839.
James L. Gillim-Elizabeth Newson, November 29, 1839.
William Jett-Mary Ann James, December 2, 1839.
Wm. Prewett-Mary W. Ford, December 3, 1839.
*Henry Tanner-Ruth Smith, December 4, 1839.
*John Chamberlain-Martha Swain, December 9, 1839.
Thos. Brooks-Peggy Kelly, December 4, 1839.
David Richardson-Mary Walker, December 21, 1839.
Jno. O. Brown-Mary A. Brady, December 26, 1839.
Wm. Nanny-Eliz. Haydon, December 26, 1839.
*Joseph C. Moore-Mary Jane Hardy, January 6, 1840.
Edwin Freeles-Frances Davidson, January 13, 1840.
James Calhoun-Eliz Clary, January 4, 1840.
Granville Underwood-Isabella Jennings, January 18, 1840.
Jos. Higdon-Ann Mattingly, January 15, 1840.
Alfred McDaniel-Rasilla McDaniel, January 25, 1840.
Richard H. Hasel-Eliza Hennings, January 23, 1840.
Peter L. Anderson-Camilla Crow, January 29, 1840.
Geo. Galloway-Sallie Spray, February 8, 1840.
Thos. Hinton-Mary Ann Stout, February 12, 1840.
Squire L. Whittaker-Susan Anderson, February 12, 1840.
Alfred Jackson-Lucy Miller, February 19, 1840.

Robert F. Miller-Almira McFarland, February 19, 1840.
*Harrison Stowers-Elizabeth Balec, February 19, 1840.
Rezin McDaniel-Cynthia McDaniel, February 22, 1840.
Moses P. Fuqua-Louisa Phelon, February 24, 1840.
*Jno. Myers-Sarah Allen Potts, February 25, 1840.
Johnnie Thomas-Nancy Ashby, February 25, 1840.
Frederick L. Bransford-Eliza C. William, February 26, 1840.
*Jno. Crabtree-Louisa Shadwick, February 27, 1840.
Geo. Sample-Elvira Stearman, February 29, 1840.
Robt. Miller-Cordelia Anderson, March 3, 1840.
Willey Nevill-Judea Ann Gabbert, March 7, 1840.
Richerson Owen-Eliz. Johnson, March 10, 1840.
Loranzo Douthitt-Patience Cardwell, March 18, 1840.
Jno. T. Roberts-Clara Walker, March 30, 1840.
Alexander Harrison-Elizabeth Williams, April 15, 1840.
Nennett D. Coomes-Camilla M. Ford, April 20, 1840.
Henry Blair-Susan Ann Roger, April 21, 1840.
Stephen Ashby-Frances Thorpe, April 28, 1840.
Silas M. Moorman, Sarah S. Talbott, May 2, 1840.
B. P. Beauchamp-Salima Lashbrook, May 4, 1840.

JESSAMINE COUNTY MARRIAGES

(Contributed by Miss Frankie Coyle, Trabue Chapter)

Records from old marriage book copied from certificates.

John Aken-Susannah Johns, August 1, 1804.
Charles Alexander-Martha Moore Madison, December 4, 1821.
Beverly Allen-Elizabeth Davis, October 30, 1806.
Charley Allen-Elizabeth Gatewood, 1785.
Francis Allen-Elizabeth Madison, November 24, 1803.
Greenberry Allen-Anney Roberts, October 12, 1815.
John Allen-Polly Williams, January 25, 1804.
Elias Alsman-Betsy Richardson, June 27, 1820.
Hiram Alverson-Elizabeth Knox, October 4, 1811 or 21.
Asberry Amos-Lucy Bryers, January 20, 1811.
Aaron Anderson-Betsy Spalden, December 22, 1818.
Daniel Anthony-Elizabeth Williams, November 28, 1805.
Alexander Armstrong-Polly Wilson, January 6, 1803.
James Armstrong-Nancy Wilson, December 19, 1805.
Andrew Arnett-Edy Walters, October 6, 1815.
John Arnett-Abby Walters, November 1814.
Michael Arnspiger-Esther Bowman (Bowmer), August 19, 1804.
Michael Arthur-Amanda McFa. Martin (or Mastin), May 24, 1822.
Thomas Ashford-Ann Hawkins, February 24, 1814.
Dudley Baker-Peggy Newman, April 29, 1815.
James Baker-Polly Davis, 1812.
Peter Baker-Isabelle Veach, August 3, 1820.
John Barkley-Olly Singleton, April 18, 1805.
Samuel Barkley-Jane Singleton, February 23, 1804.
Joseph Barnett-Rosanna Ryland, April 11, 1816.
Wiley I. Barnes-Patsy C. Perkins, December 29, 1807.
George Barr-Phebie Bryan, December 30, 1802.
William Bateman-Betsy Wilson, January 20, 1803.
Kennedy Baxter-Kitty Gerard, October 6, 1818.
John Beckum-Sally Webster, August 15, 1816.
Elijah Bell-Susan Green, December 31, 1820.

Thomas Berry-Hannah Rice, May 15, 1799.
John Bishop-Hannah Welch, 1813.
James Black-Abigail Taylor, March 9, 1804.
Moses Black-Sarah Lowry, October 14, 1801.
Robert Blackwell-Nancy Coplin, September 20, 1820.
Robert Bunton-Polly Scott, July 5, 1820.
Berry Burk-Rhoda Berryman, November 8, 1818.
Joseph Burnell-Patsy McGraith, July 4, 1812.
Jonah Burton-Martha Gilmore, August 14, 1800.
Andrew Caldwell-Mary Williams, November 6, 1817.
William Caldwell-Nancy Roberts, February 7, 1804.
Abraham Callender-Nancy Nicholson, August 9, 1807.
Isaac Callender-Lucy Nicholson, September 14, 1803.
Thomas Carr-Patsy Young, April 1, 1806.
Thomas Carroll-Rebecca A. Walters, May 15, 1806.
John Carter-Ellenor Stephens, December 21, 1813.
Joshua Carter-Mary Hite, March 14, 1815.
Landon Carter—Sarah Bunnell, November 8, 1820.
Mathias Carter-Elizabeth Empson, September 10, 1809.
Abraham Castle-Sally Price, December 22, 1801.
Asa Chambers-Jane McCarty, December 18, 1806.
John Chowning-Polly Howser, April 2, 1818.
Thomas A. Clark-Mary Anderson, November 18, 1813.
William Claybrook-Elizabeth Arnspiger, 1812.
Daniel Cloud-Nancy Owen, January 13, 1800.
David Coffman-Catherine Cassell, May 30, 1811.
William Collier-Susannah Higbee, 1816.
Thomas Collins-Polly Cleveland, 1814.
Uriah Collins-Ally Lasewell, 1810.
Andrew Coolwell-Mary Williams, November 6, 1817.
Jesse Combs-Peggy Frost, June 15, 1801.
Jonah Combs-Catherine Gatewood, July 5, 1800.
James Conner-Janey Moore, 1811.
James R. Conner-Malinda Ewing, 1813.
Isaac Cook-Polly Stephens, 1808.
Ruben Cooley-Lucy South, December 21, 1820.
Isaac Coon-Polly Stephens, 1808.
Samuel Coons-Sally Thompson, March 3, 1816.
John Copeland-Rachel Nunen.
John Corrier-Nancy Zimmerman, April 22, 1817.
Robert Coyas (Cozur)-Betsy Keller, 1808.
Braxton Blake-Hester Reed, April 25, 1811.
Daniel L. Blakeman-Fanny King, January 14, 1814.
John Boatman-Elizabeth Hunter, January 28, 1800.
Robert Boatman-Mary A. Willis, December 22, 1807.
Robert Boatman-Nancy Willis, January 5, 1802.
Jesse Boatman-Sally Hunter, June 10, 1806.
Powhattan Boatright-Lucy Utley, 1815.
Wiliam Boatman-Elizabeth Willis, March 18, 1808.
Hugh Boga-Meliss Shanklin, May 9, 1801.
William Boger-Catherine Shreve, October 10, 1815.
John Bogin-Sarah Hunter, January 18, 1800.
Michael Boner-Maria Lewis, June 26, 1815.
George Boston-Polly Walster, April 24, 1812.
Daniel Bourne-Peggy Dillon, March 20, 1801.
Robert Bowmer-Caty Supinger, December 23, 1800.
William Boyd (Bogel?)-Catherine Shreve, October 10, 1815.
Shadrack Bradshaw-Polly Bradshaw, February 27, 1805.
Rezin Brasfrow (?)-Nancy Johnson, 1785.
Raison Brasher-Sally Fields, November 18, 1803.
Joseph Brinker-Polly Roberts, September 1, 1803.
James Briscoe-Catherine Thompson, March 15, 1818.

James Brittain-Polly Newman, Novembe 24, 1801.
Paskal Broadus-Ann Deboe, December 21, 1815.
Wm. Broughton-Polly Blackford, December 21, 1815.
James Brown-Margaret D. Read, January 6, 1814.
Richard P. Bruce-Elizabeth Bullett, March 25, 1814.
Waddle G. Bruce-Elizabeth Colvard, June 2, 1808.
Moses Bromfield-Rachel Quimby, March 5, 1815.
Walter Brumfield-Sally Woorley, September 13, 1821.
William Brumfield-Mary Grow, January 24, 1802.
George Brunner-Christene Brunner, October 9, 1815.
Jacob Bruner-Mahala Grimes, January 16, 1811.
James Bruster-Betsy Blunt, March 19, 1805.
David Bryan-Mildred Kersey, April 14, 1815.
George Bryant, Elizabeth Prowell, January 27, 1802.
George Bryan-Margaret Empson, April 8, 1808.
James Bryant-Susannah Procter, February 11, 1800.
John Bryant-Nancy Ponderter (Poindexter), 1785.
Levy Buchanan-Sally Sellers, December 18, 1804.
Robert Buckner-Clary Ammony, February 15, 1799.
Simeon Buford-Agnes Barr, August 21, 1800.
Josiah B. Bullock-Mary P. Clark, January 11, 1816.
William Craig-Peggy Walters, April 14, 1805.
George Crane-Lucinda Amos, November 28, 1814.
James Cravens-Elizabeth Proctor, 1808.
John Crow-Elizabeth Clubb, December 1, 1815.
Elijah Criswell-Elizabeth Rice, January 2, 1806.
Oliver Crumwell-Lucy Elkins, October 9, 1803.
Samuel Cumley-Ruthey Starr, March 15, 1818.
William Cummins-Elizabeth Campbell, August 3, 1815.
Lawrence Jones Daily-Eliza Morrison, 1811.
Woodford Curd-Jinney West, October 10, 1800.
David Dale-Lucy Gatewood, April 13, 1817.
Richard Dally-Susannah Helander, Februay 16, 1815.
Cornelius Darnaby-Eleanor Stonestreet, March 24, 1801.
Fortunatus Davenport-Martha Moore, January 28, 1812.
Richard Davidson-Polly Handley, January 13, 1815.
James Davis-Elizabeth Hawkins, Nov. 6, 1813.
Larkin Davis-Gorfuel Scott, November 6, 1813.
Martin Davis-Nancy Rickets, May 13, 1819.
Robert Davis-Deborah Hornbuckle, November 27, 1804.
Samuel Davis-Mary Panky, June 11, 1818.
John Dedman-Peggy Sandusky, 1809.
Edward Delaney-Margaret Mitchel, 1805.
Andrew Delman-Betsy Brunner, May 19, 1816.
Asa Demos-Elizabeth Heifner (Heixner?), April 18, 1816.
Richard Dennis-Mary F. Garnett, 1812.
David Dickerson-Nancy Rice, September 21, 1801.
Fountain Dickerson-Polly Rice, July 19, 1814.
John Dickerson-Polly Covington, July 25, 1799.
Lewis Dickerson-Kitty H. Price, November 6, 1813.
William Dickerson-Ester Riser, August 4, 1806.
George Dougherty-Hannah Boyd, November 12, 1801.
John Daugherty-Elizabeth Miles, October 19, 1801.
William Dougherty-Eleanor Dougherty, 1806.
Joseph Douhunner-Elizabeth Miller, 1819.
Banoni P. Downing-Polly Finley, June 1, 1814.
Jeremiah Downing-Phoebe Stephens, (no date).
William Downs-Susan Crowder, March 22, 1804.
James Downey-Elizabeth Carson, December 10, 1800.
William Drake-Agness Cunningham, March 19, 1799.
Peter F. Drane-Lucinda Smith, January 14, 1819.

Ruben Drysdale-Sally Walker, July 13, 1815.
Absolem Duerson-Fanny Humphry, September 16, 1817.
William Duncan-Nancy Blackford, 1813.
James Dunn-Martha Morrison, December 24, 1818.
James Edwards-Matilda Edwards, April 1799.
John T. Edwards-Judith Young, January 28, 1813.
Robert Edwards-Rebecca Sodusky, October 18, 1812.
Thomas Edwards-Elizabeth Walters, May 20, 1802.
Elliott Elkin-Sally Botts, March 31, 1801.
Benjamine Elledge-Catey Reynolds, April 7, 1806.
Johnston Ellicott-Sethie Marrs, 1812.
Cornelius Empson, Eleanor Greenwood, December 14, 1818.
James Ennis-Lucinda Lewis, August 19, 1819.
William Evans-Elizabeth Thomas, May 21, 1816.
Aaron Farra-Sally Need, March 21, 1816.
Silas Favour-Mary Suls (?), 1812.
John Furgurson-Susan Barry, May 11, 1800.
John Finn-Lettie Walters, October 8, 1816.
Martin Finn-Frances Organ, March 16, 1801.
Richard Finn-Polly Cole, Jan. 23, 1805.
William Finn-Sally Walters, November 9, 1801.
John Fishback-Lucy N. Hord, December 24, 1801.
William Fisher-Elizabeth Carroll, April 13, 1802.
William Fisher-Martha Lee, June 11, 1815.
Ellis Fitzgeril-Polly Humbil, July 9, 1806.
John Flemming-Jane Rusk, February 20, 1806.
James Fletcher-Sally Scott, November 11, 1802.
Davis Floyd-Elizabet Davis, March 20, 1809.
Merrit Forbus-Mary Hughes, no date.
John Fosee-Judith Prewitt, August 16, 1815.
Edmund Foster-Betsy Hawkins, October 24, 1805.
Jeremiah Frayer-Martha Walters, October 18, 1804.
Abraham Froman-Betsy Elkin, January 21, 1806.
James Frost-Nancy Young, November 6, 1813.
Stephen Frost-Jane Walker, 1804.
Jacob Fry-Rebecca Keller, no date.
Abraham Fulkerson-Ann Stonestreet, February 24, 1807.
Samuel Gaily-Nancy Scott, October 25, 1803.
Benj. Galey-Betsy Woods, November 19, 1800.
John Garner-Jinney Moss, 1806.
Larkin Garnett-Lucy True, May 23, 1806.
William Garnett-Nancy Ward, July 17, 1812.
William Gates-Mary Dickerson, November 24, 1804.
Richard Gatewood-Sally Anderson, no date.
James Guy-Polly Barnes, November 3, 1815.
Robert Gee-Betsy Walters, March 24, 1802.
John George-Polly Heydon, March 22, 1805.
James Gete-Celia Crowder, October 16, 1815.
William Gibbins-Elizabeth Gatewood, December 12, 1819.
John Gibson-Peggy Wilson, November 25, 1802.
John Glover-Sarah Young, July 11, 1799.
Claybrook Gooch-Sarah Jeffrey, July 18, 1811.
John Gouldin-Sally Williams, January 5, 1803.
James Graham-Mary Wilson, April 2, 1807.
John Graham-Elizabeth Knowble, August 25, 1809.
James Gregg-Susan McCampbell, March 26, 1818.
Hardin Grey-Polly Conner, September 27, 1815.
Elias Griffin-Martha Huckstep, August 11, 1816.
John A. Grimes-Lucy Broadus, February 14, 1806.
Alexander Groomer-Eliza McCullin, October 6, 1817.
Robert Guy-Betsy McAfee, 1807.

John Hackett-Elizabeth Murphy, January 3, 1816.
John D. Hackney-Sally Collins, December 6, 1816.
Nathan D. Haggard-Judith Kindred, December 19, 1805.
John Hambris (or Hambrig)-Betsy Isbrel. No date.
Ezra Hammond-Hannah Farrow. March 30, 1801.
Charles Hampton-Margaret Dorrity. No date.
Stephen Hampton-Elizabeth Ficklin. September 14, 1802.
Handy Handley-Polly (Patty?) Harris, June 16, 1800.
Daniel Harris-Malinda Proctor. No date.
Lewis Harris-Nancy Davis, January 31, 1808.
Zephaniah Harris-Joahana Mitchell, December 19, 1799.
William Hartman-Nancy Cullin, February 5, 1801.
Samuel Hastand-Catherine Nave, no date.
Abraham Hatfield-Polly Combs, November 19, -8-8.
George Hawkins-Polly Murrain, November 9, 1808.
John Hawkins-Margaret Singleton, no date.
William Henderson-Sally Hawkins, November 24, 1808.
Jesse Heydon-Sarah Hawkins, August 7, 1817.
Thomas Hawkins-Polly Singleton, November 7, 1816.
Thomas Hawkins-Ann Wilmore, January 17, 1808.
Thomas Haydon-Mary Keller, January 14, 1801.
George Hendricks-Polly Bolin, January 22, 1806.
Thomas Henry-Peggy Scott, no date.
Thomas Heydon-Mary Keller, January 17, 1801.
John Hicks-Elizabeth Sandusky, January 19, 1804.
Thomas Hickman-Sally Prewitt, February 17, 1803.
James Highsmith-Catherine Woods, August 14, 1806.
Marryman Hightower-Sarah Dickerson, December 24, 1801.
Richard Hightower-Susan Gates, April 5, 1801.
James Hiller-Ann Singleton, May 27, 1801.
Green Hill-Fanny Forman, 1813.
John Hill-Elizaeth Reed, September 29, 1812.
James Hillpatrick-Margaret Scantling, July 14, 1818.
Wilson Hisel-Sarah Drake, December 25, 1800.
Michael Hockersmith-Nancy Holeman, December 26, 1799.
Henry Holbert-Mary Power, 1815.
William Holderby-Isabelle Dillon, April 10, 1800.
John Hole-Jenney Overstreet, January 3, 1807.
Archibald Jackson-Polly Parmer, no date.
Ebenezer Jackson-Nancy Chambers, July 6, 1807.
John Jackson-Ann Maxwell, December 29, 1801.
Isom Jackson-Henrietta Jimmerson, January 9, 1816.
Thomas Jefferies-Polly Johnson, October 7, 1801.
John Jenkins-Polly Peyton, September 10, 1815.
Thomas Jenkins-Tilitha Elkin, September 4, 1804.
Thomas C. Jennings-Jane P. Zimmerman, January 30, 1806.
Richard Jesse-Patsy Wright, July 1, 1817.
Elisha Jeter-Isabella Long, no date.
William Jimmerson-Salinda Willis, October 7, 1804.
Holman Johnson-Catherine Murrain, July 15, 1816.
Samuel Johnson-Peggy Hudson, October 16, 1816.
David P. Johns-Nancy Johnson, November 4, 1817.
James Jones-Nancy Rundles, December 11, 1806.
Moses Kean-Sally Eaton, November 27, 1804.
Charles Kain-Jane Holms, December 31, 1799.
Pollard Keene-Catherine Roberts, no date.
Gideon Kelly-Peggy McCarty, October 13, 1805.
Nicholas Kelly-Temperance Crumwell, January 8, 1807.
William Kelly-Sary Souduskey, no date.
Charles Kennedy-Polly Finn, October 7, 1802.
James Kennedy-Sallie Quinn, February 20, 1806.
Joseph Kennedy-Eleanor Sellers, April 9, 1799.

Edward Kerby-Eilzabeth Buiter (Butler), January 1, 1804.

Francis Kerley-Polly Butler, October 27, 1799.

Henry Kerley-Susannah Butler, October 31, 1802.

Richard Kesley-Nancy Dean, no date.

David Kersey-Tabby Moss, July 9, 1814.
Bartholomew Kindred-Hester Blake, February 5, 1815.
Edward Kindred-Sally Scott, no date.
George King-Patsy Heydon, no date.
John Krigbaum-Sarah Organs, December 25, 1816.
Spencer Holloway-Catherine Reed, April 4, 1816.
Hugh Holmes-Sally Scott, January 27, 1801.
Nicholas Holston-Rebecca Slight, June 16, 1812.
David Hoover-Nancy Hoover, March 22, 1820.
Joel Hoover-Nancy Howser, December 31, 1818.
Henry Horine-Catherine Trisler, May 4, 1804.
Joseph Horton-Fanny Hunter, no date.
Chester Howard-Polly J. McGrath, December 10, 1815.
John Howell-Nancy Baxter, December 12, 1816.
William Howell-Sarah Walters, April 26, 1806.
William Howell-Betsy Morain, February 12, 1809.
John Howzer-Polly Ansparger, January 21, 1800.
John Huckstep-Eliza Sansum, June 8, 1800.
Samuel Huckstep-Martha Crowder, March 23, 1801.
James Hudson-Betesy Proctor, January 2, 1806.
Jacob Huffer-Susanna D. Rohrer, August 19, 1804.
James Hughes-Nancy Craig, no date.
Jesse Hughes-Nancy Nicholson, March 14, 1799.
Joseph Hughes-Susan Singleton, no date.
Joseph Hughes-Lucy Singleton.
Roland Hughes-Jane Rankin, no date.
Samuel Hughes-Nancy E. Price, 1785.
Thomas Hughes-Nancy Veach, April 8, 1801.
William Hughes-Mary Neal, no date.
William Hughes-Nancy Morrison, February 10, 1817.
Frederick W. Huling-Sarah Brown, December 1, 1815.
George Hulse-Rebecca Owens, November 30, 1809.
John Hunley-Polly Mitchell, December 10, 1816.
John Hunt, Jr.,-Polly Johnson, February 12, 1801.
Samuel Hunt-Ruth Shelton, July 9, 1809.
Wilson Hunt-Sarah Drake, December 5, 1800.
Davidson Hunter-Polly Davidson, June 11, 1815.
Joseph Hunter-Sarah Coleman, May 7, 1800.
William Hunter-Betsy Hunter, February 18, 1808.
John Hunt, Jr.,-Polly Johnson, February 12, 1801.
John Lancaster-Lucy Proctor, no date.
David Lawson-Sophia McCarty, November 30, 1815.
Rowland Letcher-Sophia Gates, December 29, 1814.
John Levingston-Betsy Dixon, August 22, 1815.
George Lingenfetter-Nancy York, June 20, 1805.
William Lipsey-Margaret Fulkerson, September 18, 1800.
James Lockett-Polly Howard, March 5, 1799.
Silas Lockhart-Cittury Cannon, December 3, 1812.
Benjamine Logan-Sally Scott, December 29, 1803.
Francis Lowen-Sarah Hudson, February 18, 1808.
Melvin Lowrey-Phoebe Hiter, October 28, 1800.
John Lowry-Nancy Carroll, January 7, 1802.
John S. Lucas-Hannah Lewis, November 22, 1816.
William Lucas-Elizabeth Higbee, June 5, 1803.
James Lusk-Ellen Gilbert, May 3, 1815.
Ambrose Mannin-Turany (Lurany?) Jones, December 2, 1802.
William Marker-Peggy Hornbuckle, September 20, 1799.

Henry Marshall-Betsy Johnson, April 12, 1803.
James Marshall-Polly Howard, 1813.
Thomas Marshall-Melinda Craven, November 17, 1816.
James L. Martin-Rebecca McConnell, April 21, 1816.
John Martin-Polly Martin, no date.
Phillip Mayer-Sally Arnspeger, March 13, 1815.
Nelson Mays-Anna Turner, September 10, 1814.
George Mason-Betsy Howser, March 29, 1802.
Peter Mason-Nancy M. Hamlette, November 15, 1813.
Lindsey Mays-Patsey Simpson, January 19, 1803.
Barnett Metcalf-Letitia Martin, December 3, 1813.
Jacob Miller-Mary Hufford, November 25, 1802.
John Minor- Mary Graham, March 24, 1799.
Robert Minor-Martha Skean, October 9, 1799.
James McCarty-Nancy Lusk, April 22, 1802.
John McCoy-Susannah Moore, July 4, 1806.
Isaac McClane-Catherine Wells, January 16, 1814.
Andrews McCloud-Peggy Foley, no date.
John L. McCosby-Margaret Minor, 1813.
James McCune-Kiziah Dean, February 28, 1806.
James McDaniel-Ruth Aevis, July 23, 1812.
Jesse McDonnald-Polly Empson, May 8, 1807.
Samuel McDowell-Elizabeth Chrisman, August 13, 1811.
Robert McGrath-Peggy Daugherty, March 13, 1785.
John McKee-Ann Platt, February 14, 1809.
James McMillin-Susannah Amminy, September 19, 1799.
John McVay-Polly Hannah, 1811.
Robert Middleton-Hannah Campbell, 1813.
Robert McPheters-Jane L. McKee, March 14, 1822.
Daniel Monerod-Antonette Dufour, no date.
Charles Miner-Nancy Moss, December 3, 1806.
Aaron Moore-Rachel Black, December 15, 1803.
Abraham J. Moore-Sally Craig, August 27, 1816.
Jesse Moore-Peggy Cathers, December 17, 1801.
Joel N. Moore-Joannah Wharton Meriwether, 1815.
Moses Moore-Eleanor Black, August 13, 1801.
William Moore-Patsy Boles, April 11, 1799.
Harvey Morris-Nancy Boatman, 1813.
Samuel Morrow-Sally Caldwell, December 25, 1800.
Edward Mosley-Lucy Smith, September 3, 1815.
Robert Mosley-Mary Smith, July 18, 1819.
John Mosely-Frances Smith, October 18, 1812.
Ray Moss-Jane McKinney, December 29, 1803.
James Mott,-Hettie Walters, July 2, 1818.
John Muller (Miller)-Aggy Butler, December 17, 1814.
William Murphy-Eleanor Blakeman, 1813.
William Murrain-Lidia Overstreet, May 15, 1817.
Charley Myers-Sally Edwards, July 20, 1803.
Peter Nave-Elizabeth Hoover, December 21, 1813.
Charles Neal-Rebecca Brown, September 9, 1813.
Elijah Neel-Polly Kingut (?), 1810.
Jacob Neal-Susannah Cassell, February 19, 1818.
James Neal-Sally Hughes, no date.
James Neal-Polly Martin.
Benjamin Nicholson-Martha Gilbert, October 14, 1803.
Larkin Nicholson-Betsey McCarty, August 15, 1803.
Thomas Nicholson-Peggy Davis, May 28, 1815.
Patrick Noonan-Elizabeth Hammon, April 26, 1816.
James Nutter-Mary P. Lewis, 1816.
Thomas Nutall-Fanny D. Moore, November 27, 1806.
William Olds-Anna Welch, December 18, 1806.

David Oliver-Polly Gatewood, no date.
Archibald Organ-Polly Kruikbaum, December 23, 1816.
Gabriel Overstreet-Elizabeth Hawkins, September 8, 1806.
George Overstreet-Mary McCarty, February 4, 1819.
James Overstreet-Sally Miller, November 3, 1804.
James Overstreet-Elizabeth Kersey, May 8, 1817.
R. D. Overstreet-Jane Lowry, April 25, 1815.
Richard Overstreet-Polly Ramsey, December 29, 1803.
Samuel Overstreet-Elizabeth Hawkins, November 24, 1804.
Thomas Overstreet-Susannah Ramsy, May 15, 1816.
Samuel Owen-Kitty Rutherford, 1816.
Thomas Overstreet-Betsy Potts, September 26, 1819.
Edward Owens-Rachel Rowan, 1818.
Thomas Padgett-Betsy Scott, August 1, 1816.
Jonathan Palmer-Sally A. Lafon, July 25, 1814.
Nathaniel Parker-Clarissa Higbee, 1806.
John Patterson-Nancy Campbell, 1813.
Benjamine M. Patton-Margarit Patton, February 14, 1815.
James Patton-Sally Bourne, December 5, 1815.
James Paul-Sally Redmond, September 20, 1814.
Andrews Pattrick-Sarah Ghaskins, June 26, 1817.
William Peacher (?)-Nancy Davis, 1814.
Jonathan Paul-Eunice Griffin, March 19, 1799.
Robert Pebworth-Harding Kersey, May 2, 1816.
John Pemberton-Patsy Webster, January 19, 1818.
Jeremiah Penice-Susannah Moore, July 6, 1800.
David Perry-Nancy Burnett, October 2, 1819.
John Perry-Charity Price, July 26, 1815.
Thomas Peyton-Polly Wharton, 1818.
Robert Phillips-Rebecca Grimes, June 19, 1806.
William Phillips-Elizabeth Moss, June 28, 1800.
John Piggond-Easter Sherwood, 1785.
Edward Pilcher-Elizabeth Pilcher, February 7, 1813.
Peter Poindexter-Polly Marez, July 1, 1802.
William Poindexter-Sally Higbee, July 1, 1815.
Greenville Porter-Betsy Lanfred, January 22, 1818.
John P. Porter-Eliza McDowell, 1813.
Silas Porter-Nancy Buckannan, January 23, 1804.
William Porter-Molly Cathers, January 22, 1802.
John Portwood-Rebecca Hunter, 1813.
Harrison Posy-Sarah Hunter, November 26, 1818.
William Prather-Ruth Wilson, October 7, 1802.
Lewis Preston-Elizabeth Griffin, June 26, 1817.
Joel Prewitt-Maryanna Netherland, July 22, 1805.
Richard P. Price-Elizabeth Bullett, March 25, 1814.
Catlett Proctor-Hannah Sousky (?), February 6, 1800.
Ezekiel Proctor, Nancy Carothers, December 17, 1804.
John Proctor-Eleanor Offutt, July 5, 1804.
Thomas Proctor-Elizabeth Craig, March 28, 1815.
Uriah Proctor-Frances Sally, 1811.
Joseph Pruit-Polly Price, August 12, 1813.
Woody J. Pullman-Polly Skeene, January 3, 1807.
Isaac Raaley-Sally Skeene, July 28, 1814.
James Ramsey-Martha Williams, December 16, 1813.
John Ramsey-Mary Dune, December 29, 1805.
Jonathan Rawlings-Nancy Hornbuckle, August 21, 1806.
Samuel Redding-Nancy Knock, December 12, _____.
John Reed-Elizabeth Walker, December 31, 1818.
Peter Reed-Dulana Miller, April 9, 1814.
Gabriel Reid-Lucy Caldwell, January 18, 1811.
Joseph Renfrow-Milly Land, April 21, 1803.

Samuel Rentfroe-Nelly Hunter, August 5, 1811.
David Reynolds-Jane Moore, September 20, 1804.
Levy Reynolds-Henrietta Treder, June 17, 1818.
William Reynolds-Nancy Myers, June 26, 1817.
Henry Rhorer-Susannah Hoover, October 11, 1814.
Jacob Rhorer-Mary Hoover, June 20, 1816.
David Rice-Elizabeth Lincoln, November 14, 1805.
Richard Ridgely-Jane Price, 1811.
Jacob Rhorer-Mary Hoover, June 20, 1816.
Eliphalet Roane-Nancy A. Wilson, 1807.
Henry Robb-Milly Shelton, April 20, 1809.
Simon Roberts-Hannah Cleveland, 1815.
Henry Rogers-Betsy Haubaugh, May 26, 1805.
Jesse Roper-Catherine Williams, February 6, 1800.
William Roper-Elizabeth L. Price, 1810.
Leroy Rore-Judith Cloud, 1806.
Barritt Rucker-Elizabeth Holloway, June 5, 1803.
John Rucker-Betsy Burton, November 7, 1805.
Samuel Ruffner-Elizabeth Hiber, January 22, 1819.
Archa Rutherford-Rachel Empson, September 4, 1814.
Shelton Rutherford-Hannah Roman, 1810.
Frederick Sageser-Kitty Bruner, October 3, 1799.
Jacob Sallee-Hannah Smith, February 5, 1801.
Jacob Sally-Elizabeth Pigman, December 7, 1819.
Michael Sands (?)-Polly McDaniels, October 3, 1806.
Joel Saunders-Sally A. Moore, 1814.
John A. Saunders-Lucy Proctor, 1814.
William Schale-Patsy Elledge, May 15, 1806.
Henry Sawyers-Betsy Evins, October 16, 1817.
James Scott-Susan Zike, March 9, 1808.
John Scott-Polly Wells, June 21, 1804.
Thomas Scott-Sarah Ward, October 28, 1800.
William Scott-Julianna Shevers (?), no date.
William Scott-Nancy Frost, April 12, 1804.
Joseph Sellers-Mary Johnson, December 31, 1801.
John Shanklin-Jane Knight, August 31, 1815.
Samuel Shanklin-Elizabeth Barrick, October 3, 1805.
Greenwood Shelton-Jane Lyon, April 20, 1809.
John Shelton-Catherine Murray, March 23, 1802.
John Shelton-Hannah Hill, December 5, 1816.
William Simpkins-Nancy Wilkerson, March 2, 1815.
Nathaniel Simpson-Peggy Close, April 11, 1811.
Walter Simpson-Polly Spires, June 24, 1802.
Jeremiah Singleton-Fanny Craven, ———, 1818.
Lewis Singleton-Rebecca Roberts, January 16, 1814.
Moses Singleton-Elizabeth Lowery, August 12, 1818.
William Skeene-Cynthia Dickerson, October 6, 1815.
Abraham S. Smith-Polly Trabue, February 16, 1813.
Allen Smith-Martha Prewitt, December 2, 1819.
David Smith-Polly Proctor, April 16, 1809.
George Smith-Hannah Hawkins, October 27, 1803.
Jacob Smith-Mary Barker, June 22, 1800.
Jacob Smith-Nancy ———, October 31, 1816.
James Smith-Mariah Hanks, March 23, 1817.
John Smith-Polly Lockett, August 22, 1811.
John Smith-Elizabeth Easley, July 28, 1814.
Joseph Smith-Peggy Johnson, January 9, 1800.
Peter Smith-Peggy Ford, August 27, 1814.
Thomas Smith-Murchal (?) Lockett, April 16, 1801.
Thomas A. (or H.) Smith—Hopey Morris, ———, 1818.
Samuel Sodder-Mary Pettett, December 8, 1802.

Michael Sone-Rebecca Hulse, 1813.
George Spears-Leat Keller, March 10, 1789.
W. H. Smith-Providence Carter.
Jacob Sodusky-Martha Daugherty, 1808.
Henry Speed-Betsey Fulkerson, February 16, 1806 (or 1816).
Moses Spencer-Elizabeth Birch, May 3, 1815.
Thomas Spencer-Eleanor Moore, 1813.
Abner Springer-Nancy Hockersmith, March 26, 1811.
Absolom Springer-Nancy Moore, October 6, 1816.
Jacob Springer-Sophia Rice, June 24, 1802.
John Springer-Charlotte Jackson, January 6, 1803.
George Springer-Lucy Hockersmith, October 3, 1803.
John Starr-Sally Miner, 1785.
Andrew Staunton-Catherine Miller, July 11, 1811.
Allen Stephens-Sally Empson, December 22, 1803.
John Stephens-Catherine Caldwell, December 17, 1818.
John Stephenson-Elizabeth Akin, July 24, 1802.
Jacob Stipe-Susanna Bourne, November 7, 1815.
John D. Stockton-Patsy Spires, September 2, 1805.
John Stone-Polly Castle, December 16, 1802.
John D. Stonestreet-Betsy Pollock, October 13, 1807.
James Stotts (or Slotts)-Luerey ———, 1785.
Samuel Switzer-Polly Baker, May 17, 1813.
John Taylor-Judy Moss, May 13, 1804.
John Taylor-Magdalen Gray, 1813.
Joseph Taylor-Elizabeth Swinsher, November 13, 1803.
Benjamine Telly-Frances Isbell, March 11, 1800.
Stephen Temple-Margaret Walker, November 6, 1800.
Daniel Terrell-Elizabeth Quinby, November 13, 1800.
Alexander Thompson-Rebecca Jackson, May 24, 1818.
Andrew Thompson-Mary Evans, December 18, 1800.
James Todd-Polly Lowrey (or Lourey), November, 1804.
Jacob Todhunter-Joanna Sall, December 7, 1813.
Parker E. Todhunter-Catherine Ryland, October 21, 1818.
Isaac Tompson-Elizabeth Farra, December 17, 1812.
George I. Trabue-Betsy B. Sally, December 25, 1818.
William T. Transdail (?)-Mary Seller, October 6, 1800.
John Trisler-Fanny Reed, 1812.
Leonard Trisler-Sarah Zike, October 12, 1812.
William Trotter-Rachel Keller, August 27, 1805.
Ezekiel True-Susanna Williams, April 16, 1801 (or 1808).
James True-Polly Rese, 1813.
John True-Nancy Steward, October 27, 1805.
Robert True-Sally Williams, February 6, 1803.
John F. True-Rebecca Brown, October 27, 1816.
William Utley-Elizabeth Davis, December 17, 1813.
Jacob Veach-Polly Hilton, December 19, 1805.
James Venable-Hannah Chrisman, April 21, 1813.
John Waggerman-Barbara Howzer, March 29, 1802.
Zephaniah T. Waldin-Betsy Owen, October 22, 1816.
Alexander Walker-Betsy Scott, December 22, 1803.
David T. Walker-Caroline Lewis, July 4, 1814.
James B. Walker-Sally Lowrey, December 7, 1819.
Joseph G. Walker-Martha Scott, September 6, 1814.
John Walker-Sally Coffee, January 24, 1800.
Randolph Walker-Lucy Haydon, August 5, 1805.
Edward Wall-Hytha McGrath, July 18, 1806.
John Wallace-Lucy Need, March 21, 1816.
James H. Walsh-Nancy Wingate, February 11, 1806.
David Walters-Martha Lockhart, October 11, 1804.
Champmans Walters-Jane Lockhart, June 8, 1806.

James Walters-Elizabeth Tanner, November 17, 1806.
Parry Walters-Mary Hadley, October 14, 1802.
Stephen Walters-Polly Cooly, January 10, 1801.
John Warner-Rhoda Hunley, 1818.
Richard Waters-Betsy Stonestreet, September 17, 1815.
James Webb-Mary Coleman, December 26, 1802.
Archer Webber-Peggy Taylor, April 14, 1799.
Nelson Webster-Lucy Culler, 1814.
Lewis Webster-Betsy Webster, September 21, 1817.
Peter Webster-Nancy Blackwell, no date.
John Welch-Jane Rice, June 26, 1817.
Jacob Wells-Sally Carothers, November 29, 1818.
Richard West-Polly Hunt, July 30, 1805.
John Whalin-Mary Ann Elkin, December 24, 1801.
William Wheat-Elizabeth Huber, no date.
James White-Catherine Stephens, 1815.
John White-Nancy Bradshaw, 1802.
William White-Nancy Davis, March 21, 1816.
Jacob Wiles-Nancy Hoover, December 26, 1819.
William Wiles-Betsy Margison, November 21, 1814.
Peter Wilkerson-Polly Miller, July 23, 1802.
Benjamin Williams-Nancy Williams, October 31, 1799.
Elijah Williams-Sarah Willis, February 8, 1807.
Elijah Williams-Lucinda McGrath, May 27, 1813.
Matthew Williams-Rachel Lawson, January 2, 1806.
Milton H. Williams-Nancy Wethers, March 30, 1815.
Joseph Willis-Betsy Young, June 11, 1805.
Willis S. Williamson-Sally Mays, February 24, 1818.
Drury Willis-Polly Hunter, November 20, 1816.
James Wilmore-Jane Dillon, June 8, 1806.
Alexander Wilson-Polly Johnson, December 31, 1799.
Lawrence Wilson-Peggy Wilson, November 22, 1803.
Samuel Wilson-Sophia Anderson, 1815.
William Wilson-Polly Wilson, November 11, 1806.
Peter Withers-Evelina Price, November 8, 1818.
John Wood-Martha Ramsey, December 28, 1815.
Abijah Woods-Sally Lancaster, April 24, 1816.
John Woods-Nancy Smith, November 12, 1806.
Stephen Woods-Matilda Weber, October 8, 1818.
Robert Woodward-Polly Spencer, February 25, 1816.
Pleasant Woodson-Mary Bradshaw, April 7, 1816.
Richard Woolsey-Betsy Maynod (?), November 13, 1815.
Elijah Wright-Jennett Harris, December 5, 1799.
Martin Young-Susannah Sale, 1814.
Richard Young-Fanny Wharton, June 28, 1804.
Ruben Young-Mary Sharp, June 28, 1804.
William Young-Peggy T. Scott, December 2, 1802.
William Young-Mary Smith, April 16, 1809.
David Zike-Catherine Smith, October 5, 1815.

MADISON COUNTY MARRIAGES

(Contributed by Mrs. Joseph Head, Boonesboro Chapter)

Aley-Arefoard-John Page, February 11, 1796.
Robert Anderson-Clancy Woodruff, June 17, 1790.
Robert Allen-Nancy Cloyd, February 28, 1793.
Eceabud Ashcraft-Sarah McDaniel, November 12, 1796.
Charles Burgin-Margaret Deatherage, Rugust 3, 1790.

James Barrens-Issabel Barnes, November 10, 1790.
Jack Barnett-Peggy Davis, January 6, 1791.
Abraham Benton-Caty Prater, March 24, 1791.
William Bridges-Betsy Wright, September 1, 1791.
Benjamin Basseter-Sally Burgin, June 14, 1792.
Henry Burnham-Sally Jones, September 20, 1792.
John Bradley-Polly Roberts, November 27, 1792.
Thomas Bradly-Rachel Roberts, November 27, 1792.
William Blethe-Onee Martin, July 20, 1793.
Amos Beach-Margaret Freely, May 25, 1793.
John Black-Sara Gass, November 27, 1793.
Joshua Baseter-Nancy Nicholson, September 24, 1795.
Sherwood Burton-Rebecca Crosswhite, June 27, 1795.
Thomas Brown-Rebecca Pursley, June 23, 1796.
James Baker-Peggy Noland, August 24, 1796.
Humphrey Best-Caty Leonard, January 7, 1796.
Andy Brisco-Ann Kavanaugh, February 25, 1796.
Hiram Biggerstaff-Mary Watts, June 29, 1796.
Charles Burris-Elizabeth Kidwell, October 29, 1796.
William Caperton-Lucy Woods, December 15, 1790.
Richard Calloway-Margaret Wills, November 25, 1790.
Thomas Crage-Sarah Hall, October 6, 1792.
Daniel Chapman-Jinny Wainscott, January 24, 1793.
Andrew Coldwell-Francina Hardwick, June 5, 1795.
Jesse Clarke-Mary Fullinglove, May 12, 1796.
Vincent Carrico-Susannah Quick, February 18, 1796.
Richard Chapman-Sally Dier, June 4, 1795.
Zachariah Davis-Prudence Roberts, August 19, 1790.
John Durbin-Elizabeth Oller, April 19, 1792.
John Durbin-Patience Logsdon, April 8, 1795.
Isaac Duncan-Susannah Kavanaugh, September 24, 1795.
Soloman Dunford-Susannah Knott, January 12, 1797.
John Ellis-Elizabeth Nunnery, June 2, 1796.
Joseph Embry-Rachel Strange, June 7, 1796.
Lawrence Flourenoy-Doshea Hoy, January 13, 1791.
James Fleming-Susannah Patterson, December 4, 1792.
John Farris-Hezzy Trap, Oct. 24, 1795.
Frederick Fort-LucyMoore, March 3, 1791.
Thomas Findley-Seally Pollard, March 20, 1796.
Henry Green-Margaret Lowery, December 31, 1793.
John Gass-Ann Anderson, January 17, 1793.
John Gulridge-Ann Farris, July 23, 1793.
Bartlett Gentry-Elizabeth Timberlac, February 13, 1794.
George Goff-Agnes Cole, March 16, 1793.
John Gardner-Ann Noland, June 27, 1796.
William Griffin-Ledia Price, February 11, 1796.
Issabel Gray-John Sapp, January 6, 1791.
Abraham Hammon-Pilly Nales, May 3, 1792.
James Hockaday-Betsy Fox, August 25, 1791.
Benjamin Harris-Nancy Burgin, June 14, 1792.
John Heirs-May Turpin, January 9, 1793.
Sampson Hawk-Ellender Stockstill, September 30, 1793.
George Hubard-Polly Belen, June 2, 1796.
Francis Holly-Nancy Crock, June 25, 1796.
Thomas Harris-Rachel Barns, December 15, 1796.
Joseph Holeman-Catherine Wilson, April 8, 1790.
Richard Johnson-Mary Turner, August 18, 1796.
John James-Susannah Schouse, October 17, 1796.
Joseph Jones-Jinny Chenault, December 27, 1796.
Alexander Kennedy-Elizabeth Alford, June 27, 1793.
Isaac Kent-Lucy Hopkins, December 25, 1793.

(128)

Elijah Knightly-Elizabeth Overstreet, September 2, 1796.
Giles-Kelley-Marthaford DeJarnett, February 13, 1796.
Doury Kidwell-Ann Patton, October 25, 1796.
James Kennedy-Mary Denny, February 21, 1797.
James Lee-Hezekiah Moberly, May 5, 1795.
Thomas Lewis-Elizabeth Stone, September 29, 1796.
Peter Lee-Peggy Goff, June 6, 1796.
Patience Logsdon-John Simon, May 28, 1792.
Jeremiah Mize-Nancy Peek, July 22, 1790.
Joseph Merrett-Nancy Brooks, November 4, 1790.
Mellon Traus (Travis?)-Nancy Sims, February 17, 1791.
John Moore-Rebecca Mize, July 24, 1792.
Thomas Mannion-Nancy South, March 14, 1793.
William Moore-Elizabeth Troussdale, June 7, 1793.
William Murfee-Sara Carpenter, July 10, 1795.
William Miller-Charity King, Oct. 20, 1795.
Humphrey Mize-Betsy Hill, June 29, 1796.
Samuel Moberly-Ann Tudor, October 29, 1796.
James McLane-Polly White, September 1. 1791.
Cornelias McDaniel-Patsy Dickey, Septemeber 26, 1793.
Robert McCord (McCall?)-Pamala Harris, December·31, 1795.
Samuel McClary-Sara Crawford, May 9, 1796.
Samuel Portwood-Franky Evans, December 16, 1790.
Thomas Patterson-Hannah Adams, August 5, 1790.
Ebenezer Platt-Lucy Jett, January 9, 1791.
James Prather-Hannah Freeman, November 29, 1782.
Pleasant Prophett-May Martin, December 19, 1792.
Edward Peart-Sarah Reylee, July 20, 1793.
John Page-Aley Arefard, February 11, 1796.
Nathan Roberts-Seller White, November 29, 1792.
Daniel Ray-Patience Baker, December 6, 1792.
William Robinson-Jenny Clendenan, June 25, 1795.
Steplen Shange (Strange)-Ann Crook, January 11, 1790.
John Sapp-Issabel Gray, January 6, 1791.
John Simon-Ann Logsdon, May 25, 1792.
Thomas Stalker-Martha Allegree, January 16, 1794.
William Shackelford-Betsy Moore, March 13, 1794.
Stanton Sherwood-Kitty Drinkard, September 18, 1794.
Humphrey Sene-Susannah Gentry, July 10, 1795.
James Stewart-Jane Potts, October 13, 1796.
Roger Shackelford, Jr.-Elizabeth Stewart, April 1, 1796.
James Sims-Jemima Owens, March 26, 1796.
Richard Stone-Elizabeth Madden, October 21, 1796.
Thomas Turner-Nelly Deil, July 22, 1790.
Philip Turner-Abegail Hickman, March 17, 1791.
Thomas Tribble-Jane Phelps, August 18, 1796.
John Williams-Mary England, May 25, 1792.
Patrick Woods-Rachel Cooper, July 19, 1792.
John Williams-Betsy Collins, January 29, 1793.
William Weathers-Mary White, January 23, 1794.
Thomas Welch-Susannah Turpin, January 9, 1794.
John Williams-Winny Wiatt, May 6, 1795.
Joseph Williams-Sally Searcey, March 24, 1796.
Peter Whitkear-Emlia Bates, June 10, 1796.
Muvy Webb-Mary Burgin, May 15, 1796.
John White-Easter Tinchor, June 1, 1797.
Alexander Wylie-Hannah Patterson, January 9, 1797.
James Winders-Nancy Brown, January 12, 1797.
Joshua Yates-Martha Stewart, September 7, 1795.

NELSON COUNTY MARRIAGES

(Contributed by Mrs. J. B. Brown, John Fitch Chapter)

James Cain and Ann Davis, February 12, 1810.
Walter Cambron and Mary Finch, May 10, 1810.
Ben Chapege and Eliza Shepherd, May 7, 1812.
James Crow and Nancy Lasley, December 24, 1812.
Ralph Cotton and Rachel B. Johnson, September 12, 1812.
James Cooper and Lydie Barker, March 11, 1818.
Hugh Conway and Esther Miller, April 15, 1813.
John Clark and Amey Jenee, February 25, 1813.
Wm. B. Chowder and Elizabeth Wise, August 15, 1815.
Sandy Crow and Catherine Hughes, November 7, 1815.
Conner Cooper, and Jennie Rhodes, September 29, 1816.
Amos Coy and Nancy Huston, November 29, 1816.
David H. Cox and Catherine Foreman, August 14, 1817.
John Clayton and Marie Hayden, April 6, 1817.
Daniel Caric and Matilda Carric, April 28, 1817.
Thomas Connor and Rachel Gardener, February 10, 1818.
Martin Cutsinger and Polly Sanders, December 8, 1818.
Wm. Childs and Nancy Bridwell, May 11, 1819.
Joseph Crowe and Polly Hamilton, February 13, 1819.
Wm. Coy and Abigail Brown, February 29, 1820.
Squir Crume and Sally Cotton, October 5, 1820.

NICHOLAS COUNTY MARRIAGES

(Contributed by Mrs. W. B. Ardery, Jemima Johnson Chapter)

Sampson Archer-Polly Kincart, December 22, 1803.
Alexander Allison-Elizabeth Taylor, June 2, 1805.
Robert Ardery-Margaret Mitcheltree, February 4, 1808.
Jacob Arlewine-Kizah Dotson, January 25, 1810.
Thomas Alexander-Harriet Thomson, February 8, 1810.
William Asberry-Mary Ford, November 1, 1809.
Joseph Adamson-Jane Wilson, August 25, 1811.
William Armstrong-Nancy Lauderback, March 29, 1812.
Andrew Bunton-Elizabeth Lockridge, November 26, 1801.
Benjamin Burden-Elizabeth Tully, November 6, 1801.
John Benson-Sally Musick, Novemebr 3, 1803.
Andrew Burns-Hannah Adams, September 20, 1804.
Parker Brown-Sarah Bell, January 17, 1805.
David Bagby-Lucy Collier, August 30, 1806.
Robert Barny-Polly Bradshoe, April 21, 1808.
Henry Bonta-Jeany Fulton, August 25, 1808.
John (Tor F.) Barnet-Elizabeth McClenagan, October 13, 1808.
John Brain-Polly Boatman, April 6, 1809.
John Byers-Sarah Ray, May 12, 1809.
Appleton E. Ballard-Anne Hall, May 31, 1810.
James Brown-Polly Baker, August 2, 1810.
William Bunton-Caty Howard, November 8, 1810.
John Batson-Rachel Drummond, January 24, 1811.
Robert Beard-Margarett Davis, May 1, 1811.

John Bedford-Sally Bedinger, December 5, 1811.
Edmund Bell-Peggy Brinson, April 23, 1811.
John Barlow-Nancy Dotson, January 2, 1812.
James Bunton-Susannah Benson, October 24, 1811.
David Caldwell-Elenor McClenahan, Febraury 25, 1801.
Edward P. Crisswell-Mary Stephenson, August 6, 1801.
Dennis Conneirs- Polly Burke, February 9, 1802.
Thomas Caldwell-Sally Caldwell, June 2, 1803.
James Collins-Mary McDowell, September 29, 1803.
Overton Cosby-Susannah Hyser, June 17, 1806.
Aaron Carnehan-Elvira Mitchell, December 18, 1806.
James Carson-Isabella Mathers, January 22, 1807.
William Crawford-Elsey Doughty, June 2, 1807.
Samuel Crawford-Mary Ann Barnett, January 8, 1808.
Joseph Campbell-Sarah Davis, March 3, 1808.
Robert Caldwell-Elizabeth Howe, March 16, 1809.
David Caughley-Jemima Burden, June 23, 1810.
Lewis Clarke-Peggy Mitchell, December 13, 1810.
Overton Cosby-Susannah Haysor, June 17, 1806.
Richard Cord-Poll Madon, December 11, 1807.
John Camron-Nancy McGinnis, May 20, 1811.
Coleman A. Collier-Jane Howarton, January 30, 1812.
Isac Darland-Jenny Wilson, December 9, 1802.
Abraham Dorlan,Sally Brown, November 29, 1804.
Thomas Davis-Elizabeth Grosvenor, July 5, 1804.
Elijah Dazey-Milly M. Baskett, December 20, 1805.
Henry Dampier-Martha Davidson, Febraury 25, 1808.
Jacob Dawitt-Polly Man, July 24, 1811.
John Evans-Margaret Caldwell, January 1, 1801.
John Ellis-Lucrece Wells, June 20, 1805.
George Eidson-Mary Lilly, October 11, 1804.
Samuel Easlick, Delilah Burden, September 12, 1805.
James Ellis-Fanny Doughty, March 20, 1806.
Robert Edoing?-Nancy Metcalfe, May 1, 1806.
Joseph Earlick-Patsy Griffith, November 17, 1807.
William Elliott-Sally Turner, December 8, 1808.
Robert Ewing-Nancy Metcalfe, May 1, 1806.
Jacob Fight-Peggy Cotrill, June 6, 1805.
William Fuller-Mary Wilson, September 4, 1806.
————————— Fowler-Patsy Collier, October 30, 1805.
John Frye-Polly Gonce, February 20, 1810.
John Feeback-Nanny Richey, December 27, 1810.
Thomas Guffin-Archady Thomson, July 24, 1806.
David Gamble-Polly Sleop (Sloop), January 1, 1807.
William Godman-Elizabeth Drummons, August 25, 1808.
Benjamin Galbrath-Elizabeth Sanderson, November 24, 1808.
Thomas Gunsanles-Hetty Powell, December 25, 1811.
Joseph Grugg-Mary Cord, October 1, 1807.
John Gontz-Susannah Earliwine, November 7, 1812.
Robert Hall-Mary Thomson, April 22, 1802.
Samuel Haskett-Mary Stephenson, March 25, 1802.
Thomas Harvey-Mary Grosvenor, December 19, 1804.
George Harrison-Prudence Gamble, November 25, 1805.
William Hamilton-Mary McIntyre, March 6, 1806.
Henry Howard-Jane Saunderson, January 12, 1806.
Henry Hastings-Ann Poatchel, August 4, 1806.
Tolliver Hughes-Susannah Gamble, May 17, 1807.
Samuel Hall-Polly Potts, March 31, 1808.
Mills Hanny-Mary Smith, May 31, 1810.
James Hamilton-Peggy Turner, October 4, 1810.
William Hughes-Elizabeth Boan, March 21, 1811.

Gabriel Hase-Arabella Cord, March 20, 1811.
Mathew Howard-Ailsey White, May 12, 1811.
Titus Harris-Rosannah Cleveland, March 10, 1811.
William Hardin-Sally Duncan, February 27, 1811.
James Hillock-Susannah Snap, August 8, 1811.
Mordicai Haitley-Grace Wheeler, January 9, 1812.
Aaron P. How-Polly Caldwell, March 13, 1812.
John Harberry-Mary McClean, May 11, 1812.
Joseph A. Hopkins-Margaret Murphey, July 28, 1812.
Joshua Howard-Rebecah Pondergrass, August 27, 1812.
John Irvin-Sarah Ishmæl, May 10, 1807.
Peter Ireland-Ann Allen- September 28, 1804.
James Ishmæl-Mary McFerrin, June 21, 1804.
Thomas Ishmæl-Elizabeth McDonnald, January 1, 1808.
John Ishmæl-Elizabeth Harbet, April 4, 1809.
Thomas Jones-Jane Easley, no date, probably 1800.
John Johnson-Sarah Craig, May 28, 1801.
John Jamison-Peggy Hamilton, July 21, 1808.
Benone Jemison-Mary Catherwood, June 25, 1812.
Robert Kennady-Rebecca Carnahan, September 15, 1806.
Robert H. Kimbrough-Sally Bashell, April 14, 1807.
Samuel Long-Susannah Barlow, March 15, 1804.
Peter Mann-Barberry Jones, no date, probably 1800.
Samuel Marshall-Susannah Waggoner, July 30, 1802.
John Moore-Ester Archer, December 7, 1802.
John Myers-Ruth Smart, January 6, 1803.
Gavin Mathers-Peggy McCune, February 21, 1805.
Henry Mann-Rachel Jones, March 14, 1805.
David Myers-Frances Foster, June 19, 1805.
George W. Murphy-Sally Dean, April 2, 1807.
William Mathers-Peggy Ardery, March 17, 1808.
James Miller-Mary Davidson, September 22, 1808.
James Mathers-Susanna Nesbit, October 27, 1808.
Thomas Michell-Elizabeth Clark, November 2, 1809.
George Mountjoy-Polly Collier, October 16, 1806.
James Martin-Nancy Fight, July 22, 1809.
Lewis Myers-Rosannah Ishmæel, October 1, 1811.
John Mitcheltree-Sarah Hillock, June 4, 1811.
WilliamMcLees-Elizabeth Caldwell, February 25, 1802.
John McNiele (M. Niele)-Susannah Barnett, December 15, 1803.
Robert McCune (M. Cune)-Phœbe Ray, December 27, 1804.
Archibald McMiecah?-Elizabeth Arnold, August 1, 1805.
John McDonald-Peggy McMitchell, Febraury 23, 1809.
David McCune-Hannah Ardery, January 1, 1811.
John McCord-Sally McCarty, September 27, 1807.
John McGuire-Elizabeth Keith, January 10, 1811.
Felix McCarty-Polly Hisler, December 23, 1811.
Daniel Newcome-Christine Davidson, March 26, 1801.
Walter Neives-Rebecca Chriswell, April 24, 1811.
Henry Overby-Polly Conway, April 24, 1806.
John Oliver-Malinda Powell, July 26, 1811.
Robert Pendergrass-Ester Kilgore, September 23, 1802.
James Piper-Frances Ray, November 30, 1802.
Frederick Potts-Elizabeth Olliver, September 26, 1805.
Stephen Peyton-Nancy Doughty, April 16, 1807.
Joshua Philips-Lucinda Irvine, January 21, 1808.
Ashford Prather-Polly Brattell, March 15, 1810.
Samuel Potts-Nanay Taylor, December 2, 1810.
Peter Pickard-Nancy Tryman, April 27, 1809.
Isaac Pauley-Sarah Paugh, January 29, 1811.
Nathaniel Paramough, Polly Parsons, April 14, 1812.

Elijah Purcell-Nancy Powell, August 6, 1812.
Jeremiah Pauley-Esther Poe, May 28, 1812.
Thomas Reveal-Elizabeth McFerrin, January 21, 1802.
Solomas Richey-Rachel Davis, September 8, 1805.
Noah Richey-Phœby Arlewine, April 20, 1809.
Silas Roads-Elizabeth Carnahan, March 8, 1800.
Edward Rælesback-Martha Jinkins, April 17, 1811.
Samuel Roggers-Elizabeth Irwin, January 14, 1812.
John Saunderson-Ibby Galbreath, December 21, 1800.
John Stephenson-Martha McAnulty?, April 6, 1802.
John Swinny-Prescilla Potts, November 24, 1803.
John Scott-Elizabeth Caldwell, July 4, 1805.
William Saunders-Rebecca Plugh, January 5, 1804.
George Sparks-Rachel McClenehan, April 18, 1805.
Hugh Smith-Mary Wilson, September 4, 1806.
Mathew Scott-Jane Philips, January 3, 1806.
Robert Saunderson-Polly Howard, May 5, 1808.
George Short-Kitty Monical, July 6, 1809.
Joseph Smith-Polly Anderson, January 7, 1810.
John Smith-Mary Howe, August 3, 1809.
John Saunders-Polly Beard, March 29, 1810.
Mitchell Smith-Patsy Overby, December 27, 1810.
Daniel Snapp-Peggy Smith, January 24, 1811.
James Stockdale-Elizabeth Logan, February 4, 1811.
Phillip Stoops-Agnes Morgan, June 17, 1811.
Humphrey Smart-Polly Myers, May 28, 1811.
James Staneford-Casandra Stanerford, September 8, 1811.
Asa Shepherd-Catherine Richardson, January 21, 1812.
Mosese Thompson-Ann Atockwell, December 24, 1807.
William Truelove-Polly Mattox, November 7, 1809.
John Taylor-Mary Harding, March 21, 1811.
George Tryman (Fryman)-Margaret Snap, no date, probably 1800
John Wiley-Hannah Rouse, July 13, 1800.
John Williamson-Sarah Grosvinor, July 30, 1802.
William Wishart-Betsy Rodes, October 7, 1802.
Aaron Wiggins-Elizabeth Ward, September 23, 1804.
William Wheeler-Margaret Rotston, July 29, 1806.
William Wiggins-Elizabeth A. Wells, January 21, 1810.
Nathaniel Webster-Rachel Marsh, January 20, 1812.

FIRST SHELBY COUNTY, KENTUCKY, MARRIAGE BONDS

(Contributed by Mrs. Graham Lawrence and Miss Elizabeth V. Todd, Isaac Shelby Chapter)

Very Few Are Included in First Marriage Book—Spelling as in Bond.

1 7 9 2

3 December—John Crawford—Polly Denbe, daughter of Solomon gomery. Bond signed, Joseph Warford—att. Will Shannon.

3 December—Moses Hogland—Sarah Egin, daughter, Mary Montgomery. Bond signed, Joseph Warford—att. Will Shannon.

10 December—Barnet Reed—Susanna Stillin,. Bond signed, Robert Jeffris, Wm. Adams—att. Will Shannon.

25 December—David Demaree—Jane Kerne, daughter of Peter Kerne. Bond signed, Henry Montgomery—att. Thos. and Jas. Shannon.

No Date—John Booth—Sally Kinder. Peter Kinder—att. Wm. Butler.

No Date—Aaron Hogland—Elizabeth Ageain. James Hogland—att. Wm. Butler.

No date—John Wilson—Prudence Munro. Alexander Chambers—att. Wm. Butler.

No Date—Archibald Neal—Margaret Mogner. Bond signed, Wm. Butler.

1 7 9 3

24 January—James McCollough—Jane Perkins, daughter, John Perkins. John Perkins, Wm. Glen—att. Will Shannon.

24 January—William Perkins—Jane Glen. John Perkins, Wm. Glen—att. Will Shannon.

11 March—John Cheneworth—Mary Buskirk, daughter of Michael Buskirk. Thomas Buskirk—att. Will Shannon.

29 March—Cane Field—Miss Anne Lewis. Jonathan Cox—att. James Craig.

30 March—Joseph Warford—Mary Warford, daughter of John Warford. Jacob Underwood—att.Jas. Craig.

10 April—Jonathan Boone—Catherine Fullinwider. Ralph Vancleave —att. Jas. Craig.

15 April—Robert Lasley—Hannah McCortney, daughter, James McCortney. Culbertson Parks—att. James Craig.

18 June—Mason Watts—Deborah Ryker, consent of mother and stepfather, John Vancleave, Rachel Vancleave. Bond signed, Hugh Adams—att. Jas. Craig.

18 June—Benijah Laugherty—Miss Ralph (?) Vancleave. Ralph Vancleave—att. Jas. Craig.

7 September—Henry Brenton—Mistress Hannah Gin (Gwin?). Brackett Owen—att. Will Shannon.

23 September—George Veech—Miss Allenor (Eleanor) Bowman, daughter of John Bowman. Bond signed, John Bowman—att. Jas. Craig.

1 7 9 4

21 January—John Best—Elizabeth Whitaker, daughter of Aquilla Whitaker. Aquilla Whitaker—att.Jas. Craig.

22 January—James Swayze—Elizabeth Starke, daughter of Daniel and Elizabeth Stark. Robert Jeffris—att. Jas. Craig.

15 February—William Morris—Susanna McCortney, daughter of John and Hannah McCortney. Edward DeLaney—att. Jas. Craig.

18 February—Benjamin Boyd—Anna Lindsey.   William Hall—att. Jas. Craig.

18 February—Robert Tyler—Sarah Pritchett, daughter Jas. Pritchett. William Hall—att. Jas. Craig.

4 March—Nicholas Clines—Elizabeth Favers, daughter of Caleap (Caleb ?) Favers. Jas. Hoagland—att.Wm. Butler.

4 March—Aaron Vancleave—Elizabeth Vancleave, daughter of John Vancleave. John Vancleave—att. Jas. Craig.

6 March—Anthony Sharpe—Rachel Ellison. James Scott—att. Jas. Craig.

10 March—Thomas Infield—Anne Fullinwider. Jacob Fullinwider—att. Jas. Craig.

15 April—Edward Young—Susey McCortney, daughter of John and Hannah McCortney. Daniel Colgan—att. Jas. Craig.

23 April—John Owen—Patty Talbott. Jas. Craig.

6 May—John Ingel—Mistress Liddy Goben, widow of Joseph Goben. Isaac Whitaker—att. Jas. Craig.

7 July—Daniel McDonald—Rhody Stark, daughter of Joseph Stark. Peter Bailey—att. Dorsey Pentecost.

8 July—Matthias Cyphers—Sarah Edwards. David Edwards—att. Dorsey Pentecost.

9 August—Lewis Martin—Polly Wright. Obadiah Wright—att. Wm. Butler.

25 August—Jacob Richy—Mary Martin. John Martin—att. Wm. Butler.

30 August—Jonathan Stark—Rachel Devore. Daniel Devore—att. Wm. Butler.

25 September—Edward Wells—Phebe Paddock. Jonathan Paddock.

23 September—John Vancleave—Ernes Vancleave, daughter of Benjamin Vancleave. John Vancleave—att. Wm. Butler.

8 October—Bazil Noel—Mary Gregg. John Todd.

18 November—John Vancleave—Marjah Kerns, daughter of Peter Kerns. John Ryker—att. Wm. Butler.

18 November—William Wallace—Sarah Shannon, daughter of Thos. Shannon. Alexander Reid.

27 November—Reuben Clark—Betsey Lacefield. William Lacefield—att. Wm. Butler.

28 November—Edmond Adcock—Mary Ford. James Hoagland.

5 December—Lewis Bain—Sally Hensley. George Hensley—att. Wm. Butler.

8 December—Isaac Garrett—Elizabeth McDowell, daughter of Charles McDowell. Hugh Adams—att. Wm. Butler.

22 December—Jacob Stark—Margaret Stark, daughter of James and Hannah Stark, Jonathan Stark, Aaron Stark—att. Jas. Craig.

24 December—Jonathan Hensley—Nancy Garrett, daughter of John Garrett. Saml. Hensley.

30 December—William Thomas—Mary Cypher. Joseph Cyphers—att. Wm. Butler.

31 December—Samuel Hensley—Allefer Cooper, daughter of Leven Cooper. Saml. Cooper, Isaiah Boone—att. Jas. Craig.

1 7 9 5

7 January—Samuel Cooper—Hester Lindsey, daughter of Mrs. Nancy Wilims (Williams). Squire Boone—att. Jas Craig.

8 January—Robert Erwin—Temperance Meek. Jeremiah Meek—att. Craig.

8 January—Robert Erwin—Temperance Meek. Jeremiah Meek—att. Jas. Craig.

20 January—John Otgan—Mrs. Eliza Bell (widow). John John—att. Jas Craig.

5 February—Aquilla Whitaker—Drusey Price, daughter of Walker Price. Levi Whitaker—att.Wm. Butler.

10 February—Alexander Millin—Elnore Mayo. Alexander McClain—att. Wm. Butler.

19 March—Benjamin Applegate—Lucy Huse, daughter of Benjamin Huse. David Price.

19 March—David Price—Frances Pearse, daughter of George Pearse. Benjamin Applegate.

4 May—Jesse Crume—Jane Cyphers, daughter of Joseph and Barbary Cyphers.

21 May—Michael Wallace—Agness Shannon, daughter of Thos. Shannon. Alexander Shannon—att. Wm. Butler.

22 May—Joseph Hammond—Esther Garrett, daughter of John Garrett. Richardson Hensley.

21 July—William Ferguson—Easter Allison. Anthony Sharp—att. J. Craig.

21 July—Stephen Shipman—Margarett, daughter of John Garrett. Charles McDowell.

31 July—Allen Manson—Sarah Griffin, daughter of Ralph Griffin. Aaron Vancleave—att. Wm. Butler.

5 August—Thos. Horton—Elizabeth Heighday. George Harris; James Hoagland—att. J. Craig.

6 August—John Teigue (Teague ?)—Polly Harris, daughter of Daniel Harris. Joseph Teigue, Saml. Smock, George Harris—att. Jas. Craig.

26 August—James Shield—Elizabeth Martin, daughter of John Martin. Wm. Richy, Edward Martin—att. Jas. Craig.

28 August—Elias Neels—Mrs. Margaret Bowling. Coleman Daniel—att. J. Craig.

4 September—Tobias Wise—Mary Griggsby. Charles Griggsby—att. Will Chaplain.

6 October—Thomas Cously—Margaret Lowden, daughter of Robert Lowden. Jas. W. Hemphill, Philip Buzan.

16 December—Isaac Williams—Jane Galbreath. David Galbreath—att. J. Craig.

21 December—William Garrett—Sally Gasaway. Jospeh Hammond—att. Wm. Butler.

28 December—Ambrose Bols—Jeny McCortney, daughter of John and Hannah McCortney. Wm. Lee, John Johns.

1796

No date—William Goddard—Winney Duree, daughter of Anne Banta. Saml. Duree, Abraham Bull—att.W. Logan.

1 March—James Duley—Betsy Denbow, daughter of Soloman Denbow. John Crawford—att. Wm. Logan.

5 March—John Smith—Jane Collins. William Collins.

14 March—Spence Ford—Susanna Bright, daughter of Albertus Bright. Lewis Bright, Jas. Bright, Saml. Ford.

18 March—Abraham Kephart—Rebekah Thorn, daughter of Elizabeth Thorn. Samuel Thorn.

26 March—Adam Sill—Ann Huss. William Hall—att. Wm. Logan.

4 April—Ewel Kendall—Elizabeth Stephenson, (given in consent Stinson). James Stephenson—att. Wm. Logan.

5 April—John Eliott—Fanny Pruitt, consent of Elisha Pruitt. Jas. Logan, Joseph Pruitt—att. Wm. Logan.

6 May—Andrew Gregory—Mary Lunceford. Bland W. Ballard—att. Wm. Logan.

25 May—Wm. C. Readey—Sarah Fisher, consent of Zach Fisher. Mical Randel, Jas. Logan.

28 May—Timothy Flude—Mary Oliver. Cravin Lane—att. Wm. Butler.

1 June—Light Townsend—Betsey Diheroon. Jas. Long—att. Wm. Butler.

21 June—Noah Staples—Mary Mahurin, daughter of Silas and Sarah Mahurin. Stephen Mahurin—att.Go. I. Johnston and Wm. Logan.

28 June—Thomas Jacobs—Elizabeth Cline, daughter of John Cline. Wm. Hall, George Conn, Joseph Nelley.

28 June—John Polly—Polly White. Hugh Micklin—att.Wm. Logan.

9 July—James Robins—Mary Lastly. David Miller, Richard Elam.

14 July—William McCormick—Nancy Morton. John Wright—att. Wm. Logan.

18 July—Noah Staples—Betsey Oliver (widow). Thomas Dougherty, Aug. Carnes—att.Wm. Logan.

27 July—John Kysor—Catherine Ferguson, daughter of Catherine Ferguson. Moses Cook, Alex Rowan—att. Wm. Logan.

31 August—William Neal—Salley Blackwell. Wm. Roberts.

20 September—John Gregory—Priscilla Bracket. Hankins Bracket—att. Will Logan.

22 September—Wm. Crawford—Nancy Benbow. Jas. Dooley—att. Will Logan.

20 October—John Montgomery—Lidia Lucus, or Lukes, daughter of Abraham Lukes. Thomas Harris, Jas. Steel—att.Will Logan.

24 October—Richard Elam—Elizabeth Sorrels, daughter of Nelly Sorrels. Jas. Logan, Jas. McCampbell, Robert C. Hatton.

29 October—George Campbell—Margaret Ferguson. Campbell Ferguson—att. Will Logan.

2 November—Robert Glass—Sally Owen, daughter of Brackett Owen. Thomas I. Gwin, John Owen.

14 November—Daniel Johnston—Martha Sturgeon. James Sturgeon—att. Will Logan.

28 November—George Corn—Jane Williams, daughter of David Williams. James Kern, John Kern, James Carr—att. Wm. Logan.

19 December—Joseph Pruitt—Patsey Elliott, daughter of Robert Elliott. John Elliott, Elisha Pruitt.

20 December—Francis May—Mary McGrew, daughter of Alexander McGrew. John Dinnen, John McGrew, Anthony Denning—att. Wm. Logan.

20 December—Anthony Denning—Susanna Hoke, daughter of Henry Hoke. Wiliam Denning, Francis May—att.Wm. Logan.

20 December—Phillip Hart—Susanna Johnson, daughter of John and Rachel Johnson. John Johns, Henry Johns—att. Wm. Logan.

21 December—Denis Murphy—Sally Postleweight. James Duncan—att. Wm. Logan.

1 7 9 7

12 January—Jacob Castleman—Sarah White, daughter of John White. Pascal Hickman—att. Wm. Logan.

17 January—William Gregory—Rebekah Lain, consent of Lombard and Rebekah Lain. Philip Hart, Henry Johns—att.Will Logan.

21 January—George McClain—Ann McHenry, consent of Richard McHenry. Nicholas Cline, John McClain.

26 January—Larkin Langford—Rachel Tucker, daughter of Jacob Tucker. Wm. Tucker—att. Wm. Logan.

31 January—James Johnson—Jane Currey. Thomas Johnson.

3 February—John Leatherman—Betsey Graves, daughter of David Graves. Peter Leatherman—att. Wm. Logan.

4 February—John B. Mills—Susanna Howard, daughter of Drury Howard. Jas. McDavitt—att. Wm. Logan.

4 February—George Taylor—Betsey Leatherlain. Samuel Ray—att. Wm. Logan.

7 February—Samuel Sebastian—Sarah Carlin. Absalon Carr—att. Wm. Logan.

11 February—Elisha Langley—Jane Shepherd. Christopher Shepherd, Elisha Langley—att. Wm. Logan.

13 February—James Anderson—Mary Montgomery. Alex. Montgomery—att. Wm. Logan.

21 February—Spencer Collins—Catherine Lukes, daughter of Abraham Lukes. James Glover—att. Wm. Logan.

23 February—John Cull—Rachel McHenry. Hugh Cull—att. Wm. Logan.

27 February—Robert Benbow—Mary Ann Crawford. Wm. Crawford—att. Wm. Logan.

1 April—Adam C. Smith—Mary Baker. Martin Daniel—att. Wm. Logan.

2 April—Simeon Newman—Elizabeth Harrison, daughter of John and Elizabeth Harrison. John Long, JamesHannah, John Harrison—att. Wm. Logan.

10 April—John Harris—Mary Carmen. Caleb Carman—att. Wm. Logan.

11 April—Nathan Underwood—Betsey Wright, consent of Obadiah and Hannah Wright. Charles Baird—att. Wm. Logan.

16 April—Lewis Bright—Polly Ford, daughter of Wm. Ford. Hopkins Bright, George Boyd—att. Wm. Logan.

20 April—Ezekiel Newman—Betsey Harrison, daughter of John and Elizabeth Harrison. JamesQuirk—att. Wm. Logan.

24 April—Jesse Pendergrass—Patsey Moore (name torn). Frederick Hoff—att. Wm. Logan.

2 May—James White—Anne Glen. Wm. Glen—att.Wm. Logan.

8 May—George Burton—Rebekah Lee, consent Gershom and Rebecah Lee. Nathan Lee—att. Wm. Logan.

9 May—Jeremiah Payne—Sally McCoy, consent Wm. McCoy. Daniel Bennett—att. Wm. Logan.

22 May—Henry Boyle—Sarah Park. George Cravenson—att. Jas. Craig.

10 June—Jonathan Ruble—Hannah Leatherman, daughter of Mrs. Elizabeth Black. Jacob Ruble—att. J. Lindsay.

12 June—Henry McWade—Mary Carman. Wm. Butler, Wm. Elam.

17 June—Joseph Gregory—Polly Kendall, daughter of Thos. Kendall. Thos. Kindel—att. Will Elam.

20 June—Thomas F. Rees—Polly Bright, daughter of Albertus Bright. Lewis Bright, Spencer Ford—att. Wm. Elam.

20 June—Adam Hostatter—Hannah Hartman. Christian Hostatter—att. Wm. Elam.

3 July—William Johnson—Jenney Miller. Isaac Miller—att. Wm. Elam.

2 August—Abraham Hoff—Ann Whitaker. John Whitaker—att. Wm. Elam.

10 August—Berryman Hencely—Elizabeth Morgan. Richardson Hencely.

26 August—Wm. Owen—Lucy Cardwell. John Owen—att. W. Elam.

28 August—William Marquess—Lucy Griffin. Jas. Alle—att. Wm. Elam.

15 August—Aaron Long—Matty Sill. Wm. Tunks.

21 August—Frederick Leatherman—Polly Lastly. Jacob Wise.

24 August—David Fish—Franky Shepherd, daughter of Patsey Shepherd. Christopher Shepherd, George Hansberry.

21 August—Joseph Williams—Easter Hambleton, daughter of Wm. Elet. George Corn, William Keer.

14 August—Edmond Hencely—Polly Garrett. Wm. Garrett—att. Wm. Elam.

1 September—Elisha Lindsey—Sarah Holmes, daughter of Jas. Holmes. Nicholas Lindsey, Jesse Holmes, G. Shannon—att. Jas. Craig.

11 September—John Stevens—Sarah Pryor. James Reed—att. W. Elam.

18 September—Thomas Theobald—Patience Pendergrass. Jesse Pendergrass, Garrett Pendergrass.

27 September—John Ross—Sally Lane, daughter of Lambert and Rebecca Lane. Henry Johns, John Johns—att. Wm. Elam.

22 September—Thomas Dougherty—Jane Smith. Samuel Perkins, John Fields—att. Wm. Logan.

8 October—Samuel Smith———— David Smith—att. Wm. Elam.

14 October—AlexanderWarson—Jane McDowell. Alex. McDowell—att. Wm. Elam.

14 October—Francis Hall—Mrs. Eliza Elam. James Craig.

17 October—Obadiah Truax—Nelly Sturgeon, daughter of John Sturgeon. Robt. Sturgeon.

17 October—Comander Piles—Nancy Baker. Att. Wm. Butler.

21 October—Bazil Tegard—Ann Todd, daughter of John Todd. Jacob Ruble—att. Wm. B. Elam.

1 November—Elias Hoagland—Sarah Wood, daughter of Mary Wood. James Wardlaw—att.W. B. Elam.

3 November—Nathan Crawford—Nancy Hicks, consent of brother and sister. Drury Melone.

15 November—Crus Sut—Janey Miller. Conrad Miller—att. W. B. Elam.

13 November—James Cochren—Catherine Casey. Charles Casey.

14 November—Henry McWaid—Margaret Anderson. John Shannon—att. W. B. Elam.

15 November—Yelley Kindall—Mary Clark, consent of John and Mary Clark. Wm. Kendall, Thos. Gree—att. W. B. Elam.

16 November—Hugh McClure—Polly Lewis, daughter of Thos. Lewis. Lewis Ellison, Betsy Ellison, Jas. Logan.

18 November—Nathan Scearce—Lilly Weakley. Stephen Weakley—att. Wm. Elam.

18 November—Samuel Smock—Rachel Robins. Gerardus Ryker, Wm. Elam.

29 November—Edward Mosby—Sarah Jones Elliott. William Elliott, Wm. Elam.

24 November—Robert Cameron—Mary Ann Shields. Thos. Simpson—att. Wm. Elam.

28 November—Nathan Lee—Isabella Morrow, daughter of Wm. Morrow. Wm. Elam.

30 December—Wilford Martin—Mary Winkfeld. Francis 'M-v—att. Wm. Elam.

8 December—John Davis—Charity Bryan, daughter of J Alse Bryan. Joseph Bryan—att.W. B. Elam.

9 December—Thos. Chenoweth—Nancy Collins, daughter Collins. Richard Chenoweth.

8 December—Jas. Worthington—Hannah McPike. Saml. Perkins.

11 December—Alex. Acker—Jenney Clark. Hezekiah Pigg, Wm. Elam.

13 December—John Leverston—Mary Bryant. Alexander McNeal.

13 December—Benjamin McNew—Rachel Bryant. Jonathan Vancleave.

12 December—Will Metcalfe—Elizabeth Jones. Rich Jones.

20 December—Dickey Graves—Nelly Tilly, consent of Lazarus Tilly. Edmond Graves, Wm. Elam.

20 December—Chris Rhody—Isbell Buzan. McKinley, Will Elam.

21 December—Saml. Boyd—Agness Moon. Jas White, Wm. Elam.

22 December—Price Nuttle—Polly Ditto. Abraham Ditto.

25 December—Wm. Lock—Elizabeth Tague (Teague), consent of John Tague. Benj. Lock, Robt. C. Hatten, W. Elam.

29 December—Saml. Perkins—Polly Blake. Rich Elam.

30 December—John Lowden—Sally Carr. Jas. Carr, Wm. Elam.

31 December—Daniel Coleman—Elizabeth Connell, daughter of Jesse Connell. John Reed, Nancy Connell, Francis Connell.

1 7 9 8

(Not in First Marriage Book—Bond in Bundle)

19 January—James Brown Isbell Brown. David Miller, Elam.

22 January—Charles Baird—Catherine Tyler. Robt. Tyler, John Watson, W. B. Elam.

15 April—John Dellin—Mary Mahurin. Stephen Mahurin, Wm. Elam.

12 June—William Graham—Patsy Shillideay. George Shillideay; attorney, W. Watson.

27 July—Samuel Long—Hannah Griffith. Thos. Griffith, Wm. B. Elam.

26 July—Wm. Miller—Mildred Johnson. John Miller, Wm. Johnson, Elam.

4 August—Christian Leatherman—Barbary Hostedler, consent of Christian Hostedler.

OLD BIBLE RECORDS

HUTCHINSON BIBLE

(Contributed by Mrs. Ruby Arnsparger, Jemima Johnson Chapter).

DEATHS

James Hutchison, the father of Archibald, Sr., departed this life July 28, 1806, in 66th year of his age.

Peggy (Margaret) Hutchinson, the mother of Archibald, departed this life March 5, 1815, in 80th year of age. (This is not very legible, might be 89th year of age).

Sallie Hutchison Ware, daughter of Archibald and Catey Hutchinson, died Oct. 16, 1816.

James G. Hutchinson, son of Archibald and Catey Hutchinson, died Nov. 27, 1819.

Archibald Hutchinson, husband of Catey Hutchinson, died Aug. 31, 1831, in the 64th year of his age.

J. O. Hutchinson, son of Archibald and Catey Hutchinson, died July 24, 1834.

Catey Hutchinison, wife of Archibald Hutchinson, departed this life May 18, 1865.

Thomas Metcalf departed this life Jan. 3, 1895.

Archibald Hutchinson, son of Archibald and Catey Hutchinson, departed this life Dec. 6, 1900.

BIRTHS

Sally Hutchinson, daughter of Archibald and Catey Hutchinson, his wife, was born Sept. 22, 1796.

Hiram Hutchinson, son of Archibald and Catey Hutchinson, his wife, was born Nov. 24, 1798.

(First name not legible) Hutchinson, son of Archibald and Catey Hutchinson, his wife, born Nov. 24, 1800. (Birth not legible).

Kitty Hutchinson, daughter of Archibald and Catey Hutchinson, his wife, was born May 2, 1805.

Polly Hutchinson, daughter of Archibald and Catey Hutchinson, his wife, was born Sept. 29, 1807.

Archibald Hutchinson, Jr, son of Archibald and Catey Hutchinson, his wife, was born Oct. 21, 1809.

Jensey Hutchinson, daughter of Archibald and Catey Hutchinson his wife, was born May 21, 1812.

Catherine Metcalf was born Feb. 19, 1830.

MARRIAGES

Archibald Hutchinson and Catey Gouge married Jan. 11, 1786.

Elizabeth B. Hutchinson and Abraham Lowry married April 8, 1806.

Peggy Alsop Hutchinson and Thomas Metcalf married April 6, 1809.

Fanny Hutchinson and Robert McFatridge married May 10, 1810.

James Hutchinson (marriage recorded but not legible).

Sallie Hutchinson (marriage recorded but not legible).

BIRTHS

Archibald Hutchinson born on Friday, the 27th day of March, 1767.

Catey Hutchinson, his wife, was born in October, 1766.

Elizabeth Bell Hutchinson, daughter of Archibald and Catey

Hutchinson, his wife, was born on October 30, 1786.

Peggy Alsop Hutchinson, daughter of Archibald and Catey Hutchinson, his wife, was born Feb. 21, 1789. Birth recorded, but badly torn.

Fanny Hutchinson, daughter of Archibald and Catey Hutchinson, his wife, was born April 19, 1794.

NOTE: The record of births, deaths and marriages of the Hutchinson family as given was copied by me from the old Hutchinson family Bible, and to the best of my knowledge and belief is a true and accurate copy.

BERTHA HUTCHINSON CHAPMAN,
Newport, Kentucky.

HUTCHINSON-LOWERY BIBLE

(Contributed by Mrs. Ruby Arnsparger, Jemima Johnson Chapter).

James Hutchinson, son of Thomas Hutchinson, of St. George Parrish Spttsylvania County, Virginia, was born 1740. Departed this life July 28, 1806.

Peggy Alsop, wife of James Hutchinson, born 1740, departed this life 1815.

Archibald Hutchinson, son of James, born March 27, 1767.

Caty Gouge, wife of Archibald Hutchinson, born Oct. 7, 1766, Baltimore, Md.

Archibald Hutchinson and Caty Gouge married Jan 11, 1786, Port Royal, Va.

Archibald Hutchinson departed this life Aug. 21, 1831.

Caty Gouge Hutchinson, wife of Archibald, departed this life May 17, 1868, aged 99 years.

Abraham Lowry, son of Stephen Lowry and Catherene Lewis, was born 1781, departed this life Sept. 25, 1816, aged 35 years.

Elizabeth Lowry, daughter of Archibald Hutchinson and wife, born Oct. 30, 1786, departed this life Aug. 17, 1859.

Abraham Lowry and Elizabeth Hutchinson married April 6, 1806.

Catheren Lewis Lowry born July 25, 1807, died 1848, unmarried.

Alexander Scott Lowry, born Jan. 6, 1809, died 1854, married Miss St. Clair.

James H. Lowry, born April, 1811, married Miss Elizabeth Neal.

William H. Lowry, born Nov. 25, 1813, died 1877, married Miss Sobrina Neal.

Abraham Lowry, born May 6, 1815, married Miss Mason.

Stephen Archibald Lowry, born Jan. 28, 1817, married Miss Mary Smith.

Sobrina Neal, born 1831, died 1909, married William H. Lowry, June 3, 1862.

McROBERTS BIBLE RECORD
Lincoln County

(Contributed by Mrs. William James, Logan Whitley Chapter).

John McRoberts and Lynney Jackman were married Jan. 6, 1802.

John McRoberts was born Aug. 18, 1772—Died June 22, 1840.

Lynney Jackman was born Dec. 24, 1774—Died April 2, 1851.

Sydney S. McRoberts was born May, 24, 1807.

Hayden J. McRoberts was born July 9, 1810.

Oliver Perry McRoberts was born Dec. 4, 1815.

Hayden J. McRoberts and Martha Jane Helm married July 4, 1838.

Oliver Perry McRoberts and Marry I. Hunton married Jan. 28, 1842.

Sydney S. McRoberts and Elenora Rizer married August 28, 1839.

Andrew Wallace (son of Samuel Wallace) born Sept. 25, 1748. Died July 3, 1820.

Isham Coulter was born June 23, 1816.

Mary Moore Coulter was born Dec. 8, 1824. Died Aug. 5, 1863.

John Bingaman was born Sept. 21, 1794. Died June 20, 1867.
Jenny Bingaman was born April 16, 1799. Died April 23, 1863.
Sallie Hutchinson Bingman was born Dec. 14, 1816. Died June 26, 1883.
Nancy Kissinger Hutchinson was born June 26, 1794. Died 1869.
John Buchanan was born March 6, 1815. Died July 2, 1898.

SNODDY BIBLE

(Contributed by Mrs. Mary H. Dean, Gen. Evans Shelby Chapter)

NOTE: The family records copied from the Bible of Robert Snoddy. The Bible was printed by Mathew Cary, 118 Market Street, Philadelphia, Penn., Oct., 1802 and bought by Robert Snoddy in 1803. We know by the fact being handed down from son to son, and neighbors that knew him, that he and his brother James were with Washington during the Revolution and were with him at Yorktown at the surrender of Cornwallis. The above mentioned Bible is the property of Carey Snoddy, Owensboro, Ky., great-grandson of Robert Snoddy. Robert Snoddy's will is in file on the Barren County Court House, dated 1820.

John Snoddy came from Ireland in 1740. He married Agnes Glasgow in the Presbyterian Church in Philadelphia, Penn., Oct. 7, 1741. Later he was Justice of Peace, Washington County, Va.

MARRIAGES

James Snoddy to Fannie Wilkerson, Feb. 28, 1768.
John Snoddy to Elizabeth Sampson, March 17, 1779.
William Glasgow Snoddy to Sarah Davis, Dec. 22, 1785.
Thomas Snoddy to Hannah Davis, November, 1786.
Robert Snoddy to Sophia Shaille, 1790.
Anne Lee Snoddy to Thomas Bransford, Nov. 3, 1789.
Mary Snoddy to Robert Patton, February, 1790.
Jane Snoddy to William Gibson.
Samuel Wilkerson Snoddy to Sally Alen, Nov. 13, 1794.
Daniel Snoddy to Sarah Alen, Dec. 24, 1794.
Carey Snoddy to Mary Haselwood Wilkerson.
William Snoddy to Verlina Burgess, Dec. 13, 1804.
Sally Snoddy to Phillip Hawker, July 3, 1804.
Jane Snoddy to William Hawker, Oct. 14, 1807.
David Snoddy to Nancy Thomas, June 22, 1807.
Thomas Snoddy to his second wife, Jane Blackburn, March 20, 1806.
William Thurman to Elizabeth Snoddy, Sept. 1805. (May be 1815).
Mary Snoddy to John Myers, Oct. 12, 1812.
John Lewis to Ann Snoddy, Aug. 29, 1816.
Carey A. Snoddy to Sarah Penn Edmonds, Sept., 1820.
Samuel Snoddy to Jane Gray, Jan. 1, 1816.
John Snoddy to Ann Shirley, Feb. 26, 1824.
Polly Snoddy to Nathaniel Parrish.

CHILDREN OF JOHN AND AGNES GLASGOW SNODDY

James, born Aug. 3, 1742.
Jane, born March 9, 1744.
John, born Sept. 15, 1746.
Mary, born Sept. 18, 1748.
Samuel, born Jan. 4, 1751.
Elizabeth, born June 12, 1753.
Cary, born Aug. 6, 1755.
Robert, born Nov. 10, 1757.
Thomas, born Jan. 26, 1761.
William Glasgow, born June 22, 1763.

CHILDREN OF JAMES AND FANNIE SNODDY

Samuel, born Jan. 6, 1769.
Daniel, born June 22, 1771.
Anne Lee, born Nov. 12, 1773.
James, born April 15, 1776.
David, born May 12, 1778.
Jane, born Sept. 14, 1781.
Francis Crutchfield, born May 7, 1789.

CHILDREN OF JOHN AND ELIZABETH SNODDY

William, born Aug. 4, 1780.
Thomas, born Feb. 12, 1782.
Sally, born May 25, 1783.
Fanny, born Feb. 22, 1786.
Elizabeth, born Feb. 23, 1788.
Jane, born May 15, 1789.
Anne, born Sept. 15, 1793.
Robert, born April 2, 1795.
Mary, born June 9, 1797.

CHILDREN OF CARY AND MARY SNODDY

Sarah Hazelwood, born Jan. 4, 1790.
William, born July 26, 1793.
John Cary, born April 15, 1796.
Robert Wilkerson, born Feb. 14, 1800.
Elizabeth, born April 1, 1803.

CHILDREN OF WILLIAM AND MARY SNODDY

John, born Oct. 2, 1786.
Samuel, born Nov. 9, 1788.
Daniel, born Dec. 8, 1790.
Polly, born Jan. 13, 1792.
Agnes Glasgow, born July 17, 1793.
Elizabeth, born Dec. 19, 1797.
Glasgow, born Aug. 9, 1799.
Betsy, born Oct. 11, 1801.
Nathaniel Davis, born Dec. 23, 1803.
William, born Feb. 13, 1809.
 Sally, born Nov. 24, 1811.

CHILDREN OF THOMAS AND HANNAH SNODDY

James, born March 9, 1788.
Mary, born June 14, 1790.
Nancy, born April 4, 1792.
Elizabeth, born Jan. 3, 1794.
John Davis, born Nov. 23, 1795.
Samuel Glasgow ,born Jan. 16, 1798.
Robert Henderson, born Nov. 22, 1799.
Hannah, born March 18, 1801.

CHILDREN OF SAMUEL AND SALLY SNODDY

Nancy Cary, born Nov. 18, 1795.
Fanny Lee, born Jan. 6, 1798.
Carey Allen, born Feb. 11, 1800.
Daniel, born March, 1806.
Ann Anderson, born Sept., 1808.

CHILDREN OF DANIEL AND SARAH SNODDY

Elizabeth Austin, born Aug. 11, 1796.
Francis Turner, born Nov. 22, 1798.
Sally Cary, born Nov. 27, 1800.
Benjamin Alen, born Feb. 26, 1803.
Martha Jane, born Feb. 27, 1805.
Mary Ann, born Jan. 16, 1807.

CHILDREN OF THOMAS AND ANN BRANSFORD

Judith, born Aug. 5, 1791.
Francis, born May 13, 1794.
Martha, born Aug. 3, 1799.
Walter, born Feb. 23, 1802.
Thomas Lewis, born Nov. 29, 1804.
From Buckingham County, Va., to Barren County, Ky. Ancestors of the Bransfords and Lewis' of Nashville, Tenn.

CHILDREN OF DAVID AND NANCY SNODDY

John Phillip Barateer, born June 22, 1808.
Edward Wilkerson, born Nov. 24, 1810.
James Cary, born April 7, 1811.

CHILDREN OF WILLIAM AND ELIZA SNODDY THURMAN

Ann Sophia.
Mary Elizabeth.
Robert Cary.
John William.

CHILDREN OF SAMUEL AND JANE SNODDY

Elizabeth, born Nov. 11, 1817.
Isabella, born Feb. 27, 1819.

CHILDREN OF THOMAS AND JANE SNODDY, HIS 2ND WIFE

Jane Mathews, born Feb. 16, 1807.
Edward Blackburn, born Oct. 25, 1808.
Thomas, born Feb. 18, 1811.
Margaret and Cary. (Indistinct).

CHILDREN OF CARY AND SARAH PENN SNODDY

Mary Ann, born July 21, 1821.
William Edmonds, born Aug. 26, 1823.
Robert Carey, born Dec. 17, 1825.

CHILDREN OF ROBERT AND ANN ROGERS SNODDY

Married December 12, 1848, Glasgow, Ky., and celebrated their Golden Wedding December 12, 1898, Louisville, Ky.
Sarah (Sally), born Sept. 23, 1849 or 1850.
Florence, born Jan. 14, 1852.
Addie, born Feb. 3, 1854.
Carey, born Jan. 17, 1856.
Ann Rogers, born May 19, 1859.
NOTE: Robert Carey Snoddy and Ann M. Rogers were married in Glasgow, Ky., Dec. 12, 1846. Ann M. Rogers was the daughter of Doctor George Rogers and Sarah (Gorin) Rogers, who was a daughter of John

Gorin, Revolutionary War soldier, who gave the people of Barren County 50 acres of land, the site of Glasgow, Ky. My wife's great-grandfather surveyed the land and I have the compass he used. Sarah Gorin was one of the first children born at Glasgow, Ky., her brother, Franklin Gorin, was the first white child born in Barren County.

CAREY SNODDY.

DEATHS

Samuel Snoddy died Feb. 1, 1768.
John Snoddy, Sr., died Feb., 1784.   Agnes, his wife, died Dec. 30, 1801.
Hannah Snoddy, wife of Thomas, died March 18, 1801.
Elizabeth Snoddy, wife of John, died June 9, 1797.
Elizabeth Snoddy, daughter of Thomas Snoddy, died July, 1795.
Elizabeth Snoddy, daughter of William, died Sept. 13, 1798.
Nancy Cary Snoddy, daughter of Samuel, died Oct. 13, 1796.
Thomas Snoddy, son of Robert, died June 17, 1807.
Francis Turner, daughter of Daniel Snoddy, died April 22, 1808.
John Snoddy, died Oct. 27, 1810.
Sophia Thomas Snoddy, died Dec. 19, 1810.
Carey Snoddy, Sr., died June 12, 1822.
Robert Snoddy, Sr., died Sept. 16, 1820.
Lytie Day Snoddy, born Aug. 31, 1890, Barren County, Ky.
Ann Lee Bransford, died July 20, 18—.
Carey Snoddy, son of Robert, died July 11, 1858, at Hot Springs, Ark., buried in Cave Hill Cemetery. Louisville, Ky.
Robert Carey Snoddy, son of Carey, died in Louisville, Ky., Nov. 16, 1905. Buried in Cave Hill.

CHILDREN OF CAREY SNODDY AND RUTH HALL SNODDY

Married in Glasgow, Ky., Sept. 27, 1883.
Robert Cary Snoddy, born June 24, 1884, Barren County, Ky
Lytie Day Snoddy, born August 31, 1890, Barren County, Ky.
Hall Terry Snoddy, born March 18, 1899, Owensboro, Ky.
John Rogers Snoddy, born Dec. 8, 1900, Owensboro, Ky.
NOTE: My sons have changed the spelling of their names and it is now Snowday.
Lytie Day married E. M. Spiak, of Jacksonville, Ill., where she now lives.—Carey Snoddy.

GOODLOE BIBLE RECORDS

(Contributed by Miss Letitia Hedges, Jemima Johnson Chapter)
(Copied from the old family Bible of William Goodloe by his great-granddaughter, Mrs. Elizabeth Goodloe Stephen Spears).
Robert Goodloe, born April, 1741. Died Jan. 25, 1797.
Sarah Short Goodloe, (his wife), born Aug. 14, 1745. Died June 2, 1814.
John Minor Goodloe, born March 1, 1771.
Elizabeth Goodloe, born Aug. 17, 1773.
Henry Goodloe, born Aug. 7, 1774.
David Short Goodloe, born July 26, 1776. Died Oct. 13, 1845.
Arch Woods, born Jan. 29, 1749. Died Dec. 17, 1836.
Susan Goodloe Hart, born March 15, 1839.
William Goodloe, born Oct. 22, 1769.
Susanna Woods, born June 13, 1778. Died Oct. 2, 1851.
John Goodloe, born Dec. 12, 1796. Died March 20, 1813.
Sarah Short Goodloe, born Aug. 2, 1798.
Mourning Goodloe, born Jan. 18, 1800.
Robert Goodloe, born Nov. 26, 1801. Died June 22, 1803.

Archibald Woods Goodloe, born Nov. 9, 1803. Died at Columbia, Ark., Oct. 27, 1849, and buried Dec. 4, 1849 in his father's graveyard.

Willian Clinton Goodloe, born Oct. 7, 1805.

Henry H. Goodloe, born Oct. 15, 1807. Died Oct. 1, 1848.

Elizabeth Jones Goodloe, born Nov. 25, 1809.

David Short Goodloe, born Nov. 3, 1811.

Thomas Woods Goodloe, born Feb. 4, 1814.

Octavious Goodloe, born April 21, 1816. Died March 22, 1847.

Lucy Ann Goodloe and her twin brother, George Goodloe, born March 28, 1819.

Lucy Ann Goodloe Hart, died Jan. 2, 1843.

George Goodloe, died Oct. 13, 1836.

William Goodloe and Susanna Woods were married on the 23rd. day of Feb., 1796.

Thomas Woods Goodloe was married to Mary Webb Ware, the 17th. day of Jan., 1844.

John Goodloe died March 20, 1813, age 16 years, 3 months, and 8 days.

Robert Goodloe died June 22, 1803, age 19 months.

George Goodloe died Oct. 13, 1836.

Lucy Ann Hart died Jan. 2, 1843.

EDMUND MARTIN, SR., BIBLE

(Contributed by Miss Letitia Hedges, Jemima Johnson Chapter)

NOTE: This Bible contains also the records of the Fristoe and Johnson families.

Elijah Martin was born March 19, 1768.

Micajah Martin was born March 6, 1770.

Jeremiah Martin was born June 16, 1772.

Sarah Martin was born July 18, 1774.

Anna Martin was born October 27, 1776.

Lucretia Martin was born May 12, 1779.

Isabel Martin was born March 8, 1783.

Rachel Martin was born November 13, 1784.

Rachiel Martin was born June 6, 1785.

Milly Martin was born May 20, 1787.

Edmund Martin was born was born April 29, 1789.

Hannah Martin was born August 24, 1791.

Sarah Deeling was born July 17, 1785.

Margaret Francis Martin was born February 17, 1833.

Louisa Jane Martin was born April 11, 1835.

Louisa Jane Martin departed this life March 10, 1850, aged 14 years, 11 months.

Margaret Francis (Martin) King, daughter of Edmund Martin, Jr., and his wife, Rebecca (Stitt) Martin, departed this life, March 22, 1854, aged 21 years.

Mary Louisa King was born April 19, 1852.

Edmund Carson King, born January 22, 1854.

NOTE: Susannah Fristoe's first husband was named Duling or Deeling, died perhaps near Philadelphia. Later she married Edmund Martin, Sr., who had lost his wife, and left three children, recorded above. Susannah Fristow married Edmund Martin, Sr., in 1788.

Edmund Martin, Sr., departed this life the 28th of November, 1811. In the 66th year of his age.

Susannah Martin, consort of Edmund Martin, Sr., departed this life the 18th of July, 1821, in the 62nd year of his age. "Re-buried at Millersburg graveyard July 22, 1839."

Edmund Martin, Jr., born April 29, 1789, and his wife, Rebecca (Stitt) Martin, born December 27, 1791, married July 19, 1815.

Edmund Martin, Sr., and Susannah, his wife, married the 10th day of March, 1788.

Edmund Martin, Jr., died May 27, 1863. Aged 74 years, 28 days.

Rebecca Martin, his wife, died November 25, 1865 in the 75th year of her age.

Elijah Martin and Rebecca Boggs married November 27, 1791.

Elijah Martin departed this life August 5, 1842.

Rachel Rees departed this life November 29, 1859, in the 75th year of her age.

Milly Pollard departed this life March 16, 1863, in the 76th year of her age.

BIRTHS AND DEATHS

CHILDREN OF EDWARD AND REBECCA MARTIN

Julia James Martin was born July 13, 1813. Died Aug., 1817.

Hiram Martin was born Oct. 10, 1816. Died June, 1838.

Susannah (Martin) Johnson was born Jan. 20, 1819. Died 1894.

Mary Williams Martin was born March 10, 1821.

Jeremiah John Martin was born Jan. 26, 1823.

William Porter Martin was born March 2, 1825.

Hannah Martin was born Aug. 27. 1827. Died Aug. 30, 1827.

Samuel Fitch Martin was born Nov. 5, 1828. Died 1895.

Jeremiah John Martin died March 30, 1887.

William Porter Martin died Nov. 11, 1881.

FRISTOE RECORDS

Daniel Fristoe was born December 7, 1739.

Mary Fristoe was born September 11, 1735.

Susannah Fristoe, daughter of Daniel Fristoe and Mary, his wife, was born June 29, 1760.

Lydia Fristoe was born November 17, 1761.

Mary Fristoe was born May 22, 1765.

Thamar Fristoe was born January 17, 1770.

Thomas Fristoe was born November 27, 1767.

Ann Fristoe was born March 13, 1772.

Catherine Fristoe was born June 19, 1774.

Henry Williams, son of George and Mary Williams, was born March 10, 1779.

George Williams was born April 1, 1781.

The first daughter of Rhodin and Catherine Hord was born March 23, 1801, survived eight days.

Mary Hord was born May 7, 1802.

Thamar Hord was born January 7, 1805.

William Henry Hord was born December 9, 1807.

William Grinstead was born August 18, 1772.

Daniel Thomas Fristoe Hord was born April 10, 1810.

Rhodin Hord was born January 1, 1777, father five children.

Prudence Grinstead, daughter of William and Ann Grinstead, was born October 5, 1793.

William Grinstead and Ann, his wife, were married the 7th day of January, 1793.

Rhodin Hord and Catherine, his wife, were married Sept. 9, 1800.

Daniel Fristoe departed this life Nov. 3, 1774, in the 35th year of his age.

George Williams, Sr., departed this life July 4, 1791.

James Grinstead departed this life on Sunday evening, April 6, 1807. Aged 84 years and 4 months.

Thomas Fristoe departed this life April 23, 1815.

JOHNSON RECORDS

William Johnson was born March 1, 1774.
Isabella Taylor was born Nov. 28, 1774.
William Johnson and Isabella Taylor married in the year 1795.
Joshua F. Johnson was born Oct. 2, 1796.
Elizabeth Johnson was born Jan. 11, 1799.
John Johnson was born May 20, 1801.
Laban Johnson was born May 20, 1805.
Theophilus Johnson was born Aug. 24, 1807.
William Johnson was born Feb. 20, 1811.
James H. Johnson was born Feb. 17, 1813.
Benjamin Franklin Johnson was born April 15, 1816.
Elizabeth Johnson was married to James Stitt Dec. 19, 1816.
Laban Johnson and Frances Holladay married Feb. 8, 1831 (or 51).
Theophilus Johnson and Ann King Kennett, married Aug. 26, 1828.
James H. Johnson and Susan Martin married Jan. 17, 1838.
B. F. Johnson and Elizabeth L. Martin married Feb. 2, 1848.
William Johnson, Sr., departed this life April 28, 1856.
Isabella Johnson departed this life Sept. 25, 1856.
Joshua Johnson departed this life Dec. 22, 1835.
Betsy Stitt (formerly Elizabeth Johnson) departed this life June 23, 1870.
John Johnson departed this life April 20, 1834.
Laban Johnson departed this life March 10, 1881.
Theophilus Johnson departed this life Jan., 1841.
William Johnson departed this life Jan. 30, 1882.
James Harrison Johnson departed this life March 9, 1896.
Benjamin Franklin Johnson departed this life Dec. 12, 1887.
Susan (Martin) Johnson departed this life April 19, 1894. (She was the wife of James Harrison Johnson above).
Ann Eliza Johnson, born July 11, 1838. Died Jan. 14, 1862.
(She was the daughter of Theophilus Johnson and Maria, his wife).
Hannah Taylor departed this life Nov. 11, 1817.
Joshua Taylor departed this life Dec. 26, 1825.
Births of James H. and Susan Johnson's children:
Louisa F. Johnson, born Nov. 22, 1838.
William Henry Harrison Johnson, born Sept. 21, 1840.
Mary Rebecca Johnson, born Oct. 19, 1842.
Elizabeth Franklin Johnson, born Sept. 1, 1851.
Louisa F. Johnson to James W. Conway, married April 25, 1854.
Mary R. Johnson to James M. Collier, married Jan. 16, 1862.
William H. H. Johnson to Mary Elizabeth Judy, married Dec. 15, 1864.
Births of William H. H. Johnson and Elizabeth Judy's children:
David Clarence Johnson, born October, 1865.
Lida Belle Johnson, born July, 1867.
Lelia Johnson.
Sue Johnson.
NOTE: This included eight generations, back to Richard Fristoe, Jr., father of Daniel. 2. Daniel, father of Susannah Fristoe Martin. 3. Susannah Martin, mother of Edmund Martin, Jr. 4. Edmund Martin, Jr., father of Susan Martin Johnson. 5. Susan Johnson, mother of W. H. H. Johnson. 6. W. H. H. Johnson, father of Lida B. Johnson. 7. Lida Johnson Conway, mother of Clarence Conway. 8. Clarence Conway is father of two children.

BEDFORD TESTAMENT RECORDS

(Contributed by Miss Letitia Hedges, Jemima Johnson Chapter).

Property of Misses Margaret and Grace Donaldson, Paris, Ky.
Littleberry Bedford was born January 1, 1769.

Mattie Bedford (his wife) was born September 8, 1772.
"Children."
Thomas Bedford was born October 26, 1790.
Henry Bedford was born October 26, 1792.
Elizabeth Bedford was born December 7, 1794.
William Bedford was born December 7, 1796.
Littleberry Bedford was born July 30, 1798.
John Bedford was born July 26, 1800.
Augustine Volney Bedford was born August 18, 1802.
Franklin Povall Bedford was born August 18, 1802.
Benjamin Coleman Bedford was born August 17, 1807.
Patsy Povall Bedford was born November 26, 1809.
Archibald Moseby Bedford was born February 25, 1812.
Edwin Green Bedford was born August 27, 1814.
George Madison Bedford was born May 19, 1817.
Franklin Povall Bedford died January 27, 1828. Aged 22 years.
Littleberry Bedford (father) died August 7, 1829. Aged 6 0years.
Henry Bedford died December 10, 1840. Aged 48 years.
Elizabeth Kennedy (nee Bedford) died July 18, 1834. Aged 40 years.
William Bedford died November 24, 1842. Aged 46 years.
Archibald M. Bedford died September 17, 1860. Aged 48 years.
Augustine Volney Bedford died March 6, 1863. Aged 60 years.
Mattie Clay Bedford died March 2, 1864. Aged 92 years.
George M. Bedford died February 12, 1887.
Patsy Povall Bedford Clay died March 19, 1897. Aged 88 years.
Edwin Green Bedford died 1901.
Children of William Green Clay and Patsy Bedford Clay:
Thomas Edwin Clay, born July 20, 1830. Died July 8, 1912.
Maria Clay Colcord, born 1832.
George Clay. Died infancy.
Mary Clay. Died infancy.
William Green Clay, Jr., born 1842. (Killed in Civil War, 1863).
Sidney Bedford Clay, born August 18, 1847. Died March 6, 1918.
Mattie Clay Donaldson, born August 20, 1845. Died May 18, 1928.

WILLIAM DEPP BIBLE RECORD

Contributed by Mrs. W. B. Smith, Edmund Rogers Chapter)

MARRIAGES

William Depp and Elizabeth, his wife, married the third day of September, Amo Domini, 1789.

Nancy Depp was married to Benjamin Davidson the 20th of November, 1814.

Susannah Depp was married to Jessee Davidson the 4th day of January, 1815.

Joel W. Depp was married to Elizabeth Montague the 10th of January, 1815.

Polly Depp was married to Elijah Buford the 16th of April, 1816.

Peter Depp was married to Mary H. Courts, the 1st of April, 1817.

Elizabeth Depp was married to Thomas Winn the 17th day of January, 1820.

John Depp was married to Mary Ellis the 24th day of September, 1823.

Patsey Depp was married to James Young the 14th day of December, 1826.

Thomas Depp was married to Phebe D. Young the 17th day of December, 1827.

Permelia Depp was married—of October, in year—

Jane Depp was married to William H. Young the 17th of December, 1840.

BIRTHS

William Depp was born March 25, 1761. Son of Peter and Susanna Depp.

Elizabeth Depp, daughter of Joel and Elizabeth Walker, was born July 13, 1772.

Nancy Depp was born Sept. 5, 1790.

Elizabeth Depp was born January 17, 1792.

Joel W. Depp was born May 16, 1793.

Peter Depp was born February 14, 1795.

Patsey Depp was born April 27, 1803.

Salley Depp was born June 7, 1804.

Thomas Depp was born September 15, 1805.

Permelia Depp was born July 29, 1807.

Two daughters born November, 1809.

Jane Depp was born April 30, 1815.

Susanna Depp was born the 14th of March, 1797.

Polly Depp was born December 5, 1799.

Jane Depp was born April 30, 1815.

Margaret Buford was born January 16, 1831.

Sarah Elizabeth Winn was born the 1st day December, 1820.

Peter Henry Winn was born the 21st day of March, 1822.

James Manning Winn was born August, 1823.

Elmore Depp Winn was born the 2nd day of May, 1825.

Robert McCoy Buford was born September 28, 1825.

Nancy Austin Winn was born the 15th day of January, 1827.

Elizabeth Depp was born June 21, 1826.

Catherine Depp was born July, 1825.

Joseph Henry Depp was born January 3, 1827.

Amanda Jane Depp was born the 7th day of October, 1828.

Walter Henry Winn was born November 5, 1828.

Elizabeth W. Depp was born the 11th of August, 1831.

Simeon Buford was born March 30, 1817.

William Davidson was born November, the 11th, 1815.

William Buford was born August 20, 1819.

John Buford was born December 24, 1820.

Haywood Buford was born January 18, 1827.

BIRTHS AND DEATHS

Elizabeth Depp died December 19, 1817. Aged 45 years.

Peter Henry Winn departed this life September 8, 1823.

Marcus D. LaFayette Winn was born December 26, 1830.

William Depp died the 19th of October, 1834. Aged 73 years.

Elizabeth W. Buford was born January 25, 1834.

Haywood Buford was born August 15, 1830.

Mary Francis Young departed this life February 6, '74.

William Buford departed this life September 30, 1821.

William H. Young was born November 7, 1812.

Jane Young was born April 30, 1815.

William D. Young was born November 12, 1841.

John W. D. Young was born May 1, 1843.

Philip N. Young was born the 7th of January, 1845.

Elizabeth Jane Young was borne November 21, 1846.

(Written on margin). Amanda S. Young died April 3, 1888.

William H .Young died November 6, 1888.

Martha Depp, consort of Jamess Young, died April 26, 1846.

Mary Young was born February 28, 1848.

Emily D. Young was born June 9, 1851 and died in nine weeks.

Jane Young departed this life July 3, 1851.

George Ann Young was born December 14, 1852.

Amandy Susan Young was born March 20, 1854.

Thomas Franklin Young was born January 16, 1864.
George Ann Young departed this life August 10, 1875.

BARLOW BIBLE RECORDS

(Contributed by Mrs. W. B. Smith, Edmund Rogers Chapter).

Robert T. Barlow was born April 20, 1773.
Ann Barlow (his wife) was born October 31, 1773.
William Barlow (his first son) was born February 12, 1794.
Mary T. Barlow was born March 27, 1796.
Jemina C. Barlow was born May, 1798.
Lucy F. Barlow was born January 25, 1800.
Henry W. Barlow was born November 7, 1801.
Robert E. Webb was born January 20, 1838.
Robert H. Barlow was born November, 1803.
John P. Barlow was born October 5, 1805.
Barbara S. Barlow was born October 9, 1807.
Virginia Ann Barlow was born July, 1809.
Louisa A. Barlow was born August 1, 1811.
Elizabeth F. Barlow was born June 7, 1813.
Nancy N. Barlow was born June 9, 1815.
James J. Barlow was born August, 1819.
Frances J. McHatton was born July 15, 1840.
Joseph H. Barlow was born May 13, 1825.
W. B. Dodd was born March 17, 1821.
Susan F. Dodd was born March 28, 1828.
James C. Dodd was born March 8, 1851.
Ann E. Dodd was born December, 1853.
Mary Emily Dodd was born February 22, 1857.
Richardson Eubank was born May 10, 1791.
James E. Webb was born February 7, 1869.
Helen H. Webb was born July 2, 1870.
John N. Webb was born September 15, 1872.

MARRIAGES

Robert L. Barlow was married to his first wife, Lena Burress, December 27, 1792.
He and Ann Blunt, his second wife, were married December 22, 1804.
William B. Barlow and Barbara Lane were married Sept. 4, 1817.
Henry W. Barlow and Ann Watts were married November, 1834.
John P. Barlow and Lucinda Craddock were married April 23, 1805.
Barbara L. Barlow and E. L. Webb were married July 29, 1830.
Richardson Eubank and Lucy F. Barlow were married Dec. 15, 1836.
Alexander R. C. Hatton and Mary H. Barlow were married Oct. 17, 1839.
James J. Barlow and Parmelia A. Hollis were married Jan. 5, 1843.
Louisa Barlow and William Jones were married November, 1846.
William B. Dodd and Susan F. Eubank were married Oct. 11, 1849.

DEATHS

William B. Barlow died April, 1832.
Jemima C. Barlow died 1805.
Robert H. Barlow died October 5, 1805.
Virginia Ann Barlow died July, 1827.
Robert T. Barlow died May 11, 1841.
Barbara L. Webb died March 20, 1844.
Nancy Barlow died July 28, 1844.
Richardson Eubank died May 13, 1851.
May L. Barlow died March 15, 1847.

Louisa Jones died December 7, 1874.
Elizabeth F. Barlow died November 11, 1878.
Lucy F. Eubank died September 25, 1884.
Robert E. Webb died December 5, 1893.
James E. Webb died September 27, 1898.

REYNOLDS-RICHARDSON BIBLE RECORDS

(Contributed by Mrs. W. B. Smith, Edmund Rogers Chapter).

DEATHS

Felix A. Richardson died July 6, 1835.
Marian McQeuown died February 19, 1889.
Sallie Reynolds, wife of M. S. Reynolds, died February 20, 1837.
M. S. Reynolds died July 27, 1891, 86 years old.
Jane M., wife of M. S. Reynolds, died February 9, 1897, 88 years old.
Thompson Ann, daughter of M. S. Reynolds and Jane, his wife, died February 6, 1845.
Jane M., daughter of M. S. Reynolds, and Jane, his wife, died March 16, 1845.
W. B. Reynolds died in Anderson County, Ky., at the home of Mrs. Martha Fullerton.

MARRIAGES

M. S. Reynolds and Sallie Ritter married November 23, 1830.
F. A. Richardson and Jane M. Steele marriedApril 27, 1830.
M. S. Reynolds and Jane M. Richardson married May 6, 1838.

BIRTHS

Elizabeth, daughter of F. A. Richardson and Jane, his wife, born May 8, 1834.
Felix A., son of F. A. Richardson and Jane, his wife, born December 11, 1835.
Thompson Ann, daughter of M. S. Reynolds and Jane, his wife, born July 1, 1844.
Emma S., daughter of M. S. Reynolds and Jane, his wife, born February 20, 1840.
Jane M., daughter of M. S. Reynolds and Jane, his wife, born December 14, 1842.
Fannie E., daughter of M. S. Reynolds and Jane, his wife, born December 23, 1844.
Brice S., son of M. S. Reynolds and Jane, his wife, born October 8, 1845.
Henry Clay, son of M. S. Reynolds and Jane, his wife, born April 25, 1847.
Belle K., daughter of M. S. Reynolds and Jane, his wife, born December 7, 1848.
T. T., son of M. S. Reynolds and Jane, his wife, born March 2, 1850.
J. N., son of M. S. Reynolds and Pane, his wife, born June, 6, 1852.
M. S. Reynolds fas born June 28, 1806.
Sallie Ritter was born October 2, 1809.
W. B., son of M. S. Reynolds and Sallie, his wife, born April 12, 1832.
James W., son of M. S. Reynolds and Sallie, his wife, born September 5, 1834.
Sallie E., daughter of M. S. Reynolds and Sallie, his wife, born February 19, 1837.
F. A. Richardson was born November 3, 1807.
Jane M. Steele was born August 22, 1812.
Eliza Ann, daughter of F. A. Richardson and Jane, his wife, born April 18, 1831.

Marian, daughter of T. A. Richardson and Jane, his wife, born June 15, 1833.

LAMPTON BIBLE

(Contributed by Mrs. Mary H. Dean, Gen. Evan Shelby Chapter).

Henry Lampton was born October 25, 1760 in Culpepper County, Virginia.

Susannah Holmes, daughter of Edward Holmes and Sarah Ann Starke, was born April 9, 1766 and married Henry Lampton January 3, 1785. Children: Thomas Catlett Lampton, born May 8, 1788, married Mildred Foushee, 1813.

Patsy Lloyd Lampton, born December 29, 1790, married John Holburt, September 17, 1812.

Ann Starke Lampton, born December 21, 1792, married Samuel Kerfoot.

Edmond Holmes Starke Lampton, born December 18, 1794, married Agnes McGoffin.

Joshua Elzey Lampton, born April 5, 1797, married Kate Hall.

Sally Conway Lampton, born February 27, 1799, married Dr. Goodman.

Lucinda Ethiford Lampton, born October 17, 1801, married John Aldridge.

Walker Taliaferro Lampton, born December 6, 1804, married Sallie Schrewsberry.

Henry Monroe Lampton, born December 6, 1808, married Mariah Upton.

James Madison Lampton, born June 18, 1811, married Eliza Hunter.

Joshua Lampton, born August 24, 1779, married Jane Finnell, of Kentucky, in 1803. They had eleven children.

William, born May 25, 1804, married Miss Martha Fountain.

James, born 1806, married Jane Ridgeway, of Boone County, Mo.

John, born 1808. (Did not marry).

Samuel, born 1810.

Lewis, born 1812.

Wharton, born 1814.

Benjamin, born 1817.

Martha Jane, born September 28, 1821, married April 24, 1844 Dr. William Keith.

Elizabeth Ann, born 1823, married Orace S. Ridgeway, March 16, 1848.

Joshua, Jr., born 1825.

Susan Lewis, born 1827.

William Lampton, born 1734, married Patsy Schooler 1763 in Page County, Va. Their children:

William, born 1764, in Virginia.

John, born 1766, in Virginia.

Lewis, born 1768, in Virginia.

Benjamin, born 1770, in Virginia.

Samuel, born 1772, in Virginia.

Sallie, born 1775, in Virginia, married James Trowbridge.

Mary, born 1777, in Virginia, married William Crosswhite.

Joshua, born 1779, in Virginia.

Susan, born 1781, in Kentucky, married William McKinzey.

Wharton Schooler, born 1784, in Kentucky.

James, born 1787, in Kentucky.

Benjamin Lampton, born in Virginia, 1770, married in 1800. Children:

Jane Lampton, born 1803, married John M. Clemens (father and mother of Samuel L. Clemens—Mark Twain).

Patsy Lampton, born 1805, married John A. Quarles.

(156)

James A. H. Lampton, born 1815.

NICHOLLS BIBLE

(Contributed by Mrs. Mary H. Dean, Gen. Evan Shelby Chapter).

James Nicholls, born February 1, 1775, died February 26, 1847.
James Nicholls and Margaret Randolph married November 20, 1800.
Margaret Randolph, born October 20, 1784, died October 10, 1855.
Their children:
Elizabeth Nicholls, born December 2, 1801, died February 6, 1891.
Henry Nicholls, born November 1, 1803.
Sarah Nicholls, born November 2, 1805.
Robert Nicholls, born December 2, 1807.
Prudence Nicholls, born February 12, 1809.
Cordelia Ann Nicholls, born April 16, 1811, died January 20, 1844.
Arromenta Nicholls, born October 1, 1814.
Randolph Nicholls, born February 7, 1816.
James Nicholls, Jr., born January 26, 1818, died January 27, 1852.
John Randolph Nicholls, born November 19, 1820.
William Pinkney Nicholls, born Feb. 23, 1823, died July 30, 1880.
Catherine Nicholls, born September 3, 1829.

MARRIAGES

Elizabeth Nicholls, first to John Wickliffe Israel Godman, February 19, 1823.
Mrs. Elizabeth Nicholls Godman married second, Rollo Sullivan, July, 1863.
Henry Nicholls to Elizabeth Nicholls.
Sallie Nicholls, to Elijah Phipps, Noverber, 1834.
Cordelia Ann Nicholls, first to Charles A. Wickliffe, July 6, 1829.
Mrs. Cordelia Ann Nicholls Wickliffe, to Francis Robertson.
Arrimenta Nicholls, to Charles Robertson, March 26, 1840.
James Nicholls, Jr., to Margaret Lea, January 22, 1841.
John Randolph Nicholls, to Parthena Board, December 5, 1848.
Catherine Nicholls, to James C. Moorman, February 5, 1852.
William Pinkney Nicholls, first to Lucy Nall, February 23, 1854.
William Pinkney Nicholls, second to Sally M. Bell, Sept. 5, 1872.

BROWN BIBLE

(Contributed by Mrs. Mary H. Dean, Gen. Evan Shelby Chapter).

Robert Brown and Sally Thompson were married December 26, 1801. In the 25th year of his age and the 19th of hers. Children:
Betsy S. Brown, born November 2, 1803 (Elizabeth did not marry).
Jane Brown, born July 4, 1806, married William Pettypool.
James Brown, born February 1, 1808, did not marry.
John T. Brown, born July 21, 1809, married Eliza Dean.
William Sweptson Brown, born March 1, 1812, married Miss Bruce.
Sarah Ann Brown, born March 29, 1813, married Mr. Padgett.
Dorothy Brown, born February 24, 1816, married Mr. Nelson.
Isabella Brown, born February 24, 1818, did not marry.
Mary Catherine Brown, born May 14, 1820, married William B. Elliott first, and Henry Thornton Lampton, second.
Richard G. Brown, born December 25, 1822, did not marry.
Martha Brown, born September 1, 1826, married Dr. Hill.
Robert Brown departed this life October 11, 1840, aged 64 years and nine months.

OLD GRAVEYARD INSCRIPTIONS

Washington, Mason County, Kentucky

(Contributed by Miss Hattie Scott, Susannah Hart Shelby Chapter)

Solomon Brown died December 16, 1833, age 51 years.

John A. West, born in Cumberland County, Pennsylvania, July 12, 1797, died October 14, 1859.

David, son of Captain David and Ann Bronaugh, born in Spottsylvania County, Va., May 12, 1793.

Elizabeth, daughter of P. J. and M. A. Key, born Nov. 15, 1855, died March 24, 1862.

Elizabeth Gowen, daughter of Samuel and Sarah Tebbs, wife of Thomas Forman, born May 12, 1810, died October 17, 1884.

Edward S. Perrie, born October 3, 1803, died December 25, 1856.

Harriet, wife of Edward S. Perrie, born October 21, 1807, died January 1, 1871.

Esther Werrich, consort of Henry Werrick, died May 8, 1821, 24 years old.

———— Harris, wife of M. Edward Harris, died suddenly 14th of December, 1798, 30 years, eight months, eight days.

NOTE: Either the first wife of Edward, Sr., or the wife of Edward Harris, Jr.

George Wood, born November 19, 1753, died August 22, 1832.

Anna Wood, wife of George Wood, died October 12, 1824, aged 74 years, four months.

Lewis Gordon died May, 1844, aged 83 years.

Keziah Gordon, wife of Lewis Gordon, died December 19, 1841, 82nd. year.

Abegail Johnston, wife of Dr. John Johnston, died, 1806.

Mary Johnston, wife of Dr. John Johnston, died May 8, 1794, aged 31 years, six months, three days.

Susan Thorp died November 24, 1820, aged 65 years, eight months, four days.

Andrew Thorp died January 3, 1827, aged 68 years, two months, 19 days.

Samuel Smith died March 20, 1808 in 52nd. year of his age.

Mary Smith, wife of Samuel Smith, died 1806, aged 44 years.

Louisa Matilda Johnston, daughter of John and Mary Ann Johnston, died Tuesday, February 23, 1826, aged 19 years.

Margaret Smith, wife of Samuel Smith, died July 24, 1850, aged 83 years, 7 months, 23 days.

Arthur Fox, born February 27, 1761, died April 11, 1794, aged 33 years, 1 month, 15 days.

Reuben Merrell, died March 12, 1849, aged 78 years, 7 months, 15 days.

Jonathon Stout, died August 28, 1819, aged 55 years, 2 months, 4 days.

Mary Ann Williams, daughter of Thomas and Mary K. Williams, born, April 10, 1799, died July 1, 1822.

Richard Carwine, born, December 27, 1748, died November 19, 1813, aged 64 years, 10 months, 22 days.

Mary Ann, daughter of Mary and James Biggers.

Hannah Richett, (?) daughter of David Riche (?(, died June, 1793, in 13th year of her age.

Mrs. American Taylor, wife of Miller Taylor, born May 12, 1796, died April 23, 1826.

Mason Williams, son of Thomas and Mary K. Williams, born March 15, 1801, died November 24, 1824.

Nancy Faw, wife of William H. S. Faw, born July 23, 1802, died August 18, 1823.

William Williams, son of Thomas and Mary K. Williams, born 180—.

Israel and Martha Williams, son and daughter of Thomas and Mary K. Williams, born March 10, 1803.

Elizabeth Holloway, wife of Samuel W. Holloway, died July 26, 1813, 31st. year.

Benjamin Davis, offspring of David and Sarah Davis, who departed this life without the knowledge of————?

Samuel Forman died January 14, 1833, aged 54 years, 4 months, 25 days.

Margaret Forman, born October 5, 1783, died November 12, 1856.

Ann Basettine Judson, daughter of Gilbert and Mary D. Mason, died January 25, 1839, 4 months.

Mrs. Abi Green, wife of John Green, died September 3, 1839, aged 39 (30?) years, 9 months, 27 days.

George Mefford, husband of Nancy Mefford, died November 11, 1832, aged 35 years, 1 month, 19 days.

Sarah Merrell, died November 2, 1849, aged 38 years, 9 months.

Nancy, wife of Stephen Barclay, born April 22, 1800.

John Byers, son of John and Ann Maria Byers, died December, 1823, aged 7 months.

Isabel Bayless Dewees, daughter John C. and Maria Dewees, died August, 1824, aged 9 months, 12 days.

Samuel Forman died January 14, 1833, aged 54 years, 4 months, 25 days.

Margaret Forman, born October 5, 1783, died November 12, 1850, aged 67 years, 1 month, 7 days.

David Wood, born April 13, 1789, died 1869.

Mrs. Emma Wood, wife of David Wood, died August 29, 1840, aged 43 years, 5 months, 8 days.

NOTE: She was, before her marriage, Emma Scudder.

Benjamin Bayless, Sr., born February 14, 1774, died October 18, 1839.

Rebecca H., consort of A. W. Richey, died November 30, 1835, 26 years.

Francis Perrie, born September 13, 1772, died September 6, 1812.

Richard Rutter, born Cecil County, Maryland, died July 28, 1840, aged 74 years, 8 months, 27 days.

Joseph E. Reid, son of John and Nancy, Reid, of Virginia, born July 27, 1791, died December 15, 1810.

Thomas Parry, died 1834, aged 86?

Mary Parry, wife of James Parry, died June 15, 1841, aged 8 months.

Sally Ann Parry ,wife of James Parry, died June 15, 1841, aged 28, 8 months, 15 days.

Mrs. Mary Proctor, daughter of Samuel and Elizabeth Peck, wife of Lewis Proctor, born August 3, 1800, died January 10, 1834.

Conquest W. Owens, born July 17, 1796, died October 5, 1861.

Eliza, wife of C. W. Owens, born January 3, 1802, died February 25, 1871.

Robert Taylor, Jr., born March 4, 1806, died September 2, 1852.

Our mother, Mrs. Dolly Wood Forman, born December 14, 1786, died May 4, 1872.

Arthur Fox, son of Andrew and Mary Wood, born 1856.

Mitilda Ann Wood, born January 19, 1794, died May 25, 1878.

NOTE: Daughter of Arthur Fox, wife of Andrew Wood.

Andrew Wood, born March 11, 1777, died March, 1866.

Sarah Jones, born October 31, 1792, died April 3, 1862.

Daniel Morgan died June 27, 1833, aged 53 years.

Stephen D. Morgan, born November 23, 1809, died August 4, 1865.

Thomas Blackburn died April 16, 1848, in 76th year.

Susan M. Musick, daughter of H. G. and A. M. Music.

Stephen Treacle, born April 15, 1741, died August 5, 1814.

Nancy Cheeseman, consort of William Cheeseman, second wife, died April 1, 1833, 79 years old.

William Cheeseman, born December 15, 1741, died July 24, 1828, aged 86 years.

Mary Cheeseman, first wife of William Cheeseman, born January 24, 1736, died November 27, 1805.

Sarah Corwine, born April 3, 1761, died September 11, 1820.

James Biggers, born February 22, 1804, died July 9, 1851.

James Chambers, born September 12, 1778, died November 9, 1823.

Ann Chambers, wife of James Chambers, born February 22, 1775, died March 29, 1845, daughter of John and Margaret Armstrong.

Britton Chandler, born March 20, 1797, died February 8, 1850.

Aaron Albert, born 1819.

Sarah Rees, (?) died 1795, aged 38 (?) years.

Louisa, wife of Joel Perham, born February 13, 1804, died July 15, 1875.

Lititia Jane, daughter of Andrew and Mitilda Wood, born 1826.

Sarah C., wife of D. R. Thomas, daughter of Alexander and Rebecca Rader and granddaughter of David and Sarah Tuckwiller of Greenbrier County, Virginia, born February 25, 1833, died June 26, 1864.

Rebecca, wife of Alexander Rader, daughter of David and Sarah Tuckwiller of Greenbrier County, Virginia, who died August 22, 1844, aged 32 years.

BRADLEY BIBLE

(Contributed by Miss Mattie R. Davis, Lexington Chapter)

(In possession of Mr. G. W. Bradley, Lexington, Ky.)

Thomas Bradley, son of Robert Bradley, was born March 5, 1761.

Philadelphia, his wife, daughter of Thomas Ficklin, was born December 15, 1768.

Robert Bradley, their son, was born June 26, 1790.

William Bradley, born February 7, 1793.

Henry Bradley was born July 7, 1795.

James Ficklin Bradley born February 10, 1798.

Margaret Bradley, born May 20, 1800.

John Bradley, born November 16, 1802.

(Mary) Bradley, born February 20, 1805.

Jephthah Dudley Bradley, born February 20, 1808.

Joseph Leeland Bradley, born August 11, 1810.

Robert Henry Bradley, son of William and Mahala, born January 25, 1819.

Sarah Margaret, daughter of William and Mahala, born August 4, 1827.

Elizabeth Jane Bradley, born April 24, 1829.

Amanda Ficklin Bradley, born September 18, 1831 on Thursday.

Mary Ann Maria Bradley, born May 7, 1834.

Nancy Kirkpatrick Bradley, born October 14, 1836, Friday.

Mahala Francis Bradley, born September 20, 1842.

Maranda K. B. Bradley, born December 28, 1839.

George Thomas Bradley, born August 29, 1845, Friday.

James William Bradley, son of William and M. Bradley, born February 25, 1848, Wednesday.

Eva Lee, daughter of J. H. and M. F. Miller, born August 26, 1802.

Lillie, daughter of J. W. and R. H. Hanna, born in Dover, Ky., February 13, 1867.

Mary Mahala Bradley, daughter of G. T. and S. F. Bradley, born at Pleasant Valley, April 28, 1868, Tuesday.

Lutte Bradley, daughter of G. T. and S. T. Bradley, born September 19, 1870, Monday.

George W., son of G. T. and S. T. Bradley, born December 22, 1882.

Alice Bradley, daughter of G. T. and Margaret, born July 9, 1891.

Sarah Margaret Bradley, wife of G. T. Bradley, born November 17, 1848.

MARRIAGES

Thomas Bradley and Philadelphia Ficlin married March 5, 1788.
Their son, William Bradley, married Sally (Deakins) April 7, 1818.
Henry Bradley, son, married Maria Jenkins (January) 25, 1808.
James F. Bradley married ———— Keller February 11, 1800 (10).
William Hudleson and Margaret Bradley married June 2, 1815.
William Bradley and Mahala Kirkpatrick married February 18, 1826.
Jepthah Dudley Bradley and Ann Eliza Suggett February 6, 1834.
Margaret Bradley and B. F. Dils November 4, 1846.
Eliza Fan Bradley and James L. Bradley April 26, 1819.
Amanda F. Bradley and R. H. Conawry July 6, 1854.
Nancy E. K. Bradley and T. M. Browning July 25, 1854.
R. H. Bradley and Margaret Ann Perkins August 1, 1844, Nashville, Tenn.
Mahala T. Bradley and James H. Miller September 19, 1861.
George T. Bradley and Susan T. Redmon June 25, 1867.
———— K. Bradley and J. W. Hi———— March (Feb.) 6.
George William Bradley and Margaret Schen, June 1, 1909.
Mary Louise Bradley, daughter of G. W. and M. S., born July 9, 1914.

DEATHS

Robert Bradley, son of Thomas Bradley, died October 22, 1820.
Philadelphia, consort of Thomas Bradley, died September 13, 1823, aged 51 years.
Thomas Bradley died June, 1824.
John Bradley died September 3, 1839.
Eliza Jane Bradley died August 29, 1852.
Henry Bradley died February 8, 1859.
Eva Lee, daughter of ———————— Miller, died March 14, 1864.
James W. Bradley died November, 1883, aged 35 years.
Sallie W. Bradley died May 25, 1819, wife of William Bradley.
William Bradley died in Millersburg, Ky., August 8, 1861.
Leeland J. Bradley died Bolivar County, Miss., November 12, 1861.
Amanda F. Conway died in Millersburg, Ky., December 4, 18(-)7.
Nannie K. Browning died April 1, 1871.
Miranda K. B. Hanna died in Dover, March 28, 1875.
Mahala Bradley died at B. F. Dills, October 28, 1875.
Fannie B. Miller died in Millersburg, January 20, 1879.
Susan T. Bradley died January 6, 1884, near North Middletown.
Sarah Margaret Bradley, second wife of G. T. Bradley, died January 15, 1925.
Author J. Skillman, son of Mary Mahala Bradley and Charles M. Skillman, died August 24, 1925, Washington, D. C., at Walter Reed Hospital, buried in Arlington Cemetery. Wife, Lillie Elizabeth Martin, baby, Lillian Elizabeth.
James W. Bradley Stitt, died May 19, 1918, in Vacaville, Cal., aged 84 years.
Sarah Margaret Bradley Dills died December 13, 1914, Enid, Okla.
Robert H. Bradley died June, 1918, Franklin, Tenn.
Alice S. Bradley died January 21, 1921.

BRECKINRIDGE BIBLE

(Contributed by Miss Mattie Davis, Lexington Chapter).

Owned by Miss Laura Virginia, and Marie Louise Smith, Lexington, Ky.

Preston Breckinridge was born the 17th day of March, in the year of our Lord, 1770.

Elizabeth Breckinridge, his wife, was born March 23, 1775.

Preston Breckinridge and Elizabeth Trigg were married in the year of our Lord, 1790. (She was the daughter of Col. Stephen Trigg, who was killed in the Battle of Raisin, who was born in Spottsylvania County, Va., in 1742 and buried in Nicholas County, Ky., August 19, 1782).

Preston Breckinridge departed this life on the 11th day of December at 3 o'clock Past Meridian in the year of our Lord, 1819.

Elizabeth Trigg Breckinridge departed this life in the year of our Lord ————.

Robert Preston Breckinridge, son to Preston and Elizabeth, was born the 1st day of November, in the year of our Lord, one thousand seven hundred and ninety-four.

William Trigg Breckinridge, son to Preston and Elizabeth, was born the 10th day of February in the year of our Lord, one thousand seven hundred and ninety-nine.

Mary Ann Breckinridge, daughter to Preston and Elizabeth, was born the 3rd day of June in the year of our Lord, one thousand eight hundred and two.

Steven Trigg Breckinridge, son to Preston and Elizabeth, was born the 11th day of January in the year of our Lord, one thousand eight hundred and six.

Elizabeth Latimer Breckinridge, daughter to Preston and Elizabeth, was born the 16th day of June in the year of our Lord, one thousand eight hundred and nine.

Gabriella Jones Breckinridge, daughter to Preston and Elizabeth, was born the 13th day of June, in the year of our Lord, one thousand eight hundred and twelve.

A. L. Shotwell and Gabriella Breckinridge were married July the 30th, 1829, by the Rev. Thomas Henderson.

Mary Ann Breckinridge and Leo Tarlton married the 14th day of January, 1819.

William T. Breckinridge and Deborah M. Russell were married on the 9th day of January, 1820.

Deborah M. (Russell) Breckinridge was born the 17th day of June, 1800.

Elizabeth Latitia Breckinridge, daughter of William and Deborah, was born the 3rd day of September, 1821.

Feilding E. Dickey departed this life on the 27th of February, 1836. ried on the 8th day of February, 1827.

Betsy Breckinridge Dickey, daughter of Fielding and Elizabeth L. Dickey, was born September the 12th, 1832.

Feilding S. Dickey departed this life on the 27th of February, 1836.

Laura Louise Dickey, daughter of Fielding and Elizabeth L. Dickey, was born May the 4th, 1835.

Stephen T. Breckinridge departed this life on the 19th day of November, 1836, in the 30th year of his age.

William T. Breckinridge departed this life on the 12th day of June, 1838, in the 30th year of his age.

Elizabeth L. Dickey departed this life on the 25th day of July, 1840, at 5 o'clock in the morning in the 31st pear of his age.

Betsy Breckinridge Dickey married Sidney Rodeo Smith, September 25, 1849.

RICKETTS-DAVIS BIBLE

(Published by Mathew Carey, 1812, Philadelphia, Pa. In possession of Miss Emma Davis, Nicholasville, Ky.)

(Contributed by Miss Mattie R. Davis, Lexington Chapter)

MARRIAGES

William Davis and Martha Ricketts were married August 19, 1829.

BIRTHS

Thomas Ricketts, Sr., was born November 23, 1753.
Ruth Ricketts was born July 10, 1758.
Martha Wilson Ricketts was born March 15, 1760.
Elizabeth Ricketts, of Martha, was born January 15, 1791.
Thomas Ricketts, of Martha, was born September 20, 1792.
Robert W. Ricketts, of Martha, was born August 21, 1790.
Margaret Ricketts, of Martha, was born October 1, 1796.
Nancy Ricketts, of Martha, was born March 13, 1799.
Benjamin Ricketts, of Martha, was born July 29, 1801.
Hezekiah Ricketts, of Ruth, was born October 27, 1781.
Mary Ricketts, of Ruth, was born October 27, 1781.
Martha Ricketts, of Martha, was born August 10, 1804.
John D. Ricketts, of Martha, was born December 11, 1806.

BIRTHS

William Davis, April 5, 1801.
Martha R. Davis, August 10, 1804.
Maranda A. Davis, June 16, 1830.
Thomas A. Davis, November 9, 1831.
Elizabeth M. Davis, March 10, 1833.
William M. Davis, April 15, 1835.
Robert W. Davis, November 22, 1836.
John P. Davis, May 2, 1839.
Luther A. Davis, March 30, 1841.

DEATHS

Thomas Ricketts, August 22, 1828.
Elizabeth Ricketts Crump, August 10, 1829.
Hezekiah Ricketts, February 16, 1841.
Thomas Ricketts June, November 30, 1844.
Martha W. Ricketts, September 11, 1850.
Robert W. Ricketts, January 1, 1856.
Elizabeth M. Davis died January 6, 1860.
William M. Davis, died August 18, 1864.
William Davis, Sr., August 21, 1875.
Mary R. Roberts, February 4, 1863.
Margaret R. Baker, July 18, 1866.
Nancy R. Davis, July 3, 1873.
Martha Crews Ricketts, February 4, 1878.
Benjamin Ricketts, October 22, 1881.
Martha R. Davis, September 3, 1888.
John D. Ricketts, December 18, 1890.
Robert W. Davis, October 28, 1895.
Luther A. Davis, June 21, 1905.
Maranda A. Magee, March 19, 1897.
John P. Davis, March 30, 1911.

DAVIS BIBLE

Bible published by Kimber & Sharpless, 1825, Philadelphia, Pa. In possession of Miss Emma Davis, Nicholasville, Ky.

(Contributed by Miss Mattie R, Davis, Lexington Chapter).

BIRTHS

Henry B. Davis was born December 15, 1764.
His wife, Ann Fullilove, was born October 10, 1768.
Sally Barnes Davis was born October 16, 1789.

Elizabeth Davis Larance (middle name) was born February 6, 1792.

Allen Davis, son of Henry Davis and Nancy, his wife, was born August 27, 1794.

Martin Davis was born September 30, 1795.

Nancy Davis, daughter of Henry and Nancy, his wife, was born July 27, 1797.

Henry Davis, son of Henry and Nancy, his wife, was born April 21, 1799.

William Davis was born April 5, 1801.

Ambrose Davis was born July 25, 1802.

Polly Davis was born February 21, 1804.

Martha Davis was born August 23, 1805.

Judah Davis was born January 6, 1810.

Melese Mize was born February 20, 1815.

Troyless Mize was born September 10, 1816.

Leroy W. Davis was born February 14, 1820.

Levy Davis was born December 27, 1821.

Marthey M. Davis was born March 4, 1824.

Henry R. Davis was born March 14, 1826.

John A. Davis was born May 24, 1828.

MARRIAGES

Henry B. Davis and his wife, Nancy, married December 16, 1788.

William Mize and Salley, his wife, married April 17, 1814.

Elizabeth Brooks was married March 4 or 1 day, 1818.

Henry B. Davis and Nancy Fullilove married Dec. 16, 1788.

BIRTHS

Henry B. Davis was born December 15, 1764.

Nancy Fillilove, his wife, was born October 10, 1768.

Sallie Barnes Davis was born October 16, 1789.

Elizabeth Larance Davis was born February 6, 1792.

Martin Davis was born September 30, 1795.

Nancy Davis was born July 27, 1797.

Henry Davis was born April 21, 1799.

William Davis was born April 5, 1801.

Ambrose Davis was born July 25, 1802.

Mary Davis was born February 21, 1804.

Martha Davis was born August 23, 1805.

Judah Davis was born January 6, 1810.

DEATHS

Henry B. Davis departed this life June 20, 1838.

Nancy Davis, consort of Henry B. Davis, departed this life January 31, 1841.

Allen Davis, son of Henry and Nancy, his wife, died December 15, 1794.

Anthony Fullilove died January 24, 1803.

His wife, Elizabeth, died February 17, 1803.

Benjamin Biggerstaff died March 3, 1836.

Capt. R. Munday died February 25, 1837.

Henry B. Davis departed this life June 20, 1838.

Nancy Davis, his wife, died January 31, 1841.

BIRTHS

Robert D. Brooks was born January 1, 1820.

Nancy Brooks was born September 3, 1821.

Rachel Brooks was born February 21, 1823.
Ambrose Brooks was born July 26, 1826.
Henry D. Brooks was born March 13, 1828.

John I. Kanatzar was born December 10, 1835.
Jesse Kanatzar was born March 28, 1797.
Nancy Kanatzar was born December 19, 1825.
Elizabeth Kanatzar was born September 12, 1827.
Polly Kanatzar was born June 14, 1830.
Henry Kanatzar was born September 29, 1833.
John I. Kanatzar was born December 10, 1835.
Joseph Kanatzar was born May 21, 1838.

MARRIAGES

Martin Davis was married May 14, 1818.
Nancy Kannatzar was married February 1, 1824.
Henry Davis was married May 14, 1826.
William Davis was married August 19, 1829.

DUDLEY BIBLE RECORDS

(Owned by Newton B., and J. Burgess McConathy. Bible published by
Baird & Dillon, Philadelphia, Pa., 1812)

(Contributed by Miss Mattie R. Davis, Lexington Chapter)

MARRIAGES

Ambrose F. Dudley and Nancy Moberley were married September 11, 1827.
Allen Embry and Nancy Dudley were married October 22, 1846.
Nathaniel C. Hart and Elizabeth Dudley were married December 12, 1848.
Newton McConathy and Sallie Hart were married October 8, 1889.

BIRTHS

Ambrose F. Dudley was born May 5, 1803.
Nancy Dudley was born January 15, 1809.
Elizabeth Mary Dudley was born May 4, 1831.
Semira E. Dudley was born October 11, 1832.
Thomas P. Dudley was born November 8, 1834.
James Ambrose Dudley was born September 5, 1836.
Richard M. Dudley was born September 1, 1838.
Edwin Embry was born July 6, 1846.
Nathaniel C. Hart was born February 26, 1825.
Elizabeth M. Hart was born May 4, 1831.
Mary Ann Hart was born July 9, 1850.
Semira D. Hart was born September 15, 1851.
Bettie M. Hart was born April 14, 1854.
Sallie Hart was born June 16, 1856.
Edwin N. Hart was born August 9, 1858.
Ambrose D. Hart was born August 18, 1860.
John I. Hart, November 28, 1862.
Mattie C. Hart, November 16, 1864.
Flora S. Hart, November 20, 1866.

DEATHS

Ambrose F. Dudley died August 17, 1840.
Nancy E. Dudley died September 26, 1846.

Edwin Embry died September 13, 1847.
Semira E. Dudley died June 10, 1853.
Edwin N. Hart died October 22, 1861.
Nathaniel C. Hart died July 1, 1868.
Myra D. Featherston died March 29, 1887.
Elizabeth D. Hart died March 10, 1888.
Newton McConathy died June 3, 1895.

BIRTHS

Newton McConathy, Jr., was born April 2, 1893.
J. Burgess McConathy was born December 18, 1894.

SPRINGFIELD CHURCH
Bath County

(Inscriptions from graves)

(Contributed by Mrs. Rezin Owings, Col. George Nicholas Chapter)

Eliza J., wife of F. A. McQuithy, July 22, 1842-December 15, 1915.
(Her son) G. T. McQuithy, November 4, 1875-July 9, 1899.
Flora Jean, daughter of T. B. and F. M. Gordon, November 25, 1850-August 22, 1863.
Infant daughter of John and Miranda Harper, died July 13, 1875.
Marinda Harper, daughter of B. W. Pearce, wife of John Harper, born June 21, 1858, died June 18, 1881.
Richard Noland, November 13, 1806-January 16, 1883.
Matilda, wife of Richard Noland, August 17, 1818-May 13, 1889.
Ivanora Triplett, October 24, 1875-February 19, 1879.
Archie, son of O. P. and Manerva Lovell, September 7, 1888-May 7, 1899.
Elizabeth, wife of J. T. Morgan, 1871-1904. (Her son) J. S. Morgan, 1902-1902.
Lucy J., wife of George Gregory, November 12, 1851-August 8, 1900.
John T. Overby, Company H., 18th Kentucky Infantry.
Jennie Lou, daughter of P. S. and L. Hughart, December 6, 1880-November 29, 1882.
John A. Gudgell, May 11, 1840-May 16, 1863.
Joseph Gudgell, September 20, 1801-May 13, 1864.
Louisa J., consort of Joseph Gudgell, June 20, 1814-July 28, 1861.
Joseph Gudgell, May 10, 1858-August 1, 1858.
Elizabeth, wife of W. Williams, died February 15, 1883.
William Williams, born March 2, 1822.
Julian Williams, October 8, 1866-July 22, 1877.
Nannie J. Burns, born February 24, 1851.
John Taylor, 1863-August 1, 1891.
James Harrah, died April 30, 1821 in 61st year of his age.
William Harrah, died September 28, 1815 in the 25th year of his age.
Eliza M. Harrah, died October 7, 1821, six years old.
Mary E., wife of W. L. Boyd, September 7, 1850-May 13, 1880.
Willis Hays Groves, June 29, 1809-May 4, 1852.
Samuel B. F. Crain, August 30, 1816-January 12, 1858.
Maranda R. Crain, December 7, 1816-April 20, 1889.
Andrew English, born 17—, died April 13, 1814.
James E. Groves, March 23, 1835-December 22, 1859.
John Groves, 1772-August 24, 1847.
Minerva Jane Groves, July 6, 1814-November 27, 1847.
Mary Louisa, wife of D. R. Jones, and daughter of W. H. and Minerva Groves, born July 25, 1833, died March 18, 1851.

Lucy, daughter of G. M. and E. R. Coleman, born June 1, 1856, died June 19, 1856.

Thomas Meteer, August 18, 1775-August 19, 1847.

M. M., May 1, 1815.

John Long, June 26, 1802, aged 32 years and 9 months.

December 2, 1799, Levina Brooks, aged 18 years.

Thomas Atkinson, March 18, 1754-April 11, 1812.

Mary Galloway, February 12, 1813, aged 74 years and six months.

Betsy Shanklin, died February 9, 1815, aged 18 years.

Rebecca Moffett, January 22, 1764-July 2, 1843.

John Caldwell, died June 9, 1806, aged 65 years.

Jane Hall, January 14, 1757-July 20, 1831.

William W. Donaldson, November 8, 1811-August 15, 1881.

Rebecca B. Crooks, January 18, 1780-December 6, 1845.

Elizabeth F., wife of Robert B. Crooks, died November 19, 1849, aged 54 years, 3 months and 1 day.

Fanny K. Anderson, September 9, 1798-May 17, 1860.

Henry H., son of W. and F. K. Anderson, January 14, 1841-August 17, 1843.

Owen Myers, October 28, 1845-March 5, 1910.

Annie, wife of Owen Myers, August 17, 1838-June 3, 1899.

Barbara Bartlett, 1812-1902.

Edgar J., son of W. and F. K. Anderson, May 17, 1838-January 15, 1839.

Robert C., son of W. and F. K. Anderson, May 10, 1838-December 16, 1838.

Margaret M. Graham, consort of James M. Graham, Jr., and daughter of Ephraim and Ann Herriott, born April 11, 1810, died May 27, 1838.

Lucinda H. Graham, died May 5, 1825, aged 17 years.

Sarah Graham, died October 14, 1844, aged 71 years, 1 month and 7 days.

James M. Graham, died August 6, 1825, 56 years old.

William W. Whaley, June 29, 1837-August 29, 1838.

James Burns, September 17, 1793-August 23, 1849.

Susan, wife of Enoch Burns, died August 8, 1845. Aged about 70 years.

Enoch Burns, died May 25, 1842, aged about 74 years.

Ignatious Burns, March 6, 1798-December 26, 1849.

James T. Burns, died October 1, 1857, aged one year, one month and ten days.

John W. Burns, died October 15, 1857 in the 10th year of his age.

Leuan Saunders, November 20, 1843-May 26, 1851.

Joe Minerva Burns, December 28, 1834-June 23, 1836.

James W. Burns, February 20, 1838-March 16, 1838.

James W. Saunders, November 19, 1834-March 17, 1838.

Sarah A. Gay died May 7, 1846, aged 25 years, one month and eleven days.

William Bean, died May 3, 1846 in the 47th year of his age.

Seth, son of Edmond and E. E. Botts, August 10, 1853-January 28, 1855.

Rev. Joseph P. Howe, died July 11, 1827, aged 61 years. "Organized and first pastor of Springfield Church."

Rebecca P., wife of J. P. Howe, died May 26, 1825, aged 53 years.

Malinda, wife of Ignatious Burns, October 19, 1794-January 31, 1870.

John F. Triplett, 1804-1875. Sarah his wife, 1812-1908.

Elizabeth W. Triplett, January 10, 1803-November 2, 1874.

Sarah S. Triplett, May 16, 1806-October 7, 1885.

Margaret Lochridge, died January 30, 1835, aged 73 years.

Joseph A., son of A. and J. Simpson, August 24, 1809-June 4, 1819.

Jane Simpson, died June 8, 1854 in her 77th year.

Andrew Simpson, April 15, 1772-January 8, 1842.

Mrs. Mary Stephens, April 20, 1804-December 28, 1845.

William Simpson died September 17, 1826 in the 26th year of his age.

Alexander Simpson died July 23, 1812,aged 58 years.

Elizabeth, wife of A. Simpson, died June 25, 1805, aged 51 years.

Elizabeth J. Simpson, daughter of William J. and Mary Simpson, died July 15, 1822, in the 4th year of her age.

Rebecca W., daughter of J. and R. Cunningham, born January 16, 1813, died August 6, 1875.

Sarah Cunningham, June 6, 1807-June 14, 1879.

Mary Ann, daughter of J. and R. Cunningham, November 21, 1802-September 20, 1869.

Elizabeth A. Gudgell, September 9, 1835-September 12, 1855.

Sarah Louisa, daughter of J. and M. E. Cunningham, January 19, 1853-May 12, 1853.

John Cunningham, Jr., August 4, 1798-September 22, 1852.

Willie T., son of T. F. and Helen G. Triplett, died December 3, 1880, aged 23 days.

William L. A. Cunningham, May 8, 1880-January 5, 1881.

William Andrew Young, born January, 1832, died February 11, 1833.

Jane Y., wife of John Cunningham, Jr., June 14, 1799-May 15, 1841.

Rachel, wife of J. Cunningham, October 16, 1771-July 31, 1835.

John Cunningham, Sr., May 27, 1766-June 25, 1847.

Margaret B. Cunningham, November 21, 1800-October 10, 1827.

Amanda M. F., wife of H. L. Crooks, born November 18, 1815, died January 7, 1845.

Margaret Crooks, November 19, 1778-July 10, 1831.

Uzal Crooks, August 13, 1774-August 1, 1824.

Capt. Elisha Catlett, born February 22, 1779, died November 13, 1824.

Robert Cunningham, March 20, 1832-August 27, 1833.

Maranda, daughter of J. and S. Atkinson, June 7, 1823, died October 20, 1828.

Mary G. Moore, consort of James W. Moore, August 14, 1845, in her 20th year.

Mary E., daughter of Dr. L. and Eliza Glover, born August 9, 1833, died December 24, 1854.

James Alexander Walker, died October 23, 1840, in his 23rd year.

Sarah E., daughter of W. F. and M. D. Atkinson, March 27, 1868, March 18, 1869.

Alice B., daughter of W. F. and M. D. Atkinson, born September 1, 1872, died August 19, 1875.

Emily E., wife of James H. Groves. born October 18, 1817, died March 30, 1858.

T. R. Groves.

Jane Hill, August 22, 1788-July 4, 1825.

Capt. James Hill, March 12, 1774-May 13, 1860.

Thomas Hill, March 6, 1781-March 25, 1847.

Jane R., wife of Thomas Hill, May 9, 1798-February 19, 1883.

Sarah Jane, wife of W. T. Howe, March 31, 1829-October 29, 1848.

Robert K., son of A. L. and S. A. Garner, born December 15, 1895-died December 23, 1895.

Eliza, wife of Thomas McIntosh, born September 9, 1824, died October 4, 1899.

Infant daughter of W. W. and M. O. Warner, born May 22, 1900, died September 21, 1900.

Maude Fassett, born 1865, died 1909.

James Turner, born August 2, 1906, died August 5, 1906.

Margaret Burns, born November 15, 1850, died September 11, 1899.

Maria, wife of Enoch Burns, born February 25, 1818, died May 19, 1883.

Burnie, born July 16, 1873, died July 30, 1875.

Lucy E., born December 16, 1879, died July 30, 1875. Child of O. and J. C. Stone.

John L. Moreland, born September 24, 1860, died February 22, 1908.

James H. Milaer (?) born November 21, 1809, died May 18, 1817.

Lindorf A. Glover, born February 12, 1847, died October 15, 1912.

Mary G. Moore, consort of James W. Moore, died August 14, 1845.

Mary E., daughter of Elvia Glover, born August 9, 1833, died December 24, 1834.

William, son of Dr. D. and S. N. Walker, born June 10, 1826, died January 5, 1855.

John A. Atkinson, born February 5, 1788, died December 26, 1840.

Sarah, wife of John Atkinson, born April 13, 1799, died April 5, 1853.

Mary Ann, wife of Thomas Atkinson, born May 24, 1760, died May 16, 1844.

Lucy, wife of William Atkinson, born April 28, 1796 ,died October 9, 1851.

William Atkinson, born March 1, 1800, died February 10, 1860.

James A. Atkinson, born March 12, 1834, died October 5, 1886.

T. J. Atkinson, born November 14, 1814, died October 5, 1886.

D. Preston Walker, born October 6, 1819, died October 5, 1912.

Dr. Dan L. Walker, died January 14, 1856.

Infant of Ollie and Dora Groves, died July 15, 1912.

Levi Spencer, born April 26, 1849, died March 7, 1915.

William Steele, born February 1, 1848, died April 29, 1895.

Sarah, wife of Dr. Daniel Walker, died November 5, 1866 in her 80th year.

Joanna Walker, born August 15, 1815, died October 14, 1877.

Daniel B. Glover, born August 2, 1835, died November 23, 1911.

Eliza, wife of Dr. L. A. Glover, born August 15, 1812, died October 18, 1891.

Dr. L. A. Glover, born May 27, 1806, died March 26, 1864.

Sarah G., wife of J. H. Phillips, born February 12, 1842, died April 28, 1864.

Joanna E. Glover, born February 14, 1852, died August 30, 1864.

Joseph S. Glover, born October 6, 1844, died September 13, 1864.

Dan S. Glover, born June 24, 1896, died July 26, 1896.

William P. Glover, born November 11, 1846, died March 2, 1898.

Charles A. Glover, born January 8, 1839, died November 11, 1902.

Edwin Glover, born January 8, 1851, died February 13, 1912.

Eliza, his wife, born January 6, 1870, died July 7, 1908.

Alice Rudder, 1874-1892.

Laura Rudder, 1876-1880.

May Rudder, 1885-1889.

Eliza Rudder, 1887-1887.

Mary A., wife of James H. Faulk, born March 25, 1847, died December 25, 1890.

Leomy, wife of E. J. Steele, born May 11, 1863, died January 17, 1888.

Elizabeth, daughter of T. J. and Elizabeth Steele, born August 18, 1909, died October 17, 1910.

John Franklin, son of J. R. and Jane Tolls, born August 12, 1852, died February 27, 1853.

Elizabeth H. Tackett, born October 9, 1835, died August 30, 1882.

Sarah Cundiff, born February 1, 1877, died April 21, 1913.

Elizabeth A., wife of Omer Wilson, born July 18, 1836, died March 13, 1898.

Emma D., wife of B. H. Arnold, born April 13, 1858, died July 9, 1881.

B. Hodge Arnold, born December 18, 1851, died April 3, 1887

Mary Ann, wife of George E. Owings, born August 2, 1834, died July 20, 1872.

William B. Arnold, born February 5, 1822, died Feb. 24, 1863.

Arnold, son of T. G. and C. D. Owings, born March 22, 1875, died July 19, 1876.

Eliza, wife of Samuel D. Hodge and daughter of William and E. Atchinson, born October 26, 1815, died October 28, 1854.

S. D. Hodge, born July 28, 1800, died March 12, 1871.

Elizabeth Dabney, born in Montgomery County, January 8, 1796, died in Bath County, July 24, 1877.

Milley Bennet, died February 13, 1856, in her 65th year.

Sarah G. Rice, wife of James T. Crooks, born February 5, 1846, died February 28, 1899.

Jas. T. Crooks, born September 26, 1842, died Januar y18, 1920.

Infant son of H. D. and M. I. C. Paynter , born and died July 12, 1902.

Effie G., daughter of J. E. and S. B. Maury, born September 16, 1863, died August 5, 1866.

Samuel O. Crooks, born March 17, 1839, died February 17, 1876.

Stuart R. Crooks, born July 3, 1873, died September 16, 1875.

Tom Ed, son of G. and C. Lane, born July 12, 1872, died October 13, 1886.

Malinda O., daughter of S. O. and M. T. Crooks, born April 10, 1869, died May 5, 1870.

Henry V., son of J. T. and S. E. Crooks, born April 25, 1859, died June 29, 1865.

Julia A., wife of B. H. Graves, born January 9, 1808, died January 15, 1866.

Thomas Coleman Graves, 1830-1922.

Malinda Ann., wife of A. V. Crooks, born November 9, 1817, died August 14, 1848.

Charles Elihu, son of Rezin G. and Mary Owings, born June 19, 1842, died October 13, 1842.

Rezin G. Owings, born June 9, 1810, died April 17, 1861.

Mary Kelso Owings, wife of R. G. Owings, born October 16, 1819, died September 21, 1905.

E. G. Owings, born April 9, 1848, died August 17, 1903.

Lanville A. Brown, born January 21, 1849, died August 10, 1851.

William T. Atkinson, born February 8, 1832, died May 27, 1882.

Charles O., son of C. G. and A. B. Whaley, died February 4, 1869.

Amanda B., wife of Charles G. Whaley, born December 26, 1811, died June 16, 1864.

Frank G., son of C. G. and A. B. Whaley, born January 22, 1855, died August 9, 1858.

Infant son of J. J. and Mattie Scott, born and died December 12, 1895.

James Stinson, born September 5, 1827, died January 21, 1887.

Elizabeth Stinson, born January 17, 1835, died August 21, 1897.

Mary, wife of James P. Kirk, born July 29, 1874, died January 20, 1897.

Charles T. Mallory, born July 31, 1871, died March 24, 1839.

Thomas Marshall, son of G. E. and M. H. Guerrant, born September 2, 1839, died June 6, 1864.

William Henry, son of H. E. and M. H. Guerrant, born November 25, 1845, died May 26, 1846.

Dr. H. E. Guerrant, born in Virginia, August 15, 1805, died June 30, 1876.

Mary B. H., wife of Dr. H. E. Guerrant, daughter of Judge Elihu Owings, born September 28, 1812, died January 6, 1850.

Martha A. V., daughter of H. E. and M. H. Guerrant, born December 19, 1836, died September 25, 1838.

Mary Evelyn, daughter of H. E. and M. H. Guerrant, born February 21, 1844, died August 17, 1854.

Julia G., wife of W. B. Devault, daughter of H. E. and M. H. Guerrant, born February 22, 1847, died April 22, 1874.

Lucy O., daughter of H. E. and M. H. Guerrant, born January 13, 1849, died August 15, 1871.

Thomas Toy, born June 15, 1854, died April 12, 1915.

Florence, wife of Thomas Toy, born January 12, 1836, died June 22, 1902.

T. V. Heaton, born March 13, 1871, died May 25, 1891.

Harriet A., wife of T. V. Heaton.

Hettie, daughter of R. H. and L. Clark, born May 5, 1886, died March 11, 1886.

Infant daughter of M. G. and M. S. Foley, born and died April 22, 1891.

Elizabeth Lee, daughter of G. W. and S. Foley, born February 24, 1866, died March 7, 1884.

Marten J., son of Claude and H. J. Foley, born April 12, 1895, died March 1, 1896.

R. M. Trimble, born August 12, 1837, died February 21, 1909.

Armildia, his wife, born January 18, 1835, died February 15, 1912.

Sarah, wife of G. W. Foley, born February 28, 1836, died May 31, 1885.

James Edward Crockett, born August 14, 1887, died May 29, 1913.

Missouri B., wife of J. S. Goodpaster, born July 23, 1858, died May 13, 1892.

Fenton B., daughter of J. S. and M. B. Goodpaster, born August 26, 1886, died January 31, 1891.

Ernest, son of R. B. and M. E. Crooks, born January 28, 1871, died May 2, 1881.

Amelia P. Kirk, born December 18, 1883, died June 30, 1886.

ADAMS BIBLE RECORD

(Furnished by Mrs. W. B. Smith, Edmund Rogers Chapter)

BIRTHS

Hardin Cohorn Adams was born November 24, 1815.
Mary Ann Amandy Mansfield was born July 6, 1819.
William Thomas Adams was born January 13, 1839.
Joseph Harvey Adams was born June 16, 1841.
John Hardin Baker Adams was born October 4, 1843.
Margaret Ann Matildy Adams was born May 26, 1846.
Sarah Elizabeth Adams was born August 13, 1848.
Eligha Bird Adams was born November 17, 1851.
Mary Ann Amandy Adams was born July 23, 1855.
Samma Morgan Adams was born August 21, 1860.

MARRIAGES

Hardin Cohorn Adams and Mary Ann Mansfield married February 9, 1837.

Alonzo Pedan and Mollie Adams married October 6, 1874.

Clem McGlocklin and Emma A. Adams married December 21, 1898.

Alice B. Pedan and Shelton S. Martin were married February 5, 1908.

Ebley C. Pedan and May Faut were married October 8, 1908.

Annie W. Pedan married Roy L. Montgomery, December 31, 1908.

A. E. Pedan and Helen Webb married November 9, 1910. His second wife.

DEATHS

Margaret Ann Matildy Adams died August 9, 1855.

Sarah Elizabeth Kennedy died August 23, 1868, in Kansas.

Samuel Morgan Adams departed this life August 6, 1887, in Louisville, caused by the falling of a derrick on July 25.

Hardin Cehorn Adams departed this life August 10, 1888, at his
home on Boyd's Creek.

Mary Ann Adams departed this life March 15, 1899.

Clem D. Pedan, son of A. E. Pedan, died December 1, 1891.

Emma Pedan McGlocklin died April 1, 1907.

Mollie Pedan, wife of E. A. Pedan departed this life March 30, 1909.

LAUDRUM-BRIDGES BIBLE

(Furnished by Mrs. W. B. Smith, Edmund Rogers Chapter)

William Laudrum and Elizabeth Herndon married October 11, 1820.

DEATHS

Alexander C. C., the first, died December 12, 1831.

Evaline Francis died September 4, 1837, aged 7 years, six months
and 21 days.

Mary Dorothy died July 18, 1858, her daughter, Mary Ellen died
March 24, 1866.

Elizabeth Jane Settle died Friday, March 18,, aged 48 years, six
months, 25 days, 1870.

William Laudrum died December 20 day at 4 o'clock A. M. 1870.

Elizabeth Laudrum departed this life May 8, 1888, aged 87 years,
five months and 27 days.

BIRTHS

William Laudrum, born July 20, 1800.

Elizabeth Laudrum, born November 11, 1800.

Eilzabeth Jane, born August 21, 1821.

John Thomas, born February 17, 1823.

Sarah Ann, born May 3, 1825.

Robert Lewis, born April 3, 1827.

Mary Dorothy, born October 11, 1828.

Eveline Francis, born February 25, 1830.

Alexander Christopher C., born December 5, 1831.

Catherine Lucetta, born November 7, 1832.

Alexander Christopher C., born June 10, 1835.

Nathan Yancey, born January 27, 1837.

Olivier Francis, born May 20, 1840.

John T. Laudrum, son of Robert William, born May 24, 1856 and
died October 16, 1856.

Mary Allen Tinsley, born April 17, 1858.

Lucetta Jane, born June 5, 1859.

Mary Elizabeth, born November 25, 1861.

Condee Hackney, born March 11, 1866.

James Nathan, born November 30, 1867.

Nathan Alexander Button, born January 21, 1862.

The above grandchildren to William and Elizabeth Laudrum.

Soloman, born April 22, 1850.

Amanda Jane, born July 23, 1852.

MARRIAGES

Uriah and Sarah A. Bridges, formerly Sarah A. Laudrum, married June 15, 1848.

Samuel James and Nancy B. James, formerly Nancy B. Bridges, were married May 25, 1856.

Samuel James Bridges and Margaret Bridges, formerly Margaret Kennedy, married December 22, 1855.

William H. Bridges and Mary A. Bridges, formerly Mary A. Dickinson, married July 26, 1860.

BIRTHS

Richard Bridges was born February 12, 1798.
Ruth Bridges was born January 17, 1796. Children of above.
James T. Bridges was born May 4, 1821.
Uriah S. Bridges was born July 20, 1822.
Martha S. Bridges was born February 12, 1825.
Samuel I. Bridges was born December 7, 1826.
Thomas I. Bridges was born December 17, 1829.
William H. Bridges was born December 5, 1831.
Lorena D. Bridges was born August 8, 1833.
Nancy B. Bridges was born September 26, 1835.
James William Bridges, son of Uriah and Sarah A. Bridges, was born April 13, 1849.
John Thos. Bridges was born Sept. 28, 1852.
Thos. Jefferson Bridges, Jr. was born Nov. 27, 1853.
Nathan Lewis Bridges was born July 22, 1857.
David Morton Bridges was born March 13, 1859.
Capernia Frances James, daughter of Samuel James and Nancy was born May 22, 1857.
James Richard James was born September 30, 1858.
Ella Dow James was born August 3, 1861.
Ethan Allen James was born December 6, 1862.
Samuel Jefferson James was born April 3, 1864.
Mary Susan James was born August 11, 1866.
James Andrew Bridges, son of Samuel and Margarett Bridges, was born November 3, 1859.
Charles Morton Bridges, son of William H., and Mary A. Bridges, was born October 11, 1863.

DEATHS

Thomas I. Bridges departed this life August 5, 1853. Aged 23 years, 7 months and 18 days.
David M. Bridges, son of Uriah and Sarah A. Bridges, departed this life May 29, 1860. Aged 1 year, 2 months, 15 days.
Ella Dow James died June 22, 1863. Aged 1 year, 10 months and 19 days.
Richard Bridges departed this life May 21, 1888. Aged 90 years, 3 months and 9 days.
Ruth Bridges departed this life December 9, 1883. Aged 87 years, 10 months and 22 days.
David Morton Bridges departed this life May 29, 1860.
      Children of J. T. and M. A. Bridges:—
First born departed this life January 18, 1874.
Sarah Frances Steffee departed this life February 10, 1883.
Nathan Lewis Bridges departed this life September 19, 1883.
Ethridge Garnett Steffee, son of S. R. and S. F. Steffee, departed this life March 22, 1883.
Ruth Elizabeth Bridges departed this life August 14, 1884.
Charlie Lewis Bridges departed this life January 29, 1891.
U. S. Bridges departed this life June 18, 1905. Aged 82 years, 10 minths and 28 days.
Sarah A. Bridges died August 22, 1915. Aged 90 years, 3 months and 19 days.

Janie Bell Bridges died May 29, 1915.
H. A. Bridges died October 3, 1919.
N. Y. Laudrum died January 19, 1925.

BIRTHS

Uriah S. Bridges was born July 20, 1822.
Children of the above:
James W. Bridges was born April 13, 1849.
John T. Bridges was born November 27, 1853.
Nathan L. Bridges was born July 22, 1857.
David M. Bridges was born March 16, 1859.
Sarah F. Bridges was born April 27, 1861.
Ruth E. Bridges was born February 13, 1865.
Children of J. T. and M. A. Bridges:
First born January 15, 1874.
Minnie Bell Bridges was born October 24, 1877.
Children of S. R. and S. F. Steffe:
Ethridge Garnett Steffe was born March 12, 1882. Died March 22, 1882.

MARRIAGES

Uriah S. Bridges and Sarah A. Laudrum married June 15, 1848.
John T. Bridges was married to Martha A. Steffee February 6, 1873.
T. R. Steffee and S. F. Bridges married March 11, 1880.
J. W. Bridges and Harriett A. Bridges married Oct. 3, 1889.
Thomas J. Bridges and Laura K. Landers married Jan. 10, 1895.
J. E. Bridges and Jannie Belle Pardue married March 26, 1902.
J. E. Bridges and Allie Settle married February 7, 1917.

MEMORANDA

James Edgar Bridges, son of John T. and M. A. Bridges, was born March 26, 1883.
Children of J. W. and H. A. Bridges:
Charles Crues Bridges born January 29, 1891.
Henry Page Bridges, son of J. W and H. A. Bridges, born April 8, 1892.
Lee Bridges, born June 17, 1895.
Nettie Lee Bridges, daughter of J. E. and Janie Bridges, born April 6, 1903.
Susie Mea Bridges, daughter of J. E. and Allie Bridges, born December 7, 1917.

BOGGS BIBLE

(This record from John Boggs Bible owned by
Mrs. Louise T. Simmons, Danville, Ky.)
(Contributed by Mrs. Allen Zaring, Boonesboro Chapter)
John Boggs, born August 17, 1759, son of Robert Boggs and Margaret Robinson.
John and Elizabeth Pearson married November 3, 1776.

ISSUE

Margaret Boggs, born August 17, 1797, married Andrew Cornelson.
Col. Robert Boggs, born April 30, 1799, bachelor.
John Boggs, Jr., born February 28, 1801, bachelor.
Benjamin Boggs, born December 31, 1806, bachelor.

Hannah Boggs, born November 3, 1808, married James Noland Turley.

DEATHS

Elizabeth Pearson Boggs died April 29, 1819.
John Boggs died March 14, 1850, bachelor.
John Boggs, Sr., died April 5, 1847.
Col. Robert Boggs died December 29, 1864.
Benjamin Boggs died March 25, 1883, bachelor.
NOTE: John Boggs, Sr. born August 17, 1759 was soldier under Gen. Washington. Mrs. Jane B. Noland, Richmond, Ky., has great granddaughter, owns the uniform he wore and his razor strap.
NOTE: Mrs. William Arnold owns the oldest Bible, 1725 of Boggs, being the one of Robert Boggs and Margaret Robinson whose first child was born on ship coming from Scotland and who had four sons in war of Revolution for eight years, John, Robert, James and William Boggs. They were at Valley Forge and at the Thames in 1812. James Boggs took part as a private.
These are the pioneer families of Kentucky and some of the patents of land is still in family.
Robert Boggs,s born September 9, 1746, son of Robert and Margaret R. Boggs, married Sarah Huston. Born 1775, died Sept., 1816.
Robert Boggs and Margaret Robinson, his wife, settled in Delaware.

ISSUE

Agnes Boggs, born January 1, 1783, in Fort Harrord, died age of 84 years, unmarried.
Margaret Boggs, born December 3, 1784.
Betsy Boggs, born March 20, 1787.
Polly Boggs, born December 29, 1789.
Esther Boggs, born January 27, 1792, married Newman.
Robert Boggs, born August 8, 1793, bachelor.
Jane Boggs, born December 28, 1794, married James Bell.
James Boggs, born September 13, 1796, married Sopha Hart.
Settled on Boggs Fork in Fayette County, Ky., 1784.
Robert Boggs, Sr., born September 9, 1746, died Aug. 25, 1825.
His wife, Sarah Huston, born 1775, died 1816.
Robert Boggs, born 1712, married Margaret Robinson, Mar. 3, 1741.

ISSUE

First, James Boggs, born January 16, 1742, died in infancy.
William Boggs, born September 15, 1743.
Robert Boggs, born September 9, 1746, married Sarah Huston.
Second, James Boggs, born September 10, 1747, married Sallie Winn.
Agnes Boggs, born February 4, 1749.
Elizabeth Boggs, born February 11, 1751.
Benjamin Boggs, born March 12, 1753.
Moses Boggs, born November 12, 1856, went to Ohio.
John Boggs, born January 11, 1759.
Joseph Boggs, born January 2, 1761.
Margaret Robinson Boggs, died June 5, 1801, age 80 years.
Robert Boggs, died April 2, 1804, age 92 years.
A leaf from Bible printed 1725, owned by Robert and Margaret Boggs, now Mrs. William Arnold, Richmond, Ky.
Joseph Boggs, born January 2, 1761, son of Robert and Margaret R. Boggs.
Elizabeth Plow, born September 4, 1779, near Rightsidle, Pa., married September 8, 1807.

Margaret Boggs, born February 23, 1809, died March, 1891, married Right Glenn.

Elizabeth Boggs, born July 26, 1811, died January 2, 1828.

Benjamin F. Boggs, born July 23, 1812.

John P. Boggs, born August 10, 1813.

Mary Boggs, born October 2, 1814, died June 7, 1877, married Robert C. Cornelison.

Nancy Boggs, born April 10, 1815, died, 1843.

Robert R. Boggs, born September 2, 1817, married Margaret Galespie.

Joseph S. Boggs, born June 16, 1819, married Mary Elizabeth Turley.

William R. Boggs, born May 24, 1823, died 1897, bachelor.

James H. Boggs, born November 17, 1824, married Millie Cornelison in Missouri.

Elizabeth Plow Boggs died February 13, 1870, age 91 years.

Joseph Boggs, died July 13, 1843, age 83 years.

COULTER BIBLE

(Contributed by Miss Letitia Hedges, Jemima Johnson Chapter)

Thomas Coulter was born April 1, 1783.

Nancy Pruit Coulter was born January 3, 1790.

Dilly Coulter was born September 13, 1807.

Susana Coulter was born March 14, 1809.

Olive Coulter was born July 13, 1813.

John Coulter was born May 1, 1811.

Isham Coulter was born January 23, 1816.

Frances Coulter was born April 16, 1818.

Elizabeth Coulter was born April 7, 1820.

Polly Coulter was born December 11, 1823.

Mary Moore Coulter was born December 8, 1824, died Aug. 5, 1863.

Elizabeth Bingaman was born September 18, 1786.

Henry Bingaman was born July 8, 1790.

Nancy Bingaman was born July 14, 1792.

John Bingaman was born September 21, 1794, died June 20, 1867.

Margaret Bingaman was born April 4, 1797.

Jennie Bingaman was born April 16, 1799, died April 23, 1863.

Lewis Bingaman was born March 8, 1801.

Katie Bingaman was born January 30, 1803.

Annie Bingaman was born January 30, 1803.

Sallie Hutchinson Bingaman was born December 14, 1816, died June 26, 1883.

Nancy Kissenger Hutchinson was born 1794, died 1869.

BERRY BIBLE

(Contributed by Miss Dora Vallandingham, Big Spring Chapter).

George Berry married Jane Carter, 1783.

Their Children:

Ellen R., born 1783; William, born 1786; George C., born 1787; Jane, born 1789; Cyrill, born 1791; Henry, born 1793; Silas, born 1796; Jacob C., born 1798.

NOTE: George Berry was born in Virginia, 1759, and died in Scott County, Ky., 1839.

BARLOW-HUGHES BIBLE

(Bible belonging to Miss Lillian Hough, Paris, Ky., 1925)

(Contributed by Mrs. W. H. Whitney)

MARRIAGES

Jesse Barlow and Ann Hughes were married on the 9th day of April, 1840.

BIRTHS

Christiann Hughes was born 17th day of June, 1775 (?).
Daniel G. Hughes, son of George Hughes, was born Sept. 28, 1799.
Ralph Hughes was born January 19, 1801.
Elizabeth Hughes was born May 4, 1802.
Sally Hughes was born October 28, 1803.
William Hughes was born July 23, 1805.
Louisa Hughes was born April 22, 1809.
Polly Hughes was born December 7, 1810.
Margaret Hughes was born June 11, 1812.
Casandra Hughes was born February 8, 1816.
Jane Hughes was born July 8, 1817.
George Hughes was born September 20, 1819
Christian Hughes was born August 6, 1821.
Elizabeth Ann Garrard Johnson was born October 30, 1826.
John Thomas Barlow was born the first day of June, 1841.
James McClure Barlow was born January 14, 1843.
Mary Elizabeth Alen was born July 29, 1836.
Lucy Jane Barlow was born July 13, 1846.

DEATHS

Ralph Hughes died September 16, 1825.
James Johnson died October 28, 1827.
Sarah Johnson died April 18, 1831.
George Hughes departed this life 14th of June, 1833.
William Hughes, Jr., departed this life 23rd of July, 1833.
Eilzabeth Johnson departed this life October 9, 1832.
Sarah Ann Morris departed this life October 12, ———.

BIRTHS

George Hughes Morris was born November the 18th, 1828.
Addiliza Morris was born February the 21st, 1830.
Sary Ann Morris was born November the 24th, 1831.

DEATHS

Christiana Hughes, wife of George Hughes, died June 16, 1833.
George W. Hughes died June 20, 1875.
Polly Morris, the wife of Horatio Morris, died January 5, 1832.
Casander Hughes departed this life September 5, 1833.
Anne Barlow, youngest daughter of George Hughes, departed this life June 23, 1847.
Jane Howard, wife of Jesse Howard, died June 14, 1853.
Elizabeth Hughes died October 1, 1859.
John T. Barlow departed this life March 10, 1863.

(Printed and published by M. Carew & Son, No. 126 Chestnut Street, Philadelphia, Pa., 1818)

GRANT FAMILY BURYING GROUND
Fayette County, Ky.

(Contributed by Miss Helen Hutchcraft, Jemima Johnson Chapter)

Sacred to the memory of Sally Grant, wife of William Grant, Jr., who was born December 25, 1761, and departed this life June 7, 1779, aged 17 years, 5 months and 18 days.

Sacred to the memory of Susana H. Grant, daughter of Samuel and Jerusha Mosby, who was born in the year 1737 and departed this life August 10, 1811, aged 75 years.

Sacred to the memory of William Grant, Jr., who was born January 10, 1761 and departed this life February 20, 1814, aged 53 years, 1 month and 10 days.

Sacred to the memory of Elizabeth Boon, consort of William Grant, Sr., and daughter of Squire and Sarah Boon, who was born February 5, 1733 and departed this life February 25, 1814, aged 81 years and 20 days.

Sacred to the memory of Eliza Grant, daughter of William and Sally Grant, who was born March 25, 1793 and departed this life March 15, 1818, aged 25 years.

Sacred to the memory of Mrs. Rebecca Grant, consort of Samuel M. Grant, who departed this life July 31, 1833.

John W. Moore, born March 4, 1787, died October 13, 1844.

Joseph Mosby, born January 28, 1756, died September 7, 1848. An honest man, one of the noblest works of God.

Thomas G. Moore, born December 12, 1834. Died September 5, 1870.

D. B. RITTER BIBLE

Barren County, Kentucky

(Contributed by Mrs. W. B. Smith, Edmund Rogers Chapter)

D. B. Ritter married Mary Ann Fishburn.
D. B. Ritter was born March 18, 1787.
Amelia Ritter was born November 12, 1807.
Henry Ritter was born December 23, 1811.
Peter Ritter was born April 15, 1814.
Jemima Ritter was born October 1, 1815.
Susanna Ritter was born August 18, 1817.
Elizabeth Ritter was born September 6, 1819.
Martha Ritter was born June 12, 1824.
John Ritter was born June 12, 1824.
D. B. Ritter was born July 6, 1826.
Elizabeth May was born July 14, 1828.
Jacob Ritter was born August 19, 1830.
Paulina Ritter was born January 18, 1834.

The mother of the eleven undersigned children departed this life on the 27th day of September, in the year of our Lord, 1855.

J. D. B. Ritter and Mary Berndect (?) was married on the 13th day of July, 1856.

John W. S. Young was married to Mary Ritter, the widow of D. B. Ritter, September 16, 1879.

DEATHS

Mary Ann Ritter died September 27, 1855.
D. B. Ritter, Sr., departed this life October 26, 1865.

JOHN RITTER, SR., BIBLE

(Property of Judge Walter Evans)

(Contributed by Mrs. W. B. Smith, Edmund Rogers Chapter)

BIRTHS

December 7, 1767, John Ritter, Sr., then was born.
November 18, 1777, Delilah Ritter then was born.
Januarv 21, 1749, Wilson Ritter then was born.
October 21, 1795, Preston Ritter then was born.
February 23, 1798, Charity Ritter then was born.
December 24, 1799, Polly Ritter then was born.
May 29, 1802, Elizabeth Ritter then was born.
March 28, 1805, John W. Ritter then was born.
September 21, 1807, Matilda Ritter then was born.
January 5, 1810, Burwell Ritter then was born.
"I make this record at the age of 74 years, eight months and five
days old, John Ritter, Sr. This 12th day of August, 1842."
John W. Evans was born September 18, 1842.
George D. Evans was born October 6, 1843.
September 18, 1842, J. Walter Evans then was born.
October 6, 1843, G. Davis Evans then was born.
John Ritter and Delilah Wilson was married March 21, 1793.

DEATHS

Charity Courts died January 17, 1841.
August 23, 1844, Elizabeth Sedars died.
Delilah Ritter died October 8, 1852.
Elizabeth Wilson died February 16, 1831.
Delilah Ritter died October 8, 1852.
John Ritter died the 16th day of April, 1835.

EXTRACTS FROM OLDEST RITTER BIBLE

(Contributed by Mrs. W. B. Smith, Edmund Rogers Chapter)

The family of Abraham Ritter and Margaret Ritter:
Joseph Ritter was born April 21, 1766.
John Ritter was born December 7, 1767.
Abraham Ritter was born November 27, 1769.
William Ritter was born June 27, 1774.
Margaret Ritter was born November 15, 1776.
Isaac Ritter was born November 29, 1779.
Elizabeth Ritter was born April 2, 1782.
Rossanna Ritter was born March 16, 1784.
David B. Ritter was born March 18, 1787.
Ealcy Ritter was born October 1, 1789.
Sary Ritter was born May 8, 1792.
James Ritter was born March 9, 1795.
Nancy Ritter was born December 17, 1797.
"Joseph Ritter died December 19, 1842. The total of his days, 76
years."

EVERETT BIBLE

(Contributed by Mrs. W. B. Smith, Edmund Rogers Chapter)

MARRIAGES

William Everett, born 1785, died 1863.

William Everett and Ellender Humphrey was married the 24th day of December, 1812.

Absent Lewis and Susan Everett was married the 28th day of September, 1865.

Samuel Everett and Mary E. Riggs was married October 5, 1873.

Maria Everett and James G. Thompson were married Oct. 27, 1880.

Annie M. Smith and Frank Frei were married March 19, 1890.

Elizabeth M. Everett was married to Robert Field, 1849.

Elizabeth N. Everett, widow of Robert Field, was married to Hiram Smith, 1854.

(Annie Frie's mother).

BIRTHS

William Everett was born September 1, 1785.

Ellender Everett, wife of William Everett, was born the 12th day of September, 1793.

Eliza Jane Everett, daughter of William and Ellender Everett, was born the 7th day of October, 1813.

William James Everett was born the 13th day of May, 1815.

Joseph Everett was born the 28th day of February, 1817.

John Everett was born the 23rd day of August, 1819.

Huldy Ann Everett was born the 22nd day of August, 1821.

Thomas Everett was born the 19th day of March, 1822.

Jesse Everett was born the 7th day of July, 1823.

James H. Everett was born the 9th day of May, 1825.

Betsey N. Everett was born the 11th day of February, 1827.

Nancy N. Everett was born the 23rd day of February, 1829.

Nancey Mariah was born January 1, 1831.

Samuel J. Everett, born November 17, 1832.

Hiram Smith, born September 27, 1804.

Susannah Everett, born the 8th day of September, 1835.

Frank Frei, born July 3, 1866.

Ellen Fields was born the 3rd day of February, 1850.

Frank Everett, son of Annie and Frank Frei, was born August 10, 1902.

William Thomas Fields was born the 18th day of November, 1851.

Anna Maria Smith was born August 15, 1864.

Mary Susan Smith was born January 25, 1868.

Lucy Ellen Everett, born October 22.

DEATHS

Robert B. Fields, died January 23, 1852.

Hiram Smith, died October, 1875.

Husband of Elizabeth Everett Smith.

William James Everett, died the 28th day of August, 1817.

Joseph Everett, died —————.

Nancy N. Everett, died June 15, 1830.

Hulde Ann, died July 15, 1836.

Eliza Jane, died March 19, 1840.

William Everett, died August 29, 1863.

Ellender Everett, died September 8, 1875.

Elizabeth N. Everett Smith, died February 11, 1870.

Susan Katherine Lewis, died March 8, 1919.

Maria Everett Thompson, died November 21, 1921.

SETTLE BIBLE

(Contributed by Mrs. W. B. Smith, Edmund Rogers Chapter)

BIRTHS

Franklin Settle was born April 13, 1797.
Franklin B. Settle was born August 31, 1842.
D. P. Barclay was born July 12, 1826.
John Settle was born, 1829.
Susan B. Settle was born April 9, 1805.
Virginia F. Settle was born April 19, 1830.
Capernia Settle was born April 10, 1843.
Sarah Ella Settle was born ——————.
Franklin Barclay was born August 29, 1855.
Franklin Barclay was born August, 1856.

MARRIAGES

Franklin Settle and Susan B. Holman were married October 28, 1828 A. D.
James A. Westerfield and Virginia F. Settle were married May 31, 1850.
D. P. Barclay and Virginia F. Settle were married Oct. 30, 1855.

DEATHS

Franklin Settle, Sr., died January 9, 1857.
D. P. Barclay, died January 9, 1862.
Franklin Barclay, died August, 1856.
Franklin B. Settle, died March, 1863.

PEDAN BIBLE

(Contributed by Mrs. W. B. Smith, Edmund Rogers Chapter)

BIRTHS

Eleager Pedan was born December 13, 1796.
Sarah W. Harrison was born March 15, 1801, the wife of E. A. Pedan.
Mary Pedan was born December 7, 1820.
Benjamin G. Pedan was born November 25, 1822.
Selena Pedan was born September 21, 1825.
James M. Pedan was born April 2, 1828.
Smitha Pedan was born July 19, 1830.
John Clifton Pedan was born March 20, 1833.
Moses T. Pedan was born November 20, 1835.
Edmund H. Pedan was born August 19, 1838.
Arannah McKinza Pedan was born January 3, 1841.
George R. Pedan was born May 13, 1843.
Alonza E. Pedan was born March 13, 1847.

MARRIAGES

Eleager Pedan and Sarah W. Harrison were married in the year 1820 on the 20th day of January.
Benjamin S. Pedan and Virginia Pursley were married December 21, 1843.
James S. Scott and Salinah H. Pedan were married November 5, 1846.

Francis M. Pedan and Sintha M. Pedan were married December 24, 1850.
Eleager Pedan and Sarah Ford were married November 9, 1855.
M. T. Pedan and M. C. Francis married November 17, 1858.
G. A. Estes and S. M. Pedan married December 20, 1858.
E. H. Pedan and S. D. Watts married November 24, 1859.
James H. Pedan and Eliza J. Roberson married October 26, 1862.
Alonzo Pedan and Mary Adams married October 6, 1874.
E. H. Pedan and Bettie Broady married December 21, 1882.

DEATHS

Mary Pedan departed this life on the 16th day of September, 1823.
Arunah (?) McKinza Pedan departed this life July 26, 1844.
Sarah W. Pedan departed this life October 7, 1834.
Francis Maria Pedan departed this life November 10, 1856.
J. C. Pedan departed this life November 10, 1863.
G. R. Pedan departed this life March 19, 1864.
Eleager Pedan departed this life July 4, 1877.
Selinah H. Pedan departed this life January 13, 1859.
James H. Pedan departed this life December 9, 1898.
Clem D. Pedan, son of E. A. Pedan, died in Oklahoma City, December 1, 1891.
Emma Pedan McGlocklin, died in Franklin, Tenn., April 10, 1907.
Mollie A. Pedan, died September 10, 1909.

WASON BIBLE

(Contributed by Mrs. Ernest Dunlap, Bryan Station Chapter)

Came to Kentucky from Greencastle, Franklin County, Penn.
James Wason, born December, 1793, died December, 1810.
Mary Orr Wason, wife of James Wason, died June 14, 1822.
Jenney, daughter of James and Mary Orr Wason.
John Wason, born November 25, 1795.
James Wason, born June 12, 1798, died 1868.
Thomas Wason, born November 14, 1800, died 1842.
William Wason, born July 10, 1803, died 1833.
Samuel Wilson Wason, born April, 1806, died 1854.
Mary Ann Wason, born February, 1809.
Robert Hervey Wason, M. D., son of James Wason and Mary Orr Wason, born March 11, 1811, died October 30, 1819.

McCAW BIBLE

(Contributed by Mrs. Ernest Dunlap, Bryan Station Chapter)

The following is taken from Bible purchased in 1844 by John McCaw.

John McCaw, son of Mary Johnston and John McCaw, born May 22, 1791.
Cicely de Graffenried, daughter of Sarah Thomas and Allen de Graffenried, born July 10, 1806.
John McCaw and Cicely de Graffenried married September 19, 1822. in South Carolina.
Children of John and Cicely McCaw:
Mary Allen McCaw, born November 20, 1823, died Sept. 28, 1825.
Sarah McCaw, born January 29, 1827, married James Lane Allen, in 1856, died February 24, 1864.
Frances McCaw, born December 21, 1828, married January 28, 1851, to William H. Brand, died 1907.
John McCaw, born December 9, 1830, died March 26, 1844.

Mary Johnston McCaw, born November 24, 1832, married September 14, 1852 to R. B. Kendall, died December 27, 1881.

Twins of above unnamed, died at birth.

Carolina McCaw, born March 1, 1835, married November 22, 1859 to George B. Pickett, died January 16, 1860.

Thomas de Graffenried McCaw, born September 21, 1837 in Tennessee, married October 6, 1867 to Juliet Atkinson, died Jan. 13, 1871.

Emma McCaw, born September 8, 1839, died September 20, 1924.

Cicely McCaw, born September 30, 1841, died October 2, 1842.

Lucy McCaw, born March 22, 1844, married June 1, 1870 to Frank Woolley, died March 15, 1905.

William Robert McCaw, born May 6, 1846, married November 8, 1870 to Eloise Chesley Hance, died August 19, 1916.

Nina McCaw, born May 13, 1849, married April 16, 1872 to Edward Coleman, died March 4, 1879.

Pauline McCaw, born December 12, 1852, died October 9, 1876.

CALEB RATLIFF BIBLE

BIRTHS

(Contributed by Miss May Stone, Fincastle Chapter)

Elizabeth Ratliff, daughter of Zephaniah and Henneretta Ratliff, born April 19, 1775.

Mary Ratliff, daughter of Zephaniah and Philadelphia Ratliff, born June 2, 1781.

Ellender Ratliff, daughter of Zephaniah and Philadelphia Ratliff, born August 18, 1782.

Joseph Ratliff, son of same, born November 23, 1783.

Charles Ratliff, son of same, born July 15, 1785.

Valentine Ratliff, son of same, born November 11, 1786.

Susannah Ratliff, daughter of same, born April 4, 1788.

Margaret Ratliff, daughter of same, born December 12, 1789.

Nancy Ratliff, daughter of same, born March 10, 1791.

Coleman Ratliff, son of same, born December 13, 1792.

Caleb Ratliff, son of same was born June 13, 1794.

Zephaniah Ratliff, father of above children was born February 25, 1753.

Nancy Stone Ratliff, wife of Caleb, was born February 16, 1800.

Sanford Coleman Ratliff, son of Caleb and Nancy, born September 29, 1820.

Emily Ratliff, daughter of same, born April 23, 1822.

Richard Stone Ratliff, son of same, born June 20, 1824.

James William Ratliff, son of same, born December 24, 1825.

Elender Elizabeth Ratliff, daughter of same, born Jan. 24, 1828.

Joan Francis Ratliff, daughter of same, born Feb. 4, 1830.

Alfred S. Ratliff, son of same, born March 31, 1832.

Susan Rebecca Ratliff, daughter of same, born Feb. 15, 1834.

Caleb Newton Ratliff, son of same, born March 12, 1837.

MARRIAGES

Zephaniah Ratliff and Philadelphia Stone, March 16, 1780.

Caleb Ratliff and Nancy Stone, August 19, 1819.

William A. Brooks and Emily Ratliff, June 16, 1842.

Omar Wilson and Ellender Ratliff, May 7, 1845.

Richard Stone Ratliff and Martha A. Hickman, Sept. 2, 1846.

Jacob Gossett and Joan Ratliff, Sept. 2, 1846.

James Lane and Susan Ratliff, July 4, 1849.

James W. Ratliff and Louisiana Jones, October 18, 1858.
Caleb Newton Ratliff and Anna E. Jones, February 4, 1882.

DEATHS

Margaret Ratliff, October 30, 1794.
Valentine Ratliff, May 21, 1810.
Elender Ratliff Stone, March, 1814.
Philadelphia Ratliff, August 1, 1824.
Mary Ringo, July 10, 1826.
Joseph Ratliff, October 6, 1827.
Zephaniah Ratliff, June 8, 1831.
Susana Beard, June 23, 1833.
Nancy Ratliff Moffett, February 22, 1864.
Sanford Coleman Ratliff, March 24, 1844 or 1864.
Nancy Stone Ratliff, May 18, 1867.
Ellenor Ratliff Wilson, September 5, 1875.
Caleb Ratliff, July 12, 1878.

SCOTT GRAVEYARD

On the farm of David Bell at Scott's Station, 4½ miles from Shelbyville

(Contributed by Mrs. Clifford Walters, Isaac Shelby Chapter)

James Scott, born 1785, died 1822.
Julia Lyle Scott, Born 1786, died 1856.

ROBESON BURYING GROUND

On the farm of David Bell, at Scott Station, 4½ miles N. W. of Shelbyville

Leonard Robinson, born 1759, died 1835.

Francis Venable Robinson, born 1733, died 1821.

James Robinson, son of Leonard and Frances, born 1815, died 1830.

CROSBY GRAVEYARD

On the old Henry McMakin farm now owned by Smith on the Toods Point road, 3½ miles North of Simpsonville.

John Crosby, born May 10, 1755, died July 17, 1853.

Nancy, wife of John Crosby, born October 11, 1768 ,died June 22, 1851.

Gnoath Crosby, born July 13, 1802, died August 17, 1828.

Andrew Todd, born December 27, 1776, died August 14, 1844.

INDEX

Barns, 25, 34.
Barnet, 104.
Barnett, 18, 22, 54, 66, 85, 86, 104, 105, 106, 107, 108, 110, 112, 113, 114.
Barr, 18, 69.
Barren County Wills, 13-15.
Barrett, 15, 50, 53, 55, 58, 59, 62, 107.
Barrow, 76, 78, 81, 84.
Barry, 49.
Bartlett, 30, 105, 107, 109, 116, 167.
Bartley, 13.
Barton, 18, 31, 36, 45, 48, 53, 88.
Baseman, 53, 58.
Bassett, 105, 107, 108, 110.
Bassitt, 108.
Basye, 29.
Basey, 92, 95.
Bates, 18, 35, 105, 107, 109.
Bath Co., 97, 106, 109.
Bath County, (graveyard inscriptions), 166-171.
Batiss, 96.
Batley, 30.
Batterton, 16, 18, 19, 37, 63.
Baxter, 34.
Baughn, 109.
Bayes, 86.
Bayless, 159.
Baylor, 19.
Bayman, 48.
Beachamp, (See Beauchamp) 15.
Beagle, 66.
Beal, 41, 72.
Beall, 105, 110, 113.
Bean, 167.
Beanchamp (See Beauchamp) 39.
Beard, 30, 32.
Beasley, 16.
Beatty, 37, 87.
Beaty, 41.
Beauchamp (See Beachamp) 88, 106, 108, 112, 113, 114.
Beaver, 43.
Beckett, 19, 59.
Beckley, 109, 113.
Bedford, 19, 27, 28.
Bedford Bible, (not indexed) 151-152.
Bedinger, 27.
Bedle (Beadle) 95.
Beeler, 35.
Beldeer, 14.
Bell, 13, 19, 30, 33, 78, 79, 86, 98, 106.
Bell, 107, 109, 110, 114, 115, 136.
Bellis, 20, 26, 89.
Bellows, 42.
Benbow, 138, 139.
Bendtell, 30.

Benear, 20.
Bennet, 13, 43, 45, 52, 62, 85, 92.
Bennett, 95, 107, 110.
Bennett, 113, 115, 140.
Benson, 20.
Benton, 116.
Bernoe (Bournaugh) 24.
Berry, 43, 56, 59.
Berry Bible, (not indexed) 176.
Berryman, 27, 30, 31, 86.
Besharer, 20.
Best, 134.
Bethol, 107.
Betty, 30.
Beubridge, 86.
Bever, 67.
Bevins, 109.
Bibb, 111.
Bichols, 70.
Biddle, 17, 20.
Bigger, 85, 158, 160.
Biggs, 44, 77, 83.
Bigham, 46.
Bills, 16, 29.
Bimms, 78.
Bingham, 105, 108, 109.
Bird, 21.
Birkhead, 116.
Bishop, 113.
Black, 20, 28, 42, 89, 105, 107, 110, 140.
Blackburn, 43, 44, 65, 80, 159.
Blackwell, 105, 107, 138.
Bladsoe, 79.
Blair, 31, 33, 44, 45, 60, 61, 112.
Blake, 142.
Bland, 100.
Blandford, 114, 116.
Bledsoe, 41, 80.
Bleste, 31.
Blincoe, 110.
Blue, 20, 21.
Boardman, 21.
Boaz, 21.
Bobb, 31.
Bodkin, 45.
Bodley, 38, 39, 40.
Boggess, 23.
Boggs, 38.
Boggs Bible, (not indexed) 174-176.
Boling (Bowling) 90.
Bollock, 71.
Bols, 137.
Bonge, 78.
Bonner, 114.
Bonta, 21.
Booker, 92, 95.
Boon, 30, 31, 32, 34.
Boone, 34, 44, 92, 94, 96, 100, 112, 134, 136.
Booth, 134.

Bostian, 36.
Boswell, 41, 47, 49, 50, 53, 58, 91, 110, 111.
Boteler, 38.
Botkins, 49.
Botts, 167.
Boucher, 107.
Bouldin, 21.
Boulware, 31, 36.
Bourbon County Index to Estates, 5-12.
Bourbon County Wills, 15-29.
Bourland, 108.
Bourn, 74.
Bourne, 68, 73.
Bowen, 18.
Bowlds, 115.
Bowles, 15, 21, 23, 29.
Bowlin, 30.
Bowling, 137.
Bowman, 33, 38, 40, 134.
Bowmer, 71.
Boyd, 27, 31, 45, 46, 51, 55, 57, 65, 66, 78, 91, 96, 135, 139, 142, 166.
Boyers, 44.
Boyle, 140.
Boyles, 90, 91.
Brackin (Bracken-Brakin) 80, 95.
Bracket, 138.
Bradbourn, 31.
Bradley, 22, 37, 41, 54.
Brady, 116.
Bradford, 33, 38, 39, 40, 67, 87.
Bradley, 22.
Bradley Bible, (not indexed) 160-161.
Bradon, 61.
Bradshaw, 31, 81.
Bramblett, 22.
Branham, 86.
Brand, 18, 22, 57, 107, 112.
Brandon, 24, 44.
Branham, 18, 22, 28, 89.
Brannock, 54.
Bransford, 15.
Brant, 95.
Breckenridge, 18, 22, 29.
Breckinridge Bible (not indexed) 161-162.
Brent, 17, 40.
Brenton, 96, 134.
Breeding, 90.
Breitzell, 47.
Briant, 105, 107.
Brice, 19.
Bridges, 13, 23, 25, 77.
Bridges Bible, (not indexed) 172-174.
Bridgewater, 93.
Bright, 31, 94, 116, 137, 139, 140.
Brink, 34.

Brinson, 60.
Briscoe (Briscow) 91.
Bristoc (Bristoe) 25, 27.
Bristow, 112, 113, 115, 116.
Broadus, 29.
Broadwell, 45, 52, 55, 64.
Brock, 39.
Brockman, 51.
Brodie, 90.
Bromagene, 80.
Bronaugh, 75, 158.
Brooks, 100, 105, 112, 116, 167.
Brown, 15, 16, 17, 18, 21, 23, 25, 28, 29, 34, 35, 36, 44, 46, 56, 60, 62, 66, 77, 84, 88, 91, 105, 106, 107, 108, 114, 115, 116, 142, 158.
Brown Bible, (not indexed) 157.
Browning, 13, 14, 17, 23, 57, 59.
Bruce, 27, 31, 73, 98, 99.
Brumfield, 32.
Bruster, 32, 68, 69.
Bryan, 13, 20, 23, 24, 29, 33, 38, 40, 141.
Bryant, 25, 30, 31, 34, 36, 65, 97, 108, 109, 142.
Bryam, 14.
Buchannon, 23, 90.
Buckanan, 19.
Buckhannan, 113.
Buck, 83.
Buckley, 35.
Buckner, 44, 57, 107.
Buford, 13.
Bull, 137.
Bullett, 86.
Bullock, 31, 32, 33, 34, 91.
Bunch, 113, 114, 116.
Bundle, 14.
Bunn, 110.
Burbridge, 40, 79.
Burch, 32.
Burcham, 14.
Burchan, 14.
Burchman, 13.
Burden, 114.
Burger, 36.
Burgess, 48, 65.
Burke, 23.
Burkshire, 26.
Burns, 31, 166, 167, 168.
Burr, 16.
Burris, 24.
Burroughes (Burris) 24.
Burrow, 109.
Burton, 24, 110, 112, 114, 115, 140.
Bush, 14, 15, 30, 41, 42.
Buskirk, 91, 134.
Butcher, 81, 109.
Butler, 24, 78, 79, 80, 83, 91, 134, 135, 136, 137, 140, 141.

(187)

Buzan, 90, 137, 142.
Bye, 108.
Byers, 14, 95, 159.
Byrd, 34.

C

Cabell, 34.
Cabit, 106.
Cade, 32.
Calbert, 61.
Caldwell, 24, 32, 36, 44, 57, 79, 80, 167.
Calhoon, 40, 105, 115, 116.
Calk, 81.
Call, 24.
Callant, 59.
Calloway, 85, 114.
Calvert, 30, 37.
Calyar, 61.
Cameron, 47, 92, 141,.
Campbell, 16, 23, 25, 30, 32, 36, 40, 41, 54, 60, 65, 74, 78, 85, 94, 107, 110, 112, 114, 138.
Camper, 32.
Camron, 43, 45, 49, 54, 64.
Can, 54.
Canady, (Kennedy, 23, 25, 96, 108.
Canoy, 96.
Cantrill, 28, 77, 80, 83.
Caplinger, 95, 96.
Carbough, 57.
Carckwell (Compkwell) 87.
Cardwell, 97, 107, 140.
Carey, 49, 105, 109.
Carland, 110, 111.
Carler, 85.
Carlin, (Kerlin) 92, 116, 139.
Carlisle, 107.
Carmen, 139, 140.
Carnagy, 54, 61.
Carnes, 67, 138.
Carnine, 97.
Carpenter, 44.
Carr, 20, 27, 44, 50, 53, 92, 93, 138, 139, 142.
Carrell, 100.
Carrico, 115.
Carrington, 98.
Carrithers, 92.
Carsner, 70.
Carter, 14, 25, 32, 46, 49, 64, 85, 98.
Cartmell, 38, 40.
Cartwill, 44.
Carty, 32.
Carwine, 158.
Cary, 29, 115, 116.
Case, 82, 92.
Casey, 40, 44, 52, 62, 116, 141.
Cason, 64.

Cassaday, 114.
Castleman, 32, 92, 188.
Catherwood, 45.
Catlett, 168.
Cavender, 89.
Cavens, 39.
Chadwell, 74.
Chamberlain, 106, 108, 112, 116.
Chambers, 39, 45, 58, 59, 66, 76, 106, 109, 111, 115, 134, 160.
Chamblin, 25, 26.
Champ, 26.
Chandler, 45, 160.
Chaney, 108.
Chaplain, 137.
Chapman, 97, 111, 112, 116.
Cheatham, 79.
Cheeseman, 160.
Cheneworth, 134.
Chenoweth, 141.
Childers, 16.
Chiles, 70.
Chinn, 26, 32, 33, 43, 45, 49, 60, 62, 63.
Chinowith, 106.
Chipley, 30.
Chism, 13, 114.
Chopsherr, 52.
Chowing, 49.
Chowning, 26, 51, 54, 76.
Chrisman, 73.
Christian, 111.
Church, 112.
Clair, 52.
Clark, 34, 39, 45, 64, 81, 87, 106, 107, 110, 112, 135, 141, 142.
Clark County Marriages (not indexed; in alphabetical order) 100-104.
Clarke County, 98.
Clarke, 26, 33, 39, 42, 45, 64, 91, 99, 113.
Clarkeson, 16.
Clarkson, 16, 19, 27, 48, 62, 108, 109.
Clary, 111, 116.
Clay, 22, 27, 28, 34, 35, 36, 37, 38, 56, 107.
Clelland, 15.
Clements, 83.
Clemons (Combs) 28.
Cleoff, 31.
Cleveland, 28, 45.
Clifford, 28, 43, 52, 53.
Clifton, 95.
Cline, 93, 138, 139.
Clines, 135.
Clinkenbeard, 28.
Cloud, 28.
Clubb, 42.
Clyce, 81.
Coateney, 112.

Daley, 49.
Dance, 55, 57.
Dangerfield, 33.
Daniel, 91, 92, 106, 116, 137, 139.
Darnaby, 33, 53.
Darnall, 78.
Darnell, 77.
Darrough, 46.
Daugherty, 81, 88.
Daulton, 100.
Davenport, 32, 67, 75.
David, 46.
Davidson, 13, 106, 113, 114, 115, 116.
Daviess, 33, 105, 107, 110.
Daviess County Marriages, 104-117.
Davis, 13, 14, 20, 57, 60, 63, 77, 79, 80, 83, 84, 88, 97, 104, 105, 106, 107, 109, 111, 114, 115, 141, 159.
Davis Bible, (not indexed) 163-165.
Dawson, 25, 27, 32, 64, 108, 110, 111, 112, 113.
Day, 45, 46, 49, 54, 64.
Deck, 46.
Dedford, 27.
Deeds, (miscellaneuos) 98-99.
Dehart, 47.
Dehoney, 88.
DeLaney, 134.
Dellin, 142.
Delse, 57.
Demaree, 96, 134.
Demasters, 51.
Dement, 95.
Dements, 39.
Demmitt, 16.
Denbe, 133.
Denbow, 137.
Denning, 138.
Dennis, 109.
Dennison, 108.
Denny, 44, 92.
Denton, 115.
Depp, 13.
Depp Bible, (not indexed) 152-154.
Desha, 46.
Devore, 34.
Devore, 135.
Dewees, 159.
Dewitt, 77.
Dewitte, 83.
Dial (Dyal) 46.
Dicken, 105.
Dickens, 108.
Dickerson, 23, 63, 69.
Dickey, 21, 35.
Dickson, 56.
Diheroon, 137.

Dillin, 69.
Dills, 47, 64.
Dils, 46.
Dilse, 62.
Dingle, 33.
Dinnen, 138.
Dinwiddie, 90.
Ditto, 142.
Dixon, 66.
Doane, 58.
Dobbins, 23.
Dobins, 110.
Dodd, 13.
Dods, 95.
Dodge, 58.
Dogel, 42.
Dollerit, 109.
Dooley, 138.
Dolin, 113.
Dollin, 108.
Donaldson, 167.
Donephan, 99.
Donnell, 18.
Donoho, 40.
Dornan, 91.
Dotson, 107.
Douglas, 47, 51, 64, 85.
Douglass, 58.
Dougherty, 138, 141.
Dovney, 83.
Doway, 108.
Downing, 33, 58.
Downs, 105, 107, 109, 110, 112, 114, 115.
Drake, 80, 87.
Drummond, 38.
Drury, 108.
Dryden, 47, 61.
Dryson, 107.
Dudley, 20, 35, 37, 38, 40.
Dudley Bible, (not indexed) 165-166.
Duffee, 47.
Dugan, 61, 91, 92.
Duhamel, 34.
Duke, 14.
Dudley, 137.
Dumend, 108.
Dummidee, 72.
Dunaway, 25.
Duncan, 27, 29, 43, 47, 51, 59, 77, 62, 82, 84, 93, 105, 106, 107, 108, 111, 112, 115, 138.
Dunlap, 47, 52, 65.
Dunn, 47, 50, 55, 61, 68, 91, 115.
Dupuy, 92.
Durbin, 47.
Duree, 137.
Duval, 58.
Duvall, 45, 87.
Dyer, 109.
Dyson, 109.

(190)

E

F

Fraize, 49.
Frame, 23.
Francis, 76.
Franklin, 169.
Frazier (Frazer) 13, 22, 33, 34, 45, 53, 57, 61, 62, 63, 64, 65, 66, 105, 107, 108, 114.
Freeles, 116.
Frels, 113.
French, 109.
Friel, 114.
Friels, 107.
Fristoe, 150.
Fry, 34, 48, 56, 63, 64, 67, 110.
Fulkerson, 70, 111.
Fullerton, 34.
Fullinwider, 92, 94, 134, 135.
Fulton, 22.
Fuqua, 78, 79, 80, 81, 112, 114.
Furnish, 43, 49, 60.
Furtard, 77.
Furtad, 77.

G

Gabbard, 109.
Gabbert, 105, 108, 110, 116.
Gaines, 96.
Gaither, 106.
Galbreath, 137.
Gale, 86.
Gallagher, 100.
Galley, 63.
Galloway, 104, 105, 106, 107, 109, 111, 112, 113, 114, 116, 167.
Galoway, 114.
Gamble, 18.
Gannon, 46.
Gardner, 14.
Gardnes, 39.
Garmany, 43, 54.
Garner, 25, 57.
Garnet, 66.
Garnett, 46, 53.
Garner, 168.
Garrard, 25, 27, 37.
Garrett, 35, 57, 74, 76, 82, 92, 136, 137, 140.
Garriott, 17.
Gasaway, 92, 137.
Gass, 22.
Gates, 67, 104.
Gatewood, 37, 40, 67, 70, 88.
Gauf, 107.
Gay, 167.
Gazway ,93.
Gentry, 19, 26.
George, 26, 49, 58.
Gibney, 23.
Gibson, 17, 30, 31, 33, 41, 66, 106, 115, 116.
Gilbert, 68.

Giles, 16.
Gilison, 109.
Gillian, 34.
Gillim, 116.
Gillock, 15.
Gillon, 82.
Gilmore, 68, 105.
Gist, 37.
Givens, 26, 38, 49.
Glasgow, 48.
Glass, 94, 138.
Glem, 94.
Glen, 134, 139.
Glenn, 105,110.
Glky, 18.
Glover, 35, 78. 80, 92, 97, 106, 109, 139, 168, 169.
Goben, 135.
Goddard, 137.
Godman, 44.
Goff, 108.
Gohayn, 54.
Gooch, 53, 93, 94.
Goodloe, 34.
Goodloe Bible, (Not indexed), 148, 149.
Goodlow, 98.
Goodnight, 34.
Goodrich, 16.
Goodwin, 80.
Gordon, 42, 72, 112, 158, 166.
Gore, 113, 116.
Gorham, 18, 31.
Gormany, 43.
Gossee, 54.
Gossett, 47, 60.
Gott, 96.
Gough, 88.
Gowen 158.
Graham, 77, 83, 142, 167.
Grant 31, 50.
Grant Graveyard, (Inscription not indexed), 178.
Graves, 18, 22, 34, 35, 42, 47, 90, 139, 142.
Gray, 18, 51, 54, 65, 70, 108, 112, 116.
Gree, 141.
Green, 21, 45, 49, 72, 73, 76, 92, 159.
Greenup, 51.
Greenwall, 84.
Gregg, 135.
Gregory, 64, 95, 137, 138, 139, 140, 166.
Grey, 13, 43, 49, 55.
Grider, 14.
Griffin, 109, 110, 111, 136.
Griffing, 23.
Griffith, 17, 51, 54, 67, 88, 104, 106, 107, 109, 110, 111, 114, 115, 116, 140, 142.

Griggsby, 137.
Grigsby, 106, 107, 108.
Grinstead, 22, 81, 100.
Grimes, 18, 32, 35.
Grisby, 105.
Groghegan, 65.
Groves, 166, 168, 169.
Grubbs, 31, 50.
Guardner, 60.
Gudgell, 166, 168.
Guerrant, 78.
Gunsaulus, 49.
Guye, 55.
Gwin, 94, 95, 138.
Gwinn, 20.
Gwyn, 35.

H

Hackett, 78.
Hackley, 80.
Hadley, 112.
Haff, 94.
Hagriss,98.
Hagan, 76, 85.
Hagers, 98.
Hagerty, 39.
Haggard, 116.
Haines, 48.
Halderman, 16.
Hale, 78, 105, 116.
Haley, 35, 40.
Hall, 21, 24, 26, 35, 49, 52, 53,
    54, 61, 79, 89, 91, 92, 93, 106,
    107, 108, 111, 113, 114, 135,
    137, 138, 141, 167.
Hallet, 84.
Hallax, 29.
Ham, 87.
Hambleton, 49, 140.
Hamilton, 19, 20, 24, 26, 27, 35,
    39, 49, 61, 105.
Hammond, 136, 137.
Hamner, 114.
Hancock, 28, 35.
Haneil, 92.
Hanks, 81.
Hanna, 94, 109.
Hannah, 139.
Hannon, 49.
Hansberry, 140.
Hansbrough, 91, 92, 93, 94.
Hansford, 107, 116.
Hanson, 49.
Harbison, 69.
Harcourt, 45, 50.
Hardin, 27, 33, 84, 85.
Harding, 43, 50, 99.
Hardwick, 45.
Hardy, 116.
Hargdon, 30.
Harmon, 42, 85, 93.

Harnes, 66.
Harp, 47.
Harper, 35, 166.
Harrah, 166.
Harriett, 21.
Harriotte, 21.
Harris, 13, 14, 31, 40, 79, 89,
    106, 108, 109, 110, 111, 112,
    113, 114, 136, 137, 138, 139,
    158.
Harrison, 14, 16, 35, 36, 51, 57,
    93, 108, 110, 111, 113, 116,
    139.
Harrison County Wills, 42-67.
Harrow, 78, 79, 80.
Hart, 26, 35, 36, 105, 107, 110,
    138, 139..
Hartman, 93, 140.
Hasel, 116.
Haskins, 88.
Hasty, 82.
Hatcher, 108.
Hatfield, 114.
Hathaway, 81, 108.
Hatten, 142. (See Hatton).
Hatter, 93.
Hatton, 138. (See Hatten).
Hawes, 110, 114.
Hawkins, 26, 29, 33, 44, 49, 50,
    67, 87, 106.
Hawks, 71.
Hay, 35.
Haydon, 23.
Hayden, 65, 67, 114, 116.
Hayes, 83.
Haynes, 114.
Hay, 32.
Hays, 37, 77, 89, 113.
Haynes, 59, 79, 108, 111, 113.
Hazel, 111.
Head, 81, 106, 107, 110, 111,
    113, 114, 115.
Heading, 65.
Hearn, (Hearne) 25, 49.
Hearring, 114.
Hedger, (Heger) 46, 50, 65.
Hedges, (Heges) 19, 22, 25, 46,
    60, 79, 104, 106.
Heeles, 76.
Heighday, 136.
Heintle, 110.
Helm, (Helms) 34, 81, 104, 105,
    106, 107, 115.
Hemmingway, 110.
Hemphill, 72, 93, 95, 137.
Hencely, 140.
Henderson, 23, 30, 36, 50, 89,
    109, 114, 115.
Hendershott, 16.
Hendley, 33.
Henning, 108.
Hennings, 116.

Hennis, 23.
Hendrick, (Hendricks) 13, 48, 57, 109, 110, 113.
Hendrix, 115.
Henry, 21, 22, 23, 50, 53, 64, 87, 115, 116.
Hensley, 135, 136.
Henton, 94.
Herndon, 88.
Herren, 50.
Herring, 109.
Herriott, 167.
Heytel, 38.
Hiatt, (Hieatt) 50, 51, 65, 112.
Hicklin, 89.
Hickman, 29, 36, 47, 65, 138.
Hicks, 141.
Hiesler, 52.
Higbee, 33, 38, 39.
Higdon, 13, 14, 111, 113, 115, 116.
Higgins, 21, 29, 32, 36, 37, 81, 82, 106, 115.
Hill, 15, 29, 30, 36, 85, 90, 91, 92, 99, 115 168.
Hillems 51.
Hillock, 36.
Hillyer, 114.
Hind, 30, 51.
Hinds, 89.
Hine, 61.
Hinkson, 55, 66.
Hinton, 51, 116.
Hissley, 113.
Hitt, 17, 76.
Hoagland, (see Hogland) 92, 93, 95, 134, 135, 136, 141.
Hoblett, 31.
Hocker, 85.
Hockersmith, 69.
Hodge, 67.
Hodges, 14, 38, 49, 50, 56, 80, 140.
Hoff, 139.
Hoffman, 44.
Hogan, 73.
Hoggins, 55.
Hoglan, 108.
Hogland, 133.
Hogg, 16, 51.
Hoke, 138.
Holder, 36.
Holdings, 114.
Holeman, 66, 112.
Holland, 51.
Holley, 81.
Holliday, (Holiday), 49, 51, 80.
Hollis, 116.
Holmark, 105.
Holmes, (see Homes) 31, 33, 39, 41, 94, 106, 109, 110, 140.
Hollis, 114.

Holloway, 20, 73, 115, 159.
Holstead, 46.
Holt, 24, 25, 51, 85.
Holtsclaw, 41.
Homes, (see Holmes) 25.
Hon, 82.
Honaker, 80.
Hoover, 70.
Hopkins, 18, 29, 39.
Hopper, 79.
Horas, 66.
Hord, 20.
Horn, 110, 114.
Horne, 113.
Hornback, 21.
Horrell, 113.
Horseman, 109, 112.
Horton, 136.
Hosley, 113.
Hostater, (Hostatter) 48, 140.
Hostedler, 91, 93, 142.
Houghstatler, 93.
Hourdan, 107.
House, 20, 34, 77, 84.
Housley, 109.
Houston, 16, 18, 21, 43, 116.
Howard, 13, 17, 55, 73, 78, 93, 105, 106, 107, 108, 109, 110, 111, 113, 114, 115, 116, 139.
Howe, 14, 16, 30, 92, 167, 168.
Howell, (Howel) 72, 79, 85, 110.
Hucherson, 52.
Huchinson, 89.
Huckstip, 70.
Hudelson, 51, 64.
Hudson, 111, 112, 113, 115.
Huey, 44.
Huff, 106.
Huffman, 14, 16, 46, 58, 61, 65.
Hufford, 36, 48.
Hughart, 78, 166.
Hughes, (Huse) 26, 35, 39, 59, 74, 115, 136.
Hughes Bible, (not indexed) 177.
Hughtower, 72.
Hulet, 34, 79, 115.
Hulse, 68.
Hume, 20, 53.
Humphries, 93.
Humphrey, 24, 35, 55, 105, 108, 111, 113.
Humphreys, 38, 61, 106.
Hunt, 35, 36, 64, 81, 108, 114.
Hunter, 32, 36, 39, 59, 60, 69.
Huntington, 19.
Hurley, 61.
Huron, 99.
Husk, 106, 108, 110.
Huss, 137.
Huston, 40, 90, 104, 108, 111, 112, 116.
Hutchenson, (Hutchinson) 33,

King, 19, 28, 44, 47, 50, 53, 57, 62, 65, 72, 91, 107, 108.
Kinman, 53, 65.
Kinnaird, 18.
Kinnard, 65.
Kinkade, 53, 96.
Kinneer, 110
Kinney, 111.
Kinny, 60.
Kinsler, 52.
Kiplinger, 28.
Kirk, 76, 105, 110, 113.
Kirkham, 106, 110.
Kirkpatrick, 56, 64, 110.
Kirtley, 14.
Kirtley, 54.
Kiser, 31.
Knight, 75.
Knox, 28.
Knoz, 18.
Kyman, 32.
Kysor, 138.

L

Lacefield, 135.
Lackland, 116.
Lacklin, 115.
Lain, 139.
Lair, 54, 55.
Laird, 54.
Lamb, 39, 105, 112.
Lambert, 116.
Lamberts, 79.
Lamme, 25, 54, 66.
Lampton Bible, (not indexed), 156.
Lancaster, 108, 110, 112.
Land, 137.
Landers, 89.
Landman, 108.
Landrum Bible, (not indexed), 172-174.
Lane, 32, 80 , 81, 82 , 93, 94, 98, 109, 140.
Lankford, 21, 139.
Langhorne, 28.
Langley, 139.
Langston, 26, 27,
Lanham, 109, 110.
Lanhanm, 85.
Lankister, 77.
Lannine, 37.
Lantaman, 86.
Lanter, 54, 58.
Lanters, 112.
Lashbrook, 111, 114, 115, 116.
Lastley, 93, 134, 140.
Lastly, 138.
Latham, 93.
Latimore, 14.
Lauderback, 54.

Laugherty, 134.
Laughlin, 32, 37, 38, 54.
Lawrence, 40, 94, 106, 109.
Lawson, 90, 94.
Lay, 35, 105.
Layton, 88, 109, 112, 115.
Laywood, 114.
Leach, 23, 34, 51.
Leachman, 112.
Leaman, 110, 112.
Leatherlain, 139.
Leatherman, 93, 139, 140, 142.
Leathers, 111, 112.
Leavell, 66.
Leavy, 39.
Ledford, 80.
Lee, 77, 99, 113, 114, 137, 140, 141.
Leech, 86.
Legater, 80.
Legget, 94.
Legrand, 33, 37.
Lemaster, 93.
Lemon, 42, 53, 54, 86.
Lemmon, 52, 56.
Lenerre, 110.
Lenter, 43.
Leonard, 48.
Letcher, 113.
Leverston, 142.
Lewis 14, 37, 40, 48, 54, 58, 61, 72, 77, 83, 93, 98, 134, 141.
Liforce, 44.
Liggetts, 104.
Likens, 109.
Lillel, 54.
Lilly, 43.
Liman, 115.
Lincoln, 33.
Lincoln County, 89, 144.
Lindsay, 39, 89, 95, 140.
Lindsey, 135, 136, 140.
Lightner, 66.
Linginfelter, 47.
Linn, 65.
Linville, 96.
Lipscomb, 41.
Little 108, 112, 113, 114.
Lively, 94.
Lloyd, 110.
Lochridge, 167.
Lock, 104, 142.
Lockett, 105, 106, 111.
Lockhart, 56, 62, 68, 95, 115.
Logan, 13, 30, 36, 39, 63, 80, 87, 90, 94, 137, 138, ⋆139, 140, 141.
Loiure, 67.
Long, 31, 39, 51, 60, 79, 106, 112, 113, 137, 139, 140, 142, 167.
Longest, 113.
Longnecker, 17.

Lonney, 36.
Lorency, 77, 78.
Lorey, 58.
Lornecy, 80.
Lott 114.
Lottisman, 109.
Loury, 74.
Loux, 33.
Love, 44, 77, 84, 107.
Lovell, 166.
Lowden, 90, 92, 93, 95, 137, 142.
Lowey, 87.
Lowery, 69.
Lowery Bible, (not indexed) 144.
Lowry, 37, 38, 48, 51, 54, 56, 59, 62, 65,
Lucas, 38, 105, 109, 112, 138.
Lucket, 78.
Lyle, 23, 24, 38, 48.
Lynch, 94.
Lynn, 107, 108, 112.
Lyon, 13, 19, 27, 77, 83.
Lyons, 25.
Lyter, (Liter), 16.
Lwoen, 72.
Luckett, 14.
Ludwick, 110, 111.
Lukes, 139.
Lumpkins, 104, 106, 107, 112.
Lumpton Bible, (not indexed) 156-157.
Luceford, 137.
Lusk, 38, 108.

M

McAntyre, 106.
McAfee, 105.
McBrown, 107.
McCampbell, 75, 94, 97, 138.
McCandless, 49.
McCan,86.
McCann, 38, 47, 61.
McCannico, 46, 55.
McCaslin, 96.
McCloud, 23.
McClain, 64, 92, 94, 136, 139.
McClanahan 20, 29, 52.
McClelachan, 33.
McClintock, 16, 18, 54, 63.
McClure 19, 47, 55, 61, 89, 94, 141.
McClum, 76.
McCullough, 32, 134.
McConathy, 40.
McConnell, 17, 18, 27, 75.
McConnac, 56.
McCormack, 113, 115.
McCormick, 107, 111, 138.
McCortney, 97, 134, 135, 137.
McCory, 90.

McCoy, 20, 23, 34, 38, 57, 92, 94, 97, 104, 140.
McCown, 84.
McCracken, 36, 106, 109.
McCreery, 105, 106.
McCrocklin, 97,
McCrosky, 30, 89.
McCullah, 38.
McCullough, 38, 39.
McCutcheon, 28.
McDaniel, 16, 27, 39, 49, 55, 57, 58, 62, 64, 105, 106, 107, 108, 111, 113, 114, 115, 116.
McDavitt, 91, 95, 139.
McDonald, 38, 45, 135.
McDonnald, 112.
McDowell, 31, 37, 39, 49, 55, 94, 109, 110, 136, 141.
McDuffee, 50, 53, 65.
McElhany, 67.
McFall, 49.
McFarland, 55, 104, 105, 106, 107, 109, 110, 112, 113, 115.
McFerrin, 100.
McGarrick, 88.
McGaughey, 94, 95, 96.
McGee, 55.
McGill, 34.
McGinty, 16.
McGowan, 30, 39.
McGrath, 62, 71.
McGraw, 107.
McGregor, 36.
McGrew, 138.
McGruder, 39.
McGuire, 42, 54.
McHattan, 45.
McHatton, 48.
McHenry, 139.
McIlroy, 30.
McIlvain, 32, 40, 46, 53, 63, 78.
McIlvan, 84.
McIntire, 45, 79, 84, 108.
McItosh, 168.
McIsaac, 36.
McKay, 14, 114.
McKee 43, 64, 74.
McKeller, 53.
McKinley, 90, 92, 142.
McKinney, 48, 72, 105, 112, 113.
McKitrick, 52, 55.
McLain, (McClain), 55, 58.
McLoney, 49, 55.
McManner, 111.
McMillain, 45.
McMillen, 113.
McMillin, 43, 51, 55, 56, 58.
McMurry, 14.
McMurtry, 30, 39, 43, 53.
McNair, 32, 39.
McNalley, 112.
McNeal, 142.

McNees, 56, 58.
McNeese, 65.
McNeil, 34.
McNett, 114.
McNew, 142.
McNutt, 56.
McOlvain, 51.
McPheeters, 19.
McPike, 142.
McQuaid, 92.
McQuithy, 166.
McRoberts Bible and other records, (not indexed) 144-145.
McShane, 66.
McVar, 114.
McWade, 140.
McWaid, 141.
Maddox, 91, 96, 107, 111
Maderson,68.
Madison County Marriages, (not indexed but alphabetically arranged) 127-129.
Maffet, 57.
Magahey, 81.
Magee, 45, 56.
Magruda, 31.
Magruder, 41.
Mahan, 18, 27.
Mahon, 56, 115.
Mahurin, 137, 142.
Mais, 56.
Makemson, 56.
Malcom, 25.
Malden, 80.
Malin, 114.
Mallay, 109.
Malone, 82.
Manes, 91.
Mann 56, 57.
Manson, 136.
Maran, 49.
Marin, 49.
Margrave, 108.
Markham, 20.
Marks, 108, 111, 112.
Marlow, 116.
Marquess, 140.
Marrs, 71.
Marsh, 44, 46, 50, 52, 56.
Marshall, 34, 38, 41, 53, 57, 64, 65, 72, 99.
Martin, 15, 17, 23, 24, 26, 27, 32, 35, 42, 51, 57, 61, 62, 66, 74, 80, 91, 96, 98, 99, 100, 105, 106, 108, 110, 111, 135, 137, 141.
Martin Bible, (not indexed) 149-150.
Mascey, 76.
Mason, 38, 41, 111, 112, 159.
Mason County, 99-100.
Mason County, (graveyard inscriptions), 158-160.

Massey, 46, 47, 57.
Matheny, 17.
Mattingly, 114, 116.
Matson, 26.
Mattox, 105.
Maupin, 20.
Maurell, 13.
Maxon, 105.
May, 41, 54, 105, 106, 107, 109, 110, 111, 112, 114, 115, 138, 141.
Mayberry, 78.
Mayfield, 26.
Mayersback, 34.
Mayo, 136.
Mead, 39, 73.
Means, 81.
Medcalf, 111.
Medole, 41.
Meek, 136.
Meeks, 81, 94.
Mefford, 159.
Meglemmery, 55.
Mellean, 25.
Mellon, 86.
Melone, 141.
Menifee, 80.
Menzies, 23.
Mercalf, 108.
Mercalfe, 55.
Merchal, 63.
Merchant, 47.
Meredith, 40.
Meriwether, 91.
Merriwether, 97.
Merrell, 158, 159.
Merryman, 17.
Mertin, 72.
Metcalf, 19, 94, 96, 104, 105, 106, 107, 114, 142.
Meteer, 78, 84, 167.
Metiare, 55.
Micklin, 138.
Midleton, 13.
Milaer, 169.
Miler, 43.
Miles, 47, 97.
Millay, 107, 108, 112.
Miller, 16, 17, 21, 28, 29, 32, 39, 43, 45, 46, 47, 48, 49, 50, 51, 52, 53, 55, 57, 58, 82, 84, 86, 91, 92, 93, 94, 95, 98, 99, 107, 109, 111, 112, 114, 115, 116, 138, 140, 141, 142.
Millin, 136.
Million, (Millean) 26, 46, 59, 61.
Mills, 29, 56, 80, 113, 139.
Milner, 58, 59.
Milton, 60.
Minter, 47, 58, 63, 108.

Miscellaneous Wills and Deeds, 97-100.
Mitchell, 22, 30, 34, 40, 57, 65, 89, 95.
Mobberly, 113.
Moffett, 51, 115, 167.
Moffitt, 98.
Mogner, 134.
Monaker, 80.
Monarch, 111.
Monly, 76.
Monroe, 86.
Monrow, 42.
Monson, 55, 59.
Montague, 13.
Montgomery, 40, 77, 90, 115, 116, 133, 134, 138, 139.
Montgomery County Wills, 76-84, 98.
Moody, 31.
Moon, 142.
Moor, 74, 77.
Moore, 23, 26, 38, 39, 44, 45, 46, 48, 50, 52, 54, 57, 58, 59, 69, 91, 99, 105, 106, 111, 112, 116, 139, 168, 169.
Morehead, 73.
Moreland, 27, 107, 169.
Moren, 54.
Morin, 66.
Morgan, 32, 43, 54, 62, 80, 81, 108, 112, 114, 115, 140, 159.
Morris, 13, 39, 69, 88, 90, 108, 109, 112, 134.
Morrison, 31, 58, 60, 115.
Morrow, 53, 56, 90, 141.
Mors, 111.
Mortin, 110.
Morton, 39, 41, 93, 138.
Mosby, 16, 141.
Moseby, 15.
Mosley, 67, 78, 80.
Moseley, 86, 98, 105, 106, 107, 108, 109, 112, 114.
Moss, 113.
Motherhead, 93.
Mothrat, 107.
Mothrell, 104.
Mount, 96.
Mountague, 61.
Mountjoy, 48.
Muir, 34.
Mulberry, 87.
Mulinix, 13.
Mullen, 53.
Mulligan, 91.
Mullinix, 14.
Munro, 134.
Murley, 57.
Murphy, 57, 107, 108, 112.
Murrell, 15.
Murry, 14.

Muse, 86.
Musick, 24, 159.
Myers, 29, 52, 77, 105, 114, 167.

N

Nally, 114.
Nanny, 116.
Napper, 36, 115.
Nash, 97.
Neal, 134, 138.
Neale, 58, 87.
Neely, 58.
Neaves, 59.
Need, 73, 75.
Neels, 137.
Nelley, 138.
Nelson, 53, 106, 107, 109, 112.
Nelson County Marriages (not indexed) 130.
Nelson County Wills 84-85.
Neighbors, 104.
Nesbit, 17, 58, 59, 88.
Nesbitt, 24, 58.
Netherland, 70.
Neves, 59.
Nevill, 116.
New, 107.
Newell, 56.
Newland, 91, 94, 95.
Newman, 93, 139.
Newson, 116.
Newton, 105, 107, 110, 111, 113, 139.
Nicholas, 77, 83.
Nicholas County Marriages (not indexed, but alphabetically arranged) 130-133.
Nichols, 28, 33, 39, 42, 57, 59. 99.
Nicholls Bible (not indexed) 157.
Night, 59.
Nisbit, 59.
Nisbits, 63.
Noble, 36, 110.
Nod, 31.
Noel, 91, 135.
Nolan, 59.
Noland, 166.
Norman, 93.
Norrin, 28.
Norris, 79, 109, 113, 114.
Norseman, 112.
North, 64.
Northcutt, 25, 50, 82.
Norvell, 14.
Nourae, 84.
Nourse, 84.
Nowell, 13.
Nuckols, 14, 15.
Nunn, 113.
Nutt, 66.

Nutter, 33, 88.
Nuttle, 39, 142.

O

Oakley, 83.
Obinskain, 115.
Oden, 115.
Oder, 59.
Odin, 115.
Odon, 52.
Ogden, 95, 107.
Oglesby, 95.
Offutt, (Offull) 74,79.
Oflyn, 111.
Ohio County Wills 85-86.
Okley, 78.
O'Kelly, 75.
Olive, 26.
Oliver, 48, 59, 137, 138.
O'Neal, 91, 106.
Orear, 78, 81, 84.
Orr, 22.
Osborne, 87, 93.
Osbourne, 66.
Otgan, 136.
Outon, 35.
Overall, 105, 114.
Overby, 166.
Oversake, 49.
Overstreet, 75.
Overton, 32, 112,.
Owen, 92, 94,106, 115, 134, 135, 138, 140.
Owens, 42, 106, 114, 159.
Oxley, 36.

P

Pace, 14.
Paddock, 135.
Parman, 52.
Palmer, 28, 90, 105.
Parish, 40.
Parke, 97.
Pankey, 71.
Park, 140.
Parks, 86, 134.
Parker, 17, 21, 22, 24, 35, 36, 38, 39, 40, 47, 55, 57, 86, 112, 115.
Parmer, 49.
Parnell, 14.
Parrish, 16, 40.
Parry, 106, 159.
Pate, 111.
Paton, 55.
Patterson, 34, 38, 39, 40, 41, 46, 54, 59, 60, 63, 80, 109.
Patton, 51, 59, 69, 78, 87, 90, 91, 106.
Paulings, 87.

Pauly, 97.
Pavey, 51.
Payne, 21, 22, 32, 34, 35, 36, 37, 39, 40, 51, 63, 73, 79, 82, 93, 140.
Payton, 29, 54.
Peables, 80, 81.
Peacce, 109.
Peak, 87.
Pearce, 166.
Pearse, 136.
Pearson, 106, 112.
Peck, 47, 159.
Pedan Bible (not indexed) 181-182.
Peddicord, 109.
Pedicord, 106.
Peebles, 40.
Peel, 40.
Peers, 25.
Pelicord, 110.
Pemberton, 31.
Pence, 42, 82, 89.
Pender, 86, 113, 115.
Pendergrass, 139, 140.
Pendleton, 59, 60.
Penn, 44, 60.
Peniston, 71.
Pennington, 95.
Pentecost, 135.
Penticost, 95.
Perham, 160.
Perkins, 36, 47, 50, 58, 60, 94, 134, 141, 142.
Perrie, 158, 159.
Person, 111.
Perrin, 42, 44, 56, 63.
Peter, 13.
Pettel, 80.
Petty, 14.
Pew, 87.
Peyatt, 40.
Peyton, 21, 29, 78.
Phiegly, 91.
Phigley, 106.
Phillips, 47, 60, 75, 106, 112, 169.
Phinkston, 106.
Pickett, 22, 30, 39, 50, 60,
Pierce, 23, 45, 110, 112.
Piercy, 23, 97.
Pigg, 60, 142.
Pilcher, 40.
Piles, 105, 141.
Pipes, 116.
Pindell, 35, 60.
Pinkley, 14.
Pinkston, 105, 108, 109, 111, 112, 113.
Pitcher, 74.
Pock, 54, 60.
Pogue, 36.
Poindexter, 44, 66.

Pointer, 108, 109, 110, 114.
Poland, 96.
Pollard, 23, 44, 60, 107.
Pollock, 32, 57.
Polly, 114, 115, 138.
Polk, 39, 111.
Polke, 91, 92, 94.
Pool, 113, 116.
Pope, 35, 62.
Postleweight, 138.
Poston, 19.
Porter, 16, 23, 26, 59, 60, 63, 98, 100, 115, 116.
Poter, 76.
Pots, 109.
Potts, 95, 107, 111.
Powell, 60, 62, 95.
Powers, 52.
Prather, 94.
Preivitt, 20.
Preston, 33.
Prewett (Pruitt), 33, 68, 95, 116.
Price, 35, 38, 40, 52, 63, 72, 75, 91, 136.
Prichart, 25.
Prickett, 84.
Prichard, 90, 92.
Priest, 81, 106, 108.
Pringle, 90.
Pritchart, 81.
Pritchett, 135.
Proctor, 72, 159.
Protsman, 111.
Prudent, 16.
Pruitt, 137, 138.
Pryor, 71, 91, 140.
Pugh, 82.
Pullen, 16, 26.
Pullin, 28.
Purcell, 111.
Purdy, 17.
Pursley, 52.
Purviance, 23.
Puryor, 15.

Q

Quinn, 17.
Quirk, 139.

R

Rader, 77, 160.
Radford, 97.
Raferty, 107.
Rafferty, 110, 112, 116.
Ragan, 80.
Raine, 16, 17, 99.
Rainey, 34, 56.
Ralls, 79, 80.
Ralston, 37, 42, 43, 60, 67, 110.

Ramey, 58.
Ramsey, 72, 111.
Raney, 37.
Randel, 137.
Ransdell, 33.
Randolph, 35, 38.
Rankin, 60, 66, 99.
Rannels, (see Reynolds) 17.
Ransom, 115.
Ratliff, 77, 83, 98.
Ratliff Bible, (not indexed) 183-184.
Ravenscraft, 60, 71.
Ray, 139.
Raybourn, 28.
Raymon, 65.
Raymond, 62, 65.
Read, 84.
Readey, 137.
Reading, 51, 59.
Readnour, 61.
Redd, 31.
Redding, 95.
Reddish, 112.
Redman, 92.
Redmon, 26, 49, 61.
Reed, 30, 55, 71, 82, 92, 93, 94, 95, 133, 140 142.
Rees, 47, 95, 100, 140, 160.
Reese, 17, 50.
Reeves, 66.
Reid, (see Reed and Reid), 19, 27, 76, 96, 98, 99, 135, 159.
Reitzel, 43.
Remmington, 111.
Renick, (see Rennick), 14.
Renaker, 43.
Rennecker, 49.
Rennick, (see Renick), 39.
Reno, 61, 62.
Respess, 29.
Retzel, 43.
Reutch, 84.
Reynolds, (see Rannels), 14, 60, 97,
Reynolds Bible (not indexed), 155-156.
Rhodes, 116.
Rhody, 142.
Rice, 21, 77, 80, 83, 96, 106, 110.
Richards, 79, 112.
Richardson, 33, 40, 89, 106, 107, 109, 116.
Richardson Bible, (not indexed), 155-156.
Richart, 29.
Riche, 37, 158.
Richett, 158.
Richey, 159.
Richy, 135, 137.
Rickets, 73.

Shearman, 26.
Sheckler, 110.
Shelburn, 96.
Shelburne, 94.
Shelby County Marriage Bonds, 133-142.
Shelby County Wills, 90-97.
Shell, 43.
Shelton, 88.
Shely, 74.
Shepherd, 139, 140.
Sherman, 62.
Shickley, 111.
Shield, 137.
Shields, 62, 63, 95, 99, 141.
Shillideay, 142.
Ship, 16. 49.
Shipman, 97, 136.
Shirley, 88.
Shoemaker, 116.
Shomaker, 114.
Shop, 109.
Short, 109, 110, 111, 116.
Shouts, 116.
Shown, 106.
Shrawyer, 89.
Shropshire, 26, 58, 62.
Shuck, 96.
Shuffett, 43.
Shultz, 80, 86.
Shurts, 50, 62.
Shutt, 105.
Sidner, 17.
Sill, 92, 137, 140.
Simeon, 71.
Simieon, 33.
Simmon, 67.
Simmons, 108.
Simms, 62.
Simpson, 25, 31, 60, 61, 72, 81, 91, 96, 113, 141, 167, 168.
Sinclair, 80.
Singleton, 70, 76.
Sip, 82.
Sisk, 105.
Sketer, 30, 36.
Skidmore, 94.
Skinner, 115.
Slaughter, 111.
Sled, 96.
Smallwood, 25.
Smellser, 23.
Smieser, 43.
Smiley, 90, 96, 97.
Smiser, 45.
Smith, 13, 14, 15, 16, 18, 19, 24, 26, 27, 28, 31, 38, 40, 42, 43, 44, 45, 51, 54, 56, 60, 62, 63, 66, 67, 68, 69, 71, 78, 79, 82, 83, 84, 86, 87, 88, 89, 90, 91, 92, 94, 95, 97, 105, 109, 110, 111, 112, 113, 115, 116, 137,

139, 141, 158.
Smizer, 18.
Smock, 137, 141.
Sneed, 63, 110.
Snell, 54, 63.
Snider, 67.
Snoddy, 14.
Snoddy Bible, (not indexed), 145-147.
Snodgrass, 46, 48, 52, 53, 63.
Sodusky 69, 75.
Sonerheber, 104.
Sorreis, 91,138.
Sosh, 110.
Sparks, 18, 45, 65, 86.
Spaulding, 108.
Speak, 114.
Spears, 46, 62.
Speed, 87.
Spenser, 29, 40, 169.
Spiers, 32.
Spottswood, 15.
Spradling, 107.
Spray, 104, 116.
Spriggs, 86.
Springfield Church, (grave inscriptions), 166-171.
Spurr, 41.
Squires, 96.
Stacy, 44.
Standiford, 91, 95.
Stanly, 24, 90.
Staples, 137, 138.
Stark, 24, 135, 136.
Starke, 95, 134.
Starr, 71.
Staten, 96.
Steadycorn, 63.
Stearman, 108.
Stears, 52.
Stech, 84.
Steel, (see Steele) 80, 138.
Steele, 28, 30, 40, 41, 69, 70, 114, 116, 169.
Stell, 114.
Stephen, 75.
Stephens, 168.
Stephenson, 46, 47, 63, 89, 99, 107, 137.
Stevens, 59, 81, 108, 140.
Stevenson, 53, 59, 106.
Steward, 65.
Stewert, 14.
Stewart, 22, 50, 53, 56, 63, 70, 98, 111.
Stidham, 105.
Stillin, 133.
Stillwell, 97.
Stinnett, (Stinnet) 107, 108, 109, 110.
Stip, 28.
Stirman, 109.

Stith, 55.

Stockton, 15.

Stone, 30, 36, 41, 77, 83, 90, 91, 97, 98, 108, 112, 114, 115, 169.

Stonestreet 67, 70.

Storbridge, 78.

Stout, 36, 96, 116, 158.

Stowers, (Stowart) 114.

Strader, 18.

Strain, 108, 115.

String, 24.

Strange, 77.

Stranges, 83.

Strode, 19, 98.

Stuart, 32, 50, 63.

Stump, 64, 67.

Sturgeon, 138, 141.

Sturman, 97.

Sucker, 52.

Suddith, 99.

Summans, 77.

Summers, 29, 77, 82, 83.

Surgin, 84.

Surgis, 78.

Sut, 141.

Sutherland, 41.

Sutton, 40, 64, 66, 72, 83, 114.

Swain, 116.

Swansell, 29.

Swayze, 134.

Swearingen (Van), 29.

Swinford, 58, 60, 64.

Synder, 108.

T

Tackett, 169.

Tague, (Teague), 142.

Talbot, 23, 113.

Talbott, 17, 19, 25, 55, 89, 95, 97, 113, 114, 135.

Tanbush, 34.

Tandy, 32, 41.

Tanner, 105, 106, 108, 109, 110, 112, 113, 114, 115, 116.

Tapscott, 110, 111, 114.

Tatham,41.

Taul, 77, 79.

Taylor, 17, 21, 30, 32, 41, 45, 47, 49, 50, 56, 64, 65, 67, 78, 91, 93, 95, 99, 105, 106, 107, 109, 110, 111, 112, 113, 114, 115, 116, 139, 158, 159, 166.

Teague, 96.

Tebbs, 158.

Tegard, 141.

Tegarden, 41, 93.

Teigue, (Teague) 137.

Tenner, 113.

Tennison, 112.

Terrell, 105.

Terrill, 22.

Terry, 64.

Tharp, 89.

Thatcher, 93.

Theobald, 63, 140.

Theobalds, 23.

Thomas, 15, 21, 27, 28, 49, 63, 65, 71, 92, 93, 112, 115, 136, 160.

Thomason, 88.

Thompson, 20, 37, 41, 46, 49, 55, 58, 62, 69, 80, 87, 88, 92, 96, 98, 104, 105, 106, 107, 108, 109, 110, 114, 115.

Thomson, 99.

Thorn, 88, 137.

Thornly, 46.

Thornton, 27, 55, 64, 88.

Thorp, 158.

Thorpe, 106.

Thortin, 84.

Threshly, 31.

Thurman, 14.

Thurston, 36.

Tichenor, 91, 116.

Tidings 22.

Tilford, 94.

Tilly, 142.

Tilton, 30.

Timberlake, 44, 45, 46, 50, 56, 64.

Timmons, 106.

Tippet, (Tippett) 61.

Tisdale, 64.

Todd, 25, 32, 33, 35, 37, 39, 41, 44, 84, 92, 93, 135, 141.

Toliaferro 25.

Tolin, 79.

Tolliman, 115.

Tolls, 169.

Tomkins, 34.

Tompkins, 41, 110.

Tomlinson, 42.

Toncray, 91.

Toney, 64.

Torrance, 114.

Torrington 116.

Totten, 105.

Townsend, 137.

Tracey, 97.

Travis, 86, 104, 106, 108.

Treacle, 159.

Tredate, 15.

Tribble, 104, 105.

Trigg, 13.

Trimble, 24, 25, 50, 59, 64, 79, 80, 81.

Triplett, 32, 166, 167, 168.

Trotter, 18, 38, 39, 89.

Truax, 141.

Tucker, 55, 58, 62, 64, 91, 108, 139.

Tuckwiller, 160.
Tudor, 14.
Tull, 20.
Tullis, 57.
Tunks, 57.
Tunstall, 97.
Tureman, 100.
Turner, 40, 53, 64, 65, 68, 112, 168.
Turney, 53, 62.
Turpin, 21, 114.
Turvey, 65.
Tyler, 93, 135, 142.
Tyree, 64.

U

Underwood, 13, 93, 96, 97, 116, 134, 139.
Utler, 89.
Utley, 41.
Utterback, 82.

V

Vail, 84.
Vanada 111.
Vance, 20, 111, 113.
Vancleave, 96, 134, 135, 136, 142.
Vandarin, 17.
Van Deren, (Vanderen), 50, 53, 65.
Vandike, 105.
VanHook, 51.
Vanmeter, 111.
Vannada, 85.
Vaughan, 56.
Vaughn, 40, 112.
Veach, 53, 61, 134.
Veal, 41.
Venard, 65.
Vestal, 76.
Victor, 52.
Vinard, 49.
Virt, 83.
Vittetoe, 109.
Vittitow, 114.
Vivion, 42.
Vories, 96.
Voyles, 106.

W

Wade, 13, 14, 74, 76.
Waggoner, 63.
Wainman, 42.
Waits, (Waites), 57, 66.
Walden, 52, 112.
Walker, 13, 24, 41, 67, 72, 74, 88, 89, 96, 97, 110, 116, 168, 169.
Walkers, 68.

Wall, 42, 104, 106, 109, 111, 115.
Walls, 86.
Wallace, 16, 25, 30, 32, 34, 39, 71, 89, 96, 113, 115 135, 136.
Waller, 57.
Walter, 44, 88.
Walters, 67, 68, 72.
Walton, 47, 62.
Waltrip, 108, 109, 111, 112, 113, 115, 116.
Wand, 29.
Wapper, 79.
Ward, 18, 44, 55, 56, 65, 86, 88, 89, 107, 109, 110, 112, 113, 114, 115.
Wardlaw, 141.
Ware, 29, 113.
Warfield, 24, 45, 50, 51.
Warford, 96, 97, 113, 184.
Warfrord, 90.
Warner, 168.
Warson, 141.
Washborn, 59.
Washington, 15, 39, 76.
Wason Bible, (not indexed) 182.
Wasson, 18.
Wathen, 114.
Watkins, (Wadkins), 45, 65, 110, 111.
Watson, 32, 37, 43, 47, 51, 65, 82, 142.
Watts, 17, 73, 95, 134.
Way, 45.
Wayland, 107.
Wayman, 92.
Wayne, 116.
Weakley, 141.
Weaks, 114.
Weathers, 35.
Weaver, 40.
Webb, 20, 25, 26, 32, 61, 105, 115.
Webber, 65, 67, 83, 89.
Webster, 37, 70.
Weir, 30, 38.
Welch, 75, 111, 112.
Wells, 22, 27, 51, 73, 83, 87, 105, 112, 115, 135.
Werrich, 158.
Wesley, 80.
West, 18, 45, 55, 70, 99, 107, 158.
Westerfield, 109, 111, 114.
Whaley, 32, 33, 37, 38, 41, 167.
Wharton, 88, 89.
Whaye, 79.
Whayn, 83.
Whayne, 110.
Wheat, 20.
Whiss, 73.
Whittaker, (Whitaker), 47, 90, 92, 95, 97, 113, 116, 134,

135, 136, 140.
Whiteker, 54, 65.
White, 13, 39, 52, 64, 76, 81, 83, 106, 107, 109, 138, 139, 142.
Whitecraft, 84.
Whitecroft, 77.
Whitesides, 93.
Whitesitt, 28.
Whitley, 47, 52.
Whitney, 14, 15, 64.
Whitsitt, 82.
Whitson, 65.
Whittaker, 39.
Whitter, 109.
Wickerson, 107.
Wickliffe, 33.
Wiggins, 66.
Wiglesworth, (Wigglesworth) 44, 58, 66, 88.
Wilcockcon, 80.
Wilcox, 78, 92, 94, 96.
Wiley, 105.
Wilgns, 32.
Wilikinson, 35.
Wilkerson, 74, 76, 79, 81.
Wilkins, 41.
William, 109.
Williams, 15, 23, 24, 27, 39, 43, 44, 45, 49, 52, 54, 56, 57, 66, 68, 78, 79, 80, 83, 84, 97, 98, 106, 108, 109, 111, 112, 113, 114, 115, 116, 136, 137, 138, 140, 158, 166.
Willis, 68.
Williamson, 67, 77, 83, 92.
Wills, 79, 83.
Wills, (Miscellaneous) 97-100.
Willett, 18, 85.
Willingham, 107.
Willson, 82.
Wilman, 115.
Wilson, 14, 16, 19, 22, 24, 26, 27, 28, 30, 31, 34, 38, 40, 41, 44, 47, 51, 60, 66, 74, 75, 79, 80, 83, 86, 91, 96, 98, 107, 116, 134, 169.
Wimott, 45.
Winkeld, 141.
Winkler, 106, 107, 108, 110.
Winlock, 95.

Winn, (Win), 35, 31, 41.
Winstead, 112, 116.
Wise, 137, 140.
Withers, 54, 66, 71.
Wmy, 20.
Wolf, 58, 66.
Womack, 89.
Womal, 114.
Wood, 30, 36, 37, 43, 66, 70, 78, 86, 99, 105, 141, 158, 159, 160.
Woods, 21, 60, 77.
Woodridge, 37.
Woodson, 47.
Woodyard, 58.
Woolen, 89.
Wools, 76.
Wooten, 13.
Wordlin, 16.
Workman, 38.
Wornall, (Wornell), 25, 110.
Wortham, 31.
Worthington, 95, 106, 111, 115, 142.
Wray, 14.
Wrenn, 31.
Wright, 55, 91, 108, 109, 111, 135, 138, 139.
Wyatt, 27, 28, 81.
Wycoff, 20.

Y

Yancey, 26.
Yarnell, 66.
Yates, 34.
Yeager, 31.
Yewel, 113.
Yocum, 23.
Yoder, 84.
Young, 31, 32, 35, 39, 40, 41, 42, 49, 73, 80, 89, 95, 97, 107, 109, 111, 113, 116, 135, 168.

Z

ZELLER, 61

ZIKE, 73

ZUMMUTT, 67

ZUMWALT, 42